The Ethics of Plea Bargaining

The Ethics of Plea Bargaining

Richard L. Lippke

OXFORD

UNIVERSITY PRESS

OXFORD
UNIVERSITY PRESS

Great Clarendon Street, Oxford OX2 6DP

Oxford University Press is a department of the University of Oxford.
It furthers the University's objective of excellence in research, scholarship,
and education by publishing worldwide in

Oxford New York

Auckland Cape Town Dar es Salaam Hong Kong Karachi
Kuala Lumpur Madrid Melbourne Mexico City Nairobi
New Delhi Shanghai Taipei Toronto

With offices in

Argentina Austria Brazil Chile Czech Republic France Greece
Guatemala Hungary Italy Japan Poland Portugal Singapore
South Korea Switzerland Thailand Turkey Ukraine Vietnam

Oxford is a registered trade mark of Oxford University Press
in the UK and in certain other countries

Published in the United States
by Oxford University Press Inc., New York

British Library Cataloguing in Publication Data

Data available

Library of Congress Cataloging in Publication Data
Library of Congress Control Number: 2011939969

Typeset by Newgen Imaging Systems (P) Ltd, Chennai, India
Printed and bound by
CPI Group (UK) Ltd, Croydon, CRO 4YY

ISBN 978–0–19–964146–8

10 9 8 7 6 5 4 3 2 1

To Andrea

Acknowledgments

Early portions of this book were written while I was a Visiting Research Fellow at the Centre for Applied Philosophy and Public Ethics at Australian National University in the summer of 2007. I especially want to thank John Kleinig for initiating the visit and Tom Campbell and Seumas Miller for organizing the institutional support for it. I subsequently had the pleasure of serving two years as the Robert and Carolyn Frederick Visiting Scholar in Ethics at the Prindle Institute for Ethics, located at DePauw University. Much of the substantive work on the book was completed in that beautiful and stimulating environment. I want to thank Bob Bottoms, Bob Steele, Martha Rainbolt, and Linda Clute for making my time at the Prindle Institute so enjoyable. The students and faculty at DePauw were also extraordinarily welcoming.

Early versions of the first two chapters were read to colleagues at James Madison University, the Indiana University law school, and DePauw University. I also presented a version of Chapter 2 at the meetings of the Association for Practical and Professional Ethics, and a version of Chapter 9 at a conference on proof and truth in the law, organized by Larry Laudan, at the National Autonomous University of Mexico. I want to thank all of the participants at these events for their stimulating questions, comments, and suggestions.

Anyone who wants to write about plea bargaining must begin by studying the bible—in this case the many groundbreaking articles by Albert Alschuler on the subject. My substantial debt to his writings will be evident throughout. I remain uncertain that I have anything to say about plea bargaining that he has not already said. When the book was well under way and I believed myself to have a good handle on the topic, I began reading some of the signally important work on criminal law and procedure by the late William Stuntz. I could never think about either topic in the same way afterwards and spent many hours rethinking conclusions that I had reached and about which I had previously been quite confident. I suspect that many other scholars of the law have had the same reaction upon encountering Stuntz's writings.

I want to thank Andrew Ashworth for believing in the book enough to recommend its inclusion in his excellent monograph series. Natasha Knight at Oxford University Press was a constant source of help and encouragement as the manuscript wound its way through the OUP review process. Several reviewers for the Press offered enormously useful comments and suggestions. The final version is much improved because of their efforts.

Portions of some of the chapters have appeared elsewhere. A small part of Chapter 1 and a larger part of Chapter 2 were earlier published as "To Waive or Not to Waive: The Right to Trial and Plea Bargaining," in [2008] 2 *Criminal Law and*

Philosophy 181. My views about waiver rewards and trial penalties have evolved significantly since that article appeared. A part of Chapter 4 was published as "Response to Tudor: Remorse-based Sentence Reductions in Theory and Practice," [2008] 2 *Criminal Law and Philosophy* 259. And most of Chapter 6 appeared as "Rewarding Cooperation: The Moral Complexities of Procuring Accomplice Testimony," [2010] 13 *New Criminal Law Review* 90.

Finally, my debt to my wife, Andrea Wiley, and our children, Aidan and Emil, is incalculable. Together they keep me sane, happy, and productive.

Contents

Abbreviations

American Journal of Coparative Law	Am. J. Comp. L.
American Journal of Criminal Law	Am. J. Crim. L.
Buffalo Law Review	Buff. L. Rev.
California Law Review	Cal. L. Rev.
Cardozo Law Review	Cardozo L. Rev.
Columbia Law Review	Colum. L. Rev.
Cornell Law Review	Cornell L. Rev.
Criminal Law Review	Crim. L. Rev.
Emory Law Journal	Emory L. J.
Fordham Law Review	Fordham L. Rev.
Fordham Urban Law Journal	Fordham Urb. L. J.
Georgetown Journal of Legal Ethics	Geo. J. Legal Ethics
Georgia Law Review	Ga. L. Rev.
Harvard International Law Journal	Harv. Int'l L. J.
Harvard Journal of Law and Public Policy	Harv. J. L. & Public Pol'y
Harvard Law Review	Harv. L. Rev.
Hastings Law Journal	Hastings L. J.
Indiana Law Review	Indiana L. Rev.
Indiana Law Journal [TBC]	Ind. L. J.
Journal of Law and Economics	J. L. & Econ.
Journal of Legal Studies	J. Legal Stud.
Law and Human Behavior	L. & Hum. Behavior
Law and Inequality	L. & Ineq.
Law and Society Review	L. & Soc'y Rev.
Lewis and Clark Law Review	Lewis & Clark L. Rev.
Michigan Law Review	Mich. L. Rev.
New Criminal Law Review	New Crim. L. Rev.
New England Law Review	New Eng. L. Rev.
Northwestern University Law Review	Nw. U. L. Rev.
Oxford Journal of Legal Studies	O. J. L. S.
Pepperdine Law Review	Pepp. L. Rev.
Pittsburgh Law Review	Pitt. L. Rev.

Rutgers Law Review	Rutgers L. Rev.
Stanford Law Review	Stan. L. Rev.
UCLA Law Review	UCLA L. Rev.
University of Chicago Law Review	U. Chi. L. Rev.
University of Illinois Law Review	U. Ill. L. Rev.
University of Pennsylvania Law Review	U. Pa. L. Rev.
Valparaiso University Law Review	Val. U. L. Rev.
Virginia Law Review	Va. L. Rev.
Vanderbilt Law Review	Vand. L. Rev.
Washington University Law Review	Wash. U. L. Rev.
William and Mary Law Review	Wm & Mary L. Rev.
Wisconsin Law Review	Wis. L. Rev.
Yale Law Journal	Yale L. J.
Yale Law Review	Yale L. Rev.

Introduction

Modern legal orders have devised elaborate trial procedures aimed at separating the guilty from the not guilty among those charged with criminal offenses. They have also evolved procedures for avoiding having to conduct the trials that are supposed to perform this vitally important task.[1] In lieu of trials, individuals charged with crimes are offered various inducements to either confess their crimes or plead guilty to them.[2] Confessions typically shorten their trials; guilty pleas obviate the need for them. In the United States, trial-avoidance procedures have been in place for some time.[3] There, plea bargaining dominates charge adjudication, with approximately 95 percent of cases resolved by it. Plea bargaining in the United States is also fairly unrestrained. Prosecutors, and to a lesser extent, judges, have extraordinary discretion to offer reduced punishment to individuals who have been formally accused of crimes in efforts to convince them to enter guilty pleas. Though forms of trial avoidance are increasingly common in other countries, few of them rival the United States in equipping legal officials with the means to press defendants for guilty pleas. Perhaps due to law or custom other countries will not follow the lead of the United States. One aim of the present study is to consider why such a path seems an undesirable one to tread.

In the face of the emergence of forms of plea bargaining in Europe and elsewhere, some scholars have mounted a rearguard action against it, suggesting that any inducement offered to those charged with crimes in exchange for their confessions or guilty pleas is a breach of procedural justice and may well produce substantive

---

[1] The tension between elaborate trials and considerably abbreviated plea procedures is skillfully developed and explored by J. H. Langbein in "Torture and Plea Bargaining," [1980] 58 *Public Interest* 43.

[2] In some countries (e.g., Germany), there are no guilty pleas. However, if individuals confess their crimes, their subsequent trials will be abbreviated. For discussion of plea bargaining in Germany, see Y. Ma, "Prosecutorial Discretion and Plea Bargaining in the United States, France, Germany, and Italy: A Comparative Perspective," [2002] 12 *International Criminal Justice Review* 22, and M. Langer, "From Legal Transplants to Legal Translations: The Globalization of Plea Bargaining and the Americanization Thesis in Criminal Procedure," [2004] 45 *Harv. Int'l L. J.* 1.

[3] Legal historians disagree about when plea bargaining emerged during the nineteenth century as well as why it did so, but that it has been around since then is not much in dispute. Important recent histories of plea bargaining include G. Fisher, *Plea Bargaining's Triumph: A History of Plea Bargaining in America* (Stanford, Calif.: Stanford University Press, 2003), M. McConville and C. L. Mirsky, *Jury Trials and Plea Bargaining: A True History* (Oxford: Hart Publishing, 2005), and M. Vogel, *Coercion to Compromise: Plea Bargaining, the Courts, and the Making of Political Authority* (Oxford: Oxford University Press, 2007).

injustices.[4] Of particular concern is the possibility, and some would say likelihood, that offers of charge or sentence reductions to criminal defendants will encourage some of the innocent among them to "confess" or enter guilty pleas. There are also concerns that the negotiated settlement of criminal charges runs counter to provisions of the European Convention on Human Rights—the right against self-incrimination, the presumption of innocence, and the right to a fair and public hearing, among them.[5] These qualms about plea bargaining, whatever its form, echo those expressed for years by American scholars.[6] Plea bargaining in the United States has been subjected to withering scrutiny. Yet the practice chugs along, more or less unabated and largely unaffected by the academic debate surrounding it. Even efforts to constrain plea bargaining have at times backfired in unpredictable ways, as with the Federal Sentencing Guidelines, which were intended to limit judicial sentencing discretion and yet appear to have produced more virulent forms of charge bargaining.[7] Some scholars have suggested that attempts to reform or constrain plea bargaining are bound to fail. The primary actors within the criminal justice system—judges, prosecutors, defense attorneys, and even criminal defendants—derive too many benefits from the practice.[8] The negotiated resolution of criminal charges will go on, some predict, no matter what measures are undertaken to rein in what appear to be its excesses.

I am not convinced by such skepticism, though I am somewhat chastened by it. Whether or not it is possible to entirely eliminate plea bargaining in all its forms and varieties, I am not persuaded that it is desirable to do so. But I am no friend of plea bargaining in the unrestrained forms of it that are evident in the United States. In a nutshell, the normative position I shall advance is this: individuals charged with crimes who are willing to confess or plead guilty should be granted modest and fixed sentence discounts in exchange for doing so. Charge bargaining, and that which often accompanies and enables it, strategic overcharging, should be strongly discouraged. Trial penalties, that is, additional increments of punishment assigned to individuals who exercise their right to trial, should be prohibited. But I distinguish the loss of a

[4] See, for instance, P. Darbyshire, "The Mischief of Plea Bargaining and Sentencing Rewards," [2000] *Crim. L. Rev.* 895, and A. Ashworth and M. Redmayne, *The Criminal Process,* 4th edition (Oxford: Oxford University Press, 2010) 310–20.

[5] See Ashworth and Redmayne (n 4 above) 312–16.

[6] The literature critical of US plea bargaining practices is voluminous. Among the most important figures whose work casts plea bargaining in a mostly negative light are Albert Alschuler and Stephen Schulhofer. Some of Alschuler's many groundbreaking articles include "The Trial Judge's Role in Plea Bargaining, Part I," [1976] 76 *Colum. L. Rev.* 1059, "The Prosecutor's Role in Plea Bargaining," [1968] 36 *U. Chi. L. Rev.* 50, "The Changing Plea Bargaining Debate," [1981] 69 *Cal. L. Rev.* 652, and "Implementing the Criminal Defendant's Right to Trial: Alternatives to the Plea Bargaining System," [1983] 50 *U. Chi. L. Rev.* 931. Two key works by Schulhofer are "Is Plea Bargaining Inevitable?" [1984] 97 *Harv. L. Rev.* 1037, and "Plea Bargaining as Disaster," [1992] 101 *Yale L. J.* 1979.

[7] See J. Standen, "Plea Bargaining in the Shadow of the Guidelines," [1993] 81 *Cal. L. Rev.* 1471.

[8] See M. Heumann, *Plea Bargaining: The Experiences of Prosecutors, Judges, and Defense Attorneys* (Chicago: University of Chicago Press, 1977).

sentence discount when defendants elect trial adjudication and are convicted from the imposition on them of a trial penalty. Furthermore, before individuals are permitted to enter guilty pleas, there should be some meaningful judicial scrutiny of the state's evidence against them and the opportunity for judges to question them. Judges should elicit testimony from defendants about their crimes and ensure that defendants fully understand what they stand to lose if they waive their right to full trial adjudication of the charges against them. Our aims should be to shear plea bargaining of its excesses and constrain the abilities of state officials to engage in it, thereby forcing them to do so in more public and accountable ways.

Whether what I defend should be termed "plea bargaining" in any robust sense is a question that I do not believe the answer to which holds much interest. There is considerable variation in the language used to characterize the non-trial adjudication of criminal charges against individuals. For some, anything short of full trial adjudication will be seen as plea bargaining, even if little actual bargaining between the interested parties takes place. In this broad sense of plea bargaining, I defend it. For others, plea bargaining proper occurs only if there is considerable give and take between prosecutors (or judges, in some countries) and defense counsel over what charges are appropriate or the sentences defendants should be assigned if they are willing to admit their guilt. In this narrower sense of plea bargaining, I have little to say on its behalf. However, throughout most of the discussion that follows, I adhere to what seems the more common practice of referring to the non-trial adjudication of criminal charges against individuals as plea bargaining.

To those not familiar with the day-to-day workings of contemporary criminal justice systems, it may come as a surprise to learn that individuals accused of crimes can, to some extent and in ways that vary somewhat from legal system to legal system, negotiate the punishment that they will receive if they admit some or all of them. In part, confusion about how the criminal justice system determines the sanctions to be assigned offenders may stem from citizens having imbibed the exalted rhetoric of the criminal justice system, according to which those accused of crimes are innocent until proven guilty, beyond a reasonable doubt, in a court of law. This rhetoric makes it seem as if there is an authoritative process to which those accused of crimes must simply submit. But confusion about how the criminal justice system operates might also be produced by an understandable unease with the whole idea of punishment being something about which negotiation is possible. It might be believed or hoped that the assignment of criminal sanctions occurs according to an orderly procedure: Crimes are committed, authorities investigate and gather evidence about them, that evidence sometimes results in charges being lodged by prosecutors against individuals, the charges and the evidence for them are rigorously tested during a trial, and in cases in which defendants are found guilty, judges assign appropriate sentences. On the suppositions that the criminal law and its enforcement promote defensible societal interests, such an orderly process ensures that those interests are indeed served.

By contrast, permitting state officials and individuals accused of crimes to negotiate charges and sentences seems a procedure designed to serve their interests, but the public's interests less assuredly.

Discomfort with the negotiated resolution of criminal charges is apt to increase once the dizzying array of factors that can influence plea bargained outcomes, especially in robust plea bargaining regimes, is revealed. Legal scholars have cataloged these factors.[9] They include the strength of the evidence against defendants, the amicable relationship (or lack thereof) that exists between the prosecutor (or judge) and the defendant's attorney, the personal or political ambitions of the prosecutor, the prosecutor's or judge's caseload, the quality of a defendant's legal representation, the amount of time it will take before a defendant can receive a trial, especially if the defendant is being held on remand until a trial can occur, and the defendant's attitudes toward risk. What is striking about most of these factors is that they seem devoid of any relationship to the valid interests society has in the punishment of individuals in response to their crimes. It is as if we have set up a system of criminal laws and an enforcement procedure for them and then looked the other way as an alternative charge–adjudication scheme evolved, one which is largely indifferent to the purposes for which we originally acted.

If we ask how this indifference is likely to manifest itself, initially it is plausible to believe that plea bargaining serves up attractive deals for offenders. After all, the logic of plea bargaining would almost seem to dictate lenient outcomes. Prosecutors and judges have powerful motivations to attract defendants' guilty pleas, given the high costs of having to conduct trials. They will therefore offer defendants reductions in charges or sentences in exchange for defendants admitting their guilt. It is hard to see how such offers could fail to result in offenders being assigned sanctions that fall short of the ones they merit given their crimes. Indeed, there is evidence suggesting that plea bargaining outcomes are extraordinarily lenient at times, especially when the crimes in question are not terribly serious.[10] Again, plea practices in the United States may produce considerably more leniency than those in other countries. But 30 percent discounts for defendants who agree to plead guilty early in the charge-adjudication process are not uncommon in European countries, and such reductions cannot plausibly be seen as insignificant.[11]

---

[9] S. Bibas, "Plea Bargaining Outside the Shadow of Trial," [2004] 117 *Harv. L. Rev.* 2463, and Schulhofer, "Plea Bargaining as Disaster," (n 6 above) 1987–91.

[10] See Schulhofer, "Plea Bargaining as Disaster," (n 6 above) 1993, and J. Bowers, "Punishing the Innocent," [2007] 156 *U. Pa. L. Rev.* 1117, 1143–5.

[11] Such sentence discounts are available in England and Wales for defendants who agree to enter guilty pleas early in the adjudication process. See Ashworth and Redmayne (n 4 above) 293. Under Italian law, defense attorneys and prosecutors can reach agreements on sentences that reduce them up to one-third for defendants who waive their right to trial (though they do not enter guilty pleas) so long as the reduced sentence does not exceed five years' imprisonment. On the Italian *patteggiamento*, see Langer (n 2 above) 49–50.

However, plea bargaining might not consistently yield sentences that are milder than those appropriate given offenders' crimes. For one thing, sentence reductions will only produce undeserved leniency if the sentencing scheme itself is both ordinally and cardinally proportionate.[12] If some crimes are punished too harshly given their relative severity, or if all crimes are, then sentence concessions may do no more than reduce undeservedly stiff punishment. Beyond this, the desire to avoid having to conduct trials tempts state officials to ramp up the pressure on those charged with crimes in order to attract their guilty pleas. One way in which prosecutors do so is by overcharging. Subsequent negotiations might bring down the sentences that overcharged defendants are ultimately assigned but not to levels that can be characterized fairly as unduly or at all lenient. Also, prosecutors and judges might employ sticks as well as carrots in soliciting guilty pleas from individuals accused of crimes. The carrots come in the form of proffered charge or sentence reductions. The sticks come in the form of trial penalties, that is, extra measures of punishment which are assigned defendants who elect trial adjudication and are subsequently found guilty. Of course, defendants who plead guilty will avoid trial penalties and may gain charge or sentence concessions. Nonetheless, but for the existence of negotiated pleas and the resource savings that they promise state officials, defendants who exercise their right to trial and lose might not find themselves with sentences that partly reflect the animus of those officials rather than the seriousness of their crimes.

In short, depending on how procedural rules and legal customs structure them, plea negotiations may yield too much or too little punishment. One of the recurring themes in subsequent chapters is the care with which we must operate in conceiving the context of plea bargaining. It is one thing to assume the following: The criminal code prohibits all and only conduct that a defensible theory of criminalization justifies; the code is coupled with a sentencing scheme that is both cardinally and ordinally proportionate (or alternatively, one that is optimally crime-reductive); police and prosecutors act professionally and not overzealously in investigating and accusing individuals of crimes. It is quite another if some or all of these assumptions are rarely satisfied. Yet how we evaluate plea bargaining will be shown to crucially depend on the assumptions we make about the context in which it operates.

Delineating the issues: the forms and limits of plea bargaining

How we appraise plea bargaining will also depend on what we believe are the procedures that state officials are permitted or required to employ in their efforts to resolve cases without going to trial. It is useful, at the outset, to survey the full range of issues

---

[12] For discussion of cardinal and ordinal proportionality, see A. von Hirsch, *Censure and Sanctions* (Oxford: Clarendon Press, 1993) 18–19.

that must be confronted in setting up a system of plea bargaining. I group the issues under eight headings:

1. Availability, magnitude, and conditions of sentence discounts: The most common inducement to confess or plead guilty provided to those charged with crimes is the promise of some reduction in the sentence that ultimately they will be assigned. Yet sentence discounts vary considerably in size as well as the extent to which they are subject to negotiation. The main possibilities include having them fixed and modest, fixed and substantial, negotiable and modest or substantial, negotiable but capped (that is, not permitted to exceed some percentage of the sentence appropriate for the offense in question), where the caps can be set at high, moderate, or low levels. The magnitude of sentence discounts can also be made to depend on the point at which individuals charged with crimes signal their willingness to confess or enter guilty pleas, with larger ones allotted to those willing to do so early in the legal proceedings against them. A further significant issue is whether sentence reductions should be permitted to alter the kind of sanction imposed on individuals willing to admit their guilt, converting their sentences from, for instance, custodial to noncustodial ones.

2. Availability, magnitude, and conditions of charge discounts: Another fairly common inducement afforded criminal defendants is offers to reduce the charges against them if they will agree to admit their guilt to lesser charges or one or more of the charges left in place. Again, there are various possibilities here, ranging from an outright ban on charge reductions not warranted by an honest assessment of the evidence against individuals, to permitting prosecutors or judges almost complete discretion in eliminating charges, including serious ones, in order to salvage convictions on one or more of the remaining charges. There might also be intermediate positions, such as permitting state officials to reduce minor but not major charges, or capping charge reductions so that defendants will have to serve some percentage of the total sentence (on all charges) they would receive in the absence of such reductions. Also, as with sentence reductions, we could conceivably permit greater leniency in charge bargaining by state officials early in the legal proceedings against individuals, but take a firmer stand against it as trial dates approach.

3. Availability, magnitude, and conditions of trial penalties: As hinted earlier, it is important to distinguish rewards that individuals charged with crimes receive for admitting their guilt, from further punishment that they might incur solely for electing trial adjudication. Though the latter, so-called trial penalties are strictly avoided and viewed with disdain in many legal systems, they are not unheard of, especially in the United States. Should we permit state officials to impose them at all? If we do, should their magnitude be limited or fixed? Also, we could permit their imposition but only upon a showing by state officials that

defendants had "needlessly" demanded trial adjudication, that is, had insisted on going to trial though it was obvious that they were guilty as charged and likely knew it.

4. Availability of, and limits to, fact bargaining: In some legal jurisdictions, those charged with crimes (or more likely, their attorneys) enter into agreements with state officials regarding the facts of crimes to which the former will admit guilt. Should fact bargaining be permitted and, if it is, should there be constraints on state officials to discourage them from entering into fact bargains that significantly distort (typically, by understating) the crimes that they have convincing evidence individuals have committed?

5. Availability of pre-charge bargaining: There is evidence from some legal jurisdictions that state officials sometimes have contact with those whom they intend to charge with crimes, or their attorneys, for the purpose of discussing the charges to which individuals might be willing to admit their guilt, or the sentence recommendations that they might be willing to accept. The issues raised by pre-charge bargaining are similar to those raised by ordinary forms of charge and sentence bargaining, except that state officials who engage in pre-charge bargaining will be less likely to appear to have officially offered any concessions to the individuals whom they ultimately charge with crimes. Pre-charge bargaining will be hard to detect and discourage, but should we attempt to do so in any event?

6. Identity of the participants in plea bargaining: Jurisdictions vary with respect to the parties involved in plea negotiations. The most plausible candidates for participation are the judge or judges presiding over the case, the prosecutor(s) presiding over it, defense counsel, and the accused. Who among these should be included in a defensible plea bargaining procedure? Also, is there any reason to include the victims of crime, assuming there are any?

7. Range of criminal offenses over which plea bargaining should occur: Jurisdictions also vary somewhat with respect to the charged offenses concerning which non-trial adjudication is deemed appropriate. One option is to permit the informal resolution of criminal charges in all cases, no matter how trivial or serious. Another is to insist that cases involving the most serious criminal charges should always be subject to full trial adjudication. Other possibilities exist as well.

8. Extent of judicial vetting of charges and evidence supporting them: Legal jurisdictions that permit and facilitate non-trial adjudication vary significantly in the extent to which they require judicial scrutiny of charges levied against individuals in light of the supporting evidence mustered by police and prosecutors. Should we require only cursory review of charges and evidence in cases in which defendants confess or are willing to plead guilty? Or should we require more rigorous judicial examination of the evidence supporting the charges to which individuals are prepared to plead? Should judges be required or permitted

to question those charged with crimes, to ensure that defendants comprehend the charges against them, are likely guilty of them, and understand the rights that they forgo the exercise of if they admit their guilt?

The preceding survey simplifies matters in at least two ways. First, it makes the primary currency of plea bargaining the charge or sentence adjustments that it produces. Yet all manner of things are sometimes made the subject of plea agreements between state officials and criminal defendants (or their attorneys).[13] I shall ignore this bit of complexity in what follows, electing instead to focus on sentence and charge discounts. In the vast majority of cases resolved without trials, it is these that do the work of inducing defendants to admit their guilt. Second, and more importantly, there are forms of official interaction with individuals who have run foul of the criminal law that occur before charges are filed and cannot plausibly be described as pre-charge bargaining in the sense referred to above. For instance, in England and Wales, there is a wide variety of actions that police and prosecutors can take to divert individuals who admit their minor criminal offenses from formal prosecution.[14] Were my subject in this book trial avoidance in all its guises, I would have to analyze practices like these which precede and typically replace plea bargaining proper. However, to make things more manageable, I confine my focus to the non-trial resolution of criminal charges that have been filed or are about to be.

Though I do not urge the complete elimination of plea bargaining, I do take what will seem to many of its supporters an uncompromising stance toward it. Criminal defendants should not be encouraged or allowed to haggle with state officials about charges or sentences. State officials should not be given the tools to make guilty pleas irresistible or coerce them. But it does not follow that we should require defendants to endure trial adjudication of the charges against them. Most of them might agree to plead guilty after a hearing before a judge in exchange for modest and fixed sentence discounts. Such discounts are an appropriate recognition of their having spared the state, and their fellow citizens who support it, the costs of trials. The relatively few defendants who do insist on trials and are convicted should not be penalized for it. Instead, they should usually receive sentences based on careful assessments of the severity of their offenses.

There are some moderately persuasive arguments for giving state officials a freer hand to negotiate charges and sentences in a few cases. Though there are dangers in granting them such authority and difficulties in cabining it, we might have to confront them and address them as best we can. Nevertheless, the negotiation of charges

---

[13] For a lengthy list of concessions that US prosecutors might agree to during plea negotiations, see D. D. Guidorizzi, "Should We Really 'Ban' Plea Bargaining? The Core Concerns of Plea Bargaining Critics," [1998] 47 *Emory L. J.* 753, note 17. The list includes such things as prosecutors remaining silent at sentencing hearings, downplaying the harms to victims at sentencing hearings, or agreeing to schedule sentencing hearings before a lenient judge.

[14] See Ashworth and Redmayne (n 4 above) 167–8. See also M. Partington, *An Introduction to the English Legal System,* 2nd edition (Oxford: Oxford University Press, 2003) 104.

and sentences by the accused and state officials should remain the exception, not the rule.

I should acknowledge that some of the conclusions urged throughout this book were reached long ago by others.[15] What I hope to have done is provide them with a clearer and more sophisticated normative defense than has so far been given. Along the way, I respond in more methodical fashion to the many arguments in support of robust forms of plea bargaining, some of which appear in the scholarly literature, and some of which I devise on my own.

---

[15] See, in particular, Note: "Restructuring the Plea Bargain," [1972] 82 *Yale L. J.* 286, and Alschuler, "The Trial Judge's Role in Plea Bargaining," (n 6 above) 1154.

1

Waiver Rewards and Trial Penalties

In thinking about how we should structure plea bargaining, and in particular what tools we should supply to state officials to enable them to forge plea agreements, a crucial distinction must be drawn between their rewarding admissions of guilt from those accused of crimes and penalizing exercises of the right to trial. It is one thing if state officials are authorized to reduce the sentences of defendants, or the number or kind of charges against them, in exchange for their confessions or guilty pleas; it is quite another if those same officials are permitted to employ threats of harsher punishment against defendants who they fear might exercise the right to trial, and to act on those threats in cases in which defendants are eventually convicted at their trials. At first glance it might appear that the former, which I term "waiver rewards," and the latter, which are commonly known as "trial penalties," are two sides of the same coin. But I endeavor to show that individuals accused of crimes might decline waiver rewards without suffering trial penalties. There are ways in which we might detect the imposition of trial penalties by state officials and thwart their abilities to inflict them. The present chapter clarifies the distinction between waiver rewards and trial penalties, and illuminates the variety of the latter. Chapter 2 offers a sustained argument against permitting state officials to exact trial penalties.

Though trial penalties are difficult to detect, it is widely agreed that they are routinely assessed against defendants in the United States who insist on trial adjudication and are convicted.[1] This fact might seem uninteresting to those whose legal systems, by law or custom, forbid or strongly discourage the official imposition of trial penalties. Nonetheless, before we can determine whether countries with restrained forms of plea bargaining have adopted more defensible approaches, we need greater clarity

---

[1] I say this, but must immediately add the qualification that most of the scholars who lament the longer sentences that defendants convicted after trials receive, compared with those assigned to similar offenders who plead guilty, fail to distinguish the contribution to that differential made by foregone waiver rewards and trial penalties as I subsequently characterize them. It is thus difficult to tell what reports on the size of that sentencing differential actually tell us about the magnitude of trial penalties. Nonetheless, it does seem almost an article of faith among many legal scholars in the United States that prosecutors and judges generally seek to retaliate against defendants who elect trial adjudication and lose. See, for instance, A. W. Alschuler, "The Trial Judge's Role in Plea Bargaining, Part I," [1976] 76 *Colum. L. Rev.* 1059, 1080; C. McCoy, "Plea Bargaining as Coercion: The Trial Penalty and Plea Bargaining Reform," [2005] 50 *Criminal Law Quarterly* 67; "Note: The Unconstitutionality of Plea Bargaining," [1970] 83 *Harv. L. Rev.* 1387, and D. B. Gifford, "Meaningful Reform of Plea Bargaining: The Control of Prosecutorial Discretion," [1983] 1983 *U. Ill. L. Rev.* 37.

on how waiver rewards differ from trial penalties, as well as the distinct kinds of issues the two raise. To that end, I begin the chapter with an infamous case from the United States, one in which it seems clear that the defendant not only suffered a trial penalty, but also a fairly spectacular one.

Official tolerance of trial penalties: the Bordenkircher case

In its 1978 ruling in *Bordenkircher v. Hayes*, the United States Supreme Court upheld the life sentence of a man who had issued a bad check in the amount of $88.30.[2] The conviction on the bad check charge was Paul Lewis Hayes' third, which made him subject to the state of Kentucky's Habitual Criminal Act. For each of his previous two convictions, Hayes had served only brief stints in prison. He was not, in other words, a dangerous felon of the kind who seemed worthy of prolonged detention, and the charge of which he had most recently been convicted was hardly a serious one. During plea negotiations, the prosecutor in the case had initially offered to recommend a five-year sentence in exchange for Hayes' guilty plea on the bad check charge. The prosecutor had also made it very clear to Hayes that if he did not waive his right to a trial and accept the plea, he would go back and charge Hayes with being a habitual offender, something that the prosecutor had not done at the outset. Hayes rejected the plea agreement and the prosecutor carried out his threat. The majority on the United States Supreme Court emphasized the prior notice that the prosecutor had given Hayes of his intentions if Hayes refused the plea agreement. They also noted that the prosecutor could have charged Hayes with being a habitual offender in the first place, thereby suggesting that the prosecutor was acting pursuant to his proper authority in adding the habitual offender charge.

The *Bordenkircher* decision is remarkable in a number of ways, not the least of which is its upholding of the draconian sentence imposed on Hayes. Suppose that we set to one side questions about the wisdom of having habitual offender statutes in the first place.[3] The Kentucky statute helped produce the extraordinary outcome in the *Bordenkircher* case, but its role in doing so is not what I want to focus on in this chapter. After all, if the habitual offender law had permitted state officials to add only five or ten years to Hayes' sentence, we would still sense that Hayes had been punished, in part, simply for his having insisted upon exercising his right to a trial, a fact that the dissenting opinions in the case caustically noted.[4] Hayes' trial penalty was unusual only in being so large and explicitly threatened by the prosecutor. As such, it

---

[2] *Bordenkircher v. Hayes*, 434 US 357 (1978).

[3] For discussion of habitual offender statutes, see M. G. Turner, J. L. Sundt, B. K. Applegate, and F. T. Cullen, "'Three Strikes and You're Out' Legislation: A National Assessment," [1995] 59 *Federal Probation* 16.

[4] See especially Justice Lewis Powell's dissenting opinion in the case.

dramatically highlighted what many observers of plea bargaining in the United States believe occurs covertly and on a smaller scale in many other cases: Defendants who insist on trial adjudication of the charges against them risk being assessed an extra measure of punishment by prosecutors (or judges) who are annoyed that defendants did not take the plea deals offered to them.[5]

I have suggested that we call the charge or sentence reductions that might be earned by defendants who waive their right to trial and plead guilty "waiver rewards," in recognition of the fact that they gain something by declining to go to trial. As we have seen, there can be considerable variation in how substantial these rewards are, as well as in how they are doled out. One estimate of the sentence reductions that await compliant defendants in the United States is that of Stephen Schulhofer. He claims that individuals who waive their right to trial receive sentences that are from 25 to 75 percent lower than those who insist on going to trial.[6] If these figures are even remotely accurate, then Hayes does not appear to have been offered much of a deal by the prosecutor in his case. Indeed, we might wonder if the prosecutor's offer of a five-year sentence recommendation for writing a bad check in the amount of $88.30 was what led Hayes to balk at pleading guilty and thus take his chances with a trial.

Importantly, the percentages that Schulhofer cites are ambiguous in one crucial respect. They do not tell us whether defendants who decline waiver-reward offers and are found guilty at their trials receive sentences that are 25 to 75 percent longer because they do not receive discounted sentences or because, in addition, prosecutors deliberately recommend (and judges ratify or themselves announce) longer sentences at the culmination of trials in order to further penalize defendants for having insisted upon them. Again, it is tempting to believe that trial penalties are nothing other than lost or foregone waiver rewards.[7] But such an account of trial penalties does not help to clarify what is troubling about them. In the next section, I explain why this is so and thus arrive at a narrower and more perspicacious account of them. Doing so will put us in a better position to identify the kinds of arguments that might be offered on their behalf.

Separating waiver rewards from trial penalties

It will be useful, at the outset, to simplify things so that we can attain greater clarity about the difference between waiver rewards and trial penalties. To that end, set to

---

[5] T. W. Church, Jr. aptly terms this extra measure of punishment a "surcharge" to defendants who insist on exercising their legal right to trial, in "In Defense of 'Bargain Justice'," [1979] 13 *Law & Soc'y Rev.* 509, 520.

[6] S. Schulhofer, "Plea Bargaining as Disaster," [1992] 101 *Yale L. J.* 1979, 1993. See also J. Bowers, "Punishing the Innocent," [2008] 156 *U. Pa. L. Rev.* 1117, 1144–5, where he notes plea bargaining's lenient treatment of low-level offenders.

[7] Indeed, I once defended such an account. See my "To Waive or Not to Waive: The Right to Trial and Plea Bargaining," [2008] 2 *Criminal Law and Philosophy* 181.

one side, for the time being, questions about whether we should permit fact or charge bargaining and thus focus exclusively on the possibility that defendants who confess or agree to waive their right to trial and plead guilty might, in return, receive sentence reductions of some magnitude or other. Assume also that the sentencing scheme in place is defensible, in that the sentence ranges for the various criminal offenses are set with an eye to both comparative and absolute proportionality, or, if one prefers, in ways that are optimally crime-reductive.[8] Further, assume that defendants have not been deliberately overcharged as part of a strategy by prosecutors to put pressure on them to plead guilty rather than go to trial. Subsequently, I show how disproportionately harsh sentencing schemes and strategic overcharging can both have effects that are indistinguishable from those of trial penalties. But first we need to get clear on how trial penalties differ from foregone waiver rewards.

Suppose that defendant Henderson has been charged with armed robbery and that the statutorily defined sentence range for such an offense is a three- to six-year prison term. The lead prosecutor in the case comes to Henderson (or, more likely, Henderson's attorney) and offers to recommend a sentence at the low end of that range (say, three years) if Henderson will agree to plead guilty. The prosecutor also assures Henderson that she has spoken with the presiding judge in the case and received assurances that the judge is willing to go along with such a sentence recommendation. Against his attorney's advice, Henderson declines to take the deal and insists on going to trial. He is convicted by a jury and, post-trial, the prosecutor recommends a five-year sentence to the judge which the judge accepts. On the face of it, it would seem that the waiver reward in Henderson's case is two years and that therefore, on the flipside, his trial penalty—the extra measure of punishment Henderson receives because he elected trial adjudication of the charge against him—is likewise two years. Yet this way of looking at things obscures two different factors that might affect Henderson's final sentence.

To distinguish them, I borrow an analogy from Kenneth Kipnis. In explaining what he took to be unjust about plea bargaining, Kipnis employed an analogy involving a college professor who engaged in grade bargaining.[9] Here is how grade bargaining works: Students submit papers to which the professor gives a cursory reading. The professor then tells students that if they will waive their right to a more careful and thorough reading of their papers, she will award them a better grade than her cursory reading suggests is warranted. Suppose that student Thompson's paper appears to merit a grade of C based on the professor's cursory reading. Thompson is offered a grade of B if she will waive her right to a second reading of her paper. If Thompson refuses the grade proffer, she takes her chances with the professor's more careful reading of her paper. It might turn out that the professor will see virtues in

---

[8] For discussion of the two types of proportionality, see A. von Hirsch, *Censure and Sanctions* (Oxford: Clarendon Press, 1993) 17–19. von Hirsch uses the terms "ordinal" and "cardinal" to refer to comparative and non-comparative proportionality, respectively.

[9] K. Kipnis, "Criminal Justice and the Negotiated Plea," [1976] 86 *Ethics* 93, 104–5.

the paper that she missed the first time, in which case she will assign the paper a bet-ter grade than the C which she initially thought it deserved. It is even possible that the second, more thorough reading will convince the professor to give Thompson a grade of A on the paper. Obviously, Thompson risks losing out on the A grade if she takes the professor's bargained grade proffer. But it could also turn out that the profes-sor's second reading of the paper will confirm the cursory reading grade or, worse, will convince the professor that the paper is a poorer effort than she initially believed it to be.

Many students, faced with the choice between accepting a grade that may be somewhat better than the one they deserve and risking receiving a grade that is worse, though perhaps more in accordance with what they deserve, will jump at the opportunity to obtain the higher grade. In this way they are like many criminal defendants who are charged with crimes of which they know or suspect that they are guilty. Such defendants are willing, if not eager, to plead if they can thereby gain some measure of lenity from the court.[10] Of course, a few defendants will believe that they are innocent or hope that though they are guilty a judge or jury will acquit them. The former defendants are akin to students who believe that their papers are significantly better than the professor's cursory reading found them to be—indeed so much better that the proffered higher grade still does not, in their view, give them what they deserve. The latter defendants—ones who know that they are guilty but who hope that trials will produce acquittals—are like students who know or suspect that the cursory reading was on the mark but who hope that demanding a second reading will yield a grade outcome that is no worse than the proffered grade. Perhaps they believe, or vainly hope, that the professor will be intimidated by students who insist on a second reading, fearful that such students will turn out to be belligerent grade-grubbers who will demand conferences at which the professor must explain and justify the assigned grade in laborious detail. Such students surmise that, rather than risk having to endure such conferences, the professor will be more generous in her second reading than the paper warrants. There might also be some students who are indifferent about their grades, at least to the extent that the proffered higher grade does not succeed in motivating them to waive their right to a second reading. Such students, for whatever reasons, insist on the second reading and are prepared to live with the outcome. They are like criminal defendants who know they are guilty as charged, suspect that trials will yield convictions, but are indifferent to the sentenc-ing deals offered by state officials. Such defendants are grimly determined to make the state go through the motions of trial conviction. One suspects that defendants of this kind are exceedingly rare.

---

[10] A richly detailed account of the willingness of most criminal defendants to plead guilty in exchange for some measure of lenity from the prosecutor or judge is provided by M. Heumann in *Plea Bargaining: The Experiences of Prosecutors, Judges, and Defense Attorneys* (Chicago: University of Chicago Press, 1977), see especially chapter 4.

Kipnis offers the grade-bargaining analogy to convince us that there is something deeply suspect about plea bargaining. Grade bargaining is inappropriate because grades should be determined based on a professor's honest and careful assessment of the merits of student work. The grading of student papers is a practice that is strongly governed by desert norms, in the sense that considerations other than what students deserve because of their work are almost always irrelevant, or hardly count at all. So too, Kipnis suggests, there is something wrong with having criminal offenders' sentences determined by bargaining between them and prosecutors or judges. State officials have a responsibility to see to it that offenders are punished commensurately with the seriousness of their crimes.[11] We will subsequently spend considerable time analyzing the arguments that might be given to justify waiver rewards, including ones that defend it within a deserved-punishment framework. But, if nothing else, Kipnis's analogy helps us to see the way in which soliciting pleas with offers of waiver rewards appears troubling.

Kipnis's analogy can be developed further in order to refine our understanding of waiver rewards and trial penalties. One thing that the analogy provides is what we might term a student's "presumptive grade." This is the grade suggested by the professor's cursory reading of the paper. It is presumptive in the sense that a second, more careful reading of the paper might convince the professor to change the grade. The second reading might yield a higher grade or a lower one. Either could be fully justified given the second reading. If a student demands a second reading and the professor supplies it, and does so fairly and conscientiously, then the student has no reasonable grounds for complaint if the second reading leads the professor to revise the presumptive grade downward. This was a risk that the student took in requesting the second reading. Importantly, the lowered grade is not a penalty *for* having requested the second reading *if* the second reading is done without malice; instead it is a reasonable and foreseeable possible outcome of the second reading.

But what if the professor, irked at having to supply a second reading, consciously or even unconsciously evaluates the paper more negatively? She might actively search through the paper for flaws or shortcomings, or see the ones that she has already seen in a more negative light. Or she might decide to take out her annoyance with the student more directly by assigning her paper a lower grade than the cursory reading grade without bothering to find some pretext for doing so. It will, undoubtedly, be very hard to tell whether the professor has done things of this kind. We might even suspect that she is likely to do them, especially if she is prepared to shirk her responsibilities and engage in grade bargaining of the kind described in the first place. If she does penalize the student in one of these ways for having requested a second reading, then it would seem that the student has a legitimate complaint about the

---

[11] I put this responsibility somewhat ambiguously so that it is neutral between strongly desert-based accounts of sentencing and ones that focus more on crime reduction. Even the latter would generally have us punish more serious crimes more harshly, though for different reasons than desert-based accounts would have us do so.

outcome. Her lowered paper grade is not one she risked by refusing the grade bargain and requesting a "fair" second reading. It is instead partly a function of the professor's desire to retaliate against the student for having the temerity to request a more thorough reading of her paper. In this, we have an analogy with what I deem a trial penalty proper.

Notice this also: Students confronted by professors who offer grade bargains might reasonably worry about what will happen to them if they refuse the bargain and insist on a second, more careful evaluation. What looks like an offer might plausibly be construed by students as harboring a threat. In some cases, a grade-bargaining professor's tendency to be harder on students who request second readings will become common knowledge; word will get around that this is something students should expect. If this occurs, and the professor does nothing to combat the perception of vindictiveness on her part—or worse, encourages it by coyly denying that anything of the sort takes place when challenged by students unhappy with their second-reading grades—then at some point it will become clear that the professor is trading on her reputation for punishing students who are foolish enough to demand second readings.

Provisionally, then, we can say that a trial penalty is an additional increment of punishment imposed on defendants who are convicted after trials, one that is unrelated to the seriousness of their crimes as these are revealed at their trials. The added measure of punishment is inflicted for the sole purpose of retaliating against defendants who have elected trial adjudication of the charges against them. Waiver rewards, by contrast, are downward departures from the punishment defendants merit for their crimes, at least on the assumption that a defensible sentencing scheme is in place and that state officials attempt in a serious and careful way to assign sentences according to relevant sentencing factors under that scheme. These accounts will need to be modified later on, but for now they will suffice.

Detecting trial penalties

Depending on the legal system in which plea bargaining operates, it will be more or less difficult to detect trial penalties and, if it turns out that they are illicit, seek to discourage state officials from imposing them. Much depends on the abilities of defendants (or their attorneys) to determine what their sentences might be if they were convicted after trials and not assessed trial penalties. What is needed, in other words, is some reliable procedure for determining a presumptive post-trial sentence on each of the charges that has been lodged against an individual, where such sentences are shorn of any supplement designed to punish the individual for having elected trial adjudication. In the United States, there is no mechanism in place that enables defendants to determine the sentences they are likely to receive should they go to trial and lose. Whether this arrangement is intentional or not, it undoubtedly helps to obscure the roles that lost waiver rewards and trial penalties play in determining defendants' post-trial sentencing outcomes. In England and Wales, by contrast, defendants who come before the Crown Court can now ask judges for an "advanced indication of sentence," at plea and case management hearings.[12] This development holds considerable promise for the detection of trial penalties, as judges who assign post-trial sentences that exceed the ones they indicated earlier could be required to justify them.

There are, in fact, a variety of ways in which we might give defendants and their attorneys the means to detect trial penalties. In addition to the British procedure just described, we could require prosecutors to announce presumptive sentences when they levy charges against individuals. Such presumptive sentences would be expected to take into account relevant sentencing factors, whatever those were within the prosecutor's legal jurisdiction. If prosecutors subsequently made different sentencing recommendations post-trial, they might be expected to justify them, to show that they amounted to something other than a surcharge for defendants having exercised their right to trial.

However, it seems advisable to come up with a more formal and elaborate provisional sentencing procedure. In the first place, prosecutors rarely act alone in determining sentences, and in some legal systems they do not make sentencing recommendations at all. Judges typically play a key role in sentencing, and in some legal systems determine sentences all on their own. In this crucial respect, plea bargaining differs from grade bargaining, where the professors who announce the cursory reading grades also assign the final grades. It therefore seems a good idea to involve judges in any effort to give defendants (and their attorneys) some clearer sense of what sentences await them should they be convicted at trial. Second, and more significantly, before any post-trial sentence is indicated, there should be procedures in place to ensure both that the evidence the state has amassed supports the charges up to some level of sufficiency and that defendants fully understand what they forego if they confess or waive their right to trial. The procedures should also seek to ensure that such concessions by defendants have been made voluntarily.

To these ends, I propose a plea procedure that consists of a pre-trial hearing before a judge, one that would be initiated by defendants who indicate their willingness to admit their guilt.[13] At such pre-trial hearings, which we might usefully term "settlement hearings," the state would be expected to make a brief presentation of the evidence in support of the charges it has filed. It could also be asked to make sentence recommendations for any charges that survive scrutiny by the settlement-hearing

---

[12] See A. Ashworth and M. Redmayne, *The Criminal Process*, 4th edition (Oxford: Oxford University Press, 2010) 307–8.

[13] The pre-trial hearings that I propose have precursors in the scholarly literature. See Alschuler (n 1 above) 1122–54; Note: "Restructuring the Plea Bargain," [1972] 82 *Yale L. J.* 286; and J. I. Turner, "Judicial Participation in Plea Negotiations: A Comparative View," [2006] 54 *Am. J. Comp. L.* 199. In England and Wales, plea and case management hearings play somewhat analogous roles. See Ashworth and Redmayne (n 12 above) 307–8.

judge. To facilitate the judge's grasp of the evidence, a full dossier of the state's case, including police reports, pertinent evidence analyses, and likely witness testimony, would be delivered to the judge prior to the hearing. I would also require prosecutors to list all charges filed and dropped in the case, so that the judge could determine whether any charge bargaining has occurred between the prosecution and defense. The judge would also be expected to query the prosecution about any and all exculpatory evidence and the likely availability of state witnesses. Further, victims (if there are any) or their immediate survivors should be permitted to file affidavits describing their versions of the events under investigation. The purpose of allowing such affidavits would be to enable the settlement-hearing judge to determine whether the evidence dossier provided a full and accurate picture of the case, rather than one crafted through negotiations between prosecution and defense attorneys.[14]

During the hearing, defendants, with their attorneys' participation, would be given the opportunity to challenge the state's charges, its evidence for them, or its sentencing recommendations. In the vast majority of cases, the point of permitting defendants to do so would be to allow them to explain their side of things, dispute excessive or duplicative charges, or argue for sentences lower than those recommended by prosecutors. However, a few defendants might steadfastly protest their innocence, hoping that the judge would see things their way and throw out all of the charges. Though trials might be the most appropriate venue for defendants to challenge the state's case against them, we should not prohibit them from doing so at settlement hearings. As Josh Bowers has suggested, certain kinds of innocent defendants might be unlikely to prevail at trial.[15] Even if they do prevail, the "process costs" that trials would force them to endure might rob them of their victories.[16] Settlement hearings might offer such defendants the only reasonable prospect of escaping all punishment.

Nonetheless, most defendants who opted for settlement hearings would be expected ultimately to plead guilty to one or more of the charges against them. They would also be expected to address questions put to them by the presiding judge concerning their crimes. In other words, by requesting settlement hearings, defendants would be understood to have waived their right against self-incrimination, at least for the duration of the hearing. There seems little point in insisting on such a right if one is prepared to admit one's guilt. To protect those defendants who might decide after their settlement hearings to proceed to trial, we could prohibit the introduction at their trials of any testimony that they gave at their settlement hearings. We could

---

[14] As I envision them, such victim affidavits would not function in the ways that so-called "victim impact statements" do, that is, as attempts to influence the sentences assigned defendants who admit their guilt. Instead, the affidavits serve as a check upon the abilities of prosecutors and defendants to present a sanitized version of events to the settlement-hearing judge, one typically designed to minimize the number of crimes committed or the defendant's culpability for them.

[15] Bowers (n 6 above) 1124–32.

[16] Bowers (n 6 above) 1132–9. See also M. M. Feeley, *The Process Is the Punishment: Handling Cases in a Lower Criminal Court* (New York: Russell Sage Foundation, 1979).

also require trials to be conducted by a judge who was not involved in the settlement hearing.

The judges who conducted the settlement hearings would decide which charges, if any, to retain against defendants. Any charges dropped would be dropped without prejudice. This means that prosecutors could later re-file them if they could come up with more convincing evidence on their behalf. Settlement-hearing judges would also be expected to advise defendants about the legal rights they waive, or perhaps enjoy in more dilute form, by confessing or pleading guilty. There are legitimate questions about the standard of proof that judges should employ in making decisions about charges during settlement hearings. For the most part, I would urge a fairly low one, often referred to as the "preponderance of evidence" standard, whereby charges would be upheld by judges so long as they believed that the evidence made it more likely than not that defendants would be found guilty if they elected trial adjudication. A higher standard could be employed by judges in settlement hearings, but it is important to note that such hearings would be nothing like full trials at which judges would hear the state and defense cases in their entirety. During settlement hearings judges would be expected to do no more than ensure that there is an adequate factual basis for any subsequent admissions of guilt by defendants. Trials would remain the appropriate forum for defendants who wish to put the state's case fully to the test. However, though judges might decline to dismiss charges for which there was a preponderance of evidence, they could advise defendants that, in their view, the state's case was well short of conclusive.[17] Defendants would then be in a better position to decide for themselves whether to plead guilty or proceed to trial.[18]

Still, a stronger case can be made for insisting upon a higher evidence sufficiency standard when the charges against individuals are more serious and thus have the potential for producing lengthy prison terms. In some countries, plea bargaining is permitted only when the charges to which the accused are willing to accede produce prison sentences below a certain level.[19] The idea, I take it, is that more serious charges should be adjudicated by more formal trial processes. Mistaken convictions are not only terribly unfortunate in such cases but also costly and non-productive. I would not require trials when the charges are serious, because I am not convinced that there will be that many cases in which wholly innocent defendants will admit their guilt if they face long prison sentences. But I am not averse to requiring settlement-hearing judges to satisfy themselves that the evidence meets a higher standard in such cases. Perhaps when the sentences defendants face if convicted exceed five years'

---

[17] This might be particularly useful information in legal jurisdictions in which trial judges routinely order acquittals at the end of the state's presentation of its case.

[18] As many observers have noted, defendants are sometimes poorly represented by their attorneys. Judges at settlement hearings who advised defendants concerning their prospects at trial might help them to make more informed decisions about which course of action was in their best interests.

[19] See M. Langer, "From Legal Transplants to Legal Translations: The Globalization of Plea Bargaining and the Americanization Thesis in Criminal Procedure," [2004] 45 *Harv. Int'l L. J.* 1, 50.

imprisonment, we should insist that judges at settlement hearings find the evidence to be "highly likely" to lead to a judgment of guilt at the conclusion of a trial.

A central feature of settlement hearings would be a determination by the judge of a presumptive sentence for each of the retained charges. Presumptive sentences could conceivably come in either of two forms. They could be fairly specific, representing the judge's best estimates of the sentence he would impose if a defendant elected trial adjudication on any of the charges and was found guilty.[20] Alternatively, the judge could identify upper limits beyond which he would not go in sentencing individuals found guilty after trials.[21] The slight disadvantage to the latter approach is that it would introduce more indeterminacy into presumptive sentences. But at least those charged with crimes would have some sense of the worst sentence they would be likely to receive if they elected trial adjudication and were found guilty. Regardless of which approach is employed, the sentences announced would be presumptive only. We would need to allow judges to adjust them upwards or downwards post-trial based on additional pertinent information about defendants or their crimes that was revealed at their trials. Trials will sometimes show that a defendant's actions were more culpable or harmful than state officials initially believed them to be when they first evaluated the case in light of the relevant law. Of course, trials might also show that a defendant's actions were less harmful or culpable, in which case the appropriate response would be the assignment of a sentence lower in the relevant sentencing range. We could ensure that the announcement of presumptive sentences was not mere window dressing by requiring judges who revised them post-trial to justify doing so. Moreover, we could make upward revisions a ground for appellate review. In that way we could discourage judges from imposing trial penalties because they believe that defendants should not have insisted upon trial adjudication.

How would settlement hearings help us to mark the distinction between waiver rewards and trial penalties? Returning to our earlier example, suppose that Henderson indicates a willingness to plead guilty to armed robbery and requests a settlement hearing. The judge in the case listens to what the prosecution and the defense have to say, determines that the evidence against Henderson meets the standard of sufficiency, consults the sentencing range for armed robbery, and announces a presumptive sentence of four years' imprisonment on the armed robbery charge. Now, suppose that the legal system in which Henderson's case is being adjudicated permits sentence reductions for defendants who are willing to admit their guilt. For the sake of discussion, suppose that if Henderson pleads guilty to the armed robbery, he can get his sentence reduced to three years' imprisonment. The one-year sentence reduction is a

---

[20] Such sentences could be made more informed if defendants' requests for settlement hearings initiated the preparation of a pre-trial sentencing report by the probation office. Such reports would largely consist of biographical information about defendants and any available information about the crimes with which they had been charged. See "Restructuring the Plea Bargain" (n 13 above) 300 and 308.

[21] This is the practice in England and Wales at plea and case management hearings. See Ashworth and Redmayne (n 12 above) 303.

waiver reward—something Henderson gets in exchange for waiving his right to trial if indeed he chooses to do so. Whether such an inducement to plead gives Henderson something that he does not deserve is a complicated question, one the answer to which depends not only on the justice of the overall sentencing scheme but also on the wisdom and fairness of the judge in determining the presumptive sentence. Similarly, whether waiver rewards produce sentences that are suboptimal from the standpoint of reducing crime depends on whether sentences have, in general, been set up with a view to maximizing the benefits of legal punishment and minimizing its costs, as well as upon whether the judge has properly taken into account relevant sentencing factors in determining Henderson's presumptive sentence. But set such matters aside for now. Whatever else it does, by offering a reduced sentence in exchange for a guilty plea, the waiver reward improves Henderson's position, at least on the assumptions that he is guilty of the crime with which he has been charged and that the presumptive sentence was an appropriate one given his crime.

Suppose that Henderson declines the waiver reward, goes to trial, is subsequently found guilty, and the presumptive sentence of four years' imprisonment is ultimately authorized by the court. Has Henderson, in that case, suffered a trial penalty? My contention is that he has not. True, Henderson winds up with a sentence that is a year longer than the one he would have received had he accepted the waiver reward and pleaded guilty. But the risk of that longer sentence was something Henderson took by going to trial, just as students whose presumptive grades are C take a risk if they refuse the professor's offer of a B and are subsequently awarded their presumptive grades based on a more careful (and not vindictive) reading of their papers. Crucially, Henderson does not receive the longer sentence simply because he insisted on going to trial. He also receives it because he elected to forego the state's offer of a waiver reward. Just as importantly, Henderson does not, in the end, receive a sentence that is inappropriate, at least on the assumption that he is actually guilty and the announced presumptive sentence was based on a careful assessment of where Henderson's offense fits into the relevant sentencing range.

If the preceding conclusion is troubling, it might be because individuals who accept waiver rewards or bargained grades appear to get something they do not deserve. To many, it will seem that state officials are doing something illicit by offering such rewards, just as we are pretty sure that professors who shirk their grading responsibilities by offering students bargained grades do so. Whether or not individuals accept such offers does not seem to affect the seriousness of their crimes, in the case of criminal defendants, or the quality of their papers, in the case of students. Prima facie, there is something suspicious about a practice that produces different outcomes across individuals who appear deserving of similar ones. We have come to what I believe is the crux of the matter—whether the practice of offering waiver rewards can be defended. This topic will occupy us in coming chapters. But even if the practice of offering such waiver rewards cannot be defended, it does not follow that individuals who receive their presumptive sentences after being found guilty at trial have suffered wrongs at the hands of prosecutors or other state officials in the form of trial penalties. Robert Scott's and William Stuntz's quip that offers of sentence reductions cannot be construed as placing defendants under duress because "the choice to plead guilty is too generous to the defendant" seems correct, at least if we focus narrowly on the offer of waiver rewards in contexts in which defendants have been charged fairly and would otherwise receive sentences reflecting the seriousness of their crimes.[22] Those who plead guilty may receive better sentences than are appropriate given their crimes; but it does not follow, for the reasons we have seen, that those found guilty after trials receive sentences that are inappropriate.

However, suppose that the judge in Henderson's case imposes a five-year sentence on Henderson after he is convicted at trial of armed robbery. That is altogether different unless the judge can convincingly point to evidence revealed at Henderson's trial showing that his crime was worse than it initially appeared to be. The one-year increase relative to Henderson's presumptive sentence looks suspiciously like a trial penalty—an increase in his sentence based solely on his having elected trial adjudication. Again, a trial penalty is not the same as a foregone waiver reward; it is an extra measure of punishment the purpose of which is to penalize defendants like Henderson for exercising their right to trial. Trial penalties will typically be motivated by animus on the part of prosecutors or judges. They do not want defendants to go to trial and are prepared to employ various measures to discourage them from doing so. But we need not build reference to the motivations of legal officials into an account of trial penalties. Instead, we can say that they consist of increases in defendants' post-trial sentences, as compared with their presumptive sentences, which are otherwise inexplicable except as they function to punish defendants for having exercised the right to trial. Subsequently, we will have to amend this account if it is to accommodate the variety of trial penalties.

Importantly, on the account I am defending, there is no difference between waiver rewards and trial penalties with respect to their exerting pressure on defendants to accede to guilty pleas. Both create differentials between guilty plea and post-trial sentencing outcomes, and both can be manipulated to make the differentials substantial. But they create these differentials in distinctive ways. Waiver rewards do so by offering defendants sentences below their presumptive ones. Assuming that the sentencing scheme is defensible and judges set presumptive sentences by taking into account appropriate sentencing factors, we could even say that waiver rewards offer defendants unmerited leniency—that is, sentences lower than those which the sentencing scheme would ordinarily dictate given the nature of their crimes. Trial penalties, by contrast, pressure defendants to plead by threatening them with sentences higher than their presumptive ones. Again, assuming a defensible sentencing scheme and conscientious efforts by judges to set presumptive sentences fairly, we can say

---

[22]   R. E. Scott and W. J. Stuntz, "Plea Bargaining as Contract," [1992] 101 *Yale L. J.* 1909, 1920.

that trial penalties threaten defendants with sentences that are longer or harsher than those warranted by the gravity of their crimes.

State officials could offer waiver rewards without threatening trial penalties. The leverage over defendants such an approach would yield would be mostly a function of the magnitude of the waiver rewards offered. If state officials are permitted both to offer waiver rewards and to threaten trial penalties, the pressure exerted on defendants to plead guilty will be nearly irresistible. Yet without a presumptive sentencing scheme, it will be nearly impossible, in practice, to determine the source of the leverage exerted by state officials. Settlement hearings at which presumptive sentences are announced would allow us to detect and discourage trial penalties. Upward post-trial sentence departures would automatically be suspect and require justification. Individuals who received post-trial sentences longer than their presumptive sentences and who were not convinced by judges' explanations for the increases would be permitted to appeal their sentences.

In the absence of a presumptive sentencing scheme, we are mostly left guessing whether prosecutors have recommended, and judges have imposed, trial penalties. Most prosecutors will not act as blatantly as the one in the *Bordenkircher* case did, threatening defendants who they fear will elect trials with much longer sentences. Nor will they need to, since in some legal jurisdictions it will be common knowledge that prosecutors (and judges) do not look kindly on defendants who refuse waiver reward proffers and insist on trial adjudication of the charges against them. Criminal defendants will often, as a result, find themselves in much the same position as the students in Kipnis's analogy, who fear what grade-bargaining professors will do if they refuse their offers and make professors do their jobs.

One implication of the preceding account is worth noting. As long as we see them as two sides of the same coin, the arguments that might be given on behalf of waiver rewards will also be arguments in support of trial penalties. However, if they are distinguishable in the way I have suggested, then the arguments in favor of each will differ. What might justify prosecutors or judges in offering defendants sentences less than the ones that are appropriate given their crimes is one thing; what might justify such officials in recommending or imposing longer post-trial sentences for no other reason than to penalize defendants for having elected trial adjudication is another. Even if it can be shown that trial penalties are indefensible, plea bargaining could flourish if waiver rewards can be defended. In Chapter 2, I argue in detail that trial penalties cannot be justified. Subsequent chapters examine the defensibility of waiver rewards on the assumption that trial penalties are inappropriate.

Objections to settlement hearings

Various objections might be made against the pre-trial settlement hearings that I have proposed. Even if it is granted that such hearings would be useful in isolating trial penalties and distinguishing them from waiver rewards, their structure or feasibility might be questioned. Since I refer to such hearings throughout the remainder of the book, further discussion of their merits and practicality is in order.

Quite independently of whether settlement hearings would help us separate waiver rewards and trial penalties, having judges more actively involved in reviewing charges, the evidence for them, and determining appropriate sentences seems strongly advisable. Few who have examined the plea colloquy process in the United States, for instance, are satisfied with the extent to which judges examine the factual basis of pleas, though they are supposed to do so.[23] It is hard to believe that closer judicial scrutiny of the evidence would not improve the outcomes of the adjudication process. Prosecutors may be reluctant to drop charges once they have filed them or may be content to rely on the accumulation of charges in order to put pressure on defendants to plead guilty. Settlement hearings, in the form I have proposed, would afford defendants and their attorneys the opportunity to contest some of the charges (though presumably not all of them) as redundant or not supported by the evidence. The result in many cases would be some adjustment in the charges, bringing them more in line with the evidence. Prosecutors might also tend to recommend sentences high in the relevant sentencing ranges. Defendants and their attorneys would have the chance at settlement hearings not only to urge lower sentences but also to provide presiding judges with pertinent information in support of their claims. This, too, might work to produce outcomes that are more appropriate for defendants, given their crimes.

Granted, prosecutors are supposed to be both advocates for the public interest in containing crime and ministers of justice.[24] But many observers doubt that they can or do fulfill both of these functions effectively.[25] In the United States, where many prosecutors are elected officials, there seems a widespread tendency for them to focus on maximizing convictions at some cost to both procedural and substantive justice.[26] This tendency might not be as pronounced in countries in which prosecutors are subject to fewer or less direct political pressures. Nonetheless, having state officials, whose roles and aims are somewhat distinct, scrutinize the charges and evidence in criminal cases is likely to enhance the fairness of the adjudication process and its outcomes. Further, many criminal defendants are indigent. The quality of the legal counsel they receive is thus highly variable. Again, in the United States, those accused

---

[23]   See, for instance, Turner (n 13 above) 212–23.

[24]   In the United States, see the American Bar Association, *Criminal Justice Section Standard 3–1.2* (1980), and *Model Rules of Professional Conduct Rule 3.8* (1983). In England and Wales, there is *The Code for Crown Prosecutors*, which seems to give more emphasis to the duty of prosecutors to ensure that justice is done and, in particular, the innocent are not punished or the guilty over-punished. However, Ashworth and Redmayne (n 12 above, at 215) note some evidence that prosecutors in England and Wales at times get too close to the police and share attitudes with them such that prosecutions that should be halted are allowed to continue.

[25]   For discussion, see S. Z. Fisher, "In Search of the Virtuous Prosecutor: A Conceptual Framework," [1988] 15 *Am. J. Crim. L.* 197.

[26]   Fisher (n 25 above) 199–200.

of crimes will often be represented by overworked or underpaid attorneys.[27] In other countries, where more generous provisions are made for the defense of poor people accused of crimes, it might not be as imperative for judges to ensure that they have been properly advised and vigorously represented. Still, there are enough instances in which defendants are represented by incompetent or neglectful counsel that we should welcome greater judicial involvement in ensuring that accused persons are informed of their rights and protected against prosecutors who are sometimes a bit too eager to secure their convictions.

One likely objection to settlement hearings is that they will be inefficient. Such hearings will inevitably use up precious time and other resources that judges and prosecutors have in short supply. The main virtue of the more unencumbered forms of plea bargaining that exist in countries like the United States is that they enable state officials to process a high volume of criminal cases. Settlement hearings would take more time than standard plea colloquies, or so it would seem, and thus the courts would be more clogged than they already are.

It must be conceded that settlement hearings would slow the charge adjudication process. Of course, almost any alteration in unfettered plea bargaining practices that would require the courts to scrutinize more closely charges, evidence, and sentences will have such an effect. That hardly constitutes sufficient grounds for rejecting reforms, especially if they would not unduly impede the workings of the adjudication process and improve it in other respects. Importantly, there are already jurisdictions in the United States that employ mechanisms similar to the hearings that I have proposed, and the new plea and case management hearings in the Crown Courts of England and Wales likewise interpose judges between prosecutors eager to resolve cases and defendants who might be tempted to quickly accede to their wishes.[28] Yet it does not seem likely that efficient case-processing will be significantly impaired by such measures. Any requirement that the courts ensure the voluntary character of confessions or guilty pleas, and that defendants fully understand what they are giving up by conceding their guilt, will complicate and lengthen the charge adjudication process. Settlement hearings will only marginally increase the burdens of ensuring procedural and substantive justice.

Nonetheless, given the fact that conducting such hearings will add incrementally to the costs of charge adjudication, it might be suggested that they would make more sense if the charges in question were more serious rather than less so. Why should we require judges to review charges and the evidence for them, and issue presumptive sentences, when the charges will yield no more than modest fines in the event that the accused admit their guilt? Still, it will be hard to draw a clear line separating less

[27] S. Bibas, "Plea Bargaining Outside the Shadow of Trial," [2004] 117 *Harv. L. Rev.* 2463, 2476–82; and Schulhofer (n 6 above) 1988–91.

[28] For accounts of these hearings in the United States, see Turner (n 13 above) 247–56, for discussion of the state of Connecticut's plea bargaining system and judicial participation in it. On plea and case management hearings in England and Wales, see Ashworth and Redmayne (n 12 above) 307–8.

and more serious offenses. It would seem that any charges that might produce a custodial sentence should be reviewed by a judge in light of the evidence that state officials have been able to amass. Further, even convictions for relatively minor offenses can stigmatize individuals or add to their previous convictions in ways that might have repercussions for them further down the road. Hence, I would err on the side of providing at least brief settlement hearings in all cases excepting those for which the likely sanctions are clearly insignificant. A fallback position would be to provide them for any case in which the possible sanctions exceed some specified fine or other official imposition.

The idea that judges will rein in prosecutors or other state officials who zealously pursue convictions will be greeted with skepticism by some. It might be thought that judges will too often go along with prosecutors' sentencing recommendations which, we should assume, will tend to be high. Judges, too, will want to conserve their scarce resources. They will not want unnecessary trials and so might tend to side with prosecutors' sentencing recommendations in order to put pressure on defendants to enter guilty pleas.[29] Defendants who declined to plead guilty and thereby sacrificed any waiver rewards on offer would face the prospect of somewhat artificially elevated sentences, even if their post-trial sentences were not increased relative to their presumptive sentences. In effect, trial penalties would be built in to presumptive sentences and would dampen the enthusiasm of defendants for trial adjudication.

I am not convinced that judges would invariably go along with prosecutors' high sentence recommendations. Again, in jurisdictions in which there are pre-trial hearings akin to those I have proposed, it does not appear that judges simply accede to prosecutors' charging decisions or sentencing recommendations.[30] When judges are given a more central role in the charging and sentence-setting process, they appear to take it seriously. In standard plea colloquies in the United States, judges often find themselves in the essentially passive position of ratifying agreements worked out ahead of time between prosecutors and defendants or their attorneys. In the settlement hearings I envision, prosecutors would present the charges and evidence for them, defendants or their attorneys would respond, and it would then be up to judges to set the final charges and announce presumptive sentences. We might reasonably hope that judges would be emboldened by their more significant role in the adjudication process to display their own independent judgment regarding the charges and sentences appropriate to defendants' criminal misconduct.[31]

Admittedly, the preceding argument does not quite address the concern about the ways in which prosecutors' and judges' interests in avoiding trial adjudication coincide. But it should be noted that the leverage that state officials have to induce guilty pleas is a function of the differentials they can create between plea bargained and

---

[29] Heumann offers a useful analysis of judicial incentives to encourage plea bargains in *Plea Bargaining* (n 10 above) 127–52.

[30] See Turner (n 13 above) 254.   [31] A point made by Alschuler as well (n 1 above) 1132.

post-trial sentences. In subsequent chapters I show that there are cogent arguments for keeping waiver rewards modest. If those arguments are persuasive, then in a properly constituted charge adjudication regime, state officials would not be able to gain much leverage by setting presumptive sentences at inflated levels. Even if prosecutors invariably asked for high presumptive sentences and judges ratified them, prosecutors would no longer be able to substantially discount them and thereby create powerful incentives for defendants to plead guilty. True, defendants who were found guilty after trials would likely receive longer sentences, but not much longer ones. This might encourage more of them to opt for trial adjudication and the possibility of acquittal, especially if they believed that their announced presumptive sentences were unduly harsh. Prosecutors and judges would have to be careful about inflating sentences or they would be faced with more defendants willing to contest the charges against them in court.

It might be suggested that judges should not only announce presumptive sentences during settlement hearings but also actually negotiate the charge or sentence discounts that defendants will receive if they agree to admit their guilt.[32] In that way, defendants would acquire reasonable assurance about the outcome they face if they plead. However, there is another way in which to signal to defendants what sentences they will receive if they waive their right to trial and plead guilty. Suppose that waiver rewards were kept fixed and modest. Under such a scheme, defendants who knew their presumptive sentences would be able to figure out the sentences they would receive if they pleaded guilty. Moreover, we would avoid the possibility that judges would negotiate inappropriate charge or sentence discounts, ones that are inconsistent with the sentencing scheme's aims. And we would reduce the impact of the many factors that now figure in plea bargained outcomes, factors that often have no discernible relation to penal purposes.[33]

A further, significant objection to settlement hearings cites the conflict of interest that they would potentially create for the judges who participated in them. At the hearings, judges would be apprised of the charges against defendants and the evidence for those charges. They would also hear from defendants themselves, some of whom would openly admit their guilt on all the charges against them, and others of whom would do so to some of the charges. Also, some defendants would admit their guilt but contest the prosecutors' sentence recommendation. After all of this, it is hard to believe that judges could effectively grant such defendants the presumption of innocence if their cases ultimately went to trial. Yet that is what they might be expected to do if, after the hearing, defendants elected not to enter guilty pleas.

As we have seen, one solution to this problem is to require that any judge who participates in a settlement hearing for a defendant be barred from presiding over the subsequent trial of that defendant on the same or a reduced set of charges.[34] At least

---

[32] Alschuler (n 1 above) 1124.   [33] See, for instance, Bibas (n 27 above) 2470–531.
[34] This is the procedure in Connecticut, as noted by Turner (n 13 above) 248.

in urban jurisdictions, such a requirement should be feasible. In rural ones, however, it might be more difficult to implement.[35] In any case, we ought to be cautious about concluding that participation in a settlement hearing makes impartiality by judges at subsequent trials impossible or unlikely. As Albert Alschuler has noted, judges often have to make rulings on the admissibility of incriminating evidence.[36] In cases in which they exclude such evidence, we do not require or expect them to recuse themselves from subsequent trials of the defendants in question, though they have been privy to evidence that suggests, perhaps strongly, that the defendants are, in fact, guilty. Judges are supposed to remain impartial in spite of what they have seen, and few question whether they are capable of doing so.

Assuming that we have a firm grasp of the difference between waiver rewards and trial penalties, and a mechanism for distinguishing them, the remainder of this chapter is devoted to further development of our understanding of trial penalties and the forms they can take. Unfortunately, they are not confined to post-trial sentences that unaccountably exceed presumptive ones.

Charges added consequent to failed plea negotiations

The prosecutor in the *Bordenkircher* case did not offer one pre-trial discounted sentence to defendant Hayes only to recommend a post-trial sentence that was considerably longer. Indeed, the prosecutor did not wait until after the trial to act; upon Hayes' refusal to accept the initial offer, he immediately went back and added the additional, habitual offender charge. His doing so had all the earmarks of an attempt to impose a trial penalty. It appears to have been motivated by animus and no further evidence about Hayes or his crimes had come forward in the meantime, evidence which might warrant the levying of the additional charge. The majority opinion in the case weakly defended the prosecutor, noting that he could have filed the habitual offender charge at the outset if he had so chosen. True enough, but the fact is that the prosecutor chose not to do so and no evidence emerged to suggest that Hayes had committed further or worse crimes.[37] It is hard to see how any reasonable conclusion can be drawn other than that the prosecutor sought to exact an enormous surcharge for Hayes' insistence on trial adjudication.

Though the *Bordenkircher* case is atypical, it illustrates one of several forms that trial penalties can take. Many criminal defendants face multiple charges and might, as a result, find themselves face to face with prosecutors who offer them some combination of reduced charges and sentences in exchange for guilty pleas. Up to this point, I have ignored the complications raised by multiple charges, but it is necessary

---

[35] See Turner (n 13 above) 248–9.   [36] Alschuler (n 1 above) 1110.

[37] Justice Powell's dissent in the *Bordenkircher* case seems on the mark. He saw the threat to lodge the habitual offender charge as inappropriate given Hayes' crime and past record, claiming that it was an attempt "to discourage and then to penalize with unique severity his exercise of constitutional rights." See *Bordenkircher v. Hayes* (n 2 above) 373.

to confront them and thus begin to clarify whether and when charge bargaining, so-called, involves attempts by legal officials to impose or threaten trial penalties.

Let us begin with a simplified though probably not all that unusual scenario. Suppose that Zimmerman has been charged with three criminal offenses. Suppose also that Zimmerman has not been strategically overcharged by the prosecutor in order to increase the pressure on her to plead guilty. Instead, Zimmerman appears to have committed three separate offenses and is charged pursuant to them. Suppose also that defendants can, if they wish to do so, request settlement hearings at which presumptive sentences on charges will be determined by a judge.[38] Assume further that the jurisdiction in question has a defensible sentencing scheme and that the presumptive sentences announced by the judge are fair, based on reasonable assessments of where Zimmerman's conduct fits into the sentencing range for each of her (alleged) offenses. After the hearing, the prosecutor comes to Zimmerman and offers to drop two of the charges in exchange for a guilty plea by Zimmerman and a lenient sentence recommendation on the remaining single charge. Set to one side, for the time being, the propriety of such proffered charge bargains. Nothing I say here should be taken to defend them. Instead, my aim in raising them at this point is simply to clarify our understanding of trial penalties.

Suppose that Zimmerman refuses the combined offer of the charge and sentence reduction, proceeds to trial, is found guilty on all three charges and receives the presumptive sentence on each. Does Zimmerman suffer a trial penalty? No, not on my account, though Zimmerman does receive a longer sentence for having elected trial adjudication of the charges against her, and perhaps a much longer one, depending on the extent to which the jurisdiction in question permits judges to impose consecutive sentences, or, short of that, something other than concurrent ones. Conviction on multiple charges is a risk that Zimmerman took. Her longer sentence, assuming it is longer, is not a trial penalty. It is explainable by reference to her having been convicted on three as opposed to fewer charges. Moreover, the longer sentence does not appear motivated by any desire on the part of the prosecutor to punish her further for having chosen to go to trial. Of course, if the judge raises the post-trial sentence on one or more of the counts of which Zimmerman is convicted, that may indicate an effort on the judge's part to impose a trial penalty. It will then be incumbent upon the judge to explain the post-trial sentence by reference to features of Zimmerman's criminal conduct that were revealed at her trial. If the judge can do so satisfactorily, then we might have to conclude that no trial penalty has been exacted. If the judge cannot convincingly explain the higher sentence, then we will suspect otherwise.

This brings us to a further complication. Suppose that upon Zimmerman's refusal of his waiver-reward offer, the prosecutor goes back and adds more charges against

---

[38] For the time being, I ignore crucial questions that must be confronted concerning whether concurrent, consecutive, or additive sentences should be preferred in cases of defendants facing sentencing on multiple counts.

her. The likely consequence of the prosecutor's doing so is that Zimmerman will face a longer sentence if she is convicted at trial. This, of course, is precisely what the prosecutor did in the *Bordenkircher* case, though apparently without much hope that doing so would bring Hayes to heel. But some prosecutors who add charges subsequent to a defendant's initial refusal of a waiver reward do so to ramp up the pressure on defendants to plead guilty. Is their doing so tantamount to the threat of a trial penalty? It is hard to see how it can be anything but that, one which may be acted on if the defendant does not acquiesce but instead proceeds to trial and is ultimately found guilty. Admittedly, there will be some cases in which it will be defensible for prosecutors to add charges subsequent to the refusal of a waiver-reward offer. New evidence linking the defendant to further crimes might emerge after prosecutors make their initial offers. Prosecutors might then act appropriately by adding charges regardless of whether or not defendants accept the initial offers. Yet in the absence of new evidence linking defendants to additional criminal conduct, it is difficult to see how adding charges subsequent to the refusal of a plea offer is anything other than a threatened trial penalty. And notice, such a conclusion seems warranted even if the prosecutor could have levied additional charges against the defendant from the start, just as the prosecutor could have done in the *Bordenkircher* case.

The possibility that charges might be added subsequent to a defendant's refusal to accept a prosecutor's waiver-reward offer shows that the presumptive sentencing device outlined previously will not enable us to detect and discourage trial penalties in all of their forms. The courts could, after all, issue presumptive sentences on each of the charges subsequently added. Defendants might be convicted at trial on those charges and receive the relevant presumptive sentences. It would thus appear that defendants had not incurred trial penalties in spite of the charges added in retaliation for their refusals to accept plea deals. Hence, trial penalties do not consist solely of unjustified upward modifications of presumptive sentences. They also consist of charges added subsequent to a defendant's refusal to accept a waiver reward where those charges lack any foundation in newly emergent evidence about the defendant's criminal conduct.[39]

One way to try to ferret out and discourage imposition of this new type of trial penalty would be to require prosecutors to offer written explanations for any charges against a defendant that they add subsequent to a settlement hearing that is not followed by a guilty plea by the defendant. Defendants could then ask the courts to scrutinize such explanations, either as part of a second settlement hearing or at a preliminary trial hearing. We could also make the addition of charges in these circumstances an automatic ground for appeal of a sentence in cases in which defendants were ultimately convicted of such charges. Still, these are decidedly less than perfect

---

[39] Another possibility is that prosecutors might review existing evidence and decide that the defendant's conduct warrants further charges. Though the additional charges might be warranted in some cases, it will be difficult to resist the suspicion that in most they constitute a trial penalty.

devices for detecting and limiting trial penalties of this kind. Prosecutors might be able to assemble a plausible case for any charges that they add, one that makes doing so appear something other than an attempt to threaten or impose a trial penalty. Judges, too, will want to avoid trials and so might give prosecutors the benefit of the doubt in evaluating their explanations of added charges. But we might hope that by imposing these requirements of accountability on prosecutors and judges, we could discourage them from the more blatant attempts to penalize defendants who exercise their right to trial.

Strategic overcharging

Unfortunately, prosecutors might be able to evade scrutiny of their charging decisions by employing a different strategy, that of overcharging defendants to begin with. Numerous legal observers contend that prosecutors in the United States routinely engage in the practice of strategic overcharging.[40] Overcharging might exist in other countries as well.[41] When they strategically overcharge, prosecutors do not simply respond to the evidence that individuals have committed one or more crimes. Instead, they select charges partly with an eye to putting pressure on defendants to plead guilty. Such overcharging takes different forms. Sometimes prosecutors charge individuals with a more serious version of an offense (e.g., first-degree homicide as opposed to second-degree homicide) than the evidence warrants.[42] At other times, prosecutors charge individuals with multiple counts of an offense when they could just as easily charge them with a single count.[43] Prosecutors also overcharge by accusing individuals of numerous overlapping or duplicative offenses, or by charging them with a central offense and a number of so-called "ancillary" offenses.[44] These latter two forms of overcharging are the most insidious and difficult to combat. In jurisdictions in which prosecutors are urged to charge individuals with the "highest and most" offenses that the evidence supports, the existence of overlapping, duplicative, and ancillary offenses can produce lengthy lists of charges, all of which might be supported by at least some evidence.

There are, it should be admitted, legitimate reasons why prosecutors might initially overcharge defendants, only to later drop some of the charges against them. For instance, prosecutors might have only weak or partial evidence for some of the initial charges they file, but believe that further investigation by the police or other

---

[40] See W. J. Stuntz, "The Pathological Politics of Criminal Law," [2001] 100 *Mich. L. Rev.* 505, 519–20; Alschuler (n 1 above) 85–105; and T. L. Meares, "Rewards for Good Behavior: Influencing Prosecutorial Discretion and Conduct with Financial Incentives," [1995] 64 *Fordham L. Rev.* 851, 868–70.

[41] Ashworth and Redmayne report evidence of strategic overcharging in England and Wales (see n 12 above) 299.

[42] Alschuler refers to this as "vertical" overcharging (n 1 above) 86.

[43] Alschuler refers to this as "horizontal" overcharging (n 1 above) 87.

[44] This new form of charge stacking is emphasized by Stuntz (n 40 above) 519–20. See also D. Husak, *Overcriminalization: The Limits of the Criminal Law* (Oxford: Oxford University Press, 2008) 22–3.

officials will eventually produce the evidence needed to fully substantiate them.[45] If that evidence is never produced, prosecutors might eventually drop the unsubstantiated charges. It will look as if they intentionally overcharged the defendant to begin with, but it can be plausibly claimed that they acted appropriately in filing more rather than less charges. Prosecutors who behave in this way are simply erring on the side of caution, since they do not know what further evidence might emerge about the defendant's conduct. This is not the kind of overcharging that is thought especially worrisome by legal commentators. For it is not overcharging with a view to putting pressure on defendants to accept proffered charge or sentence reductions in exchange for pleading guilty.

Strategic overcharging confronts defendants with the prospect of lengthy sentences, ones that prosecutors may have little real interest in imposing.[46] Of course, if such sentences are deserved, based on the culpable criminal conduct of individuals, then prosecutors have done nothing amiss. But it seems increasingly clear to many observers that prosecutors in the United States are prepared to threaten defendants with sentences that exceed those which their (and, in some cases, anyone's) criminal conduct warrants.[47] This especially will be true in legal systems in which non-concurrent sentencing policies are commonplace, and in which, therefore, those found guilty on multiple counts will have their sentences added together in some way or, worse, assigned consecutively.[48] Faced with fearsome sentences, defendants will find prosecutors' offers of waiver rewards—in the form of charge or sentence reductions or both—to be sorely tempting. Again, the combination of charge-stacking and generous waiver rewards can open up vast differentials between plea bargained and post-trial sentences. That is the whole point, of course—to put nearly irresistible pressure on defendants to accede to guilty pleas. As with adding charges subsequent to earlier, failed plea negotiations, charge-stacking blurs the difference between waiver rewards and trial penalties in ways that a presumptive sentencing scheme might not be capable of fixing.

It is possible that judges at settlement hearings will throw out duplicative or overlapping charges, but we have no guarantee that this will occur. They might instead leave most charges in place and announce presumptive sentences accordingly. Defendants who refuse to plead guilty and are convicted on multiple counts might

---

[45] Similarly, prosecutors might file charges not knowing that crucial evidence for some of them subsequently will be ruled inadmissible by the presiding judge. Again, if the relevant charges are then dropped, it may look as if prosecutors deliberately overcharged defendants.

[46] A point made by W. J. Stuntz in "Plea Bargaining and the Criminal Law's Disappearing Shadow," [2004] 117 Harv. L. Rev. 2548, 2554.

[47] See Stuntz (n 40 above) 594–6, and N. J. King, "Constitutional Limits on Successive and Excessive Penalties," [1995] 144 U. Pa. L. Rev. 101.

[48] Y. Ma notes that neither German nor French law permits the imposition of consecutive sentences in multiple charge cases, thus reducing the incentives prosecutors have to overcharge. See "Prosecutorial Discretion and Plea Bargaining in the United States, France, Germany, and Italy: A Comparative Perspective," [2002] 12 International Criminal Justice Review 22, 34 and 38.

be assigned the presumptive sentence on each of them. Again, nothing will seem amiss, yet the resultant sentences cannot reasonably be construed as resulting solely from the refusal of waiver rewards by defendants. The outcomes will be worse, in part, because defendants were charged in ways that threatened them with punishment which no sober assessment of their criminal conduct would have shown to be warranted.

Consider again, in this context, the grade-bargaining analogy. Believing that some students will stubbornly insist on a second reading of their papers, professors might initially propose grades that are lower than the ones their cursory readings actually lead them to believe are appropriate. Suppose that a professor's cursory reading tells her that a student's paper is a C, but she believes or fears that offering the student a bargained grade of B will not suffice to gain the student's consent to forego a second reading. The professor thus tells the student that her cursory reading suggests that the paper should be assigned a D. If the student will agree to waive his right to a second reading, she will assign him a B. It is hard to imagine that students will not jump at the offer of bargained grades in such circumstances. For one thing, the artificially lowered cursory reading grade is bad enough, absolutely speaking, that many students will strongly want to avoid receiving it. A grade of C is one thing; at least it is a passing grade. But a D grade is intolerable. For another, the gap that the artificial lowering of the cursory reading grade creates between it and the proffered bargain grade is so large that it will be hard for students to pass on the bargain. Indeed, some of them will believe, mistakenly, that they are being rewarded handsomely for waiving their right to a second reading. There seems little doubt that the professor's artificially lowering of students' presumptive grades is manipulative and immoral. The beauty of the strategy is that it frees the professor from having to rely on explicit or implicit threats of a second-reading penalty.[49]

In a similar way, strategic overcharging enables prosecutors to threaten or exact trial penalties even if they are deprived of upward post-trial sentence revisions and the possibility of adding charges subsequent to settlement hearings that do not eventuate in guilty pleas. This third variety of trial penalty thus further complicates my account of them. On the one hand, like upward revisions of presumptive sentences and added charges, strategic overcharging belies what seems the proper relationship between the criminal conduct of individuals (or the evidence for it) and the behavior of the state officials charged with punishing them. The (provable) criminal conduct of individuals remains constant; yet state officials contrive charges that threaten inappropriately harsh punishment in order to convince defendants to waive their right to trial. If such threats succeed, as they no doubt often do, then defendants might escape sanctions that are ill-matched with their crimes. But defendants who persist in exercising their right to trial are not only threatened with such sanctions,

---

[49] Of course, some professors might employ both strategies—that is, artificially lowered cursory reading grades and threats of second-reading penalties—to put pressure on students to accede to bargained grade offers.

they will likely see them imposed if they are convicted. On the other hand, it seems a stretch to say that overcharging is motivated by animus on the part of prosecutors, as added charges and recommended post-trial sentence increases so often are. Perhaps overcharging is a kind of "anticipatory animus," a way of saying to criminal defendants "Do not mess with me!" But it is not overtly retaliatory in the ways that added charges or enhanced post-trial sentence recommendations tend to be.

Strategic overcharging may be the most insidious way of threatening or exacting trial penalties and, thus, the one most difficult to detect and discourage. Again, we might hope that judges, at settlement hearings, will cull some of the overlapping or duplicative charges before they set presumptive sentences on the remaining ones. But we have no guarantee that they will eliminate all of them. One way to neutralize the trial penalties that strategic overcharging threatens is to limit the potential sentencing impact of conviction on multiple charges. Concurrent sentencing policies, where offenders have to serve only the sentence for their most serious crime, with sentences for their other crimes served concurrently, would do the most to deprive prosecutors of the pre-trial bargaining leverage provided by strategic overcharging. Let prosecutors charge defendants with as many crimes as they wish, so long as all the parties know that the worst sentencing outcome will be the one stemming from conviction on the most serious charge, and prosecutors will quickly lose much of their incentive to overcharge.[50] Short of such an approach, sentencing policies that gave those convicted of multiple crimes steep "bulk discounts" for conviction on charges beyond the most serious one would likewise work to limit the incentives prosecutors have to overcharge.[51] In the absence of sentencing schemes that effectively limit the incentives prosecutors have to engage in strategic overcharging, we might have to rely on provisions in prosecutorial codes of ethics that strongly condemn the manipulation of sentences with an eye to extracting confessions or guilty pleas from those accused of crimes.[52] Of course, the influence of such codes is apt to depend on localized legal culture or the commitment of state bureaucracies, if and when they exist, to monitor and oversee the practices of the prosecutors they employ.

---

[50] However, the possibility of charging individuals with more serious crimes than the evidence merits would remain a source of over-punishment.

[51] The prospects and problems of bulk discounts are usefully discussed by J. Ryberg, "Retributivism and Multiple Offending," [2005]11 *Res Publica* 213. See also my "Retributive Sentencing, Multiple Offenders, and Bulk Discounts," in M. D. White (ed.), *Retributivism: Essays in Theory and Policy* (Oxford: Oxford University Press, 2011) 212.

[52] See *The Code for Crown Prosecutors*, Crown Prosecution Service 2004, Provision 7.2, according to which "Crown Prosecutors should never go ahead with more charges than are necessary just to encourage a defendant to plead guilty to a few. In the same way, they should never go ahead with a more serious charge just to encourage a defendant to plead guilty to a less serious one." The American Bar Association's *Criminal Justice Section Standards* related to the prosecutorial function are more ambiguous, with Standard 3–3.9 (f) stating "The prosecutor should not bring or seek charges greater in number or degree than can reasonably be supported with evidence at trial or than are necessary to fairly reflect the gravity of the offense."

Suboptimal sentencing schemes

To this point we have been assuming that the criminal prohibitions enforced by the legal system are attended with defensible sanctions—ones that are either proportional with the seriousness of any outlawed conduct or optimal if our aim is to reduce the frequency of such conduct. Yet there is no guarantee that existing sentencing schemes are so idyllic. They could systematically under-punish or over-punish the kinds of conduct that are appropriately criminalized. The former possibility might seem remote. In the United States, most legal observers lament the ways in which the criminal justice system threatens and employs excessively long sentences.[53] Developments elsewhere in the world are likewise ominous if our concern is to limit the damage done by penal sanctions.[54] How might the tendency for sentencing regimes to over-punish offenders affect our thinking about waiver rewards and trial penalties?

For the most part, it will not alter the conclusions I have urged in this chapter. Prosecutors operating in the context of unduly punitive sentencing schemes will continue to lodge charges and, if the legal system in place permits it, make sentence recommendations. Defendants who request settlement hearings will have presumptive sentences set by judges on whatever charges are retained. If they refuse to plead guilty in exchange for waiver rewards, go to trial, are found guilty, and assigned their presumptive sentences, defendants do not suffer trial penalties. And if they can rely on this generally being the case, it seems fair to say that they are not threatened with them either. Of course, the sanctions imposed on them might be unjust or cost-ineffective. But that is due to the defects in the sentencing scheme itself. Even defendants who plead guilty in exchange for waiver rewards might not receive sentences that are deserved or optimal if our aim is to reduce crime cost-effectively. Waiver rewards in such a context might be a source of leniency but not of undeserved or suboptimal leniency. All they will do is diminish unjust or cost-ineffective punishment.

Nonetheless, the existence of harsh sentencing schemes will make it easier for prosecutors to pressure defendants into pleading guilty without resorting to threats of trial penalties. Suppose that the way in which such schemes work is by having wide sentence ranges for the various types of offenses. Sentences at the bottom of the range for a given type of crime might not be excessive; only those at or near the top of the range are. Prosecutors could attempt to exploit the scheme by routinely recommending presumptive sentences that were at or near the top of the range. Criminal defendants, facing unduly harsh sentences, would presumably be more tempted to accept waiver

---

[53] See M. Tonry, *Thinking about Crime: Sense and Sensibility in American Penal Culture* (Oxford: Oxford University Press, 2004); J. Q. Whitman, *Harsh Justice: Criminal Punishment and the Widening Divide between America and Europe* (Oxford: Oxford University Press, 2003); and E. Currie, *Crime and Punishment in America* (New York: Henry Holt, 1998).

[54] See A. von Hirsch and A. Ashworth, *Proportionate Sentencing: Exploring the Principles* (Oxford: Oxford University Press, 2005) 79–80 for concerns about increasingly harsh sanctions in England and Wales. Whitman (n 53 above) notes a toughening stance toward criminal offenders in parts of Europe, at 69–70.

rewards that offered them lenity in exchange for pleading guilty. The only protection defendants would have against this tactic would be to have judges at settlement hearings adjust presumptive sentences downward so that they were no longer excessive. We might hope that judges would do so. However, whether they would adjust them far enough so that defendants' presumptive sentences were truly appropriate given their crimes is uncertain. We might surmise that they would not, that the overall harshness of the sentencing scheme would work to inflate presumptive sentences. Even if we were to eliminate prosecutorial sentence recommendations and simply have judges determine presumptive sentences, the sentencing scheme might exert some upward push on sentences. If higher presumptive sentences were coupled with offers of substantial waiver rewards, this would create nearly irresistible incentives for defendants to plead guilty. The combination of the two would likely yield guilty pleas by defendants at a frequency that matched those produced by the combination of trial penalties and waiver rewards. Hence, state officials would not have to threaten trial penalties under such a sentencing scheme. The scheme would, in effect, do the dirty work for them. Of course, this assumes something I have not yet shown—that trial penalties are indefensible and their use by state officials is unjustified.

Concluding remarks

Understanding the difference between waiver rewards and trial penalties is crucial to grasping the dynamics of plea bargaining. Waiver rewards consist of reductions in the sentences appropriate for offenders' crimes within a sentencing scheme. However, whether waiver rewards grant defendants unmerited leniency depends to a considerable extent on the defensibility of the sentencing scheme in place at a given time. If that scheme is excessively harsh, waiver rewards might do no more than reduce disproportionate or cost-ineffective punishment.

Trial penalties are different. They are not foregone waiver rewards. Instead, they consist of post-trial sentence increases designed to punish individuals for having elected trial adjudication.[55] When they take the form of added charges or post-trial sentences which exceed presumptive ones, it may be possible to detect them and discourage their imposition. When they stem from strategic overcharging, a presumptive sentencing scheme will be unlikely to detect them or dissuade prosecutors from threatening and exacting them. Our best hope in such circumstances might be judges who are willing to scrutinize charges at settlement hearings and pare down

---

[55] Another kind of trial penalty, though one which does not directly affect an offender's sentence, involves efforts by state officials to manipulate the "process costs" of legal punishment. For instance, prosecutors might seek to delay the advent of trials for defendants held on remand in order to pressure them to accede to guilty pleas. See Bowers (n 6 above) 1142. See also C. G. Brunk, "The Problem of Voluntariness and Coercion in the Negotiated Plea," [1979] 13 *Law & Soc'y Rev.* 527, 546.

redundant or overlapping ones so that the crimes individuals are punished for reflect their actual criminal conduct.

Having distinguished trial penalties from waiver rewards, we are now in a position to consider what can be said both for and against having them. To some it will seem obvious that trial penalties are unjustified. However, there are various arguments than can be made on their behalf. Chapter 2 is devoted to an examination of them. Subsequent chapters focus on the character and magnitude of waiver rewards.

2

Against Trial Penalties

Chapter 1 distinguished waiver rewards from trial penalties and surveyed the forms the latter can take. Waiver rewards were characterized as reductions in charges below those which state officials believe to be supported by the evidence, or discounts from the presumptively appropriate sentence for a given charge. Trial penalties consist of added charges or increases in sentences which are intended to discourage exercise of the right to trial or punish defendants for having done so. As I have indicated, the failure to carefully separate waiver rewards and trial penalties has led many commentators to conflate the distinctive rationales for them. The considerations that might be advanced on behalf of permitting state officials to offer waiver rewards are one thing. They will be the focus of discussion in later chapters. The considerations that might be advanced on behalf of threatening or exacting trial penalties are quite another. They are the focus of the current chapter.

Again, it might seem obvious that individuals should not have penalties inflicted on them solely for exercising the right to trial. But it is important to move beyond this intuition to see what might be said on behalf of trial penalties and grasp what those arguments presuppose about the abilities and knowledge of prosecutors (or other state officials). Trial penalties can be defended, to the extent that they can be defended at all, only on the assumption that state officials have extraordinary powers of discernment and judgment. Yet it seems unwise to presume that such powers are widespread among them. Moreover, since other arguments against trial penalties are persuasive, I conclude that inflicting or threatening them is an indefensible exercise of the state's authority to punish criminal offenders.

In order to put ourselves in a better position to evaluate the methods employed by state officials to induce guilty pleas, it will be useful to first sketch an account of the moral basis of the right to trial, to show what normative grounding can be given to this important legal right.[1] In the course of developing this account, the private

---

[1] The account of the moral right to trial that I develop is largely instrumental in character, though I agree that in their pursuit of goods like truth, justice, or crime reduction, trials are appropriately constrained by the need to protect or preserve other goods. For defense of a non-instrumental account of trials, see A. Duff, L. Farmer, S. Marshall, and V. Tadros, *The Trial on Trial (Vol. 3): Towards a Normative Theory of the Criminal Trial* (Oxford: Hart Publishing, 2007). For discussion of the merits of competing accounts of trials, see M. Redmayne, "Theorizing the Criminal Trial," [2009] 12 *New Crim. L. Rev.* 287. I do not believe that, in the context of the debate about plea bargaining, much turns on which account of

and public values served by trials will be identified. Doing so will deepen our appreciation of what we stand to lose if trials are not conducted at all or not in sufficient numbers within the legal system.

Moral basis of the right to trial

That individuals have a legal right to trial is widely accepted. Though there is some variability from country to country regarding what this legal right entitles individuals accused of crimes to expect, its core requirements are neatly summarized in Article 6 of the *European Convention on Human Rights*. Those charged with crimes must be given a fair, public hearing within a reasonable period of time. They must be presumed innocent until proven guilty. They must be presented with the specific charges against them and the evidence for those charges. They must be given the opportunity to respond to the charges and the evidence for them with the aid of professional legal assistance, and must be provided such assistance if they cannot afford it. They must have the right to compel witnesses to appear on their behalf.[2] Further, case law has established that the standard of proof to which the state should be held is a stringent one.[3]

We can begin to flesh out the moral basis for this legal right by thinking about what we hope to accomplish in setting up and maintaining a criminal justice system. Assume that we do so, for the most part, in order to punish conduct by individuals that is harmful to others or predatory upon their interests.[4] Many countries punish a wide variety of actions that are unrelated, or at most indirectly related, to securing the important interests of persons, but let us ignore that fact for the time being. There is ongoing debate about whether our ultimate aim in punishing harmful or predatory conduct is to keep it in check, ensure that those who engage in it receive just punishment, or promote some other purpose altogether. I shall sidestep that controversy as well.

There are two obvious things that we should design the criminal justice system to do, whatever we conceive its ultimate goals to be in punishing offenders. First, we must ensure that it is reasonably effective at apprehending and charging criminal suspects. We must therefore give some individuals within the criminal justice system the authority and resources to investigate crimes, levy charges against individuals believed to have committed them, and pursue those charges until they are in some way formally resolved by the courts. Police and prosecutors are the initial

---

the trial proves to be most defensible. Settlement hearings, as I have described them, will perform some of the functions of trials.

[2] *European Convention for the Protection of Human Rights and Fundamental Freedoms*, Article 6.

[3] See *Barbera, Messegué and Jabardo v. Spain* (1989) 11 EHRR 360.

[4] I assume that some *mala prohibita* will also be defensible, though see Douglas Husak's critical discussion of them in his *Overcriminalization: The Limits of the Criminal Law* (Oxford: Oxford University Press, 2008) 103–19.

actors on this stage. The powers that we give them are formidable ones, as they must be if they are to do their jobs. We must also provide them with enough incentives to exercise these powers, which we do if we provide the officials who occupy these roles with adequate financial compensation and social status. Indeed, there is some reason to believe that police and prosecutors tend to have too much incentive to do their jobs. The tendency toward overzealousness, on the part of state officials charged with apprehending and prosecuting suspected offenders, is a long-standing concern in some countries.[5]

Second, we must devise a charge adjudication scheme that will work systematically to separate the guilty from the innocent and assign the former appropriate sanctions. There is controversy about how best to accomplish both of these tasks. One thing seems clear, however: neither police nor prosecutors can be trusted, all by themselves, to make reliable authoritative judgments about the guilt or innocence of those charged with crimes. In the first place, they are hardly disinterested parties once charges have been filed, having already formed at least provisional judgments that certain individuals are guilty of crimes. Police and prosecutors are not to be blamed for this, as we want them to be, to some extent, advocates on behalf of the public interest in reducing crime or giving offenders what they deserve. That is why we give them the authority, resources, and incentives to get the ball rolling, so to speak. Secondly, and just as important, we know that police and prosecutors are fallible in making their provisional judgments of guilt. Even if they act professionally and wholly in good faith, they make mistakes. Thirdly, we know that they do not always act professionally or in good faith. Evidence of police and prosecutorial incompetence, corruption, and malfeasance is not hard to come by. All of this points toward the abundant wisdom in having some more disinterested (some would say "impartial") third party to adjudicate charges against criminal defendants—somebody to whom the evidence against defendants can be presented and who has not already formed provisional or, worse, final judgments concerning their guilt or innocence.

The preceding considerations do not quite get us to a moral right to trial on the part of individuals charged with crimes. They may show only that there is abundant good sense in having trials. But suppose that the basic moral rights of individuals carry with them presumptions against their infringement or curtailment except in instances where doing so can be shown to be justified.[6] The moral right to liberty, for instance, is not an unlimited right. Individuals exceed the bounds of their rightful liberty when they assault others or steal from them. The law should both protect basic moral rights and define their proper limits, though we might fervently hope that in delineating their limits legislators will be guided by defensible normative theories.

---

[5] See, for instance, S. Z. Fisher, "In Search of the Virtuous Prosecutor: A Conceptual Framework," [1987–88] 15 *Am. J. Crim. L.* 197, 204–7, and A. Ashworth and M. Redmayne, *The Criminal Process,* 4th edition (Oxford: Oxford University Press, 2010) 70–4.

[6] Douglas Husak employs a different tack, arguing that there is a moral right not to be punished, one that must justifiably be overridden. See his *Overcriminalization,* (n 4 above) 92–103.

When individuals exceed the limits of their moral rights as they are defined by the criminal law, they are liable to punishment, which can be viewed as justifiably curtailing their moral rights to liberty or property.[7] Yet even on the assumption that it makes sense to conceive of legal punishment as justifiably curtailing rights in this way, curtailment is not justified in any given case simply because individuals are suspected of crimes or charged with them. It is justified only if state officials can demonstrate to an authoritative and disinterested party that the individuals in question have exceeded the legally defined bounds of their moral rights. The standard of proof is then the relevant test for the adequacy of the state's demonstration that the accused are appropriately subject to punishment. On this account, the moral right to a trial is a second-order right, one necessitated by the basic moral rights of individuals in conjunction with the fallibility—or, worse, incompetence, corruption, or malevolence—of the state officials authorized to investigate crimes and charge citizens with them.

Granted, this account does not necessitate any particular form that the impartial and authoritative adjudication of criminal charges must take, let alone that it should consist of trials and specifically jury trials. Nor was it meant to, since there is considerable room for debate about the optimal form of the fair adjudication of criminal charges against individuals.[8] My aim in this section is the more limited one of motivating the need for such adjudication, and thereby to explain why we should scrutinize attempts by state officials to induce criminal defendants to forego formal and impartial inquiry into the charges against them. Trials have traditionally been the preferred means of authoritative and impartial charge adjudication. It is useful to consider why this is so.

Trials have the potential to produce a wide range of private and public goods. First and foremost, if the individuals charged with crimes are actually innocent of some or all of the charges against them, trials might yield full or partial acquittals that are of obvious benefit to the accused and to others who care about or depend on them. Yet the public also benefits from full or partial acquittals of the innocent. Unjust or excessive punishment is burdensome—in both direct and opportunity costs—to those who have to pay for it. For the most part, ordinary, law-abiding citizens will shoulder the burdens of legal punishment, whether justly or unjustly inflicted.

There are other public goods that flow from criminal trials as well. Critics of plea bargaining argue that, in the absence of criminal trials, the state's case against defendants is not tested, or not tested vigorously, and so police or prosecutorial incompetence, corruption, or malfeasance are not exposed, often to the considerable detriment

---

[7] Here I sidestep the debate over the death penalty. The idea that punishment can be conceived of as curtailing basic rights will not work for the right to life in any case. Life cannot really be curtailed, if by that we mean that its exercise can be limited. Of course, life can be ended, even if it cannot be curtailed.

[8] Albert Alschuler has surveyed some of the alternative adjudicative methods available in his "Implementing the Criminal Defendant's Right to Trial: Alternatives to the Plea Bargaining System," [1983] 50 *U. Chi. L. Rev.* 931.

not only of defendants but also the general public.[9] Unreasonable searches and seizures, sloppy police work, biased investigations, or dishonest police testimony are all more likely to be exposed when cases go to trial. Guilty defendants may gain unjust acquittals when the courts exclude tainted or improperly obtained evidence, but the public is thought to benefit in the long term by having state officials who are more circumspect about performing investigations or running roughshod over the interests of the individuals they investigate. Jury trials, in particular, may also discourage abuses of legislative or executive power, by ensuring that the criminal law and its enforcement do not depart too widely from communal moral norms.[10] In the United States, at least, jury nullification has a long if somewhat controversial history.[11] When legislative bodies pass criminal laws that the public does not support, or prosecutors seek to enforce them in ways that seem unduly harsh or prejudicial, juries may refuse to convict. In so doing, they send vital messages to state officials about the public's limits of tolerance for perceived abuses of state power. Of course, juries might also nullify good-faith exercises of police or prosecutorial powers with which they simply disagree.

Trials, and specifically jury trials, also promote public goods by increasing participation by members of the community in the criminal justice system and making the process of guilt determination more visible. They thereby educate members of the community about fair and dignified procedures, and reinforce the importance of such key notions as the presumption of innocence and the standard of proof incumbent upon the state in criminal trials.[12] And notice, trials may yield these public goods even if defendants are guilty as charged and convicted, or are innocent and wrongly found guilty.

It must be conceded that some of these public goods will be produced so long as there are sufficient trials in the aggregate. There is no need to provide all charged defendants with trials in order to be reasonably assured that criminal justice officials do not illicitly invade the privacy interests of citizens, for instance. But the existence of these public goods shows that the value of trials extends beyond exoneration of the innocent or partly innocent. This should make us more cautious about endorsing the arguments for waiver rewards and trial penalties that we will shortly confront. Notice this also: prosecutors and judges rarely will be in an ideal epistemic position to discern whether, and to what extent, trials will promote private and public goods.

---

[9] As Alschuler notes, criminal trials encourage genuine advocacy by defense lawyers in ways that plea bargaining does not. Such advocacy may expose flaws and irregularities in the state's case that will be glossed over in the rush to reach a plea agreement. See "The Changing Plea Bargaining Debate," [1981] 69 *Cal. L. Rev.* 652, 692–3.

[10] Note: "The Unconstitutionality of Plea Bargaining," [1970] 83 *Harv. L. Rev.* 1387, 1395–7.

[11] A. W. Alschuler and A. B. Deiss, "A Brief History of the Criminal Jury in the United States," [1994] 61 *U. Chi. L. Rev.* 867, 871–5. For a powerful critique of jury nullification, at least in the context of the US legal system, see A. D. Leipold, "Rethinking Jury Nullification," [1996] 82 *Va. L. Rev.* 253.

[12] Cf. A. R. Amar, *The Constitution and Criminal Procedure* (New Haven, Conn.: Yale University Press, 1997) 122.

Even if they were in that position, they would face inevitable conflicts of interest in deciding whether defendants should be allowed to go forward with trials given the drain on their resources that doing so will exact. Generally speaking, defendants are in a better position than anyone to know whether, or to what extent, they are innocent of the charges against them. They also will be considerably more motivated than prosecutors and judges to expose what they believe to be official misconduct or overreaching. They stand to gain, sometimes unjustly, if improperly obtained or processed evidence against them is excluded. Also, they will be more sensitive to the ways in which state exercises of power impinge on their interests or are discriminatory in intention or effect. If anyone should have the final say about whether a trial should take place, it is defendants. But the existence of trial penalties makes their exercise of that prerogative an extraordinarily risky one.

It will be objected that some defendants abuse their power to elect trial adjudication. Defendants who are guilty as charged and who know it do us no favors by insisting on trial adjudication. Even if there is some residual value in putting the state's evidence to the test in such cases, it might seem that it is too meager to justify the burden and expense of trials. Still, as we will see, it does not follow that individuals whose trials produce little of public value should be punished for insisting upon them. And especially it does not follow that prosecutors or judges should be permitted to impose additional penalties on such individuals simply because they believe that the trial demands of these individuals were unjustified.

The variety of defendants and the hazards of unilateral imposition of trial penalties

In Chapter 1, I outlined a procedure, in the form of settlement hearings at which judges set presumptive sentences, that could be used to detect and discourage trial penalties. In this chapter, we examine the reasons for going forward with such a procedure. In the meantime, though, let us suppose that trial penalties are threatened and exacted covertly by prosecutors (and judges) in the usual ways, ones that make it difficult for us to discern the contribution that they make to post-trial sentencing outcomes.

The main argument that might be offered in support of state officials implicitly or explicitly threatening trial penalties is this: Many of those charged with crimes are guilty and they know it. Trial adjudication of the charges against them serves no useful purpose and, if they are wrongly acquitted, as many of them hope that they will be, thwarts just punishment and effective crime control. True, the individuals in question may have a legal and even a moral right to a trial. But having a right does not entail that every exercise of it is defensible, all things considered.[13] If we assume

---

[13] See J. Waldron, "A Right to do Wrong," [1981] 92 *Ethics* 21, and R. Bronaugh, "Is There a Duty to Confess?" [1998] 98 *Newsletter on Philosophy of Law* 86, American Philosophical Association.

that prosecutors or judges will sometimes be in a position to tell which of the criminal defendants before them have needlessly demanded trials and thus squandered the public's resources, then it might seem appropriate for prosecutors to threaten trial penalties in order to discourage such defendants from pursuing trial adjudication. If guilty defendants realize that they are likely to pay a steep price for demanding trials that serve no useful purpose, they will be disinclined to press ahead. Those who do press ahead and are the recipients of trial penalties get what they deserve for having put state officials, and the public on whose behalf they act, through the effort and expense of needless trials.

The weak point in the preceding argument is readily apparent. It persuades, if it persuades at all, only if we concede that state officials are sometimes in a position to tell which of the defendants who demand trials are guilty as charged and so wasting the criminal justice system's resources. We need not deny, of course, that there are defendants who, by demanding trials, do precisely that. The question is whether prosecutors or judges can be trusted to identify them. It must be conceded that in a few cases, they will be able to do so with some certainty. Consider cases in which highly probative evidence against defendants is excluded by the courts because it was acquired illegally. Defendants who almost certainly would have been found guilty if that evidence had been ruled admissible might reasonably conclude that its exclusion gives them a chance at a (mistaken) acquittal. Suppose that they are nonetheless found guilty and now it is time for the prosecutor to recommend a sentence and the judge to act on that recommendation. To some it will seem justifiable for state officials to exact trial penalties from such defendants.

One problem is that such cases are likely to be somewhat rare. They will be rarer still if we acknowledge what we must—that there will be instances in which highly probative evidence that has been excluded is not what it seems. Police or evidence analysts make errors in acquiring or producing evidence. In a few cases, police or investigators plant or fabricate it. In more cases, they lie or "shade the truth" when they take the witness stand.[14] Prosecutors and judges will be in a poor position to fathom whether or when these kinds of things have occurred and thus might exact trial penalties from defendants who were not "needlessly" demanding trials. Yet even granting that there will be a few cases in which prosecutors or judges know (or have overwhelming evidence for believing) that defendants are up to no good in demanding trials, it will be exceedingly difficult to cabin their authority to impose trial penalties. For their part, prosecutors may be too inclined to think that all of the defendants who demand trials are guilty as charged and are therefore wasting their and the public's resources. Judges, too, have crowded dockets and their experience will tell them that the vast majority of individuals who go to trial are, in fact,

---

[14] See, for instance, M. Punch, "Police Corruption and Its Prevention," [2000] 8 *European Journal of Criminal Policy and Research* 301, and S. Z. Fisher, "Just the Facts, Ma'am: Lying and the Omission of Exculpatory Evidence in Police Reports," [1993–94] 28 *New Eng. L. Rev.* 1.

guilty.[15] None of this bodes well for the kind of narrowly tailored use of trial penalties by prosecutors or judges that the argument outlined above defends.

Furthermore, many criminal defendants will quite reasonably exercise their right to trial. Some will do so because they know that they are innocent of the charges against them (or of some of the charges). They may not know why they have been targeted by the police or charged by the prosecutor. They only know that they did not commit the crime or crimes in question and hope that trials will vindicate them. Other defendants who know that they are not entirely innocent will insist on trials because they believe that they have been deliberately overcharged by prosecutors as part of a strategy to put pressure on them to plead guilty to a subset of the charges. In some of these kinds of cases, the charge reductions offered by prosecutors in exchange for guilty pleas will still be perceived by defendants as imposing excessive punishment on them given their criminal acts. Such defendants may believe that they have little recourse but to go to trial in order to achieve some partial exoneration and thereby avoid unduly harsh punishment. Other defendants will insist on trials because they believe, even if mistakenly, that they are innocent of the charges against them and hope that a trial will demonstrate that. Such defendants might believe that they have legitimate excuses for the ways in which they acted, or were justified in acting as they did, or did not cross the line separating legal from illegal conduct. In addition, some defendants might know (or reasonably believe) that they are guilty of the charges against them but desire trials because they want to use them as forums to put the state's laws (or its enforcement of them) on trial. Such defendants have little hope of being found innocent, but they see trials as opportunities to make political statements of some importance to them. Some of these defendants will be pursuing objectionable or hopeless causes, but it seems doubtful that we would be willing to say this about all of them. Moreover, even if we believe that there are better ways in which to effect political change, there might nonetheless be cases in which all other avenues of attempting to do so are blocked to some citizens.

In light of the considerable diversity of criminal defendants who might elect trial adjudication of the charges against them, it would seem advisable to require a more open, formal process to determine which among those ultimately found guilty are suitable recipients of trial penalties. We could make it a criminal offense for individuals to elect trial adjudication when they know (or should have known) that they are guilty as charged and no plausible justification for having proceeded to trial is offered by them. To many this will appear to add insult to injury But more to the point, making it a distinct offense would highlight the contentious claims that would have to be established by the state in order to make the charge stick. Not only would the state have to show that a defendant had no reasonable basis for demanding a trial, but

[15] See K. A. Findley and M. S. Scott, "The Multiple Dimensions of Tunnel Vision in Criminal Cases," [2006] 2006 *Wis. L. Rev.* 291, 330. Findley and Scott make this point in relation to prosecutors, but presumably it holds for judges as well.

it would presumably also have to show that defendants knew this (or should have known it). In the absence of such knowledge, it is not apparent how defendants could be understood to have acted culpably in insisting upon trials.

Instead of having a formal, open procedure for establishing the truth of claims to the effect that defendants have needlessly and unjustifiably demanded trials, current practices in the United States permit prosecutors and judges unilaterally to determine whether such claims are true—or, worse, to exact trial penalties without even bothering to do so. Moreover, the officials who make these determinations are the same ones who will have participated in the trials that produced guilty verdicts against defendants. Whether those officials can be sufficiently impartial in deciding whether defendants have needlessly demanded trials ought to be questioned. The fact that defendants have ultimately been found guilty by the courts does not show that they did anything wrong in exercising their right to trial adjudication. But we might surmise that such adverse outcomes will be enough to convince many prosecutors and judges that defendants were up to no good in demanding trials.

Further arguments against trial penalties

At this point, I set to one side the epistemic problems that we face in determining which of those criminal defendants found guilty after trials demanded them unjustifiably. These problems may well be insurmountable, but it is important to go further and consider the case against trial penalties independently of them. It may be impossible to accurately impose trial penalties. But I hope to show that even if it were possible, we should not impose them.

In the first place, as Jeremy Waldron has shown, it does not follow from the fact that a person has wrongly exercised a moral or legal right that he or she should be punished for having done so.[16] It is easy to conceive of other cases in which we might agree that persons acted wrongly in exercising their rights, and in so doing forced public officials to expend scarce resources, yet we will balk at punishing the persons for having so acted. For instance, individuals might exercise their moral and legal rights to free speech in ways that most of us would agree are deeply offensive—in public demonstrations, for instance, designed to do little more than convey hateful or intolerant messages about other citizens. Given the incendiary character of the speech, there might need to be some expenditure of public funds to provide police protection for the demonstrators or to reroute traffic away from or around them. It is one thing to require demonstrators to apply for a permit and pay some modest fee for the public services provided. It is another to believe that their objectionable exercises of their rights to free speech should be prohibited and punished. And it is another still to believe that though their wrongful speech is not legally proscribed, it is permissible for public officials to seek to penalize them because they are annoyed at having to

16 Waldron (n 13 above) 29.

expend the resources to protect or facilitate their speech, or, perhaps more charitably, deem themselves the rightful guardians of the public's resources.

Second, even if we are convinced that it is appropriate to somehow mark the difference between criminal defendants whose trials are (allegedly) pointless and defendants whose trials are not, we need not do so by imposing longer sentences on the former group of defendants. Assuming that we can reliably identify them, we could, instead, send such defendants a bill at the culmination of their trial proceedings, one which reflected the costs of their trials. Such defendants might be charged on a per diem or partial per diem basis, the latter since some trials will be quite brief. Why does sending such defendants a bill seem, in fact, more appropriate than assigning them longer sentences? Because trial penalties have little to do with defendants' crimes and much to do with penalizing defendants who are alleged to have squandered scarce public resources. This is a point worth elaborating.

Whatever we think about defendants who demand pointless trials, their doing so does not change the essential character of the criminal act (or acts) of which they are accused. How could it, since the decision to opt for trial adjudication is one made well after the cessation of the criminal conduct that is the focus of official inquiry? Yet one would think that the appropriate basis for assigning sentences to offenders is their criminal conduct—the behavior that the charges attempt to legally characterize. Again, trials may sometimes reveal that defendants' criminal conduct was worse than state officials initially believed it to be. In such cases, I have conceded that presumptive sentences might reasonably be revised upward. But such revisions are grounded in a more accurate accounting of defendants' criminal acts prior to their having been arrested and charged. They are thus altogether different from longer sentences imposed on individuals solely for having elected trial adjudication.

If trials are deemed in some cases to squander public resources, the appropriate response is to seek reimbursement from the defendants who insisted on having them. Indeed, if we are prepared to say that state officials are in a position to determine which defendants uselessly demand trials, it would not seem to matter, for the purpose of seeking reimbursement, whether the defendants in question were found guilty or acquitted. Even those (wrongly) acquitted might be sent a bill at the culmination of their trials. If that is not counter-intuitive enough, a further twist should be noted. It seems counterproductive to impose trial penalties, in the form of longer sentences, on individuals if our concern is to conserve scarce public resources. After all, the public will likely have to foot the bill for the longer sentences that result. Perhaps the idea is that by threatening such penalties, we will not have to act on the threats very often. Most defendants will plead guilty if offered waiver rewards, especially if by refusing them they risk much longer sentences. Trial penalties might therefore operate to conserve public resources in most cases, though not all.

In response to the suggestion that defendants who needlessly demand trials might be required to pay for them, it will be objected that many of the individuals convicted of crimes are poor to begin with. The public is unlikely to collect trial fees from such individuals, and so it is reasonable instead to assign them longer sentences. But this can hardly be a convincing rationale for permitting trial penalties to be assigned across the board to defendants who uselessly demand trials. At the very least, we should inquire into whether defendants have the means to pay trial fees. We should also, it seems, offer them the option of paying the trial fees rather than, without further ado, imposing longer sentences on them. Maybe they will not be able to pay such fees all at once, but some arrangement for doing so in installments might be worked out. Trial penalties in the form of longer sentences will punish the poor more harshly simply for being poor.

Furthermore, most defendants will have already partially paid for their trial costs in advance when they paid their taxes. Part of what tax revenues do is fund the police, prosecutors, judges, and criminal courts. In short, even if some defendants should pay for their trials, many of them will have prepaid. It might be objected that criminal offenders are not exactly honest, tax-paying citizens. If they pay income taxes at all, they are apt to under-report their income (especially if much of it is illegally obtained). I doubt that we know to what extent these claims about offenders are true. But in any case, it will be difficult for even the most dedicated tax-evaders to avoid paying some taxes—in particular, sales and property taxes. Those who own no property of their own but rent from others who do will likely pay property taxes indirectly as they make their rental payments. So, offenders, as taxpayers, help to establish and maintain the court system but then are to be charged for using it. That seems odd.

Finally, suppose that it can be shown that trial penalties are defensible and that more punishment (as opposed to the assessment of fees) is the appropriate way to exact them. Trials do impose significant costs on prosecutors, the courts, and therefore the public. But it seems likely that most criminal trials will be relatively brief. Some will last only a few hours; others will take somewhere between a few days and a week.[17] A few will last longer, but they are apt to be the exceptions rather than the rule. Now the problem is this: Standard trial penalties, which may add substantially to the sentences assigned post-trial to individuals who are convicted, will often turn out to be disproportionate—indeed wildly so—given the costs imposed on the public by allegedly useless trials. Adding years to an offender's sentence, at substantial cost to the offender, the offender's family, and to the public who must pay for the offender's prolonged imprisonment, punishes the offender excessively for the costs that the offender's trial imposed on the public.[18] At most, it would seem that some

[17] Criminal trials in the United States are usually estimated to last two to five days. Yet this figure seems likely to be somewhat high, since the few cases that go to trial are probably the more complicated ones or ones for which the state has less than conclusive evidence. Many trials in so-called "dead bang" cases would likely be fairly brief.

[18] R. Jonakait cites a study of the Los Angeles County court system which estimated that the average daily cost of a criminal trial was $9,500. See his *The American Jury System* (New Haven, Conn.: Yale University Press, 2003) 97. That is a substantial amount, to be sure, and if a trial lasts a week, the total costs will exceed $60,000. But the costs of a single year's additional imprisonment are likely to be greater, especially if all of the direct and collateral costs are taken into account. Also, plea bargaining itself is not

very modest increase in the offender's sentence would more than adequately punish him or her for the "crime" of insisting on a trial.

Summing up, it would seem that prosecutors or judges are on very shaky grounds in threatening and imposing trial penalties. Such penalties do not reflect, in any systematic way, the criminal acts of defendants, likely cannot be imposed fairly without assuming prosecutors and judges to have superhuman powers of discernment, punish defendants when they should be, at most, assessed trial costs, ignore the fact that defendants have already partially prepaid such trial costs, and will likely penalize them disproportionately for the costs of a trial. If all of this is not bad enough, we might add that trial penalties appear to enable prosecutors and judges to shirk their responsibilities. It is, arguably, one of the principal tasks of prosecutors and judges to provide criminal defendants with trials when they elect to have them instead of pleading guilty, just as it is one of the principal tasks of college professors to grade carefully the papers that they have assigned. We can perhaps understand why prosecutors or judges might offer defendants inducements to plead guilty, though whether and to what extent their doing so can be justified remains to be seen. But it is hard to understand why such officials should be allowed to threaten and punish defendants who do nothing more than require them to perform their jobs.

Trial penalties as a means to fair outcomes?

We should not conclude just yet that prosecutors and judges can never justifiably employ explicit or implicit threats of trial penalties. There is an intriguing argument suggesting that they should be permitted to do so as a means of achieving fair outcomes in a wide range of cases. So far, we have been assuming that trial penalties will produce sentences that exceed the ones that are presumptively appropriate in a given case. But what if threats of trial penalties were employed precisely so that they would not have to be carried out, as part of a strategy by state officials to pressure defendants to plead guilty and accept sentences that are closer to the ones that their criminal conduct actually merits?

In later chapters, I contend that waiver rewards for pleading guilty should be kept at modest levels. Suppose that once a settlement hearing had been held and a presumptive sentence set, no criminal defendant could receive a waiver reward for pleading guilty that was greater than a 10 percent reduction in his or her presumptive sentence on any given charge.[19] Critics of such a proposal might conjecture that such modest waiver rewards will not suffice to induce many criminal defendants to plead guilty.

cost free, as Albert Alschuler has shown, so those costs would have to be subtracted from total trial costs. For a discussion see Alschuler (n 8 above) 939–40.

[19] I leave aside, for now, the problems raised by conviction for multiple offenses and, in particular, the vexed question of whether multiple offenders should be assigned concurrent or consecutive sentences, or something in-between.

There simply will not be enough for them to gain by doing so and thus they will insist on more expensive and time-consuming trial adjudication. As I subsequently show, there are reasons to doubt this conjecture, but for the sake of argument, let us assume that it is plausible. Permitting prosecutors to threaten trial penalties and judges to carry them out would increase the sentence differential between trial and non-trial adjudication. More defendants would, in light of this increased differential, waive their right to trial and plead guilty.

To see how this might work to produce appropriate outcomes, let us return, once again, to the grade-bargaining analogy. Suppose that the professor's cursory reading of a paper suggests that it merits a grade of C. Suppose that the professor initially contemplates offering the student a discounted grade of B- if the student will waive her right to a second reading, but worries that such an offer may not be enough to motivate the student to accept the bargained grade. Suppose, therefore, that when she notifies the student of the cursory reading grade, the professor also lets it be known that she does not look kindly on requests for second readings. If the student is not inclined to believe this, then she should consult with former students who made such requests. Now the student must fear that she will wind up with a C- or even a D on the second reading. She will therefore be considerably more motivated to accept the B-. Of course, the professor could have reduced her risk of having to provide a second reading by offering the student a larger waiver discount, say a bargained grade of B as opposed to B-. But her doing so would produce an outcome that is more at variance with the cursory reading grade. If the cursory reading grade is more in line with what the student deserves for the paper, then the outcome obtained by the threat of a second-reading penalty is superior to that which would be obtained by the offer of a more generous waiver reward. Granted, there is something underhanded about how the professor has gone about things. But her underhandedness eventually leads to a more optimal outcome, at least on the assumption that the cursory-reading grade accurately reflects the merits of the paper.

If threatened trial penalties operate in a similar fashion, then they, too, might help to ensure that the defendants who admit their guilt receive sentences that are more in line with what they deserve. Many offenders might not be willing to plead in exchange for modest waiver rewards, and larger ones will produce substantial deviations from appropriate sentences. But modest waiver-reward offers, coupled with implicit or explicit threats of trial penalties, might yield appropriate sentencing outcomes, whether such outcomes are measured according to crime reduction or deserved punishment criteria.

The first thing to notice is that this strategy will lead to suboptimal outcomes in cases in which defendants ignore threats of trial penalties, insist on going to trial, and are convicted. Even if we assume that such defendants were guilty to begin with, they will receive sentences that exceed, perhaps by some significant margin, presumptively fair or optimal ones given their crimes. Prosecutors and judges would have little choice but to exact the trial penalties in such cases or risk creating the perception that their trial penalty threats are empty. This disadvantage to the strategy could be conceded by its proponents but portrayed as one that must be weighed against its advantages. By employing the strategy, state officials would be able to induce many more defendants to plead guilty and receive sentences closer to the ones that were optimal. By contrast, if those officials were prohibited from threatening trial penalties, then they would probably have to conduct more trials. Not only would some guilty defendants thereby gain acquittals that are in error, but prosecutors and judges would be unable to process as many offenders through the system, given their limited resources. If the reduction in convictions turned out to be substantial, then that would have to be counted against schemes in which trial penalties were disallowed.

However, there are other problems with permitting state officials to strategically employ threats of trial penalties. A few individuals charged with crimes will be innocent. Others will be charged with crimes that are more serious or numerous than those they actually committed. The added pressure to plead guilty created by threats of trial penalties means that more of these kinds of defendants will acquiesce in guilty pleas or plead guilty to more serious or numerous crimes than otherwise would do so, at least if we imagine the alternative to be one in which state officials were authorized to offer only modest waiver rewards. This adds to the miscarriages of justice that the proposed strategic use of threats of trial penalties would create.

Also, though having to conduct fewer trials might extend the resources that state officials have at their disposal, a reduction in trials is not an unalloyed good. As we have seen, trials serve to keep police and prosecutorial misconduct or overreaching in check. They also educate the public about the meaning and value of due process and provide the public with opportunities to influence the course of criminal justice. Though these virtues of trials might seem unrelated to optimal sentencing outcomes, it does not take much imagination to see how they could work to produce them. If police or prosecutors were emboldened by the lack of public or judicial scrutiny of their conduct to run roughshod over suspects' due process rights, we might see an increase in the number of individuals wrongly charged, wrongly convicted, or convicted of crimes that are unrelated to those they actually committed.

Furthermore, we should question whether prosecutors, in particular, could be trusted to aim at optimal or just sentencing outcomes if they were permitted to use trial penalty threats. We might reasonably worry that most prosecutors would be focused more on gaining convictions than achieving fairness in sentencing outcomes.[20] Worse than this, to the extent that they are focused on sentencing outcomes, some prosecutors might be intent on maintaining the appearance that they are tough on crime. Threats of trial penalties might be used by prosecutors to

---

[20] The notion that prosecutors focus primarily on amassing convictions is widespread in the legal literature. See, for instance, W. J. Stuntz, "The Pathological Politics of Criminal Law," [2001] 100 *Mich. L. Rev.* 505, 534. See also B. L. Gershman, "The New Prosecutors," [1992] 53 *Pitt. L. Rev.* 393.

push sentences higher, rather than to achieve just outcomes. Consider the defendant Hayes in the *Bordenkircher* case. The initial offer made to him by the prosecutor (a five-year prison sentence) was not exactly generous, given the paltry sum Hayes had stolen by writing a bad check. It is plausible to believe that the offer was so meager because the prosecutor knew he could wield the threat of a substantial trial penalty if Hayes did not comply. Of course, the threat in this case was atypically large. Perhaps few prosecutors would employ such threats and fewer judges would ratify them. Nonetheless, the argument that we are considering, allowing prosecutors to utilize threats of trial penalties, assumes that they will do so to achieve just outcomes. To the extent that they are not focused on such outcomes, the argument is weakened.

Let us take stock. We are comparing the overall sentencing outcomes in two different schemes, one that permits state officials to employ offers of modest waiver rewards, and one that permits them to supplement such offers with threats of trial penalties. The most important defect in the former scheme is that it would yield more trials of individuals, some (probably unknown) percentage of whom would be unjustly acquitted. Prosecutors and judges who could employ threats of trial penalties would be able to dissuade at least some of those individuals from electing trial adjudication. But by reducing the number of trials, threatened trial penalties would deprive us of some of the public goods trials produce. Such threats would also induce a larger number of innocent, or partly innocent, defendants to plead guilty, which produces miscarriages of justice. And whether threats of trial penalties would yield just outcomes depends on whether state officials could be trusted to employ them wisely and judiciously, with an eye to ultimately arriving at such outcomes. Finally, when those officials were forced to act on their threats, as they usually would be when defendants were found guilty at trial, the sentencing outcomes would be at variance with presumptively appropriate ones.

I conclude that the argument for permitting state officials to employ threats of trial penalties in order to achieve a superior set of sentencing outcomes is not terribly persuasive. In any case, if our concern is to help prosecutors and judges conserve their limited resources and thereby increase the quantity of criminal cases they can process, the alternative is to allow substantial waiver rewards to be awarded to defendants who agree to plead guilty. One signal advantage to such rewards is that defendants who went to trial and lost would usually fare no worse than receiving their presumptive sentences. They would not receive sentences longer than the ones they deserved or which were optimal simply because they chose trial adjudication. Of course, they would receive sentences that were longer—and perhaps much longer—than their counterparts who agreed to admit their guilt. Whether in light of that fact, as well as others, more robust waiver rewards can be defended is the subject of coming chapters. But at least such rewards would not tend to produce outcomes in which individuals were punished more harshly than was appropriate given their crimes.

The exception that proves the rule?

There is one kind of case in which it might seem advisable to allow state officials to threaten, and if necessary, exact trial penalties. Suppose that an individual has been charged with a serious crime. The evidence against him that is likely to be admissible at trial, while strongly suggestive of his guilt, appears somewhat short of demonstrating it beyond reasonable doubt. However, the prosecutor is in possession of evidence that establishes his guilt conclusively. Unfortunately, the crucial evidence has been or is likely to be excluded by the court, or is no longer such that the prosecutor can use it should the case go to trial. Perhaps it was obtained through the improper execution of a search warrant by the police, or obtained in circumstances in which the police did not have probable cause for a search, though that judgment is contested by the police and is, any impartial observer would have to admit, a close call. Or perhaps a key witness for the prosecution has died under mysterious circumstances, ones strongly suggesting malfeasance on the part of the defendant. A prosecutor who could offer such a defendant only a modest waiver reward would have a hard time convincing him to plead guilty. Even offers of more substantial waiver rewards might not suffice. The defendant might be smart or brazen enough (or well-advised by his attorney) to surmise that if he goes to trial, he will likely be found innocent of the charges against him. The prosecutor would fear such an outcome, and so might be tempted to go for broke. She might inform him that if he insists on going to trial and is found guilty, she will recommend a very long sentence. The point of such a threat would be to make the defendant think twice about taking the risk of a trial. The threat might not work, of course. Indeed, the most compelling argument against allowing prosecutors to employ threats of trial penalties in these kinds of cases might be that they are likely to prove futile. Defendants who are disinclined to plead guilty in exchange for generous waiver rewards are unlikely to be cowed by threats of trial penalties. But suppose that such threats were sometimes effective. If it is granted that prosecutors, on occasion, will be in the position to know that they are dealing with scoundrels, should it not be conceded that threats of trial penalties are, in such circumstances, justified?

I suspect that it should be, but we must be very careful to note what does and does not follow from this concession. First of all, it yields only an exceedingly narrow warrant for the use of threatened trial penalties. Prosecutors will rarely be in the privileged epistemic position that has been described. And there is considerable danger in allowing that they are ever in it, since it will be tempting for them to believe that they are more often in such a position than they really are. That brings us to the second point. If we permit prosecutors to make use of trial penalty threats in a few cases, it will be difficult, in practice, to circumscribe their authority to do so. The difficulties in ensuring that prosecutors will exhibit self-restraint in the use of such threats might lead us to conclude that it is unwise to grant them the authority in the first place.

Third, in the case described, the crime in question was assumed to be a serious one. We might balk at granting prosecutors the authority to threaten trial penalties if the crimes that will thereby be resolved are minor. Trials, as we have seen, promote both private and public goods of various kinds, and even trials of "obviously guilty" defendants do so. Improper police conduct, for instance, can be revealed and sanctioned by the courts at trials of very bad and very guilty individuals. The attainment of public goods such as these is jeopardized when prosecutors are allowed to threaten defendants with trial penalties. Prosecutors arguably have a duty to not only attempt to secure substantively just outcomes in the cases that come before them, but also to do so in ways that respect and ensure due process.[21] Threats of trial penalties might yield just outcomes in a few cases but do so at some cost to due process, assuming that due process requires improperly obtained evidence to be excluded. We might be more sanguine about the ways and extent to which threats of trial penalties sin against due process if the cases resolved by them involve grave criminal offenses. But if the offenses to be punished are less serious, it is less clear whether what we would gain by punishing offenders is worth the costs to due process.

Trial penalties and duress

One of the long-standing points of contention about plea bargaining concerns whether, as a practice, it pressures criminal defendants unduly into waiving their rights to trial. Critics of plea bargaining assert, more or less vigorously, that it is often coercive.[22] John Langbein even likened it to the medieval practice of torturing defendants who refused to confess their crimes.[23] Those who defend plea bargaining admit that prosecutors' offers of reduced sentences or charges are difficult for defendants to resist, but do not see how offering to make defendants better off can possibly be seen as coercion.[24] This particular debate about plea bargaining has been plagued, I believe, by the failure to distinguish clearly between waiver rewards and trial penalties.[25] Waiver rewards are usually not coercive. They tend to improve the

---

[21] B. A. Green, "Why Should Prosecutors Seek Justice?" [1999] 26 *Fordham Urb. L. J.* 607, 634. See also J. Kleinig, *Ethics and Criminal Justice: An Introduction* (Cambridge: Cambridge University Press, 2008) 115.

[22] See K. Kipnis, "Criminal Justice and the Negotiated Plea," [1976] 86 *Ethics* 93; J. H. Langbein, "Torture and Plea Bargaining," [1980] 58 *Public Interest* 43; and C. Brunk, "The Problem of Voluntariness and Coercion in the Negotiated Plea," [1979] 13 *Law & Soc'y Rev.* 527.

[23] Langbein (n 22 above) 52.

[24] See A. Wertheimer, "The Prosecutor and the Gunman," [1979b] 89 *Ethics* 269, and R. E. Scott and W. J. Stuntz, "Plea Bargaining as Contract," [1992] 101 *Yale L. J.* 1909.

[25] The two authors who come closest to doing so are Brunk (n 22 above) 547, and T. W. Church, Jr, "In Defense of 'Bargain Justice'," [1979] 13 *Law & Soc'y Rev.* 509, 520. Brunk argues that there must be no inflation of sentences post-trial beyond the "normal" ones (547). Yet Brunk's very useful discussion is hampered by his indecision about whether to stick with a moralized or a non-moralized account of coercion. In places he claims that defendants are coerced if their choice situations are worsened by prosecutors' actions, where "worsened" means that they are threatened with higher sentences than are "normal." In other places he claims that defendants' choice situations are "worsened" if prosecutors threaten them with additional penalties that are morally unjustified. The former interpretation seems vulnerable to the ubiquity of trial penalty threats. They are "normal." Only the moralized conception

situation of defendants, although, as we have seen, there will be circumstances in which they may conceal threats of trial penalties. Trial penalties, by contrast, are invariably coercive, especially when they threaten defendants with sanctions that exceed those appropriate given the criminal conduct in which they have engaged. If my arguments in this chapter are persuasive, prosecutors who resort to them in any of their varieties exceed their moral remit.

To clarify and develop these claims, consider an exchange between a critic of plea bargaining and a partial defender of the practice. In addition to claiming that plea bargaining was likely to yield substantively unjust outcomes in many cases, Kenneth Kipnis made the bolder claim that the practice was coercive, because it put criminal defendants in a dilemma similar to that of ordinary citizens confronted by gunmen who demand "your money or your life." Defendants, just like mugging victims, must choose between a smaller, though certain loss and a larger, though more uncertain one.[26] Notice, though, that Kipnis's argument does not distinguish the contribution to the dilemma faced by the defendant made by waiver rewards as distinguished from trial penalties. In a response to Kipnis, Alan Wertheimer claimed that though gunmen act unjustifiably when they confront hapless citizens with such choices, prosecutors do not do so when they confront defendants with offers of charge or sentence reductions, at least assuming that prosecutors have acted pursuant to their legitimate authority in charging these individuals in the first place.[27] According to Wertheimer, the baseline against which the gunman's actions are to be assessed is the citizen's situation prior to the gunman's arrival on the scene. Relative to that baseline, the gunman's proposal is a threat because it makes the citizen worse off. In contrast, the baseline against which the prosecutor's proposal is to be assessed is the defendant's post-charge predicament. Relative to that baseline, the prosecutor's proposal of a waiver reward is an offer (or as Wertheimer terms it, a "promise") and likely a welcome one for most guilty defendants (though one, as Wertheimer admits, coupled with the declaration of a unilateral plan to pursue trial adjudication of the charges against the defendant if he or she refuses the waiver reward).[28]

Wertheimer's response to Kipnis seems correct, up to a point. Prosecutors are authorized to charge individuals against whom they have reasonably compelling evidence and they do nothing wrong by acting on that authority. They might also be justified in offering defendants discounted sentences in exchange for guilty pleas. That remains to be seen. Yet even if waiver rewards cannot be justified, they are not reasonably construed as threats. They offer defendants reductions in charges or

of coercion—the one according to which defendants are coerced if they are threatened with additional sanctions that are unjustified—enables us to make sense of the way in which trial penalties are coercive. Church (520) rejects what he terms a "surcharge" on the exercise of the right to trial, by which he means an additional penalty recommended or imposed on defendants for their refusal to plead guilty.

[26] Kipnis (n 22 above) 99.

[27] Wertheimer (n 24 above) 276. See also his "Freedom, Morality, Plea Bargaining, and the Supreme Court," [1979a] 8 *Philosophy and Public Affairs* 203, 223.

[28] Wertheimer (n 24 above) 275.

sentences, ones to which they may not be entitled in many cases, given the character of their criminal conduct.[29] They thus improve the situations of most defendants.[30] Even those defendants who are wholly or partially innocent are not made worse off by waiver-reward offers, though they are put in a difficult bind by them. Of course, we must assume here, as Wertheimer seems to, that defendants have not been strategically overcharged to begin with.[31] If they have been, then it is much less clear whether waiver rewards offer them things to which they are not really entitled.

However, even if waiver rewards offered to appropriately charged defendants do not coerce them, things are different if such rewards are coupled with implicit or explicit threats of trial penalties. Wertheimer notes that duress has two components. One is a psychological component, according to which defendants are placed under duress by prosecutors' proposals if they find it psychologically difficult to refuse to accept a plea offer.[32] Wertheimer concedes that waiver-reward offers satisfy this first condition of duress. But initially, at least, he denies that they satisfy the second, moral condition, which holds that a proposal puts the recipient under duress only if that proposal is immoral or unjustified.[33] Since they improve a defendant's condition, prosecutors' bi-conditional proposals are unlike the ones made by muggers. Perhaps so, but what if prosecutors' proposals contain implied or explicit threats of trial penalties? Such threats do not improve a defendant's situation in the way that offers of waiver rewards tend to. Instead, they raise the prospect of defendants finding that they are worse off than their criminal acts merit simply because they have exercised a legal and moral right.

Granted, prosecutors might not carry through on implied or explicit threats to recommend post-trial sentences that are harsher than offenders' crimes merit. By the same token, muggers might not carry through on their threats to harm those who do not turn over their money. And professors who offer grade bargains may not, if required to perform a second, more careful reading of papers, grade them more harshly in retaliation for being asked to do their jobs. But few of us would be inclined to doubt that muggers who make such threats in the first place, or professors who rely on implied or explicit threats of harsher second readings of papers, act coercively in doing so. Prosecutors (or judges) who rely on threats of trial penalties do not seem to be acting any differently.

---

[29] I am here assuming that defendants have not been overcharged by prosecutors as part of a strategy to put pressure on them to plead guilty.

[30] See especially Scott and Stuntz (n 24 above) 1920, where they note that it seems odd to view substantial waiver rewards as coercive since they are "too generous to the defendant..."

[31] Wertheimer is explicit about this in "Freedom, Morality, Plea Bargaining" (n 27 above) 229.

[32] Wertheimer (n 24 above) 271.

[33] Near the end of his discussion, Wertheimer agrees with Kipnis that prosecutors' offers of waiver rewards may be "incapable of yielding just decisions" and hints that this may show that such offers are unjustified. If they are, then the second, moral condition of duress may be satisfied and so guilty pleas may be reached under duress. See n 22 above, 279. But this seems to confuse two very different things—whether waiver rewards can be justified and whether they are coercive. My view is that they may be unjustified but that they are not typically coercive. Only trial penalties are coercive.

It might be objected that there is a crucial difference between muggers and their victims and offenders who find themselves confronted by prosecutors offering waiver rewards and wielding threats of trial penalties. Those charged with crimes, if they are guilty of them, could have avoided finding themselves in this predicament by having refrained from offending in the first place. In this way they are different from the victims of muggers who presumably have not done anything illegal by venturing out onto the streets. Criminal offenders, it might be claimed, have advance warning that prosecutors will charge them with crimes, offer them waiver rewards, and overtly or covertly threaten them with trial penalties. We should not have much sympathy for them if they persist in offending anyway and find themselves face to face with prosecutors who act roguishly.

The preceding objection is flawed on two counts. First, simply having advance warning that individuals will issue unjustified threats does not transform those threats into legitimate proposals. If muggers take out advertisements in the newspapers warning citizens that they will be out in force over the next few evenings, that would not make their subsequent mugging activities justified. That much seems clear. Notice, by the way, that the lack of justification would be especially evident in the case of citizens who did not read the relevant advertisements. Such citizens would be like innocents wrongly accused by prosecutors (and threatened with trial penalties if they do not accede to prosecutors' waiver-reward proffers). Second, individuals who offend are reasonably understood to have taken the risk of being charged with crimes by prosecutors and assigned sanctions proportional with the seriousness of their criminal wrongdoing. But saying that is very different from saying that they are reasonably understood to have taken the risk of being assessed a surcharge for having chosen to exercise their legal and moral right to trial adjudication, especially where the surcharge produces harsher sentences than their crimes merit or than would have been assigned in their absence.

There is another difference between criminal defendants and mugging victims that is worth noting. Mugging victims will presumably know that refusals to comply with the demands of those who accost them place them at risk. But it is conceivable that some criminal defendants will not know or suspect that if they refuse prosecutors' offers of waiver rewards, they are apt to get harsher post-trial sentence recommendations. Such defendants will not believe that they are being threatened by prosecutors and so will not confront the hard choice that such threats create, though they will have to decide whether or not to risk a trial with its likelihood of a non-discounted sentence. Analogously, there might be some students who are unaware of how the grade-bargaining professor's ire at being made to provide a second reading of their papers is likely to affect their grades. Such naïve defendants and students may not find out until afterwards, probably to their chagrin, that more was going on than they believed when proffers were made to them. All we can say about them is that they did not feel threatened when such proffers were made. It does not follow of course, that either prosecutors or professors act appropriately in imposing additional penalties upon those who require them to do their jobs. Moreover, defendants and students of this kind will presumably be rather rare. Usually there will be others around—defense attorneys in the case of criminal defendants—who will set them straight on the risks that they face.

It also might be argued that it does not follow from the mere fact that threats are immoral that any agreements reached in response to them are legally unenforceable. Michael Philips contends that there are cases in which A immorally threatens B in order to gain B's assent to do X, but in which A might have legal grounds for recovering damages from B if B subsequently reneges on the agreement to do X.[34] Philips' example involves an art dealer who is in the possession of materials of great sentimental value to an artist. Because the dealer wants the artist to display her work in the dealer's gallery, something which the artist is strongly disinclined to do because she regards the dealer's gallery as crassly commercial, the dealer threatens to destroy the materials in order to gain the artist's compliance. Suppose that the artist reluctantly signs an exclusive agreement to display her art in the dealer's gallery, only later to breach the agreement by displaying her artwork elsewhere. Philips admits that the dealer's threat was immoral, but questions whether it is clear that a judge would act properly by refusing to enforce the agreement it produced. Philips elaborates this point by noting that "some political philosophers would hold that law and morality ought not be so intimately and thoroughly connected—i.e., that so long as A acts within the framework of certain minimal moral constraints, he ought to be permitted to induce B to enter into an agreement by any means he chooses; and that, other things equal, these agreements ought to be legally enforceable."[35] It is not altogether clear what Philips intends by the terms "minimal moral constraints," but presumably he believes that we should balk at enforcing agreements that result from threats of overt physical coercion. Since the art dealer employs nothing of the sort, his threat does not make his agreement with the artist legally invalid due to duress.

Philips' point is, I would grant, a sensible one in the abstract. We might not want to have the courts invalidate all agreements borne of what appear to be immoral threats, regardless of the kind of immorality involved. In his example, part of what gives us pause about what the courts should do if the artist fails to honor her agreement is that the art dealer appears to have come into possession of the materials prized by the artist in some legitimate way. Perhaps the dealer purchased them from someone else or found them in an abandoned home or warehouse. In any case, since they are in the dealer's possession, we might believe that he can do with them as he wishes, including destroy them. His property rights entitle him to that much. Of course, we might also agree with Philips that his threat to destroy them in order to get the artist to

[34] M. Philips, "The Question of Voluntariness in the Plea Bargaining Controversy: A Philosophical Clarification," [1981–82] 16 *Law & Soc'y Rev.* 207, 216.

[35] Philips (n 34 above) 218.

comply with his wishes is dastardly. But since he would be within his legal and possibly moral rights to destroy the artwork, we might balk at having the courts invalidate
the agreement produced by his threat. We might also wonder if the artist could not
have attempted to purchase the valued materials from the dealer so that she would
not be susceptible to his threats. She had an option, in other words, besides submit-
ting to his threats, even if it was not a terribly promising one, since the dealer would
no doubt have demanded a steep price for the materials or simply refused to sell them
to her. Furthermore, the artist could have walked away from the dealer's threat and
plausibly hoped that he would not act on it. Other than sheer vindictiveness on his
part, he would stand to gain little from doing so (and more by selling the materials if
he could find a buyer for them).

Once we have fleshed out the example in these ways, we can begin to see how
it differs in significant respects from cases in which prosecutors threaten criminal
defendants with trial penalties if they do not accept offers of waiver rewards. First
and foremost, it is doubtful that, for the reasons laid out in some detail previously in
this chapter, prosecutors are rightfully in the possession of trial penalty threats. There
is, in effect, no honest way for prosecutors to come by or use them. Trial penalties
add to the punishment those convicted at trial receive, though their trial demands
do not fundamentally alter their crimes. Second, prosecutors, unlike art dealers, are
plausibly understood to be under an antecedent obligation to pursue justice in their
dealings with criminal defendants.[36] They are not to maximize the number of convictions they are able to obtain come what may. The reasons for this are obvious
enough. Prosecutors are entrusted with enormous power which they are expected
to use wisely and fairly. There are no similar expectations with respect to art dealers, who are not public officials. Third, in plea bargaining, defendants have no other
options besides accepting offers by prosecutors—which most of them do eagerly—or
refusing them and risking conviction at trial. There is no possibility of their neutral-
izing the leverage that a threatened trial penalty gives the prosecutor by "purchasing"
it. Moreover, prosecutors have nothing to lose—and, in fact, quite a bit to gain—by
carrying through on their threats to impose trial penalties. In this way they are unlike
the art dealer whose destruction of the prized property would not only deprive him
of future leverage but needlessly ruin what he could sell to someone else. For all
of these reasons, Philips' claim that agreements obtained through immoral threats
might still be legally enforceable does not seem persuasive in relation to prosecutors
who menace defendants with trial penalties.

---

[36] See Green (n 21 above) 612–24. Also, see Crown Prosecution Service, *The Code for Crown
Prosecutors*, 2004, Principle 2.3, and the American Bar Association, *Criminal Justice Section Standards*, 1992
"Prosecution Function," Standard 3–1.2 (c).

A lingering doubt

Suppose it is conceded that trial penalties are coercive. Some will argue that waiver rewards are no different, especially when they consist of substantial charge or sentence discounts. Such discounts create sentencing differentials that will sorely tempt the accused to give in and admit their involvement in crimes. What does it matter whether the differentials stem from proffered waiver rewards rather than threatened trial penalties? Pressure to confess or plead guilty is the same whatever its origins, or so it might be claimed.

I would not deny that waiver rewards make confessions or guilty pleas enticing and that they can make them terribly enticing if they are permitted to become quite large. In subsequent chapters, I mount an extended argument for keeping waiver rewards fixed and modest. If that argument succeeds, then individuals accused of crimes would not have to face overwhelming pressure, borne of outsized waiver rewards, to confess or plead guilty. Nonetheless, it might be objected, what does it matter that the enticements will not be as powerful? If they exist at all, they raise the risk that some innocent or partly innocent defendants (in the sense of being innocent of some of the charges against them) will forego trials and admit their guilt. Perhaps defendants who confront state officials who offer them smallish waiver rewards in exchange for guilty pleas do not exactly find themselves in the position of mugging victims threatened with "your money or your life." Instead, they confront more genteel muggers who threaten "your money or a hard knock on the scull." Most defendants will accede to guilty pleas even if the rewards for doing so are modest, just as most citizens will hand over their money to more genteel muggers.

In thinking about this objection, it is important to keep in mind that most of its force derives from the contemplation of defendants who are innocent of the crimes with which they have been charged. Those who are guilty have risked finding themselves in the predicament in which they are quite reasonably confronted with criminal charges by state officials. Further, waiver rewards offer them benefits in the form of reduced punishment for their crimes. Again, in this respect, waiver rewards, regardless of their magnitude, are unlike trial penalties as I have characterized them, since the latter involve an extra measure of punishment apportioned post-trial that is unrelated to the revealed character of individuals' crimes. Thus, it is hard to see how guilty defendants are being "mugged" by state officials who do nothing more than offer them reduced punishment in exchange for admitting their crimes.

It must be conceded, though, that waiver rewards of any size will put some pressure on innocent defendants to enter guilty pleas, as well as on defendants who mistakenly believe that they are innocent. Yet, in the first place, it is hard to imagine how we could ever completely eliminate all pressure on defendants to admit their guilt. Trials themselves will be costly to defendants, in a variety of ways, ranging from attorneys' fees (assuming defendants are not indigent), to the stresses and strains of the process and the public embarrassment of having the state's case made clear for all to see.[37] Defendants held on remand until their trials will endure added hardships. Some defendants, including some innocent ones, might plead guilty to avoid having to bear these kinds of costs, even if they could not get any sentencing concessions in exchange. True, even modest waiver rewards increase the pressures on defendants somewhat, but arguably not to the point at which they are clearly overbearing. Second, there is no guarantee that innocent defendants will prevail at trials if they elect to go through with them in efforts to exonerate themselves. In the United States, for instance, it is estimated that the state wins close to 80 percent of felony cases that go to trial.[38] In England and Wales, the percentages are better for defendants whose trials are held at the Crown Courts, with an estimated 45 percent of defendants gaining acquittals.[39] Still, a conviction rate of 55 percent is far from insignificant. We might speculate that the percentage conviction rate will be lower when defendants are, in fact, wholly innocent, but even a 20 or 30 percent chance of conviction is enough to make many defendants pause. Hence, it is not clear that having the option of a sentence discount for a guilty plea makes innocents charged with crimes altogether worse off.

Third, and most importantly, I shall argue that there are any number of powerful reasons why permitting state officials to offer and manipulate substantial waiver rewards is a morally suspect practice. It is a practice that is unlikely to enhance the deserved punishment profile of the criminal justice system as a whole or optimize crime reduction. Also, it is not a practice that makes sense if we believe that those remorseful for their crimes merit leniency. Further, it is not a practice to which state officials, who understand and are committed to the principles upon which the legal system is founded, should have recourse when the evidence against individuals whom they suspect of crimes is short of conclusive. Modest and fixed sentence discounts for guilty pleas will fulfill many of the purposes served by more robust forms of plea bargaining and will not put much pressure on the innocent to waive their right to trial. In short, the charge that waiver rewards are "coercive" obscures more than it illuminates, and it may do so even if the rewards in question are allowed to become large and variable. If they are kept modest and fixed, so that no official can manipulate them and thus step up the pressure on defendants to accept them and plead guilty rather than go to trial, then the notion that defendants are being improperly pressured to forego the right to trial seems strained.

---

[37] See M. M. Feeley, *The Process is the Punishment: Handling Cases in a Lower Criminal Court* (New York: Russell Sage, 1979), and J. Bowers, "Punishing the Innocent," [2007] 156 *U. of Pa. L. Rev.* 1117.
[38] Stuntz (n 20 above) 570.   [39] Ashworth and Redmayne (n 5 above) 294.

Concluding remarks

Trial penalties are, in the vast majority of cases, unjustified infringements upon criminal defendants' moral and legal rights to trial. Prosecutorial reliance on them, whether explicit or implicit, exerts pressure on criminal defendants that is tantamount to duress. Such threats must be distinguished from offers of waiver rewards and the longer sentences defendants risk when they do not accept such offers. Waiver rewards promise reduced punishment. Assuming that individuals are charged with crimes appropriately, based on the evidence that police and prosecutors have managed to obtain, and not overcharged or threatened with disproportionately long sentences to begin with, waiver rewards improve defendants' positions beyond what they can reasonably expect or demand given the circumstances. Trial penalties impose longer sentences on defendants for reasons that have nothing to do with their criminal conduct and everything to do with their insistence upon trial adjudication of the charges against them. I conclude that such penalties are impermissible and that we should adopt measures to detect and discourage them. Pre-trial settlement hearings, at which defendants' presumptive sentences are set by judges, are a device that would enable us to do both of these things in some instances. In succeeding chapters, I assume that such a device is employed and operates effectively.

It bears repeating that the defensibility of plea bargaining as a practice does not turn entirely on the question of whether trial penalties can be justified. Even if prosecutors could be dissuaded from exacting or threatening them, plea bargaining could persist in modified form if they were permitted to offer waiver rewards. Numerous arguments have been advanced in defense of waiver rewards. The remainder of this book takes up those arguments.

3

Waiver Rewards and Deserved Punishment

Plea bargaining does not depend on the threat or reality of trial penalties, as I have defined them. It can persist so long as state officials are permitted to offer criminal defendants rewards in exchange for agreeing to plead guilty. Waiver rewards consist of sentence discounts assigned to criminal defendants willing to admit their guilt, or reductions in the charges against them below those warranted by the evidence. Both may be offered to defendants. It is not uncommon in the United States, where plea bargaining takes robust form, for prosecutors to file a series of charges against individuals, the total sentences for which would be fearsome if the individuals in question were found guilty on all counts. Instead of insisting that defendants plead guilty to all of the charges against them, prosecutors may offer them a mix of charge and sentence discounts, one that dramatically reduces the punishment that they are likely to be assigned by the courts.

In this chapter we take up the questions of whether, and to what extent, waiver rewards cohere with a retributive, or desert-based, approach to the justification of legal punishment. At first glance, they do not appear to do so. Sentence reductions, by their very natures, offer defendants what appear to be undeserved leniency. As we saw in Chapter 1, if presumptive sentences are set at settlement hearings, they are to be based on a pre-trial assessment by the judge of where defendants' alleged crimes fit into the prescribed sentencing range. Once presumptive sentences have been set in this way, it is not apparent why, on a retributive approach to sentencing, we would permit prosecutors to offer reductions. If our aim is to punish offenders proportionally with the seriousness of their offenses, then what legitimate purpose would be served by waiver rewards in the form of sentence reductions? Again, Kenneth Kipnis's grade-bargaining analogy illuminates the problem with such punishment discounts.[1] In the analogy, students are offered grades on papers that are better than the ones to which they are presumptively entitled so that instructors will not have to go back and read carefully the papers that they have assigned. Such a scheme will seem bizarre to anyone who believes that student grades should reflect the merits of their work.

Similarly, if state officials believe that there is evidence implicating a defendant for several crimes, why should they be permitted to eliminate one or more of the charges

---

[1] K. Kipnis, "Criminal Justice and the Negotiated Plea," [1976] 86 *Ethics* 93, 104–5.

in exchange for guilty pleas? Granted, to some it will seem unnecessary or excessive to have individuals convicted on multiple charges serve the sum total of the sentences for their crimes. If offenders are forced to serve their multiple sentences consecutively, they might have to spend most of the rest of their lives in prison. Nevertheless, it seems odd, from a deserved punishment perspective, to have a charge-adjudication scheme that effectively allows state officials to act as if individuals did not commit crimes when there is clear evidence that they did.

After outlining the general contours of a desert-based approach to legal punishment, two plausible defenses of waiver rewards are developed and examined. The first holds that criminal defendants who are willing to acknowledge their guilt and spare us the expense and other burdens of trials might reasonably be given some modest reduction in their sentences. Though this might be the most plausible rationale for waiver rewards, it is both limited and not entirely unproblematic, for reasons that will be made clear. The second defense holds that, by inducing guilty pleas, waiver rewards enable state officials to mobilize their scarce resources so that they can then be deployed to mete out deserved punishment to many more offenders. Although this defense of waiver rewards has some intuitive appeal, it must be developed in ways that carry us well beyond the vague notion that such rewards enable us to expand deserved punishment. Three dimensions are distinguished along which the deserved punishment profiles of waiver reward schemes are to be evaluated. Various schemes are then analyzed along these dimensions to determine which is apt to produce the best overall profile.

In evaluating waiver reward schemes, it is crucial to identify the background conditions against which such rewards are assumed to operate. In the first part of the chapter, I stipulate a set of ideal background conditions. Where such conditions obtain, it will not prove an easy task to defend waiver rewards, especially large and variable ones. I contend that if our aim is to produce an optimal deserved punishment profile, we would do better to discourage charge bargaining and keep sentence reductions at low levels. Toward the end of the chapter, I re-evaluate the various waiver reward schemes in light of the possibility that such ideal background conditions might not obtain. In societies in which over-punishment is the norm, large and variable waiver rewards might be the only, though decidedly imperfect, way in which to limit the infliction of undeservedly harsh criminal sanctions.

Desert-based approaches to the justification of legal punishment

There is a surprising variety of retributive or desert-based approaches to legal punishment's justification.[2] Rather than defend any one of them, I shall employ an abstract

---

[2] Prominent contemporary retributive accounts of legal punishment include H. Morris, "Persons and Punishment," [1968] 52 *Monist* 475; J. Murphy, "Marxism and Retribution," [1973] 2 *Philosophy and*

characterization of the key elements to such an approach, one which should be congenial to many, if not most, of the more fully elaborated accounts in the literature. Most of these elements will play central roles in my subsequent analysis of waiver rewards. The discussion in this section will go over what may be familiar ground for some readers. Yet doing so will be useful in setting up and clarifying the analysis of waiver rewards to come.

Let us begin with what may appear to be a trivial point, though, as we will see, it turns out to be anything but that when we confront the vast array of criminal prohibitions that exist in some societies. If legal punishment is to be deserved in any meaningful sense, then it must not be for conduct that merely happens to be legally prohibited, but for conduct that, on some normatively defensible account of the criminal law, should be prohibited.[3] Individuals do not deserve to be punished for violating legal prohibitions unless what they disallow is the commission of significant wrongs. Such wrongs usually consist of actions harming the important interests of others. But they might also encompass conduct that thwarts social coordination, undermines support of needed institutions, or disrupts the fair allocation of access to scarce societal resources.[4] No clear-thinking retributivist regards punishment as deserved simply because individuals have violated legal prohibitions, no matter how unjust or otherwise indefensible those prohibitions turn out to be.

Assuming a set of defensible criminal prohibitions, the sanctions attaching to their violation must be devised and administered so that they are proportionate with the seriousness of offenses. There are two dimensions to proportionality in sanctions.[5] First, ordinal proportionality requires the appropriate scaling of sanctions and offenses. More serious crimes should be punished more harshly than less serious ones, where crime seriousness is typically taken to be a function of both the harm done (or threatened or attempted) by offenses and the culpability of the offending agent. Roughly equivalent crimes should be punished commensurately. All of this is consistent with sentence ranges for each of the different kinds of offenses, with final sentences to be determined by the sentencing judge, who takes into account the details of a given crime and facts about the offender who committed it. Second, there is cardinal proportionality, which concerns what Andrew von Hirsch terms the "anchoring point" of the sentence scale, or what we might term its "absolute"

Public Affairs 217; W. Sadurski, *Giving Desert Its Due* (Dordrecht, Netherlands: D. Reidel, 1985); G. Sher, *Desert* (Princeton, NJ: Princeton University Press, 1987); J. Hampton, "A New Theory of Retribution," in R. G. Frey and C. W. Morris (eds.), *Liability and Responsibility: Essays in Law and Morals* (Cambridge: Cambridge University Press, 1991) 377; R. A. Duff, *Trials and Punishments* (Cambridge: Cambridge University Press, 1986); and M. Moore, *Placing Blame: A General Theory of the Criminal Law* (New York: Oxford University Press, 1998).

[3] See D. Husak, *Overcriminalization: The Limits of the Criminal Law* (Oxford: Oxford University Press, 2008) 82–3.

[4] The wrongs in such cases are not direct wrongs against individuals, but against the community, in the form of non-cooperation in a scheme of mutual benefit or unfair use of a scarce resource.

[5] See A. von Hirsch, *Censure and Sanctions* (Oxford: Clarendon Press, 1993) 18–19.

level of severity.[6] Two or more sentencing scales might satisfy the requirements of ordinal proportionality and yet differ dramatically with respect to how harshly or mildly they punish offenders overall. Imagine a sentencing scale that ran from a small fine to a three-year maximum prison sentence for even the worst offenses. Contrast that with a sentencing scale that ran from a minimum three-year prison sentence for minor crimes all the way up to life imprisonment under conditions of solitary confinement for the worst crimes. Both might satisfy the demands of ordinal proportionality. Cardinal proportionality requires us to solve the vexing problem of just how much punishment the various types of crimes merit absolutely, as it were.[7] Fortunately, once we have solved that problem for any given type of crime, we can, in principle, work out the rest of the sentence scale by reference to considerations of ordinal proportionality.

Setting to one side the difficulties raised by cardinal proportionality, it is worth noting that there is disagreement about how much ordinal proportionality should be demanded from a sentencing scheme. Some, like von Hirsch, believe that it is very important to try to punish like offenders alike.[8] Significant variations in sanctions among like offenders create problems of comparative injustice that we should seek to minimize. Others, while not exactly welcoming such comparative injustices, seem prepared to tolerate them within a wider range, especially if we can thereby achieve more flexibility in the kinds of sentences assigned offenders.[9] According to such theorists, we should be open to assigning different kinds of sentences to individuals who have committed roughly equivalent crimes if doing so is responsive to their different needs or circumstances. Given that evaluation of the comparative severity of sentences is not an exact science anyway, such theorists seem to think that we should not be too concerned with achieving equal sentencing outcomes for like offenders.

Desert-based approaches to legal punishment's justification have traditionally been focused intently on achieving accurate outcomes in the arena of criminal justice. It is thought crucial not only to have legal procedures in place that reliably tend to separate the guilty from the innocent, but also ones that assign the former proportionate sentences. Still, retributivists recognize that any humanly devised criminal justice system will make mistakes. Sometimes the innocent will be convicted of crimes, or the guilty will be assigned punishments that are harsher or more lenient than they deserve. What is crucial is that such mistakes should be aberrations and not

---

[6] von Hirsch (n 5 above) 38.

[7] For discussion of this problem, see von Hirsch (n 5 above) 36–46.

[8] See A. von Hirsch, "Proportionality in the Philosophy of Punishment," [1992] 16 *Crime and Justice: A Review of Research* 55, 76.

[9] See M. Tonry, "Proportionality, Parsimony, and Interchangeability of Punishments," in R. A. Duff, S. Marshall, and R. P. Dobash (eds.), *Penal Theory and Penal Practice* (Manchester, UK: Manchester University Press, 1992) 59. See also N. Morris, *Madness and the Criminal Law* (Chicago: University of Chicago Press, 1982), chapter 5.

systemic.[10] In other words, they should represent occasional malfunctions of a set of legal procedures designed to distinguish the innocent from the guilty and assign appropriate sentences to the latter. For instance, a low standard of proof in criminal cases might be deemed problematic because of its demonstrable tendency to produce erroneous outcomes. Importantly, it is not just the formal procedures in place for adjudicating charges that will matter to retributivists. Even if such procedures work reasonably well once individuals are arrested and charged with crimes, prior decisions made by police, investigators, and prosecutors have the potential to skew deserved outcomes. If the state officials who initiate criminal proceedings against individuals are, for instance, biased by racial or class considerations in making arrest or charging decisions, then the criminal justice system will predictably produce inequitable outcomes. In short, comparative injustices can result from pre-trial actions by state officials, not solely from defects in charge adjudication.

Finally, retributive punishment has an expressive quality that makes sense only against certain background assumptions about offenders. Punishment both censures and imposes hard treatment.[11] Yet we meaningfully censure the conduct of individuals only if they are capable of moral self-governance and have acted freely in committing crimes. The requirement of moral self-governance is the basis for retributive support of the insanity defense, as well as its proscription against punishing infants, children, and the mentally disabled.[12] It also explains why retributivism struggles to defend the punishment of those with psychopathic personality disorder.[13] The requirement that individuals have acted freely in committing criminal acts explains why retributivism supports defenses based on duress or necessity, since some criminal prohibitions are violated in circumstances in which individuals have no reasonable options except to offend.[14] More controversial is the question whether, or to what extent, severe and continuing social deprivation undermines the case for the retributive punishment of some of the individuals who have violated legitimate criminal prohibitions. Many retributivists believe that it does, either by undermining the capacities of persons for moral self-governance or by forcing near-duress choices

---

[10] The distinction between systemic and aberrational miscarriages of justice comes from Kipnis (n 1 above) 102.

[11] von Hirsch (n 5 above) 9–13.

[12] Consider von Hirsch's claim that legal punishment is not meaningfully inflicted on "tigers," in his *Censure and Sanctions* (n 5 above) 11. For discussion of the liability requirements of retributive theory, see R. L. Lippke, "Mixed Theories of Punishment and Mixed Offenders: Some Unresolved Tensions," [2006] 42 *Southern Journal of Philosophy* 273.

[13] See J. Murphy, "Moral Death: A Kantian Essay on Psychopathy," [1972] 82 *Ethics* 284; R. A. Duff, "Psychopathy and Moral Understanding," [1977] 14 *American Philosophical Quarterly* 189; and C. Fine and J. Kennett, "Mental Impairment, Moral Understanding, and Criminal Responsibility: Psychopathy and the Purposes of Punishment," [2004] 27 *International Journal of Law and Psychiatry* 425.

[14] See S. J. Morse, "Deprivation and Desert," in W. C. Heffernan and J. Kleinig (eds.), *From Social Justice to Criminal Justice: Poverty and the Administration of Criminal Law* (New York: Oxford University Press, 2000) 114, 125–8.

upon them.[15] These concerns about social deprivation might serve as the basis for some mitigation in the punishment meted out to socially deprived offenders.

Rewards for acknowledging guilt

In thinking about whether waiver rewards can be defended on a desert-based approach to the justification of legal punishment, it will be helpful initially to employ a number of simplifying assumptions. First, set to one side the half-loaf cases, ones in which the primary concern of prosecutors in plea bargaining is not to conserve their resources but to secure guilty pleas from defendants against whom the state's evidence is short of conclusive. The half-loaf cases are examined in Chapter 8. For now, assume that the cases under consideration are those in which prosecutors have evidence that is likely sufficient to gain convictions should defendants elect trial adjudication. Second, assume a somewhat idealized social and legal context, one in which the criminal prohibitions enforced are defensible and the sanctions attaching to their violation are proportionate. Assume also that individuals have not been deliberately overcharged by prosecutors as part of a strategy to put pressure on them to accede to guilty pleas. In other words, let us suppose that prosecutors engage in "veridical charging," that is, charging aimed solely at accurately capturing (in light of the defensible criminal prohibitions that exist) each of the criminal acts that they have plausible evidence defendants have committed. The concept of veridical charging makes more sense if we imagine that the criminal law lacks the overlapping, redundant, or ancillary prohibitions that facilitate so much contemporary overcharging.[16] Hence, assume that we have in place a simplified and pared down criminal code, one which aims at prohibiting conduct that is clearly and significantly harmful to others or disruptive of needed forms of social coordination and cooperation. It might be objected that these simplifying assumptions take us too far from the current social reality of criminal prosecutions. Perhaps that is so. Subsequently they will be relaxed, but for now we should avoid cluttering the analysis of waiver rewards with concerns about the ways in which contemporary criminal justice systems overcriminalize and over-punish.

The most straightforward argument for granting waiver rewards in the form of sentence reductions to defendants who admit their guilt is this: Most of the defendants who are inclined to waive the right to trial are guilty and they know it. For such defendants, trials are very likely to produce convictions, though a few veridically

---

[15] The classic formulation is Murphy's (n 2 above) 231. For a more recent version of the view, see R. L. Lippke, *Rethinking Imprisonment* (Oxford: Oxford University Press, 2007) 84–98. For skepticism about the ability of social deprivation to undermine deserved punishment, see Morse (n 14 above) 140–53.

[16] For discussion of the problems raised by overlapping, redundant, and ancillary criminal prohibitions, see, W. J. Stuntz, "The Pathological Politics of Criminal Law," [2001] 100 *Mich. L. Rev.* 505, 537. See also Husak (n 3 above) 21–3.

charged defendants, against whom the state has convincing evidence, might succeed in gaining acquittals. Defendants who are guilty and who acknowledge their guilt, rather than insisting on the ritual of a costly and time-consuming trial, might reasonably be given some concession in the form of a sentence reduction. Bear in mind, trials are burdensome to others besides prosecutors and judges.[17] The resources that are expended on trials come from taxpayers whom, we might assume, are already called upon to support the provision of other public goods. Also, trials are onerous and sometimes traumatizing to the witnesses who have to testify at them, and inconvenient to the citizen jurors who are drafted to sit through them and ultimately render verdicts. If guilty defendants spare us the expense and bother of having to conduct "useless" trials, then at least they do not add insult to injury by committing criminal acts and then forcing us to prove their guilt.[18]

Still, even if this argument for sentence reductions is persuasive, it may support only modest waiver rewards in the vast majority of criminal cases. True, trials are costly in a variety of ways but not that costly. Many of them will last only a day or two; some will not last that long. Having judges, rather than juries, hear the evidence in cases in which lesser crimes are involved would further reduce the costs of trials.[19] Moreover, plea bargaining is not cost-free.[20] The settlement hearings that I have proposed will impose additional burdens on state officials and the public who supports their activities, though those burdens will probably not begin to approach the ones generated by trials. Perhaps we should show some lenity to defendants who acknowledge their guilt and spare us the expense and other burdens of having to conduct criminal trials. But large sentence discounts would seem disproportionate, much as substantial trial penalties imposed on defendants who elect trial adjudication and lose were shown to be in Chapter 2.

It should be noted that in England and Wales, defendants who agree to plead guilty early in the charge-adjudication process are eligible for larger sentence discounts, up to 30 percent, than those who do so later.[21] Defendants who plead guilty just prior to their trials, and thus cause what are known as "cracked trials," typically receive sentence discounts no greater than 10 percent. In some ways, this practice makes sense on the rationale for waiver rewards currently under consideration. The closer state officials get to having to conduct trials, the more they have invested in preparing

---

[17] A. Wertheimer notes other costs of trials in his "Freedom, Morality, Plea Bargaining, and the Supreme Court," [1979] 8 *Philosophy and Public Affairs* 203, 207.

[18] Though again, as I noted in Chapter 2, even trials of the factually guilty might produce public goods of various kinds.

[19] S. J. Schulhofer, "Is Plea Bargaining Inevitable?" [1984] 97 *Harv. L. Rev.* 1037. However, consider the example in England and Wales of the Magistrates' Courts, which handle the overwhelming majority of criminal cases, but which are seen to suffer from deficiencies in providing full and fair hearings for defendants. For discussion of those deficiencies, see A. Ashworth and M. Redmayne, *The Criminal Process,* 4th edition (Oxford: Oxford University Press, 2010) 323–5.

[20] A. W. Alschuler, "Implementing the Criminal Defendant's Right to Trial: Alternatives to the Plea Bargaining System," [1983] 50 *U. Chi. L. Rev.* 931, 939–40.

[21] Ashworth and Redmayne (n 19 above) 293.

for them, and the more potential witnesses have had to ready themselves or travel some distance to testify. If we are rewarding defendants who admit their guilt for sparing us the expense and other burdens of having to conduct trials, then those who spare us more such expenses and burdens should receive larger discounts. In addition, it is postulated that defendants who delay their guilty pleas until the last moment are waiting to see if the state's witnesses against them will actually appear for their trials. If they do, defendants accede to guilty pleas. If they do not, they might decide to risk trials. Yet it seems that we ought to discourage this behavior by defendants, and reducing waiver rewards for late pleaders is believed to do just that.[22]

However, there are reasons to doubt the desirability of such a graduated waiver-reward scheme, in spite of its apparent coherence with the rationale for waiver rewards currently under consideration. True, some defendants will be up to no good in delaying their guilty pleas. But not all of them will be. Some will be innocent or will sincerely believe themselves so. Their reasons for declining to swiftly enter guilty pleas are surely understandable and it is not clear why they should be pressured to accede to the state's wishes before they are ready to do so, or resigned to doing so. Other defendants will know that they are guilty of some or all of the charges against them, but for various other understandable reasons will be disinclined to admit their guilt. They might be charged with sexual offenses that are highly stigmatizing, or with violations of fiduciary relationships. Coming to grips with their having committed such offenses might take some time, especially since acknowledging them will be enormously damaging to the esteem in which they are held by others.[23] A few defendants may simply be in deep denial about what they have done, unable to admit it to themselves or others. For all of these reasons, I lean against the British scheme of progressively declining waiver rewards. Even "cracked trials" are less costly than real ones. Moreover, the state will be spared the expense of subsequent appeals in the vast majority of guilty-plea cases. These savings ought to be sufficient to earn late-pleading defendants the same sentence discounts as their earlier-pleading counterparts.

Still, the possibility that some defendants who agree to plead guilty might be factually innocent would seem to raise problems for a defense of waiver rewards premised on the notion that pleas save us the expense and bother of criminal trials. It is nonsensical to say of such defendants that by pleading they are "acknowledging their guilt," or that they should be rewarded for sparing us the burden of having to prove it. Practically, of course, it will be difficult to distinguish such defendants from the vast majority of defendants who are guilty and of whom it makes sense to say such things. We might hope that modest waiver rewards will be less likely to attract guilty pleas from the innocent. Further, we might believe that judges at settlement hearings will ferret out weak cases and drop charges in them, thus freeing some factually innocent

---

[22] Ashworth and Redmayne (n 19 above) 295.
[23] See A. W. Alschuler, "The Changing Plea Bargaining Debate," [1981] 69 *Cal. L. Rev.* 652, 666, where he notes that for some defendants "the act of putting the noose around their own necks is simply too difficult."

defendants from having to confront the dilemma of whether to plead guilty or go to trial and risk greater punishment. But there is no guarantee that all factually innocent individuals will either have the charges against them dropped or elect trial adjudication. Indeed, the process costs of trials might persuade some such defendants to plead guilty, even in the absence of waiver rewards.[24] Unsatisfactory though it might seem, I do not see any good reason for rejecting modest waiver rewards even if they will induce a few innocent defendants to enter guilty pleas.

Importantly, the rationale for waiver rewards currently under consideration does not appear to support the reductions in charges which are a staple of some plea bargaining regimes. It is one thing for defendants to acknowledge their guilt on the charges against them and receive something in return in the form of slightly reduced sentences. It is another for them to acknowledge their guilt on some of the charges against them in exchange for state officials dropping other charges which those officials have reason to believe are supported by the evidence. When charges are dropped in this fashion, defendants do not have to admit any of the further crimes that they may well have committed. This is a good deal for many defendants, but it is hard to see why they should be regarded as appropriately rewarded when what they have done is evade responsibility for some of their criminal acts.

Though the notion that defendants who admit their guilt rather than forcing the state to prove it merit some reduction in their punishment has much to be said for it, two objections to it ought to be considered. One of them draws upon the analogy with grade bargaining discussed in Chapter 1. It is not apparent, it might be argued, why students who save their professors from the burdens of having to provide more careful assessments of their papers deserve the better grades that they receive. In fact, many will believe it to be obvious that they do not deserve them. Why, then, should criminal defendants be deemed deserving of the waiver rewards that they might be granted for waiving the right to trial? This objection initially appears persuasive, but there are significant differences between students and criminal defendants which weaken its force. Students who hand in assigned papers have done nothing wrong by completing their assignments, unlike criminal defendants who are guilty as charged of having violated legitimate criminal prohibitions. Also, by declining second, more careful readings of their papers, students cannot be said in any sense to avoid compounding their wrongs. In this way they are unlike the criminal defendants who know they are guilty and whose trials will produce few public goods and expend significant resources. We therefore might be justified in granting modest sentence concessions to criminal defendants who spare us the burden of needless trials, though we would balk at giving students higher grades for declining more careful readings of their papers.

---

[24] See J. Bowers, "Punishing the Innocent," [2008] 156 *U. Pa. L. Rev.* 1117, 1132–42, and M. M. Feeley, *The Process is the Punishment: Handling Cases in a Lower Criminal Court* (New York: Russell Sage, 1979) 199–243.

However, this brings us to a more telling objection. Acknowledging guilt and sparing the community the myriad costs involved in having to prove it are actions that occur some time after the commission of crimes. As such, it is not apparent how they are appropriate retributive grounds for the mitigation of punishment. They do not affect either the harm done, threatened, or attempted by offenders, or the culpability with which they acted in committing their crimes. Granted, offenders who agree to plead guilty do not compound their wrongs—that is, add to them by insisting upon trial adjudication. But by not adding to them they do not essentially change them, or so it would seem. Some theorists maintain that offender remorse, which also occurs post-offense, is an appropriate mitigating factor in sentencing.[25] However, one can acknowledge guilt and forgo a trial without feeling or exhibiting remorse. Moreover, as I show in Chapter 4, remorse too is a dubious basis for waiver rewards, especially ones handed out at the time of sentencing.

In spite of this difficulty with the acknowledgment-of-guilt argument, my hunch is that it accounts for the almost universal practice of granting sentence concessions to criminal defendants who admit their crimes.[26] There seems something almost primeval about the willingness of persons to submit to authority, rather than contest it, which elicits lenity, even if such lenity is not strictly speaking deserved. Yet before we accept guilt acknowledgment as the most plausible basis for waiver rewards, we must consider another way in which they might be defended within a desert-based approach to punishment's justification. As we shall see, this alternative defense initially appears to support more substantial sentence reductions and even charge bargaining.

Expanding deserved punishment

Though the context in which we have been examining waiver rewards is an idealized one in many respects, it has nonetheless been assumed that prosecutors and the other state officials on whom they depend to investigate and process criminal charges have finite resources at their disposal. These resources might be increased somewhat, but they are unlikely to be expanded dramatically since enforcement of the criminal law must compete against other goods that the state is responsible for securing for its citizens. State officials will be unable to pursue charges against all of the individuals in society who appear to have committed crimes. Fortunately, police and prosecutors have considerable discretion in determining the individuals against whom they institute formal legal proceedings.

---

[25] S. K. Tudor, "Why Should Remorse Be a Mitigating Factor in Sentencing?" [2008a] 2 *Criminal Law and Philosophy* 241.

[26] For discussion of the ubiquity of the practice of granting concessions to defendants who admit their guilt, see Tudor (n 25 above) 241–2, and M. Bagaric and K. Ameraskara, "Feeling Sorry?—Tell Someone Who Cares: The Irrelevance of Remorse in Sentencing," [2001] 40 *The Howard Journal* 364, 366–7.

It is sometimes taken as an obvious point that state officials cannot provide trials for all of the individuals charged with crimes. But, in fact, whether limited resources impose such a constraint on state officials is not conceded in all quarters. Stephen Schulhofer grants that having to conduct jury trials for all defendants would put a tremendous strain on prosecutors and the courts. However, he claims that many persons accused of crimes could receive some meaningful, independent evaluation of the evidence against them through brief bench trials.[27] Albert Alschuler suggests that all individuals charged with felonies might be afforded jury trials, with only modest increases in the budgets of prosecutors and courts.[28]

By contrast, those who defend plea bargaining are confident that it saves state officials significant resources which can then be employed to increase the number of cases processed.[29] Trials of any kind, and especially jury trials, are expensive and time-consuming. Granted, plea bargaining is not cost-free, but having to conduct trials for a substantial portion of the numerous defendants against whom prosecutors have brought, or might bring, charges would quickly sap their resources, leaving them ill-equipped to pursue charges against other individuals whose conduct also merits punishment.

My working assumption will be that the proponents of plea bargaining's efficiency are correct—or at least correct enough to make the second desert-based argument for waiver rewards worthy of consideration. If they should turn out to be incorrect, or correct in a limited way because waiver rewards enable state officials to only marginally expand the pool of punished offenders, then the argument that we are about to consider will be seriously compromised. Again, waiver rewards consist of downward departures from the presumptively deserved punishment of offenders. They must therefore be viewed with some suspicion by retributivists.

In this section, I examine the use of sentence reductions in expanding deserved punishment. Charge reductions will be addressed in the next section. The link between the reduced sentences offered by prosecutors in exchange for guilty pleas and the expansion of deserved punishment seems straightforward enough.

Defendants who plead guilty in exchange for sentence reductions will usually not receive all of the punishment that they deserve for their crimes. As such, waiver rewards count against a charge-adjudication scheme's ability to produce an optimal deserved punishment profile. However, defendants who plead guilty in exchange for sentence discounts will receive some portion of the punishment that they deserve, at least on the assumption that they are actually guilty of the offenses to which they plead. In addition, the resources that state officials save by not having to conduct trials enable them to process a significantly larger number of cases through the

---

[27] Schulhofer (n 19 above) 1062–82.   [28] Alschuler (n 20 above) 937–48.

[29] See R. E. Scott and W. J. Stuntz, "Plea Bargaining as Contract," [1992] 101 *Yale L. J.* 1909, 1932. In "Pathological Politics" (n 16 above) Stuntz claimed that guilty pleas "are enormously cheaper" than trials, 636–7. See also the United States Supreme Court's claim that plea bargaining has become essential to the processing of criminal cases in *Santobello v. New York*, 404 U. S. 257, 260 (1971).

criminal justice system. The result will be that more individuals who merit punishment will receive all or part of it, the latter because many of them will also be induced to plead guilty by offers of waiver rewards. Even if the additional offenders prosecuted successfully do not receive all of the punishment that they deserve for their criminal acts, the use of waiver rewards permits state officials to expand deserved punishment. Moreover, once cases are resolved through negotiated settlements, they typically are not subject to further appellate review. That, too, conserves resources for state officials, resources they can utilize to see to it that more offenders get some or all of the punishment they deserve.

Such a forward-looking, aggregative approach to meting out deserved punishment will not sit well with all retributive theorists. Unlike the previous argument, which treated sentence concessions as rewards for defendants who acknowledged their guilt and saved us the expense and bother of trials, the current argument justifies them as instrumental in expanding the overall amount of deserved punishment that the authorities are able to assign. For such an approach to make sense, it must be permissible for state officials to trade off desert claims—to give some offenders less punishment than they deserve in order to use the resources conserved to give other, and presumably more serious, offenders some of the punishment they deserve. If one views desert claims as stringent in the demands they make upon state officials, then such trade-offs will be viewed with skepticism. On some desert-based approaches, state officials should see to it that the offenders whom they manage to apprehend and convict should receive all of their just punishment, and that is the end of it.[30] However, other desert theorists recognize that in the real world of limited resources, we might have to accept some compromises. The overall volume of crimes in any given society is likely to be such that it will be difficult for the authorities to apprehend and punish all the perpetrators without massive public investment of resources in the criminal justice system. Deserved punishment claims compete with one another as well as with other justice claims of equal, if not greater, significance. The more we spend on the criminal law and its allied institutions, the less will be available for education, health care, and decent housing for all citizens. Recognizing all of this, we might interpret retributivism as requiring state officials to marshal their limited resources to dole out more rather than less deserved punishment, even if this means that they must be willing to forgo imposing some of it on certain individuals in order to impose it upon others.

Still, an approach that treats deserved punishment claims as subject to trade-offs need not, and probably cannot, be grounded in a simple, aggregative consequentialism. To flesh this out, it will be useful to introduce some measure of deserved punishment, even if it is something of a contrived one. Suppose, therefore, that all

---

[30] My thinking about these matters has been shaped by M. T. Cahill's very useful discussion in "Retributive Justice in the Real World," [2007] 85 *Wash. U. L. Rev.* 815. See also D. Markel, "Are Shaming Punishments Beautifully Retributive? Retributivism and the Implications for the Alternative Sanctions Debate," [2001] 54 *Vand. L. Rev.* 2157.

criminal sanctions take the form of prison terms measured in months. Suppose also that all months in prison are the same. Imprisonment does not become easier as time goes by, or harder as an offender's release date nears. We can refer to one month of deserved imprisonment as a "deserved punishment unit" (or DPU, for short). None of this should be taken to suggest that we can arrive at a precise estimate of how many DPUs any given offender merits. In practice, we might be capable of making only rough estimates. For purposes of the present analysis, I ignore that complication.

One dimension along which we might assess a criminal justice system's deserved punishment profile is its overall output of DPUs. What I shall term "overall DPUs" will be a function of the number of offenders sentenced and the number of DPUs each of them is assigned in a given period of time. Accordingly, one charge-adjudication scheme will be judged superior to another if, for the same period of time, it produces more overall DPUs than the other. But retributivists will also be concerned with a further aspect of an adjudication scheme's punishment output. They will want us to arrange things so that like offenders are treated alike, or at least roughly so, thus introducing a "comparative justice" dimension to the analysis. Simply put, offenders will be punished alike if they receive comparable DPUs. A charge-adjudication scheme could produce very high levels of overall DPUs, but do so in ways that create significant comparative injustices. Desert theorists might prefer a scheme that was more comparatively just, even if its overall DPU output was somewhat lower. It is, I would concede, unclear how to rank these two desiderata against one another, especially since both can vary by degree. I shall simply treat them as of coequal importance in the analysis that follows. Doing so seems in keeping with one of the central tenets of retributivism—that more punishment is not necessarily better than less of it; much also depends on how the punishment is distributed.

Complicating things further, there is arguably a third dimension to a criminal justice system's deserved punishment profile that should be considered. To see this, imagine a charge-adjudication scheme that succeeded in assigning a large number of offenders during a given time period some punishment, though only a very small percentage of their deserved punishment. Would retributivists regard such a scheme as a success? It might, after all, produce high overall DPUs (by assigning lots of offenders some of their deserved punishment), and we can imagine that it would not fare too badly when it comes to comparative justice. Suppose that it assigned about the same smallish percentage of deserved punishment to each like offender. The defect in such a scheme appears to be this: In assigning offenders only a small portion of their deserved punishment, it makes a mockery of their crimes. This will be most evident with respect to serious crimes. Imagine that murderers and rapists, though punished, received only brief jail terms or were simply given fines. Sure, some punishment might be better than no punishment in such cases, but barely so. Whatever its difficulties, the notion of absolute justice plays an ineliminable role in retributive accounts of punishment and sentencing. Offenders must be assigned sanctions at least somewhat commensurate with the seriousness of their crimes, both comparatively and non-comparatively. This suggests that retributivists might also want to consider the average percentage of DPUs assigned offenders by a charge-adjudication scheme. One scheme should be judged superior to another, other things being equal or roughly so, if it produces a higher percentage of DPUs per offender. Indeed, even if a scheme with a higher average percentage DPUs per offender produced somewhat less overall DPUs than another scheme, desert theorists might reasonably prefer the scheme that gave each of the offenders to whom it assigned some punishment more of the punishment they deserved. Of course, as the differences in overall DPUs between the two schemes become more pronounced, there might come a point at which one scheme with a lower average percentage DPUs per offender, but much higher overall DPUs, would be preferred.

In short, if we are to determine the defensibility of waiver rewards based on their potential for expanding deserved punishment, we shall have to examine more than the sum total of the deserved punishment outcomes that they produce. We also have to weigh their implications for the comparative and absolute justice of outcomes.

Waiver rewards come in various sizes. In certain countries, the United States foremost among them, sentence concessions granted to defendants who agree to plead guilty are often substantial. It appears that sentence reductions as great as 50 to 75 percent are available to defendants willing to plead guilty.[31] They are also negotiable rather than fixed. Prosecutors have considerable discretion in deciding the magnitude of sentence reductions to offer, at least so long as they are not constrained by Federal Sentencing Guidelines.[32] I shall refer to charge-adjudication systems that countenance such large and variable waiver rewards as systems having "Robust Discount" (RD) schemes.

We can contrast such generous waiver-reward schemes with three alternatives. The first is one in which there are no waiver rewards, in the form of sentence reductions, provided to defendants who confess or agree to plead guilty. Under this scheme, prosecutors announce charges and judges set presumptive sentences on any charges that remain after their review of the evidence. Defendants either agree to plead guilty, in which case they receive their presumptive sentences, or they elect trial adjudication. Of course, if they do elect trial and are subsequently found guilty, they might receive longer or shorter sentences than their presumptive ones, depending on what their trials reveal about the character of their criminal conduct. But usually defendants found guilty at trial will receive their presumptive sentences. I call this the "No Discount" (ND) scheme.

---

[31] S. J. Schulhofer, "Plea Bargaining as Disaster," [1992] 101 *Yale L. J.* 1979, 1993.

[32] For discussion of how the Federal Sentencing Guidelines in the United States have altered the plea bargaining landscape, see J. Standen, "Plea Bargaining in the Shadow of the Guidelines," [1993] 81 *Cal. L. Rev.* 1471. Standen notes that though the Guidelines limited prosecutorial discretion with respect to sentences, they did not rein in their charging discretion. Hence, reduced levels of punishment are still available to defendants willing to plead guilty.

Alternatively, defendants might receive fixed sentence discounts if they agree to plead guilty and forgo trial adjudication of the charges against them.[33] Obviously, we can get slightly different fixed schemes depending on the magnitude of the sentence discounts provided. But let us suppose that defendants who agree to plead guilty receive 10 percent sentence discounts from their presumptive sentences in exchange for doing so. I refer to this as the "Fixed Discount" (FD) approach.

A third scheme is similar to the second one, except that instead of fixed sentence discounts for guilty pleas, it caps the reductions that defendants can receive in exchange for pleading guilty.[34] Prosecutors and defendants negotiate under the cap. Again, depending on how high or low the cap is set, different capped schemes can be generated. For purposes of discussion, let us suppose that the cap is set at 20 percent, such that defendants who agree to waive their right to trial and plead guilty can receive up to a 20 percent discount from their presumptive sentences.[35] I call these "Capped Discount" (CD) schemes.

We probably cannot design or implement an experiment to test the four different charge-adjudication schemes identified. We are thus left to speculate about how they would each function in producing deserved punishment. The clearest way in which the RD scheme appears advantageous is that it gives state officials enormous discretion and thus flexibility in the deployment of their limited resources. If initial waiver-reward offers are refused by defendants, they can be sweetened in order to attract guilty pleas. Contrast that with the predicament of prosecutors under the ND scheme. Under it, state officials are not permitted to deploy sentence discounts in order to attract guilty pleas. If we assume that this will result in a marked increase in demand for the trial adjudication of charges, then without concomitant increases in the budgets of prosecutors and the courts, the ND scheme will yield fewer successful prosecutions of offenders than the RD scheme and thus lower overall DPUs. Proponents of robust forms of plea bargaining would have us believe that the losses in overall DPUs will be quite large were the only options available those of pleading guilty or going to trial. Again, for the sake of argument, suppose that they are correct about this.

Still, this virtue of the RD scheme appears less impressive if we compare it with the FD or CD schemes. In both of these, individuals charged with crimes would receive sentence reductions in exchange for their guilty pleas. This would undoubtedly induce some of them to forgo trial adjudication. Indeed, there is well-known literature on plea bargaining suggesting that most individuals charged with crimes are reluctant to go to trial.[36] They are guilty more or less as charged and they know

---

[33] As suggested by Schulhofer (n 31 above) 2003.

[34] See O. Gazal-Ayal, "Partial Ban on Plea Bargains," [2006] 27 *Cardozo L. Rev.* 2295.

[35] Gazal-Ayal supports more substantial sentence reductions, in the 35–50 percent range (n 34 above) 2338–9.

[36] See M. Heumann, *Plea Bargaining: The Experiences of Prosecutors, Judge, and Defense Attorneys* (Chicago: University of Chicago Press, 1977) 69–75; C. McCoy, *Politics and Plea Bargaining: Victims'*

it. They might have to sit in jail for quite some time until their trials occur. Even if they gain acquittals, the "process costs" of doing so may rob them of their victories. Many defendants are therefore willing to plead guilty if they can receive some sentence discount in exchange for doing so. The only question might be how much of a discount is necessary in order to elicit their pleas. Both the FD and CD schemes offer them some. The RD scheme offers them more but how much more is needed to achieve high levels of overall DPUs?

Some evidence that individuals charged with crimes will accept more modest discounts can be gleaned from countries in which plea bargaining operates in more restrained fashion. As we have seen, defendants in England and Wales who plead guilty early in the charge-adjudication process can thereby obtain no more than 30 percent sentence discounts. Those who wait until the beginning of their trials to plead might earn only 10 percent discounts. Nonetheless, upwards of 90 percent of defendants in the Magistrates' Courts and 70 percent of defendants in the Crown Courts plead guilty, and some of them must be pleading guilty for little more than a 10 percent sentence discount.[37] This suggests that less robust sentence discounts may well suffice to motivate many defendants to forgo trial adjudication, especially in legal systems from which they can expect no further lenity. Granted, in the United States, robust plea bargaining practices will likely have generated the expectation among criminal defendants that substantial sentence discounts are available. Knowing that larger sentence discounts can sometimes be had, defendants there might hold out for them, signaling (whether truly or falsely) that they are willing to go to trial if state officials do not sweeten the deals offered to them. The question is whether most would adjust to a more modest sentence discount scheme, and so plead guilty in exchange for less. No doubt there would be an adjustment period, but the example of other countries suggests that smaller sentence discounts are unlikely to provoke intransigence by defendants and thus massive increases in the demand for trials.

If most defendants offered some discount from their sentences will agree to confess or plead guilty, then the overall DPUs produced by the FD and CD schemes might approach that of the RD scheme. Keep in mind that we are operating with

---

Rights in California (Philadelphia: University of Pennsylvania Press, 1993) 49–74; and Bowers (n 24 above) 1132–7.

[37] Ashworth and Redmayne (n 19 above) 294–4. However, Ashworth and Redmayne note that charge bargaining goes on in England and Wales, which means that some defendants plead guilty in exchange for more significant sentence reductions. M. Langer reports that under the Italian *patteggiamento*, sentence reductions for defendants willing to negotiate with prosecutors cannot exceed one-third of the regular sentence (and can only be given if the sentence after the reduction does not exceed five years' imprisonment). Also, under the Italian scheme, charge bargaining is prohibited. Though relatively new, the *patteggiamento* was utilized in one-quarter to one-third of cases. See Langer's "From Legal Transplants to Legal Translations: The Globalization of Plea Bargaining and the Americanization Thesis in Criminal Procedure," [2004] 45 *Harv. Int'l L. J.* 1, 50.

the assumption that offenders have been charged veridically and so not overcharged in ways that might lead them to believe it worth challenging a subset of the charges against them. Nevertheless, we should err on the side of caution and assume that the RD scheme will give us some significant advantage in overall DPUs compared with Fixed and Capped Discount schemes.

Before we concede this point entirely, however, it is important to see how the magnitude of the discounts granted by the RD scheme could potentially rob it of its ability to produce higher overall DPUs. Suppose that a given jurisdiction has 100 offenses of a given type over a one-year period. Suppose also that the deserved sentence for each of these offenses is six months' imprisonment. Under the RD scheme, assume that the authorities could arrange for punishment of 90 of the 100 offenses by offering those who were arrested and charged sentence discounts that averaged 50 percent. To simplify things, I shall ignore the disposition of the remaining cases that proceed to trial. Prosecutors would probably win more of them than they would lose. Setting those cases to one side, the RD scheme would yield 270 DPUs (90 offenders punished multiplied by 3 DPUs each) overall. Now, compare that with the outcomes produced by the CD and FD schemes. Assume that the CD scheme would yield only 70 guilty pleas. This significantly reduced number of guilty pleas would be attributable to the smaller sentence discounts it offers those charged with the offense in question. Assume that each of those who pleaded guilty under the scheme would receive the full 20 percent sentence discount, meaning that each would be assigned a sentence of 4.8 months. The scheme would nonetheless produce 336 DPU (70 offenders punished multiplied by 4.8 DPUs each) overall. Suppose that the FD scheme would produce 60 guilty pleas. Each defendant who pleaded guilty would be given the fixed 10 percent discount, meaning that each would be assigned a sentence of 5.4 months' imprisonment. The FD scheme would thus yield 324 DPUs overall.

How can it be that the CD and FD schemes might outproduce the RD scheme, in spite of the latter's significantly greater ability to generate guilty pleas? The answer, of course, is that the former two schemes grant defendants who plead guilty smaller waiver rewards than the RD scheme. The RD scheme pays a price, in terms of overall DPUs produced, for its much more generous waiver rewards. Granted, it might turn out that the difference between the number of guilty pleas generated by the RD scheme, as contrasted with the CD or FD schemes, will be much larger than the ones I have assumed. Or it could turn out that the average waiver reward under the RD scheme will be smaller, say in the range of 40 percent. In either case, the RD scheme might come out ahead in its production of overall DPUs. But what this shows is that the touted ability of RD schemes to produce more guilty pleas, even significantly more of them, does not, of itself, guarantee that they will produce greater overall DPUs. Incidentally, the possibility that substantial waiver rewards might be granted under the RD scheme is not a fanciful one. Most of the cases processed by the criminal justice system involve fairly low-level crimes, ones for which prosecutors have almost no interest in having to conduct trials. As a consequence, the evidence suggests that prosecutors who have the luxury of offering large and variable waiver rewards will be inclined to do so.[38]

Furthermore, when we turn to the other two dimensions along which we are to evaluate the competing waiver-reward schemes, it seems clear that the RD scheme will not fare as well as its three competitors. Consider the average percentage DPUs per offender. Obviously, the greater the sentence discounts that are on offer, the greater the potential losses in percentage DPUs per offender we are likely to see. Along this dimension, the ND, FD, and CD schemes all appear stronger, though the lattermost, if the caps are set high, will produce results similar to those of the RD scheme. Again, it is not clear why, in evaluating the competing schemes, we should prefer one that produces more overall DPUs to one that produces a higher average percentage DPUs per offender. Perhaps if the overall DPUs as between two schemes is considerable, whereas the difference in average percentage DPUs per offender between them is slight, we should prefer the scheme that gives us the greater overall DPUs. But that is only one possibility; many others can be imagined.

Complicating matters further is the third dimension along which we must evaluate the schemes, that of comparative justice. Here again, the RD scheme, which permits substantial and variable sentence discounts, will not tend to fare well compared with the alternatives. Even if a sentencing scheme is set up so that it is proportionate both cardinally and ordinally, its use in practice may lead to significant comparative injustices. As we saw in the Introduction, the plea bargaining literature has vividly cataloged the many, at times extraneous, factors that affect negotiated settlements, especially when sentence bargaining is freewheeling.[39] These include the workloads of prosecutors, the diligence or knowledge of defense attorneys, the amicable relationship, or lack thereof, existing between prosecutors and defense attorneys, and the degree to which defendants are risk averse. All of these factors produce variances, sometimes wide ones, in the sentences ultimately negotiated between criminal defendants (or their attorneys) and prosecutors. Further, they are extraneous factors because they have little to do with the seriousness of the crimes that the individuals in question have committed. Even if there is disagreement among desert theorists about how strongly we should insist on comparative justice in sentencing outcomes, substantial variations in sentences among like offenders are undesirable and therefore ought to be avoided.

If we focus on the comparative justice of the sentences meted out to offenders, then the ND and FD schemes will get higher marks. Both reduce the impact of extraneous factors in sentencing and thus ensure that like offenders who plead guilty are punished alike. Further, we should prefer a more modest FD scheme to one with

---

[38] See Bowers (n 24 above) 1143–5.
[39] See, for instance, S. Bibas, "Plea Bargaining Outside the Shadow of Trial," [2004] 117 *Harv. L. Rev.* 2463.

discounts of greater magnitude, since this will reduce further the disparities in sentencing between like offenders who plead guilty and those found guilty at trial. Indeed, on this score, the ND scheme gets the highest marks, since it ensures that the form of charge adjudication chosen has no impact on the sentences individuals receive (unless, of course, trials reveal things about defendants' crimes that warrant departures from presumptive sentences). By contrast, the RD scheme will produce substantial and highly variable differences in sentencing between like offenders who plead guilty and those who are found guilty at trial.

Also, as between the FD and CD schemes, the former will tend to minimize comparative injustices and so might appear preferable, other things being equal or roughly so. Under CD schemes, the extraneous factors affecting sentence bargains would continue to play some role. Under a FD scheme, defendants would confront a stark choice: either plead guilty and receive the fixed discount or go to trial and risk receiving the presumptive sentence (or a sentence somewhat more or less severe than that). There would be no negotiations, at least not with regard to sentences. Of course, there would still be some differences in sentences among those who were convicted of like offenses. Those who waived their right to trial and pleaded guilty would receive discounted sentences compared with like offenders who went to trial, were found guilty, and received their presumptive sentences. But these differences would be much less significant than under the RD scheme. And the only way to eliminate them entirely would be to adopt the ND scheme. If we assume that the ND scheme would produce significantly lower levels of overall DPUs, then the real choice will be among the schemes that give defendants something in exchange for agreeing to plead guilty.

Even if we opted for a FD scheme as the one most optimally in line with the complex imperative to impose deserved punishment on offenders, there is room for debate about the magnitude of the fixed discounts to be made available. It might turn out that in order to achieve levels of overall DPU that were reasonably close to those of the RD scheme, we would have to go with moderate fixed discounts, say in the 20 to 30 percent range, rather than with low fixed discounts, say in the 10 percent range. One way to find out which is preferable would be to offer the lower fixed discounts and monitor the frequency with which they were accepted versus the frequency with which trials were demanded. Of course, a marginally greater demand for trials initially might not show very much, especially if more robust waiver rewards have previously been the norm. We might want to give the new regime some time to become familiar to criminal defendants and accepted as "the way things are." Even if the demand for trials remained somewhat higher, that might not convince us to increase the magnitude of the fixed discounts, especially if the demand could be met without too much additional strain on current court capacities. There are good reasons, after all, to resist offering larger discounts and thus to see if we can manage in spite of some increased demand for trials.

The problem of innocent defendants

To this point I have ignored a problem that for many is one of the signal strikes against plea bargaining. One clear drawback to granting state officials wide discretion in determining the magnitude of waiver rewards is that it enables them (inadvertently, let us suppose) to pressure factually innocent defendants to enter guilty pleas.[40] Faced with significant differences between their announced presumptive sentences and the steeply discounted ones they will receive if they plead guilty, innocent defendants will often quite reasonably conclude that they cannot risk going to trial. If prosecutors were not permitted to offer such defendants highly enticing deals, more of them would presumably elect trial adjudication of the charges against them and some of them would be acquitted. Yet as proponents of more robust waiver rewards are quick to point out, some of the innocent defendants who elected trial adjudication would be convicted and they would usually receive their presumptive sentences. Such defendants would, as a result, wind up considerably worse off than if they had pleaded guilty and received steeply discounted sentences.

Furthermore, factually innocent defendants might be loath to go to trial independently of the longer sentences they are subject to if convicted. As Josh Bowers has persuasively argued, the majority of such defendants will have been arrested and charged because they are known recidivists.[41] When the police do not know the identities of those who have committed crimes, they "round up the usual suspects." Once these individuals have been arrested and charged, prosecutors are reluctant to believe their protests of innocence. As a result, prosecutors will stubbornly resist dismissing charges against such defendants. Yet as defendants of this kind contemplate going to trial, they encounter unpalatable options: If they take the stand to testify as to their innocence, prosecutors might attempt to introduce their past criminal records to impeach their testimony. How easy it will be for prosecutors to do so depends on the legal jurisdiction in question. In the United States, prosecutors' prospects are relatively good, especially if defendants attempt to introduce evidence of their good character, or if the introduction of defendants' past records falls under one of the exceptions permitted by the Federal Rules of Evidence.[42] In England and Wales, their prospects are dimmer though perhaps less so than they used to be.[43] The worry for defendants who have unsavory pasts is that if jurors get wind of them, it will have prejudicial effects.[44] The risk that their past records will be revealed might in some cases convince defendants to remain silent during their trials. Yet doing so is

---

[40] For discussion, see Gazal-Ayal (n 34 above) 2302–7, and Bowers (n 24 above) 1120–1.

[41] Bowers (n 24 above) 1124–32.

[42] See C. B. Mueller and L. C. Kirkpatrick, *Evidence*, 3rd edition (New York: Aspen Publishers, 2003) 182–4.

[43] See R. Ward and O. M. Davies, *The Criminal Justice Act 2003: A Practitioner's Guide* (Bristol, UK: Jordan Publishing, 2004) 81–114.

[44] For discussion, see R. O. Lempert, S. R. Gross, and J. S. Liebman, *A Modern Approach to Evidence Law,* 3rd edition (St Paul, Minn.: West, 2000) 323–31.

not without its own risks, as jurors might want and expect defendants to speak to the charges against them.[45] Faced with these options, recidivists who have been wrongly charged might be best off under a waiver-reward scheme that offers them substantial leniency in exchange for their guilty pleas.

Keep in mind that we are, for the time being, setting to one side the half-loaf cases, ones in which prosecutors recognize the questionable character of the evidence they have against the individuals whom they have charged with crimes. We are assuming, instead, that prosecutors (or judges) are motivated to offer sentence bargains by their desire to conserve their limited resources. The question we face, then, is this: If prosecutors had evidence against innocent defendants that was good enough to go to trial with, what would be the likely impact on such defendants of proposals to cap or fix sentence discounts at levels lower than the norm under more robust schemes of sentence bargaining?

Notice that two of the dimensions along which we have been comparing the alternative waiver-reward schemes drop out of the picture when the focus is on factually innocent defendants. There are no gains to overall DPUs produced when we punish such defendants since, by hypothesis, they do not deserve any punishment. Instead, the RD scheme simply has the advantage of producing less undeserved punishment. For similar reasons, there is no point in concerning ourselves with the contribution to average DPUs per offender made by the punishment of such individuals. Since none of them deserve any punishment, all we can say is that the RD scheme appears likely to produce lower percentage levels of undeserved punishment. With respect to comparative justice, it appears that the Fixed and Capped Discount schemes will do better in the somewhat perverse way of ensuring that the innocent who plead guilty will receive sentences akin to their factually guilty counterparts who likewise enter pleas. The RD scheme cannot boast of that stilted virtue. Still, it does seem that if we cannot altogether avoid punishing the innocent, at least we should punish them comparably with real offenders who commit similar crimes. It is bad enough to impose punishment on the innocent. It is worse to allow their punishment to be partly determined by factors that are systematically unrelated to the seriousness of their alleged crimes.

Nevertheless, the RD scheme has an edge when compared with the alternatives in relation to factually innocent defendants. It will likely yield lower, though more variable, sentences for those among them willing to plead guilty. That might well be the majority of such defendants. Also, whether Capped or Fixed Discount schemes will encourage more defendants of this kind to go to trial might depend on such things as the rules concerning the introduction of character evidence and the availability to them of competent legal counsel. If Bowers is correct, many recidivists mistakenly

---

[45] It has often been taken as a given that jurors will think worse of defendants who decline to testify at their trials and therefore be more inclined to convict them. But for evidence that this might not be true, see L. Laudan and R. J. Allen, "The Devastating Impact of Prior Crimes Evidence and Other Myths of the Criminal Justice Process," [2011] 101 *J. Crim. L. & Criminology* 493.

charged with crimes have little to gain, and much to lose, by going to trial. Most might have to accept the smaller discounts that the FD and CD schemes would make available. A few wrongly accused defendants might dig their heels in and demand trials if they could not get more for their guilty pleas, and some might earn acquittals. Yet we should probably assume that many would not.

If this is a victory for the RD scheme, it is a meager one. For one thing, the dangers of trial adjudication for wrongly charged individuals could be dramatically reduced by having legal rules that make it difficult for prosecutors to impeach individuals' testimonies by introducing evidence of their past criminal records. There are reasonably compelling arguments for having such rules quite independently of their impact on plea bargaining.[46] Also, the number of cases in which prosecutors wrongly charge redicivists and have fairly conclusive evidence against them is apt to be small. More often the cases in which recidivists are charged mistakenly will be ones in which the evidence against them is weak.[47] Prosecutors will want to negotiate pleas for precisely that reason, not to conserve their resources. Again, these more common kinds of cases will be examined in Chapter 8. Finally, and most significantly, the advantage to RD schemes in this subset of cases consists of their potential to minimize undeserved punishment, not expand deserved punishment. Few are likely to defend large and variable waiver-reward schemes on such a slender basis alone.

Charge bargaining

To this point, we have been considering waiver rewards in the form of sentence discounts. It is time to introduce the further complication of charge discounts. Again, for the time being, assume that prosecutors have veridically charged individuals with multiple crimes, rather than charging them as part of a strategy to put pressure on them to plead guilty. Individuals are veridically charged if the evidence suggests that they have, in fact, committed several distinct offenses and the prosecutor's charges are honest attempts to formally characterize them. There will be cases in which prosecutors initially file multiple charges against individuals because they believe that they have plausible evidence of their having committed several criminal acts, only later to drop some of the charges because the evidence is deemed insufficiently probative after further investigation. This adjustment in charges based on prosecutors' reassessments of the evidence is not charge bargaining as I understand it, even if it results, in part, from consultations with defense counsel. Defense attorneys might point to the flimsy evidence for one or more of the charges, or offer plausible accounts of their clients' conduct such that it no longer appears illegal or culpable. We should want

---

[46] See, for instance, R. Friedman, "Character Impeachment Evidence: Psycho Bayesian [!?] Analysis and a Proposed Overhaul," [1991] 38 *UCLA L. Rev.* 637.

[47] As Albert Alschuler has noted, the availability to prosecutors of large waiver rewards means that they will be able to pursue more cases in which the evidence against individuals is weak and nonetheless gain convictions. See Alschuler (n 23 above) 687–8.

and expect prosecutors to be responsive to the unfolding evidence in precisely these ways. There is, admittedly, a fine line between defense attorneys suggesting that their clients would be willing to plead guilty to reduced charges, and their exposing the weaknesses in the state's case such that prosecutors, all on their own, agree to drop some of the charges. But there is, in principle, a crucial difference between these two sequences of events, even if, in practice, it may be difficult to tell which of them has occurred.

Charge bargaining proper occurs when prosecutors offer to drop charges for which they believe they have reasonably compelling evidence, evidence that might well stand up at trial and convince a judge or jury of the defendant's guilt, in exchange for the defendant's agreeing to plead guilty to one or more other charges. Again, set to one side the half-loaf cases, in which prosecutors agree to drop charges in exchange for guilty pleas because they are not convinced that, should the defendant elect trial adjudication, a judge or jury would find the defendant guilty beyond reasonable doubt. The focus in this chapter is on charge bargaining motivated solely by the desire of state officials to avoid trials and thereby extend their abilities to mete out deserved punishment.

One issue that we must confront at the outset is whether there are any intermediate options between permitting charge bargaining, more or less at the prosecutor's (or perhaps the court's) discretion, and banning it outright. There might be. In some countries, once prosecutors have filed charges, they either lose control of cases entirely or there is a presumption that they will not drop charges.[48] If prosecutors subsequently do drop charges, they are required to explain to the court presiding over the case why they have done so. This presumably works to discourage charge bargaining without banning it completely.[49] Nevertheless, I will, for the most part, assume that our two primary options are either to permit it at the prosecution's (or perhaps a judge's) discretion or to ban it. Near the end of the section, a proposal to limit charge bargaining, without prohibiting it entirely, is discussed briefly.[50]

---

[48] See Y. Ma, "Prosecutorial Discretion and Plea Bargaining in the United States, France, Germany, and Italy: A Comparative Perspective," [2002] 12 *International Criminal Justice Review* 22, 33.

[49] Nevertheless, there would remain the possibility of "pre-charge bargaining," whereby prosecutors and defense attorneys would find ways to negotiate over which charges might initially be filed by the former.

[50] Another option, suggested by Tracy Meares, is to tie prosecutors' salaries to their charging decisions. Meares' proposal is that prosecutors be given modest salary increases if the final charges to which defendants in their jurisdictions ultimately plead or are found guilty of are reasonably close to those that were filed initially. Meares' proposal is aimed at curbing overcharging, but it might also be employed to reduce charge bargaining in cases in which defendants are veridically charged. It would not ban charge bargaining completely, but attempt to constrain it. However, the financial incentives Meares' scheme involves are minimal, and so one wonders how effective they would be in convincing prosecutors, who have powerful motivations of other kinds to engage in charge bargaining, to refrain from it. Moreover, the scheme seems vulnerable to the objection that it is unlikely to prevent "pre-charge bargaining." For Meares' proposal, see her "Rewards for Good Behavior: Influencing Prosecutorial Discretion and Conduct with Financial Incentives," [1995] 64 *Fordham L. Rev.* 851.

Complicating matters further, at this point, is a thorny problem in the area of retributive sentencing theory: Do such theories require sentences in multiple-charge cases to be served consecutively, or do they permit what have been termed "bulk discounts"?[51] Bulk discounts are reductions in the total sentences in cases involving multiple charges, such that individuals convicted of several crimes receive something less than the sum total of the sentences for each charge. Such discounts can be steep if defendants convicted on multiple charges have to serve only the sentence for the most serious charge, with the sentences on the other charges served concurrently. They will be less steep if those convicted of multiple charges are required to serve some portion of the sentence on each charge. Though I will not pause to defend it here, my view is that retributivists cannot consistently support concurrent sentencing policies in all cases, though they can do so in some.[52] The hard cases, for retributivists, are those in which individuals plead guilty or are convicted of numerous serious crimes, each with its own identifiable victim or victims. Though retributivists might be able to support some bulk discounting of sentences in the cases of such multiple offenders, they cannot support concurrent sentencing of them. To do so would fail to acknowledge each of the victims of the offender's separate crimes. Still, I admit that mine is a controversial position. The question is how to proceed with an analysis of charge bargaining without begging the question as to which account of sentencing in multiple-charge cases is correct.

My strategy is to divide the analysis. In the first part, I assume a concurrent sentencing scheme according to which, individuals who plead or are found guilty of multiple charges are required to serve the sentence for the most serious charge, with the remaining sentences served concurrently. In some countries, concurrent sentences in multiple charge cases are the norm.[53] It is worth noting that such a sentencing practice dramatically reduces the incentives prosecutors have to stack charges, since by doing so they gain little additional leverage over defendants in plea negotiations. Still, in other countries, non-concurrent sentencing schemes exist. Thus, in the second part of the analysis, I assume such a scheme, one in which such individuals receive bulk discounts for multiple offending but nonetheless have their sentences totaled up so that the final sentence exceeds, by some non-negligible margin, that which they would have received under concurrent sentencing schemes. In both parts, we should assume that though defendants charged with multiple crimes have the option of going to trial, they are disinclined to do so because the odds of their prevailing are long.

---

[51] For discussion, see N. Jareborg, "Why Bulk Discounts in Multiple Offence Sentencing?" in A. Ashworth and M. Wasik (eds.), *Fundamentals of Sentencing Theory* (Oxford: Clarendon Press, 1998) 129, and J. Ryberg, "Retributivism and Multiple Offending," [2005] 11 *Res Publica* 213.

[52] See R. L. Lippke, "Retributive Sentencing, Multiple Offenders, and Bulk Discounts," in M. D. White (ed.), *Retributivism: Essays in Theory and Policy* (Oxford: Oxford University Press, 2011) 212.

[53] See Ma (n 48 above) 34, where he notes that under French sentencing law, consecutive sentences in multiple-charge cases are not permitted. The same, he later notes, is true in Germany (see p. 38).

Under a concurrent (or mostly concurrent) sentencing scheme, it would be possible for prosecutors routinely to drop one or more of the serious charges against defendants without its having much effect on either the overall DPUs or the average percentage DPUs produced per offender.[54] So long as one or more of the most serious charges were kept in place, guilty pleas garnered in this fashion would make their maximum possible contribution toward total DPUs and average DPUs per offender. Also, comparative injustices would be minimized, since all of those who pleaded guilty would do so to one or more of the most serious charges against them. The catch is this: Under concurrent sentencing schemes, charge bargaining is likely to motivate defendants to waive their right to trial and plead guilty only if state officials drop the most serious charges against them. It is, after all, the most serious charges that will produce the longest sentences. The dropping of less serious charges, or a subset of the more serious ones, will not yield significantly reduced sentences if any of the more serious charges is retained. Yet if prosecutors, eager to avoid trials, regularly agree to drop the most serious charges, retaining only the less serious ones, then the losses to overall DPUs and average percentage DPUs per offender will be considerable. The losses in overall DPUs might be made up if the resource savings from some cases enable prosecutors to process a large number of other cases in which they retained the most serious charges against the defendants. It is plausible to believe that the resource savings from dropping the more serious charges in some multiple-charge cases will be considerable. Trials in multiple-charge cases will be longer, on average, and so cost prosecutors and other state officials more of their resources. Still, it appears that dropping serious charges can never be more than an occasional strategy for prosecutors, or else the overall DPU losses and decreases in average DPUs per offender will mount up in ways that are not at all promising if our concern is to optimize deserved punishment. Furthermore, if prosecutors drop all of the most serious charges in a few cases, but not as a general rule, this will generate sizable comparative injustices in sentencing. Some offenders who commit quite serious offenses will receive little of their deserved punishment, whereas the majority of such offenders will be assigned sentences commensurate with their most serious crimes.

Recall that we are ignoring the half-loaf cases and focusing on ones in which prosecutors appear to have the goods on multiple- and veridically charged defendants. Arguably, prosecutors would do better in terms of obtaining higher overall DPUs and average DPUs per offender by standing their ground and refusing to drop the most serious charges against defendants under concurrent sentencing schemes. Modest sentence discounts on each charge could be made available to defendants, but that is all. Prosecutors could also reveal more to defendants' attorneys about the evidence they have and thus hope to convince them (and their clients) that going to trial

[54] It could be argued that dropped charges, though not affecting sentences in a concurrent sentencing scheme, would create misleading public records of the crimes committed by individuals. Such misleading records might have implications for subsequent sentencing decisions, especially in sentencing regimes that employed recidivist premiums.

and gaining acquittals are exercises in futility.[55] Some defendants would stubbornly insist on trials, but it seems likely that many would not and so would agree to plead guilty in exchange for some sentencing lenity. Notice also that the more prosecutors in such cases were willing to dicker on the serious charges, the more the ultimate sentencing outcomes would be affected by the many extraneous factors mentioned previously. Some defendants would manage to get better deals than others, though the former would be no more deserving of reduced punishment. If we focus on the comparative justice of sentencing outcomes, a general reluctance to engage in bargaining about more serious charges would clearly be preferable under concurrent sentencing schemes.

Next, consider sentencing schemes that are non-concurrent and which therefore require individuals convicted of multiple offenses to serve as least a portion of the sentence for each of the charges to which they plead guilty. Under such schemes, charge bargaining would potentially be a boon to multiple-charged defendants. Even if prosecutors balked at dropping the most serious charges against individuals, their agreeing to drop some or all of the less serious ones might shave off months or years from offenders' total sentences. Charge reductions, if combined with sentence reductions, could provide defendants with powerful incentives to plead guilty. And if bulk discounts existed but did not tend to be very large, then charge reductions would be even more meaningful to defendants. Of course, each dropped charge would entail some lost overall DPUs and negatively affect average percentage DPUs per offender—more so if prosecutors dropped some of the more serious charges.[56] The dropping of serious charges could thus never be more than an occasional strategy, or else prosecutors would be forgoing the infliction of too much deserved punishment which it is unlikely they could make up for with subsequent convictions. But it is possible that prosecutors would use their charging discretion judiciously, offering modest charge discounts, at least initially. Such charge discounts, in combination with sentence discounts, would attract guilty pleas from many multiple-charged defendants. Guilty pleas would enable state officials to process further cases, thus increasing overall DPUs. If charge bargains were generally kept small, the increases in overall DPUs that they might yield would not come at too great a cost to average percentage DPUs per offender.

Still, it would be exceedingly difficult for prosecutors who utilized charge discounts to keep ultimate sentencing outcomes from running badly foul of the comparative justice constraint. By hypothesis, each dropped charge would subtract something from a defendant's overall deserved sentence. Further, the extraneous factors that tend to affect plea negotiations would continually exert their influence. Although it would be difficult to compare offenders who have been charged with multiple crimes

---

[55] Bibas argues for more liberal pre-trial discovery on both sides (n 39 above) 2531–2.
[56] This assumes that under non-concurrent sentencing schemes, offenders deserve to receive some sentence on each of the counts on which they are convicted.

in order to discern whether their sentencing outcomes consistently reflected the seriousness of all of the crimes that they have committed, it would be highly fortuitous if like multiple offenders received like total sentencing outcomes. If prosecutors were allowed to drop charges, including more serious ones, and offer sentence reductions (varying in their magnitude) on some or all of the remaining charges, they would have to be incredibly diligent about tracking the overall impact of DPU gains and losses in each case to ensure even roughly similar outcomes across a range of similar multiple offenders. We might reasonably doubt that they could or would be so diligent. Also, the combination of charge and sentence discounts would open up potentially huge differences between the sentencing outcomes of defendants who pleaded guilty and those who were convicted after trials. Multiple offenders, differing only with respect to whether they waived or insisted upon trial adjudication, would be assigned vastly different sentences. This is bad enough from the standpoint of comparative justice; it is worse if we imagine, as we probably must, that sometimes the defendants confronting such sentencing differentials might be entirely innocent of the crimes with which they have been charged.

It would thus appear advisable to try to limit charge bargaining under nonconcurrent sentencing schemes. One way to do so would be to cap the sentence reductions that could be made available. Suppose that defendants, at settlement hearings, were informed of the presumptive total sentence they faced if convicted on all counts, where the contribution made by each count to the total sentence was made clear. We could then set a maximum percentage reduction in the total sentence that could be obtained through charge bargaining. Defendants and prosecutors (or judges) would be permitted to negotiate charges under the cap. If the cap were kept low (say 25 percent or less of the total sentence), prosecutors would not be able to bargain away the most serious charges, or at least not many of them. This would mean that each case resolved would come closer to its maximum contribution to overall DPUs. Average percentage DPUs per offender would also remain relatively high and comparative injustices would be kept in check.

There is an obvious practical difficulty with such a proposal. It may not be possible, in lots of cases, for state officials and defendants to reach an accord on the charges to which the latter will plead that keeps their total sentences under the cap. The minor charges, if there are any, might carry sentences that do not add up to much. None of the more serious charges could be dropped without exceeding the cap.

Setting aside this practical problem, there are policy issues to consider as well. Should we permit state officials to drop charges (under the cap) and offer sentence discounts on any charges agreed to by defendants? Defendants would thereby earn double discounts for pleading guilty. In addition to appearing unseemly, such double discounts would open up significant sentencing differentials between defendants who pleaded guilty and defendants convicted after trials, once again raising comparative justice concerns. Why not, instead, simply permit defendants to receive fixed sentence discounts on each charge to which they agree to plead guilty? Such fixed sentence discounts could then be added together to reduce the overall sentences assigned to defendants who plead guilty to multiple charges. This would lessen, although not eliminate entirely, the differences in final sentences among defendants, whether they pleaded guilty or were convicted after trials. Moreover, additive sentence discounts in multiple-charge cases would enable us to avoid the problem with charge bargaining alluded to earlier—that it rewards defendants without requiring them to acknowledge all of their criminal conduct. Again, it is one thing to believe that we should grant some sentencing lenity to defendants who admit their guilt and spare us the trouble and expense of trials. Sentence concessions for guilty pleas do just that. It is another to reduce the punishment of individuals who refuse to acknowledge their guilt on one or more of the charges for which state officials have convincing evidence. Charge bargaining by state officials involves them in such a seemingly more dubious enterprise. If additive sentence discounts are sufficient to motivate multiple-charged defendants to plead guilty in most cases, then they might reasonably be preferred to charge discounts of any kind.

What general conclusions might we draw about charge bargaining? It would appear that within concurrent sentencing schemes, there are stronger reasons to discourage than to tolerate it. Defendants under such a scheme would be motivated to plead guilty rather than go to trial only if the most serious charges were dropped. Yet the dropping of serious charges would produce significant overall DPUs losses, lower average DPUs per offender, and often yield substantial comparative injustices. Under non-concurrent sentencing schemes, it would also seem that bargaining away the more serious charges is problematic, even if it is less of a necessity because defendants might be motivated to plead guilty if state officials dropped lesser charges. My sense is that we should, at the very least, attempt to limit charge bargaining under non-concurrent sentencing schemes so that offenders who plead must do so to the bulk of the charges against them and especially the most serious ones. Better yet, we should eschew charge bargaining altogether and instead offer fixed sentence discounts to individuals on each of the charges of which they formally acknowledge their guilt.

Waiver rewards in the non-ideal world

The analysis so far has taken place against a set of idealized background assumptions: The criminal prohibitions being enforced are defensible, such that individuals who violate them can be meaningfully said to deserve punishment. Sentencing regimes have been devised and set up so that they are proportionate, both cardinally and ordinally. Defendants have all been veridically charged, and so not overcharged in ways that might result in their being convicted of so many offenses that their cumulative sentences are clearly disproportionate with the seriousness of their criminal acts, and so undeserved. Furthermore, defendants have been presumed capable of moral self-governance and to have had viable paths other than offending down which to pursue their interests. Given these background assumptions, the question has been whether, and to what extent, waiver rewards, which represent downward departures from presumptively just sentences, can be justified. I have urged restraint in the use of waiver rewards, arguing that modest and fixed sentence discounts, or perhaps charge discounts confined to a smallish percentage of offenders' overall deserved punishment, would be preferred by retributivists.

In examining waiver rewards within the confines of a retributive or desert-based approach to punishment, we have generally taken two things for granted: First, because they constitute downward departures from deserved punishment, waiver rewards stand in need of justification; and second, that processing more offenders through the criminal justice system tends to increase the amount of deserved punishment produced. But what if the operations of existing, less-than-ideal criminal justice systems confound both of these assumptions? What if waiver rewards do not give offenders less than what they deserve, but instead ensure that they will receive less undeserved punishment? And what if by processing more individuals through the criminal justice system we do not give more individuals what they deserve because of their crimes, but instead increase the amount of undeserved punishment that we inflict on our fellow citizens? Then what?

How could it be the case that enabling state officials to process more cases might produce undeserved punishment? In any number of familiar ways. First, real-world criminal justice systems might prohibit conduct that no defensible theory of criminalization warrants. This is not an idle concern. Numerous political and legal theorists argue that existing societies prohibit and punish conduct that they have no business interfering with.[57] Rounding up and punishing more of the individuals who violate such suspect criminal laws will not in any meaningful way increase overall DPUs or percentage DPUs per offender. Though we might prefer that the individuals (unjustifiably) punished for violating such prohibitions are punished similarly, comparative justice is not much of a virtue when punishment is, by hypothesis, undeserved in the first place.

Second, existing societies might attach sanctions to defensible criminal prohibitions that are disproportionate, either cardinally or ordinally or both.[58] Punishing the individuals who violate such prohibitions increases overall DPUs up to the point where the sanctions cross the line and become disproportionate. After that, inflicting punishment does not increase overall DPUs and should be thought to count against it. Retributivists will not support a sanction scheme that routinely achieves

---

[57] See, among others, Husak (n 3 above) 4–17; Stuntz (n 16 above) 515–18; and J. Feinberg's four-volume study of the limits of the criminal law, most especially *Harm to Others* (New York: Oxford University Press, 1984), *Harm to Self* (New York: Oxford University Press, 1986), and *Harmless Wrongdoing* (New York: Oxford University Press, 1990).

[58] It is possible, of course, for existing sanction schemes to impose disproportionately mild sanctions, which would create problems of a different kind for the justification of waiver rewards. However, few commentators believe that overly mild sanctions are the problem we face, especially in countries such as the United States. See, for instance, the figures cited by Husak on the increasingly lengthy sentences given offenders in the United States (n 3 above) 18–19.

more than 100 percent DPUs per offender. Similarly, they will not value a sentencing scheme that treats like offenders alike by punishing all of them, or significant subsets of them, disproportionately.

Third, independently of disproportionate sentencing schemes, some legal systems, that of the United States being foremost among them, tolerate and often facilitate strategic overcharging by prosecutors. As we have seen, overcharging is aimed at putting pressure on defendants to accept negotiated settlements, especially in legal jurisdictions that have non-concurrent sentencing schemes. In some cases, it will also be a means of attempting to score political points with an electorate that is particularly outraged by the criminal conduct of individuals.[59] We might hope that excessive charges will be dropped during plea negotiations, or pared down by judges in settlement hearings or by juries when cases go to trial. But it seems doubtful that such fortuitous outcomes will inevitably occur. This means that some individuals will wind up on the receiving end of sentences that are disproportionately long, even if the statutorily attached sanctions are proportionate to begin with. Of course, if they are not, then the combined effect of overcharging and disproportionate sentences for each offense will be spectacularly long sentences.

Fourth, existing societies might display considerable indifference to the fact that many offenders come from severely socially deprived backgrounds.[60] Severe social deprivation is arguably a potent ground for the mitigation of legal punishment. Diminished opportunities undermine the voluntariness of conduct, including criminal conduct. I have argued elsewhere that such diminished opportunities, while not equivalent to duress, are sometimes close to duress.[61] The severely socially deprived do have options other than criminal offending, but not many and not very good ones. Though their conduct may be marginally voluntary, it is not strongly so. We should therefore be prepared to mitigate their punishment in recognition of the disproportionately high number of hard choices that they have to make. Such mitigation could take numerous forms, including sentence reductions and more rehabilitative prison conditions than are currently the norm.

Severe social deprivation is also destructive to the development and flourishing of moral self-governance in individuals. The stresses of social deprivation make it difficult for adults to nurture their children properly, including their capacities for moral sensitivity and self-control. Worse than this, broken homes and care-givers with self- and other destructive tendencies abuse and neglect children, with devastating

---

[59] Long sentences have expressive functions in addition to being effective threats against defendants who might be tempted to insist on their right to trial adjudication.

[60] This is true of the United States, where, as Stephen Morse has noted, the criminal law for the most part treats responsibility as "binary," meaning that all agents whose abilities are not severely impaired are held responsible. Defenses of diminished responsibility are rare and generally unavailable based solely on claims of social deprivation. See Morse (n 14 above) 144. Richard Delgado argues for social deprivation as a legal defense in " 'Rotten Social Background': Should the Criminal Law Recognize a Defense of Severe Environmental Deprivation?" [1985] 3 *Law & Ineq.* 9.

[61] Lippke (n 15 above) 84–8.

consequences for their long-term moral development.[62] Crime-ridden neighbor-hoods are not only poor at monitoring the conduct of children and young adults, they also furnish negative role models that glorify violence, impulsiveness, and self-aggrandizement. To the extent that individuals emerge from this environment with compromised capacities for moral self-governance, they are not quite proper subjects of retributive punishment if and when they offend. We need not believe that they will be altogether unfit for punishment. They may have some capacity for moral self-governance, though one that is weak or exercised in spotty fashion. But they fall short of the kinds of beings thought to deserve punishment for their criminal acts on retributive accounts of legal punishment. Assuming that some or all of their deficiencies in this respect are not their fault, some mitigation of their punishment would seem to be in order. Unstinting punishment of the severely socially deprived is akin to the disproportionate sanctioning of offenses. Moreover, the injustices of such unmitigated punishment will be exacerbated if the sanction scheme is too harsh to begin with, offenders are routinely overcharged by prosecutors, or the crimes in question should not really be considered as crimes in the first place.

Granted, the preceding points require considerably more elaboration and defense than I have given them. But suppose that each of them could be sufficiently sup-ported. How might this affect our thinking about the argument that waiver rewards are justified because they enable prosecutors to expand deserved punishment? The answer to this question depends on the extent to which such departures from the ideal conditions for deserved punishment obtain in a given society. We can conceive of societies whose only failing in this regard is that they have some dubious criminal prohibitions which are rarely enforced, or a few sanctions that are disproportionate given the crimes to which they are attached, or which have isolated pockets of social deprivation which is not too severe. But what about societies that exhibit all of these departures from the background conditions for deserved punishment, though per-haps to varying degrees? Observers of the criminal justice system in the United States argue that it, and the larger social system of which it is a part, manifests all of these failings and to a significant extent.[63] Suppose that they are correct about this. What would be the implications of their claims for the defense of waiver rewards based on their usefulness in expanding deserved punishment?

On the one hand, if a significant number of individuals are charged with crimes that should not be criminal offenses in the first place, or threatened with dispropor-tionate sanctions for conduct that should be criminalized, then robust waiver-reward schemes might be a tremendous boon to such individuals. Large sentence or charge discounts might be the only available means by which they could hope to have their

---

[62] See E. Currie, *Crime and Punishment in America* (New York: Henry Holt, 1998) 120–30. See also Delgado (n 60 above) 24–34.

[63] See, for instance, Currie (n 62 above). For a pessimistic evaluation of the performance of the broader social and political system in England and Wales, see M. Cavadino and J. Dignan, *Penal Systems: A Comparative Approach* (London: Sage Publications, 2006) 73–5.

unjust punishment reduced. Moreover, substantial waiver rewards would likely yield punishment outcomes that were less unjust than those produced by trial adjudication or more modest waiver rewards. In particular, the modest sentence and charge discounts I have claimed are more defensible under ideal conditions would do considerably less to insulate individuals from undeserved punishment. Of course, large and variable waiver rewards will produce lower levels of unjust punishment in ways that are highly uneven. All of the extraneous factors identified earlier will affect final sentencing outcomes. As a result, robust waiver-reward schemes would be rife with comparative injustices. But we might reasonably prefer such schemes, with all their faults, to the alternatives if they produced less average undeserved punishment per offender and less undeserved punishment overall.

On the other hand, if the availability of large and variable waiver rewards enables state officials to expand significantly the number of offenders to whom they are able to assign some punishment or other, that might count against such rewards under non-ideal conditions. Stated simply, from the mere fact that more individuals are punished we cannot reasonably infer, under non-ideal conditions, that more deserving offenders are punished. There is, it should be noted, some reason to believe that any expanded punishment capacity that robust waiver-reward schemes yield will be utilized by state officials to pursue less serious, and perhaps more dubious, kinds of offenses. Serious *mala in se* offenses will always attract the attention of police and prosecutors.[64] Such crimes are too salient for them to ignore. Public interest in the arrest and punishment of those who commit such crimes is intense, and state officials will be unwilling to risk the political backlash that would result from failure to pursue serious offenders aggressively. Moreover, we should probably assume that state officials will be motivated to see to the punishment of such offenders for reasons that go beyond the risks to their careers or reputations if they fail to do so. This suggests that any expansion in punishment capacity produced by robust waiver rewards will be felt by individuals who have committed less serious *mala in se* offenses, ignored prohibitions that derive from legal paternalism or legal moralism, or violated *mala prohibita*. From a deserved punishment perspective, some of these prohibitions will be among the most morally suspect ones. In spite of that, their violation may be attended with relatively harsh sanctions.

What is worse, inequitable enforcement of the criminal law is likely to be more common when the offenses in question are primarily against morals or involve petty forms of theft or dishonesty. Serious *mala in se* offenses will be aggressively policed by the authorities no matter who commits them. But punishment is less urgent when offenses are less serious, and so the authorities will have more discretion in deciding whom to arrest and charge. The poor, immigrants, and the otherwise socially marginalized will be targeted disproportionately for criminal prosecution of such

---

[64] See W. J. Stuntz, "Plea Bargaining and the Criminal Law's Disappearing Shadow," [2004] 117 *Harv. L. Rev.* 2548, 2563–4.

crimes.[65] Such inequities need not be the result of prejudice or animus on the part of the police, though there is no use denying that these are often factors. They can also result, as William Stuntz has shown, from simple facts about where certain individuals commit such crimes.[66] Crimes committed on the streets are easier to detect and acquire evidence about than crimes committed in suburban homes or urban penthouses. What this suggests is that any expanded punishment capacity that robust plea bargaining yields will be employed disproportionately against individuals in society whose lives are already difficult and whose punishment is therefore more problematic.

Robust waiver-reward schemes might thus have both positive and negative effects on the allocation of deserved punishment under non-ideal conditions. They might reduce to some extent the infliction of undeserved punishment on those convicted of crimes. But if the increased capacity to punish is exercised in the pursuit of less serious offenders who are poor or otherwise socially marginalized, or whose crimes should not be treated as such or punished as harshly in the first place, then robust waiver-reward schemes will also increase undeserved punishment. In light of the latter possibility, it might seem that having a charge-adjudication scheme with reduced capacity to process cases is preferable under non-ideal conditions.

Still, I suggested earlier that large and variable waiver-reward schemes might not enable state officials to process many more cases, relative to more modest waiver-reward schemes. I do not wish to go back on that point. Hence, modest waiver-reward schemes might not produce substantially fewer cases of undeserved punishment. Such schemes would still produce smaller comparative injustices, even under non-ideal conditions. But I have to concede that they would likely do so at the expense of longer sentences assigned to those willing to plead guilty. On the assumption that those longer sentences are often undeserved, then such schemes would in this respect produce more undeserved punishment than large and variable waiver-reward schemes. In other words, in the real world, the arguments that I have mustered in favor of more restrained forms of waiver rewards may be somewhat less convincing than they are under ideal conditions.

Yet if the preceding concession appears something of a victory for robust waiver-reward schemes, it is crucial to notice how far we have come from the second argument for them which we analyzed. That argument held that downward departures from just punishment were justified because they enabled prosecutors or other state officials to deploy their limited resources in ways that would expand deserved punishment. What we are now saying is something very different—that what might or might not be downward departures from just punishment are less undesirable than they initially seem because they produce less undeserved punishment overall. Such a

[65] See D. Cole, *No Equal Justice: Race and Class in the American Criminal Justice System* (New York: New Press, 1999).

[66] W. J. Stuntz, "Race, Class, and Drugs," [1998] 98 *Colum. L. Rev.* 1795.

stilted defense of large and variable waiver rewards is what we should expect, given the perverse tendency of some existing criminal justice systems routinely to inflict undeserved punishment.

Concluding remarks

The primary lessons that we should take away from this chapter are these: If the conditions for just punishment obtain, then more modest waiver-reward schemes, with their tendencies to produce relatively high levels of overall DPUs, higher average percentage DPUs per offender, and fewer comparative injustices, are preferable to more robust waiver-reward schemes. Under less than ideal conditions, robust waiver-reward schemes might do better than more modest ones in one crucial respect: They will reduce the amount of unjust punishment meted out per individual charged with, and convicted of, one or more crimes. However, robust schemes will still produce larger comparative injustices than more modest schemes under non-ideal conditions. And if robust schemes deliver on their promise to help state officials process significantly more cases, they might produce more unjust punishment overall than more restrained and thus less efficient waiver-reward schemes.

A secondary lesson emerges from the preceding discussion as well. Charge-adjudication schemes operate in the service of larger social and criminal justice systems. If those systems are reasonably well functioning, then limiting the discretion of state officials to negotiate waiver rewards seems a good strategy for obtaining deserved punishment outcomes. However, if those larger systems are badly flawed, it will be much harder to determine how discretion in the allocation of waiver rewards will affect punishment outcomes.

4

Remorse and Waiver Rewards

In Chapter 3 we saw that criminal defendants who acknowledge their guilt and save us the costs of trials by pleading guilty might be rewarded with modest sentence reductions. There is something about declining to put state officials and other citizens through the expense and bother of trials when individuals know that they are guilty anyway that speaks well of them and so might incline us toward more lenient treatment of them. Again, it is bad enough to have committed criminal offenses and very bad to have committed serious ones. But it is worse to protest one's innocence or, short of that, force the state to prove one's guilt at trial when one knows that the state's charges are veridical. Though such rewards might have somewhat dubious retributivist credentials, it was nonetheless conceded that they have considerable intuitive appeal.

The idea that criminal defendants might be rewarded for acknowledging their guilt sounds remarkably similar to an argument that is well known in the plea bargaining literature. According to that argument, defendants who plead guilty exhibit remorse for their crimes and are thus properly rewarded with reduced punishment. Yet, as I noted in the previous chapter, the remorse rationale for sentence concessions presumes more about accused persons who are willing to plead guilty than does the acknowledgment-of-guilt rationale. The latter says and assumes nothing about defendants' attitudes toward their crimes. In particular, it does not depend on their believing that what they did was wrong and feeling truly contrite for having so acted. Individuals can acknowledge their guilt and spare us the costs of trials without believing or feeling such things at all. They might simply realize that the state properly has them in its clutches and there is little hope of escaping the punishment that attaches to the criminal prohibitions they have violated. The remorse argument, by contrast, ties sentence reductions to the manifestation by defendants of certain specific psychological states that are believed to be legitimate grounds for leniency.

It seems fair to say that the remorse argument in favor of plea bargained sentence concessions has mostly been treated with a combination of amusement and contempt by legal scholars.[1] The practical problems with implementing such a policy have

---

[1] See A. W. Alschuler, "The Changing Plea Bargaining Debate," [1981] 69 *Cal. L. Rev.* 652, 661–9; C. McCoy, "Plea Bargaining as Coercion: The Trial Penalty and Plea Bargaining Reform," [2005] 50 *Criminal Law Quarterly* 67, 73–82.

figured prominently in their analyses. It will be exceedingly difficult for anyone, let alone prosecutors and judges who must process an imposing number of cases, to distinguish genuine remorse from mental states that, behaviorally speaking, are nearly indistinguishable from remorse—shame, chagrin or embarrassment at having been arrested and charged, or guilt that is unaccompanied by some kind of remorse. Worse than this is the fact that once offenders figure out that sentence reductions are available if they feign remorse, many of them will be quick to do so to ward off more severe punishment for their crimes. Also, it seems preposterous to believe that the courts make any real effort to distinguish the genuinely remorseful defendants who are willing to plead guilty from the calculating ones who realize that it is in their best interests to do so. Stephanos Bibas and Richard Bierschbach summarize the point nicely: "Our criminal justice system works as a speedy assembly line: It plea bargains cases efficiently and maximizes punishment for the limited resources available."[2] Even if there were reliable methods of distinguishing remorse from its imposters and imitators, it is a mistake to confuse state officials' encouragement and acceptance of guilty pleas with serious efforts to employ those methods. Plea bargaining is mostly about "moving the caseload" and very little about detecting and responding to genuine remorse.

The practical problems with instituting a remorse-based waiver-reward scheme are serious, though perhaps not quite conclusive. Bibas and Bierschbach believe that we have passably reliable ways of identifying truly remorseful offenders.[3] They also propose procedures that the courts could employ to make such identifications, procedures that do not require judges to have extraordinary powers of discernment.[4] Such procedures might even be used in cases in which outcomes have been plea bargained. But even if Bibas and Bierschbach are correct in thinking that the practical problems with remorse-based sentence reductions could be overcome, the deeper philosophical question of whether remorse is an appropriate ground for the mitigation of legal punishment remains. It is this question that is the primary focus of this chapter. Although legal scholars have raised and discussed it, my aim is to give it more systematic treatment.

On some accounts of the justification of legal punishment, it appears exceedingly difficult to defend sentence mitigation for remorseful offenders. How offenders feel after the fact of having committed their crimes would seem to make little difference to how they ought to be punished. On other accounts, it may be possible to defend remorse-based sentence mitigation. Yet even on these more remorse-friendly accounts, I contend that it makes little sense to reduce repentant offenders' punishment

---

[2] S. Bibas and R. A. Bierschbach, "Integrating Remorse and Apology into Criminal Procedure," [2004] 114 *Yale L. J.* 85, 88.

[3] Bibas and Bierschbach (n 2 above) 140–1. See also S. K. Tudor, "Remorse, Reform, and the Real World: Reply to Lippke," [2008b] 2 *Criminal Law and Philosophy* 269, 271.

[4] Importantly, Bibas and Bierschbach agree that sentence reductions might not be the most defensible way of encouraging remorse and apology within the criminal justice system (n 2 above) 104–9.

at the time of sentencing. True remorse requires offenders to undertake meaningful efforts at reforming their lives. Whether or not they have undertaken such efforts can be determined only after they have served at least part of their sentences. Once it is clear that their remorse has produced meaningful efforts at self-reform then, and only then, might we be justified in reducing offenders' punishment. Yet this conclusion, if correct, implies that the waiver rewards that are the stock-in-trade of plea bargaining are not the kinds of sentence mitigation that should go to the remorseful. For such rewards are given up front, as it were, not once it is clear that remorse has borne fruit in the form of character reform.

Two preliminary points

To forestall confusion, two initial points might be made. First, in thinking about whether remorse is ever a defensible basis for state officials offering reduced punishment during the plea negotiation process, it seems clear that our focus should be on waiver rewards in the form of sentence rather than charge reductions. No matter how genuinely contrite offenders are about their crimes, it is hard to see how this could ever serve as a legitimate basis for state officials dropping charges against offenders and thus acting as if there were no reason to believe that they actually committed the crimes in question. Indeed, those who defend remorse-based mitigation appear to assume that it should take the form of sentence rather than charge reductions. Still, one slight complication with this should be noted. There are, as we have seen, significant problems with overcharging by prosecutors in some legal systems. We might want prosecutors who have overcharged individuals to pare away some of the duplicative or ancillary charges that the proliferation of criminal statutes makes it possible for them to lodge. But the grounds for encouraging such responsible charging decisions by prosecutors are entirely independent of the ones that support remorse-based mitigation. Hence, it will be assumed throughout this chapter that the only kinds of waiver rewards that offender remorse is capable of supporting are sentence reductions. This will, to some extent, simplify the analysis.

Second, it might be argued that remorse and consequent apology should play more significant roles than they do in many contemporary criminal justice systems. Restorative justice theorists have insisted on this point for some time, and some of them have even appeared to suggest that remorse, apology, and the making of amends by wrongdoers should replace legal punishment as we know it.[5] Though we might not wish to go that far, a persuasive case can be made that remorse and apology by offenders should be encouraged in the criminal justice system because of the key roles they play in morally educating offenders, validating the interests of victims,

---

[5] For a useful summary of developments in restorative justice theory, see J. Braithwaite, "Restorative Justice: Assessing Optimistic and Pessimistic Accounts," [1999] 25 *Crime and Justice: A Review of Research* 1.

and healing the injuries to social trust and cooperation caused by crimes.[6] Nothing I say in this chapter should be construed as gainsaying these important points. Legal scholars have noted the ubiquity of sentence mitigation for defendants who are willing to admit their guilt.[7] It has even been suggested that we might test theories of legal punishment by their ability to explain remorse-based mitigation.[8] Theories that cannot account for the practice should be deemed inferior to those that can. But it is crucial not to confuse the social value of remorse and apology—which we might want the criminal justice system as a whole to encourage—with the question of whether remorse should serve as a basis for the mitigation of sentences.[9] Remorse and apology might be promoted within criminal justice systems in numerous ways other than by granting offenders sentence reductions. Indeed, for reasons that will soon become apparent, the availability of such reductions may undermine genuinely repentant responses as much as encourage them. My view is that sentence mitigation for the remorseful is an easy, if somewhat confused, way of acknowledging the social values that apology and remorse serve. Yet when such mitigation is offered to offenders solely on the basis of their willingness to enter guilty pleas, it demeans apology and remorse as much as it honors them.[10]

What is remorse?

There is general agreement that individuals experience remorse when they recognize that their conduct has violated legitimate moral standards enforced by criminal law, admit fully and candidly their role in wrongdoing, regret it sincerely, are disposed to apologize and make amends for it, and are committed to undertaking changes in their behavior (or its supportive attitudes and values) which will make their breach of the standards substantially less likely in the future.[11] It is crucial here that the individuals in question embrace the relevant standards as their own and not view them simply as conventions they must obey or suffer the consequences. Individuals are not remorseful if they grudgingly accept the relevant standards or are resigned to having their behavior judged by others according to such standards. The remorseful are also

---

[6] See Bibas and Bierschbach (n 2 above) 109–21.

[7] S. K. Tudor, "Why Should Remorse Be a Mitigating Factor in Sentencing?" [2008a] 2 *Criminal Law and Philosophy* 241, 241–2, and M. Bagaric and K. Ameraskara, "Feeling Sorry?—Tell Someone Who Cares: The Irrelevance of Remorse in Sentencing," [2001] 40 *The Howard Journal* 364, 366–7.

[8] Tudor (n 7 above) 242.   [9] Again, see Bibas and Bierschbach (n 2 above) 109–21.

[10] Consider in this regard J. Baldwin and M. McConville's report on British offenders who had pleaded guilty, though many of them continued to protest their innocence, in "Plea Bargaining and Plea Negotiation in England," [1979] 13 *Law & Soc'y Rev.* 287, 300. Baldwin and McConville conclude that "for these defendants, the guilty plea reflected bitterness and cynicism far more than genuine remorse."

[11] See A. Duff, *Trials and Punishments* (Cambridge: Cambridge University Press, 1986) 66–8; I. Thalberg, "Remorse," [1963] 72 *Mind* 545; and S. Tudor, "Accepting One's Punishment as Meaningful Suffering," [2001] 20 *Law and Philosophy* 581. For a thorough and insightful analysis of remorse (or, as he terms it, "repentance") see N. Smith, *I Was Wrong: The Meanings of Apologies* (Cambridge: Cambridge University Press, 2008).

different from those who are fearful of the consequences they face from disobey-
ing the standards or who are ashamed at having been caught at doing so because of
the social disapproval they incur. More importantly, remorse does not consist solely
of individuals sincerely regretting their behavior, especially if this does not issue in
attempts at reform. We rightly doubt claims of remorse when wrongdoers return to
old patterns of behavior or when they continue to associate with other bad actors.[12]
Such doubts will be affirmed if we observe wrongdoers repeating their mistakes.
At that point, protestations that, once again, they are remorseful for their wrongs
will be less believable, especially in the absence of serious efforts at self-reform. The
remorseful need not have fully reformed themselves, but they must at least have taken
the first steps toward doing so.

Unfortunately, as has already been remarked, the behavioral indices of remorse
are often indistinguishable from those of other conditions or states. More unfortunately still, most adults will long ago have learned how to mimic remorse, as a
way of countering and reducing the disapproval of parents or teachers who enforce
standards that children or young adults sometimes little understand or accept. Also,
unlike other conditions or circumstances that might properly mitigate punishment,
there are few "objective" indicators of genuine remorse that the law can require the
accused to establish in criminal cases. Compare, in this regard, the claims of provo-
cation that are sometimes offered as partial defenses in homicide cases. Such claims
are unlikely to prove successful in the absence of witnesses or physical evidence to
bolster them. Sincere protestations by defendants that they felt insulted or threatened, in the absence of buttressing evidence, are apt to be viewed with skepticism
by judges and juries. However, there is little that the genuinely remorseful can do to
distinguish themselves from their imitators. We are rightly suspicious of displays of
penitent attitudes or behavior in those who face longer sentences if they cannot gain
remorse-based mitigation. Even efforts to compensate victims are inconclusive. And
testimony by relatives and friends is likely to be tainted by sentiment, self-interest,
or guilt by association. But again, the difficulties here are ones that we should not
allow to scotch all further inquiry into the defensibility of remorse-based sentence
reductions.

Retributive arguments for remorse–based sentence mitigation

Contemporary retributive theories of legal punishment do not treat as self-evident
the proposition that those found guilty of crimes deserve proportionate punishment;

---

[12] Tudor challenges this point, arguing that though a genuinely remorseful offender should "feel the
moral pull" toward reform, there might be some cases in which the person "cannot do much to try to
effect such reform" (n 3 above) 270. Tudor would, it seems to me, have to say more to convince us that
remorse uncoupled from sincere efforts at reform is genuine.

instead they provide various explanations concerning why the guilty merit punishment. Some of those explanations would appear to afford little support to remorse-based sentence mitigation.[13] This is especially true for versions of retributivism that focus on punishing offenders according to the wrongfulness of the acts they have committed, whether punishment is deemed necessary to deprive offenders of the unfair advantage they have taken over others, to annul the false moral messages that their crimes have communicated, or censure offenders for their wrongdoing.[14]

On standard versions of retributivism, the wrongfulness of criminal acts is taken to be a complex function of two factors—the harm that the acts caused (or threatened or attempted) and the culpability with which offending agents acted. Offender remorse has little bearing on the former. If it is to gain a toehold within such theories, it must be shown to diminish offender culpability. The problem is that culpability, as it is usually construed, has to do with the extent to which offenders can plausibly be seen as the agents of the harm their acts caused, threatened, or attempted. Deliberate homicide is more blameworthy, on these accounts, and so more culpable than negligent homicide because agents who engage in the former are more invested in the harmful outcomes than those who engage in the latter.[15] Those who murder deliberately not only want the harm to eventuate, they take the necessary steps to see to it that it does. Those who kill through negligence act in ways that foreseeably increase the risks that death will result. The negligent are therefore less culpable than the deliberate because they do not intend or act deliberately to produce harmful consequences. Remorse, even if it is genuine, is something that offenders presumably feel after their crimes have been committed—perhaps immediately after, but nonetheless after the event. Therefore, it is hard to see how it has any bearing on the culpability with which the offender acted. We can imagine those who commit deliberate homicide reacting with extreme regret to the deaths of their victims. But it is not clear why the authorities should be moved by such remorse to punish murderers less, given what they have done. In the words of two critics of remorse-based sentence mitigation, the

---

[13] A point made by J. Murphy in relation to what he terms "grievance theories" of retributivism, theories that hold that punishment is deserved for "responsible wrongful acts." See his "Repentance, Punishment, and Mercy," in A. Etzioni and D. E. Carney (eds.), *Repentance: A Comparative Perspective* (Lanham, Md.: Rowman and Littlefield, 1997) 143, 149.

[14] Unfair advantage versions of retributivism are defended by H. Morris, "Persons and Punishment," [1968] 52 *Monist* 475; J. Murphy, "Marxism and Retribution," [1973] 2 *Philosophy and Public Affairs* 217; W. Sadurski, *Giving Desert Its Due* (Dordrecht, Netherlands: D. Reidel, 1985); and G. Sher, *Desert* (Princeton, NJ: Princeton University Press, 1987). Communicative versions of retributivism are defended by J. Hampton, "A New Theory of Retribution," in R. G. Frey and C. W. Morris (eds.), *Liability and Responsibility: Essays in Law and Morals* (Cambridge: Cambridge University Press, 1991) 377; R. A. Duff, *Trials and Punishments* (Cambridge: Cambridge University Press, 1986); and Jami L. Anderson, "Annulment Retributivism: A Hegelian Theory of Punishment," [1999] 5 *Legal Theory* 363. The notion that legal punishment censures wrongful conduct is defended by A. von Hirsch, *Censure and Sanctions* (Oxford: Clarendon Press, 1993) and with A. Ashworth in *Proportionate Sentencing: Exploring the Principles* (Oxford: Oxford University Press, 2005). However, von Hirsch's theory includes a prudential supplement in the form of hard treatment as a deterrent.

[15] See H. Gross, *A Theory of Criminal Justice* (New York: Oxford University Press, 1979) 77–88.

authorities would seem to respond more properly to such remorse by saying: "Feeling sorry? Tell someone who cares."[16]

The preceding conclusion is not accepted by all who defend remorse-based sentence mitigation. Steven Tudor develops an argument for such mitigation by first drawing our attention to the role of remorse in informal, non-punitive settings.[17] Suppose that a person who has committed a wrong against another person encounters the victim's reproach and experiences genuine remorse. Tudor contends that the person wronged should modify his reproach in response to the evident remorse of the person who has wronged him, adjusting or modulating his speech: "the purpose of the reproach changes from seeking to gain the wrongdoer's attention and point out what he has done, to acknowledging his remorseful acknowledgment of what he has done."[18] All of this is consistent, of course, with the victim continuing to explain the wrong to the perpetrator and pressing the perpetrator for a fuller explanation of his conduct and an apology for it. But Tudor suggests that failure to respond to the wrongdoer's remorse would be disrespectful.[19] Tudor then attempts to transfer his reasoning in this informal case over to the formal setting of legal punishment. Judges too, in handing out sentences, should respond to the differences between genuinely remorseful offenders and those who are unrepentant. Prison officials might likewise modulate their treatment of remorseful inmates, thereby treating them differently from how they treat defiant or recalcitrant inmates.

As Tudor admits, however, the claim that those who reproach others should modulate their attitudes toward, and treatment of, the remorseful does not quite get us to the conclusion that the remorseful should be granted sentence reductions. Legal authorities could, after all, treat the remorseful differently in what they say to them or how they comport themselves in relation to them, without altering the amount or kind of legal punishment that they mete out to them. Hence, Tudor argues that the offender's present blameworthiness is not simply a function of the seriousness of his offense, but also his "present worthiness of being blamed (rebuked, censured, reproached) *now* for what he did then, and that can be modulated by many factors that lie outside the crime itself and relate to the personal circumstances of the offender."[20] Sentencing judges should "take into account not just the crime (as subject matter of the communicative act) but also the nature or condition of the interlocutor."[21]

Subsequently, in his attempts to show why one of Antony Duff's arguments against remorse-based sentence reductions fails, Tudor elaborates the preceding argument. Duff sees a criminal sentence as the officially prescribed apology for the crime in question—the appropriate penance that must be served by the offender for the wrong she committed. Since the remorseful offender has no less need to apologize than the unremorseful one, the former deserves no reduction in her sentence. In response,

---

[16] Bagaric and Ameraskara (n 7 above) 364.   [17] Tudor (n 7 above) 249.
[18] Tudor (n 7 above) 249.   [19] Tudor (n 7 above) 249.
[20] Tudor (n 7 above) 250 (his emphasis).   [21] Tudor (n 7 above) 252–3.

Tudor admits that a remorseful offender has no less to apologize for than does an unremorseful one, but contends that the former's sentence might be reduced in recognition of the fact that "there is already apology at least latent in the offender's remorse..."[22] Since the remorseful offender has already expressed some of the required apology, her sentence should be shortened to reflect that.

However, Tudor's argument that an offender's blameworthiness at the time of sentencing should take into account factors that lie outside the crime and relate to the personal circumstances of the offender is not developed in sufficient detail. Consider some of the other mitigating factors that do seem relevant within retributive approaches to sentencing. The youthfulness of an offender, while perhaps lying "outside the crime itself," is usually regarded by retributivists as a mitigating factor in sentencing. So, too, the particularly difficult personal or family circumstances of an offender, especially if they are thought to have precipitated the criminal conduct, might be thought relevant to determining an offender's level of culpability. Conversely, the fact that the current offense is the latest in a long series of similar offenses, while lying outside the crime itself, has been defended as an aggravating factor in sentencing.[23] What Tudor needs to do is convince us that the specific factor he points to—offenders' post-crime attitudes toward their offending—is likewise a relevant sentencing factor. Crucially, the other factors just mentioned are all ones in place, as it were, at the time of the offense. They provide evidence either that the offenders in question were less blameworthy as they committed their offenses (because young or under extreme stress) or more blameworthy as they did so (because no longer able to claim that they did not understand the nature of the offense or made a single, impulsive mistake in committing it). Post-crime remorse is unlike these other factors, and so seems a somewhat dubious candidate for grounding sentence mitigation.

It is tempting to respond to the preceding point by arguing that offenders' contrition at least shows that they are not irredeemably committed to wrongdoing.[24] Surely we should recognize the difference between genuinely contrite offenders and those who are defiant or unfeeling by modulating the punishment that we assign to the former. Stephen Garvey poses the following thought experiment. Suppose that you are a sentencing judge and before you are two brothers who are identical twins, each of whom is equally culpable for a murder.[25] One (Brother A) has never shed a tear for what he has done and "now stands before you stone-faced."[26] The other (Brother B) is extremely remorseful. He wanted to confess and plead guilty but his lawyer talked him out of it. If A and B are the same in all other respects, should not the judge impose a lesser sentence on B than A? Yet how can we make sense of the intuition

---

[22] Tudor (n 7 above) 255.   [23] See von Hirsch and Ashworth (n 14 above) 149–55.

[24] See Bibas and Bierschbach (n 2 above) 94.

[25] S. P. Garvey, "Punishment as Atonement," [1999] 46 *UCLA L. Rev.* 1801, 1857.

[26] Garvey (n 25 above) 1857.

that the judge should do this unless we believe, like Tudor, that present remorse is an appropriate sentence-mitigating factor?

Even if we knew more than Garvey allows us to do—for instance, that B is genuinely remorseful and thoroughly committed to undertaking the changes in his life that would make him a better person, while A is not only unrepentant but scornful of his "weaker" brother who has surrendered to his remorse—I am not convinced that the thought experiment shows that we should punish B less than A. We need to know a lot more in order to determine what the two brothers deserve. Was B initially reluctant to commit the murder but led along, or, worse, badgered or intimidated by A into participating? If so, then B might plausibly be viewed as less culpable for the murder, not because he is now remorseful, but because he was pressured into it at the time. Or was B equally if not more committed to the murder but then chastened by the sight of the victim's grieving family? If so, then it is not at all clear why B should receive less punishment than A. Their actions seem equally blameworthy and B's regret comes too late to save him. It might be said that at least B shows that he is not lost to us, in the sense that he is beyond hope as an unrepentant killer. Perhaps so, but then it begins to look as if some concern with crime reduction is being illicitly smuggled into the argument. Those who are lost to us, in the way that A appears to be, are especially worthy candidates for more prolonged incapacitation in ways that the repentant are not. Yet incapacitation, all by itself, is not supposed to be the aim of retributive punishment.[27]

We must also ask whether A is "stone-faced" because he is an unrepentant psychopath. If so, then not only is it not clear that he should receive more punishment than B, but also it may not make sense to retributively punish A at all. Retributive theory presupposes that the individuals who are properly liable to legal punishment are responsive to moral considerations, at least up to some minimal level. This means that they must be capable of recognizing and acting on moral considerations, or else legal punishment, as an institutionalized expression of moral condemnation, makes no sense in relation to them.[28] Psychopaths are, in this regard, no different than non-human animals, infants, or the severely retarded, none of whom are fit subjects for retributive punishment. Further, given these familiar facts about retributive theory's liability requirements, there is something deeply incoherent about assigning B less punishment than A. Brother B, after all, is evidently not a psychopath, which means

---

[27] Some retributivists have offered arguments for limited forms of preventive detention. See, for instance, R. A. Duff, "Dangerousness and Citizenship," in A. Ashworth and M. Wasik (eds.), *Fundamentals of Sentencing Theory: Essays in Honor of Andrew von Hirsch* (Oxford: Clarendon Press, 1998) 141, and Duff's *Punishment, Communication, and Community* (Oxford: Oxford University Press, 2001) 170. For doubts about Duff's retributive argument for preventive detention, see my "No Easy Way Out: Dangerous Offenders and Preventive Detention" [2008] 27 *Law and Philosophy* 383, 391–9.

[28] See J. Murphy, "Moral Death: A Kantian Essay on Psychopathy," [1972] 82 *Ethics* 284; R. A. Duff, "Psychopathy and Moral Understanding," [1977] 14 *American Philosophical Quarterly* 189; and C. Fine and J. Kennett, "Mental Impairment, Moral Understanding, and Criminal Responsibility: Psychopathy and the Purposes of Punishment," [2004] 27 *International Journal of Law and Psychiatry* 425.

that he was capable of being moved by the powerful moral considerations against the murder in which he participated. Yet he, unlike A, appears to have ignored or suppressed them more actively.[29] It makes sense to ask of B, "How could he have done this?" in ways that it does not make sense to ask this of A if A is a psychopath. Killing other people is just one of the things that psychopaths do when the calculus of their self-interest gives them the go-ahead. But it is not supposed to be one of the things that individuals with moral consciences do. If they are cognizant of the relevant moral considerations but ignore or push them from their thoughts, this makes them seem worse, in a way, than those who lack all access to such considerations. It is therefore hard to see how, under these assumptions, one can make a case for punishing B less than A.

Another possibility, of course, is that A is not a psychopath but that he simply realizes that there is no excuse for what he has done. He stoically accepts the punishment coming his way, because he realizes that it is just, and is unwilling to make a "show" of his remorse, unlike his weaker, more emotional brother. Maybe A feels some remorse but says to himself, "too little, too late." In this case my intuitions are not at all clear as to which of the brothers should be punished more and which less, or whether they should be treated any differently at all.

What the preceding discussion shows, I believe, is that Garvey's thought experiment is otiose as it stands. The difference in the two brothers' reactions is so stark that we cannot help but ask for additional information about them. Yet, depending on the information that we imagine receiving, the rationale for granting B a sentence reduction is either dubious or seems to be based on his level of culpability for the murder, not his subsequent remorse.

It has also been suggested that those who are genuinely remorseful for their crimes, in effect, punish themselves and so do not merit as much state-inflicted punishment.[30] If the aim of retributive legal punishment is to inflict suffering on offenders that is commensurate with the suffering they unjustly impose on the victims of their crimes, then the remorseful who feel terribly about their moral failures already experience some portion of what they deserve to suffer. For the state to inflict on them the full measure of their otherwise deserved punishment would thus result in their suffering disproportionately harsh punishment.

One odd implication of this argument is that the more morally sensitive offenders are, the less the punishment they should be given for their crimes. Psychopaths or those who are morally corrupt would therefore tend to receive the longest sentences for crimes, while those who are exquisitely attuned to the moral implications of what they have done would receive shorter sentences, perhaps dramatically shorter ones. Yet again, one might think that the reverse is true, since those who are responsive

---

[29] A point made by Bibas and Bierschbach (n 2 above) 107–8. Indeed, they argue that the insanity and diminished responsibility defenses exist because some wrongdoers do not fully appreciate the wrongfulness of their conduct, and so are less blameworthy than those who do.

[30] See Duff (n 14 above) 289, and Murphy (n 13 above) 158.

to the moral considerations against what they do, but who persist in offending in spite of this, deserve more, not less, punishment. More to the point, the argument presupposes that the aim of retributive punishment is to inflict suffering on offenders that is commensurate with the suffering they caused the victims of their crimes. Yet most contemporary retributivists would likely dispute this interpretation of retributive punishment's purpose. Some see punishment as an officially imposed penance for offenders' crimes and reject the idea that remorseful offenders are less in need of having to serve their penance.[31] Others contend that retributive punishment is designed to annul the false moral messages sent by crimes.[32] Since the false messages remain "out there," so to speak, regardless of how offenders feel about those messages after their crimes, it is not apparent how such communicative versions of retributivism would support remorse-based sentence reductions. And so on. Indeed, it is hard to think of a contemporary retributivist who urges a "suffering for suffering" approach to the justification of legal punishment. Such an approach would be decidedly at odds with standard retributive thinking that treats crime seriousness as a function of both harm *and* culpability. The "suffering for suffering" rationale appears to ignore culpability altogether.

However, there might be versions of retributivism that offer some support for remorse-based sentence reductions. One of these has been elegantly developed by Antony Duff. According to Duff, in punishing offenders we encourage them to come to recognize the wrongfulness of their past conduct, repudiate it, and undertake sincere efforts at reform such that they will avoid further wrongdoing. Criminal sanctions, on this account, aim at inducing a "repentant understanding" of the wrongfulness of the offender's actions.[33] Not only are offenders to be brought to regret their earlier wrongdoing, they are to serve a penance in the form of hard treatment, during which time their remorse is to be deepened and turned toward moral reform. Duff holds out the possibility that imprisonment, in separating serious offenders from the community, might (if properly structured, which in reality it often is not) provide them the opportunity to both reflect on their wrongs and begin the process of becoming "reconciled to the Good," in the sense of taking steps to modify the desires and attitudes that brought them into conflict with the law in the first place.[34] As such, hard treatment might enable offenders to solidify their embrace of the moral norms by which the criminal law is, at its best, animated. Duff is clear that such moral reform cannot be forced on offenders, but must be consistent with respect for their autonomy. He is also careful to note that many current types of criminal sanctions cannot plausibly be cast as capable of inducing a penitent understanding of the kind he endorses.

---

[31] This is Duff's view in *Punishment, Communication, and Community* (n 27 above) 120–1, though he qualifies it by noting that in some cases, an immediate repentance by an offender for a crime might be a proper ground for mitigating her punishment. The immediate repentance shows the crime to have been a "momentary aberration" (p. 120).

[32] See Hampton (n 14 above) 398.   [33] Duff (n 14 above) 246.   [34] Duff (n 14 above) 258.

In *Trials and Punishments*, Duff seemed to embrace the possibility that genuinely remorseful defendants might be afforded sentence reductions. Setting aside the obvious practical difficulties in determining which offenders were contrite, Duff suggested that the genuinely remorseful offender "has already done part of the work of punishment for herself: she has recognized and repented her crime, and subjected herself to the pain of remorse…"[35] Duff adds, "it [her contrition] may show that she is less in need of punishment, since she is already punishing herself."[36] This, of course, seems to be the argument that we have just considered and rejected. Yet it might be construed differently and in a way that is more plausible. Duff notes that repentance "is not simply something one does and is then finished with; the task of coming to understand, to repent, and truly to disown my crime may be a long and arduous one (that is why we need penances—to help us to face up to our crimes, to repent them adequately, and to express our penitence to others)."[37] The idea seems to be that genuinely remorseful offenders have started down the path toward a penitent understanding of their crimes and, as such, are somewhat less in need of the full measure of punishment merited by their acts.[38]

This line of argument fits nicely with Tudor's claims about the more informal cases of wrongdoing and blame in which it does seem appropriate to leave off "punishment" of the truly contrite. Suppose that someone has wronged you, but that she now comes to you and expresses what appears to be genuine contrition at having done so. Suppose that in addition to apologizing profusely, she also offers to make amends in some appropriate way. Should you leave off "punishing" her in all of the informal ways in which we exhibit our displeasure with those who have wronged us? Tudor appears to be correct in urging modulation of the way in which you address the wrongdoer. Her remorse does make her different from someone who does not understand the wrong she has done or who refuses to acknowledge it or apologize for it. And in the case of relatively minor wrongs, an apology and some effort to make amends might well suffice. Yet I believe that Tudor analyzes these informal cases inadequately. Further consideration of them reveals more conditions that must be satisfied for the remorseful to merit reduced informal punishment and

---

[35] Duff (n 14 above) 289.   [36] Duff (n 14 above) 289.   [37] Duff (n 14 above) 289–90.

[38] It is worth noting that in his later work, Duff takes a more skeptical view of remorse-based sentence reductions. In *Punishment, Communication, and Community* (n 27 above), Duff insists that sentences are not to be indeterminate, but are to be set by the seriousness of offenses. He subscribes to von Hirsch's view, according to which the censure that punishment expresses must be proportional to the severity of the crime. As we have seen, such an approach leaves little room for remorse as a factor in sentencing, and this is a view that Duff, for the most part, embraces. Duff also notes that policies of offering reductions for remorse will tempt offenders to feign it, and put pressure on innocent defendants to plead guilty to avoid the harsher sanctions given the unrepentant. Finally, Duff argues that punishment has a dual purpose— "to communicate repentance forcefully and adequately to others, as well as to induce and strengthen it" (p. 121). But he insists that his account does not involve two distinct stages, one whereby punishment induces repentance, and a second whereby it communicates it. Such an account might support reductions for those already repentant, since they would have already satisfied the first stage. Instead, "the whole sentence serves the dual purpose of inducing and expressing repentance" (p.121). For the genuinely remorseful, the first purpose would simply be achieved earlier.

more complications for implementing sentence concessions in the law than Tudor acknowledges.

If the wrongs in such informal cases are to be analogous with those with which the law is concerned, we must imagine them to be fairly substantial, suggestive of more active malevolence. They might also repeat previously wrongful conduct. If the wrongs are of these kinds, we might reasonably refuse to reduce offenders' punishment once their remorse becomes evident. Why is this? For one thing, we might wait to see if they actually make amends. More than this, we might want to see from them meaningful efforts at self-reform—attempts to alter or extinguish the desires or dispositions that led to the wrong. Again, we take such efforts to be partly constitutive of genuine remorse in many kinds of cases. A serious or repeat wrongdoer who expresses remorse, makes amends, but undertakes no further efforts at self-reform seems disingenuous. She knows the drill, so to speak—that she must apologize and make amends when she commits a wrong—but is not committed to doing anything to avert future wrongs. What this points toward, I believe, is the need for some indeterminacy in the duration of the "punishment" imposed on her. We have good reason to take a "wait and see" attitude toward her, to determine whether she truly understands the wrong she has done and is chastened by her remorse. This is not something we can discern at the point at which she first expresses remorse, even if it is heartfelt. Nor is it clear from her efforts to repair whatever damage she has done.

Yet if we are to carry these lessons over to the law's dealings with criminal offenders, they do not bode well for a policy of remorse-based reductions handed out at the time of sentencing. Even if we set to one side the difficulties in distinguishing real from feigned remorse, it is simply too soon to tell whether genuinely remorseful offenders have fully embraced the lessons that they are supposed to take away from the official censure of their wrongdoing. Some offenders who are genuinely remorseful for their crimes may be weak-willed or irresolute, and so prone to further offending. Others may be repeat offenders toward whom a "wait and see" attitude seems eminently sensible. Though the genuinely remorseful might be on their way toward resuming full standing in the community, they may not be there yet. They might still need to be monitored for some time, to see if they are making real progress toward their re-embrace of the relevant moral norms.

In short, remorse-based sentence reductions might make some sense, but only within the context of an indeterminate sentencing scheme. In such a scheme, sentences initially would be based on the seriousness of offenses, but then (to use Tudor's term) "modulated" in accordance with offenders' progress toward a fully repentant understanding of their crimes. Yet the pitfalls with such indeterminate sentencing schemes are well known.[39] Their institutionalization would entail granting legal

---

[39] See A. Hirsch and L. Maher, "Should Penal Rehabilitationism Be Revived?" in A. von Hirsch and A. Ashworth, *Principled Sentencing: Readings on Theory and Policy,* 2nd edition (Oxford: Hart Publishing, 1998) 26.

authorities the power to monitor offenders and their progress toward a fully repentant understanding of their crimes. Once the authorities were satisfied that offenders were making substantial progress, whatever that means exactly, they would then reward them with sentence concessions. We might reasonably believe that such powers will not (and perhaps cannot) be used wisely by state officials.

Suppose that we set to one side the problems with granting state officials powers that we have reason to suspect they will not exercise carefully or fairly. There is the further difficulty with the potentially distracting or corrupting effects of such indeterminate sentences. Ideally, it seems that what we want offenders to do is focus on the penitential tasks before them, rather than worry about when their sentences will be completed. But even the most earnestly repentant offenders, when faced with indeterminate sentences, would likely wonder when they might be released from them. Not only will this distract them from their penitent tasks, it might tempt them to feign reform rather than work at it. Truly remorseful offenders should, it seems, be largely indifferent to sentence reductions, focused instead on their own reform. Indeed, we might be especially wary of offenders who seek out reductions or, worse, bargain for them.[40] All of this suggests that the optimum arrangement might consist of sentence reductions bestowed by the authorities in ways that are largely unpredictable. They would be like grace, granted to offenders whom the authorities determined had sufficiently regained their attachment to the good.

This brings us to a further difficulty: We might doubt that state authorities are appropriate overseers of the moral reform of offenders. To go back to Tudor's informal case, it would not be unusual or troubling for the person who was wronged to engage in some close questioning of the wrongdoer and her attitudes. The person wronged might want to know more fully why the wrongdoer acted as she did, how she feels now about what she did, what she plans to do about it, what she has done about it, how she feels about her wrongdoing in retrospect, and so on. For it may be that only by asking such questions can the victim gauge the depth of the wrongdoer's understanding of her wrong and her commitment to reform. Of course, the wrongdoer can refuse to cooperate in such inquiries. She can decide to endure the unabated "punishment" doled out by the person she wronged, or can break off the relationship entirely and avoid further interactions with the wronged person. Yet these are not options open to criminal offenders whom the state has detained. They would presumably have to answer the official sentence monitor's possibly intrusive questions about their attitudes and conduct, questions that it would be necessary to get answers to if the monitor was to properly determine whether a sentence reduction was in order. At least they would have to answer to such an authority if they were to have any hope of a sentence reduction. Whether such close supervision of the condition of offenders' moral selves is a legitimate function of liberal democratic societies is a point that has been forcefully pressed by Andrew von Hirsch and Andrew Ashworth.[41] Such

---

[40] Cf. McCoy (n 1 above) 81.   [41] von Hirsch and Ashworth (n 14 above) 92–109.

societies are not religious orders that individuals have joined and to whose probing interest in the moral health of their souls they have voluntarily subscribed.

One further point merits discussion. Near the end of his analysis, Tudor takes up the question whether the lack of remorse should be an aggravating factor in sentencing. After all, if the remorseful are to receive sentence reductions, should not the unremorseful have their sentences enhanced? Though he admits that his remarks do not fully address the issue, Tudor counsels against such sentence enhancements. He suggests that sentences for offenses should initially be set by their seriousness (presumably taking into account the two dimensions of harm and culpability). The remorseful should receive some discount from the baseline sentences in recognition of their currently reduced blameworthiness. Yet the unremorseful should not have their sentences raised above the baseline, since there are numerous reasons why offenders might not exhibit genuine remorse. In particular, some convicted of crimes might be innocent (or falsely believe themselves so), and it would be inappropriate to penalize such offenders over and above what the baseline dictates.[42] We should, Tudor argues, distinguish such offenders from "defiant gloaters" and psychopaths who are "simply incapable of feeling remorse."[43]

Yet Tudor's argument against treating lack of remorse as an aggravating factor in sentencing can be turned back on his claim that remorse-based sentence reductions are defensible. First, a policy of sentence reductions for remorse would not be any fairer to the unfortunate individuals who faced wrongful conviction than a policy that treated lack of remorse as an aggravating factor. The innocent would surely perceive the advantages of appearing remorseful, since failure to do so would mean they would face the full measure of punishment for their "crimes." Second, a policy of sentence reductions for the remorseful would impact other types of offenders unfairly. Psychopaths, who are seemingly incapable of remorse and yet not responsible for their condition, would (unfairly it seems) have to endure the full measure of their sanctions, unless we were prepared (as we might need to be) to exclude them from retributive punishment altogether. More importantly, as we saw in Chapter 3, there will be offenders who are not terribly remorseful for their crimes for reasons that have nothing to do with their being defiant gloaters or hardened recidivists. Some of them might reasonably believe that society has no legitimate business criminalizing the conduct in which they have engaged, or believe that though it does, it routinely enforces the relevant prohibitions inequitably. Some might (not unreasonably) believe that society leaves them with few other viable options than to engage in lucrative but illegal activities. Others might have weak or stunted moral consciences because they are the victims of severe social deprivation, with all of its destructive effects on moral development. It is, at the very least, debatable whether a policy of

---

[42] Tudor (n 7 above) 256.
[43] Tudor (n 7 above) 256–7. It is not clear from the text whether Tudor thinks that psychopaths are properly subject to retributive punishment.

remorse-based sentence reductions is fair to these types of offenders. If it is unfair to automatically exclude some or all of them from remorse-based sentence reductions, we will be left with an unpalatable dilemma: Either we give sentence reductions to just about anyone who pleads guilty or is found guilty at trial but who claims to have some reason for deserving a reduction, or we compound the already difficult tasks facing the officials charged with implementing the sentencing scheme. Not only will they have to distinguish the remorseful from the unremorseful, they will have to determine which of those in the latter category should nevertheless be deemed eligible for sentence reductions. Given the formidable difficulties in making these kinds of determinations fairly and judiciously, it seems better to forgo remorse-based mitigation altogether than to entrust state officials with these powers.

Remorse and crime reduction

Remorse-based sentence reductions might also be defended by those who subscribe to the crime reduction approach to legal punishment's justification. Of the three ways in which punishment is alleged to reduce crime—deterrence, incapacitation, and rehabilitation—such reductions seem most defensible from the standpoint of offender rehabilitation. Genuinely remorseful offenders, it might be argued, will be more susceptible to rehabilitation than those who are semi-remorseful or unremorseful. In particular, those who are truly contrite about their crimes will be better motivated to participate in, and profit from, prison treatment programs designed to reduce their drug or alcohol dependency, teach them anger management techniques, train them for future vocations, and the like. As such, they will be rehabilitated more quickly than those who refuse to accept responsibility for their crimes or, worse, are defiant in the face of official findings that they violated the law and are thus subject to punishment.

The preceding argument is an intuitively attractive one. Nonetheless, we might want to see some empirical confirmation of its crucial claim that the genuinely remorseful will tend to make better use of rehabilitation programs provided by the state than the unremorseful. It is possible, though perhaps not likely, that many of the remorseful will never get beyond the point of feeling repentant about their crimes. As we have seen, having the appropriate moral reaction to one's crime is but the first step down the road to reform. Even if the empirical evidence supported the central claim in the argument, there is other information that we would need if we were to award sentence reductions to the remorseful at the time of sentencing. We would need to know how much more quickly, on average, they were rehabilitated compared with their unremorseful counterparts. Without that information, we would not be in a position to calculate appropriate sentence discounts. If we knew, for instance, that remorseful offenders were rehabilitated, on average, 20 percent faster than unremorseful ones, then we could award sentence discounts that reflected that. One complication that we might anticipate is this: It could turn out that remorseful offenders who commit certain types of crimes are reformed at different rates to those who commit other types of crimes. That would require us to award variable sentence discounts to the remorseful, depending on the type of offense they have committed. A further complication is the possibility that, even within offense types, remorse as a mitigating factor might have to be weighed against aggravating sentencing factors, such as recidivism. Intuitively, it would not seem wise to reward the same sentence discounts to first-time remorseful offenders and recidivist remorseful offenders. The latter will have shown themselves to be irresolute or weak-willed, in spite of their remorse. As such they are candidates for lengthier sentences and rehabilitation stints.

Again, one alternative to bestowing sentence discounts on the remorseful at the time of sentencing would be to grant the discounts once they have been rehabilitated—that is, once their remorse has been put to good use by penal authorities in efforts to alter the habits of thinking and acting that got them in trouble in the first place. This, as we have already seen, is an imperfect option as well, since it would grant prison officials or parole boards considerable discretion in determining which offenders should be released from completing their sentences. Not only would this open the door to inequitable decisions based on factors such as race, gender, or ethnicity, but also the prospect of completing their sentences sooner rather than later might undermine offenders' sincere efforts at reform. Moreover, it would seem that remorsefulness is not really doing much of the work in this case. What matters is offender progress at reform, not how they felt about their crimes immediately after committing them. This suggests that we should leave off punishing all those who have turned their lives around, whether they were initially remorseful for their crimes or not.

Beyond these problems, there are others. As we saw in the previous section, some offenders who exhibit little remorse for their crimes are not suitable candidates for rehabilitation. The wrongly convicted, for instance, are not in need of rehabilitation, and yet denying them remorse-based sentence reductions—whether from the outset or once they have been successfully rehabilitated, whatever that might mean in their cases—would only compound the injustices done to them. Something similar would be true for individuals who are guilty of conduct that should not be criminalized in the first place. In the case of severely socially deprived offenders, predicating sentence reductions on their remorse or efforts at reform suggests, somewhat misleadingly, that they are solely to blame for the predicaments they find themselves in. Perhaps such offenders are not entirely blameless for the choices they have made due to their underdeveloped moral personalities or the meager opportunities available to them. But insisting that they demonstrate remorse or undertake efforts at reform as conditions of their receiving reduced punishment seems insensitive to the compromised character of their lives.

Crime reductionists would also have to consider the possibility that genuinely remorseful offenders should not be punished at all, as opposed to receiving reduced sentences, especially if their punishment takes the form of imprisonment.

Imprisonment notoriously makes many offenders worse, isolating and sometimes alienating them from society, subjecting them to demeaning or brutalizing treatment that hardens them, or exposing them to other offenders who teach them anti-social attitudes or criminal proclivities and skills.[44] Maybe we should avoid punishing the genuinely remorseful simply because punishment is apt to make them more, not less, likely to reoffend. Of course, the genuinely remorseful might be thought more capable of resisting or more inclined to resist these effects of incarceration, focusing instead on their rehabilitation. But many societies make a poor showing of offering prison inmates rehabilitation that is adequately funded and well administered. In fairness, crime reductionists need not, and probably would not, support the existing forms of imprisonment found in many countries. They could therefore argue that the risk that imprisonment would make genuinely remorseful offenders worse could be minimized in more humanely and constructively organized prisons. But even under the best of prison conditions, there will be some risk of deleterious effects on the remorseful that crime reductionists would have to countenance.

Suppose that in spite of all the preceding problems and doubts, remorse-based sentence reductions of some kind would be supported by the rehabilitative branch of the crime reduction approach. It would still have to be shown that such reductions comport with the other modes of crime reduction, namely deterrence and incapacitation. With respect to general deterrence, there might be some concern that sentence reductions of any kind will marginally diminish the incentives that would-be offenders have to desist from crime. However, the evidence that there is a correlation between longer sentences and reduced offending is weak, at best.[45] Thus, if remorse-based sentence reductions were modest in size, it is doubtful that they would conflict in any way with general deterrence. Those offenders who were less than genuinely remorseful would continue to receive the full measure of their sentences in any case and would thus serve as more than adequate reminders of the risks of offending (to anyone susceptible to deterrence).

It is harder to say how specific deterrence, the idea that those who have experienced punishment firsthand will be more motivated to avoid risking it in the future, would be affected by sentence reductions for the remorseful.[46] On the one hand, the

---

[44] Consider T. Mathiesen's claim that imprisonment more often "debilitates" than rehabilitates offenders, in his *Prison On Trial*, 2nd edition (Winchester, UK: Waterside Press, 2000) 53. For a lucid account of the debilitating psychological effects of imprisonment on individuals, one that calls into doubt their abilities to return to normal lives, see C. Haney, *Reforming Imprisonment: Psychological Limits to the Pains of Imprisonment* (Washington, DC: American Psychological Association, 2009).

[45] See A. von Hirsch, A. E. Bottoms, E. Burney, and P. O. Wikstrom, *Criminal Deterrence and Sentence Severity: An Analysis of Recent Research* (Oxford: Hart Publishing, 1999), and D. S. Nagin, "Criminal Deterrence Research at the Outset of the Twenty-First Century," [1998] 23 *Crime and Justice: A Review of Research* 1.

[46] Bibas and Bierschbach note that "psychology, psychiatry, sociology, and criminology have not empirically linked expressions of remorse and apology to a decreased need for specific deterrence of particular offenders" (n 2 above) 106.

unremorseful would continue to experience their full sentences, and one suspects that the genuinely remorseful would receive a sufficient sentence to provide them with the kind of supplemental prudential reasons to avoid future wrongdoing upon which special deterrence relies. Still, if among the genuinely remorseful there were some offenders who were irresolute or weak-willed, longer sentences might provide them with stronger prudential incentives to avoid further wrongdoing. Such stronger incentives are ones that they appear to need. Thus, the case for remorse-based sentence reductions might depend to some extent on our ability to subdivide the genuinely remorseful or, failing that, on estimates about the proportion of the irresolute or impulsive among them. Notice that genuinely remorseful offenders who were irresolute or impulsive could conceivably be worse bets for desistance from future crime than less remorseful offenders who were more responsive to prudential incentives. Since the focus of special deterrence is not on reforming offenders, it might turn out that some less than genuinely remorseful offenders could be induced to desist from crime out of fear more quickly or reliably than their more remorseful (but less prudent) counterparts who commit similar crimes. In that case, it is the former who would be the better candidates for sentence reductions, though not ones based on remorse.

The inability to predict, in advance, which of the genuinely remorseful are impulsive or weak-willed, and so in need of stronger prudential incentives to refrain from offending, would seem to point us away from remorse-based sentence reductions awarded at the time of sentencing. In response, it might be suggested that we could continue to award sentence reductions at the time of sentencing if we simply denied them to recidivists, even genuinely remorseful ones. We would, after all, have some reason to believe that such offenders would be unlikely to follow through on their efforts at self-reform. The problem with this proposal is that some first-time offenders, even if they are remorseful, will likewise fail in their efforts at self-reform. Remorse-based sentence reductions granted at the time of their sentencing would therefore not be optimal if our aim were to reduce future offending. We might therefore prefer that, if reductions are to be awarded, they should be predicated on real progress at self-reform. But that again points us back toward remorse-based reductions granted by state officials once some part of offenders' sentences has been served. Since we might doubt whether state officials will be able to determine with any accuracy whether offenders have made progress at self- reform, the most sensible approach might be to eschew remorse-based reductions altogether.

With regard to incapacitation, the genuinely remorseful would, in general, seem less dangerous than the semi-remorseful or unremorseful and therefore less in need of restraint. Again, however, this conclusion would have to be qualified if among the genuinely remorseful there were significant numbers of irresolute or impulsive individuals. Such offenders might be in as much need of restraint as unremorseful ones, and thus not ideal candidates for sentence reductions. Unless we could somehow separate out irresolute or impulsive remorseful offenders, the problems they pose do not bode well for a policy of sentence reductions handed out at the time of sentencing.

It would seem, therefore, that though special deterrence and incapacitation, as modes of crime reduction, are consistent with remorse-based sentence reductions, they do not lend much support to reductions granted at the time of sentencing. Yet there is a deeper problem with the crime reduction analysis which has so far gone unnoticed. We have been proceeding as if sentences for offenders were somehow set—by reference to what considerations has not been made clear—and then posing the question whether remorseful offenders might be deemed eligible for discounts. But surely a more plausible way to view the crime reduction approach to sentencing is this: Sentence ranges are determined by weighing the benefits of punishment, in the form of deterrence, incapacitation, and rehabilitation, against its many costs and burdens. Since there are many different kinds of offenses for which sentence ranges would have to be set, the exceedingly complex task of weighing the good and bad consequences of shorter or longer sentences, as well as the consequences of the different types of sentences (broadly, custodial or non-custodial) available, would have to be carried out in relation to each type of offense. There are reasons to doubt that this weighing can be done in relation to any given type of offense, let alone in relation to all of them.[47] At present we probably lack the empirical information that would be required to determine the deterrent, incapacitation, or rehabilitative effects of shorter versus longer sentences for any given type of offense. More than this, we may not have the cognitive abilities to combine all of the data and competing considerations into the type of overall analysis that a systematic crime reduction approach envisions.

But set these doubts about the feasibility of the crime reduction sentencing project aside and suppose that we were able to produce a fully articulated sentencing scheme. Suppose also that it had as one of its features a sentence range for each type of offense. It seems plausible to believe, for the reasons outlined earlier, that among the factors that might serve as a basis for assigning a given offender a sentence lower in the range would be his or her genuine remorse for having committed the crime in question. Of course, there might be other factors (e.g., a long history of offending) that would counsel us to assign the offender a sentence higher in the relevant range. All of these factors would have to be weighed by the judge charged with determining a presumptive sentence for an offender, given the charges he or she faces. The problem is that once the presumptive sentence was determined, it would not make any sense to grant the offender a further, remorse-based reduction. The offender's remorse would already have been taken into account in determining the presumptive sentence. In

---

[47] Some of these reasons are discussed in my *Rethinking Imprisonment* (Oxford: Oxford University Press, 2007) 40–50.

this way, the crime reduction approach to sentencing seems different from desert-based approaches, which initially focus on the factors of harm and culpability (as the latter is normally understood) in determining sentence ranges. On desert-based sentencing schemes, it at least makes sense to think about awarding the remorseful some discount from their presumptive sentences because their remorsefulness may not already have been factored into the determination of their sentences. But on a crime reduction approach, it will already have been factored in. A further remorse-based discount would be redundant.

Conclusions

Let us take stock: The most defensible form of remorse-based sentence reductions appears to be one in which they are awarded by state officials who deem an offender's progress toward moral reform substantial enough to warrant some easing off of his sentence. There are numerous problematic tasks that such a policy would necessitate state officials having to perform: separation of the genuinely remorseful from those who feign it or exhibit one of its simulacra, figuring out why those who do not exhibit it have this failing, and discerning the strength of an offender's reattachment to the good in the form of progress at moral reform. We might reasonably doubt the abilities of state officials to perform any of these tasks adequately and responsibly, let alone all of them. Moreover, performance of these tasks would require these same officials to conduct potentially intrusive inquiries into the lives of offenders, their thinking about their conduct, and their emotional reactions to it. Offenders who failed to cooperate with these inquiries could not, for a variety of reasons, simply be deemed unremorseful and ordered to serve their full sentences. State officials would have to inquire into the reasons for their non-cooperation, to ensure that they did indeed reflect poorly on offenders, and thus were legitimate bases for denying them sentence reductions.

My conclusion is not that a policy of sentence reductions for remorse cannot, in principle, be defended, though I have underscored the many difficulties in mounting such a defense. But it should be apparent that defending such a policy does not place us remotely in the vicinity of a defense of the kinds of waiver rewards offered criminal defendants in exchange for their guilty pleas. Few prosecutors or criminal court judges appear to make anything more than casual efforts to discern whether defendants who are willing to plead guilty are actually remorseful for their crimes. We can imagine them taking more pains in this regard and could set up procedures that would encourage if not require them to do so.[48] Such procedures would no doubt slow the plea bargaining process considerably, and so we might wonder how long support for requiring them would remain strong. In any event, such procedures

---

[48] Again, see Bibas and Bierschbach (n 2 above) 140–1.

would not tell us what we need to know about offenders if remorse-based mitigation is to be defensible. For what we need to know about them is not how repentant they are immediately after their offenses are committed, but whether and how successfully they make use of their repentance to effect lasting changes in their lives. And that is something we may only find out about them some time after they have completed their sentences.

5

Waiver Rewards and the Reduction of Crime

In Chapters 3 and 4, defenses of waiver rewards premised on the expansion of deserved punishment and the mitigation of punishment for the genuinely remorseful have been examined. Neither type of defense succeeded in showing that more robust forms of plea bargaining, forms which grant state officials considerable discretion in bestowing variable and substantial waiver rewards on defendants in exchange for their guilty pleas, are justified. Robust plea bargaining produces larger absolute and comparative injustices than more constrained forms of it. And though easing off punishment of the genuinely remorseful makes sense on some accounts of legal punishment's justification, discounts granted to them at sentencing do not.

The conclusions reached in previous chapters might not trouble defenders of substantial and negotiable waiver rewards. They might contend that the most formidable defense of such rewards has yet to be examined. That defense invokes the crime-reduction approach to the justification of legal punishment, holding that robust waiver rewards enable prosecutors to process their caseloads more efficiently, thereby strengthening the deterrent signals sent by the criminal justice system. If legal punishment is the "price" of crime, then robust waiver rewards facilitate the swift transmission of price information to potential offenders. As Frank Easterbrook quips, it is "more costly to try a case than to settle it."[1] Trials slow the administration of punishment, and if they were required for all accused individuals, they would likely bring the criminal justice system to a standstill. Waiver rewards keep the administration of justice flowing smoothly. Since potential offenders receive quicker and more reliable signals about the hazards of offending, more of them are persuaded to desist from it.

The crime reduction defense of substantial and variable waiver rewards will be evaluated in two stages. In the first stage, the legal and social status quo will be treated as a given and, more importantly, as a mostly benign force if our overriding concern is to keep harmful and predatory behavior in check. In other words, current criminal prohibitions will be taken as legitimate, and existing sanction levels will be deemed, if not entirely optimal, at least not obviously suboptimal if our overriding aim is to limit crime at reasonable cost. These assumptions are contentious, as even some defenders

[1] F. H. Easterbrook, "Criminal Procedure as a Market System," [1983] 12 *J. Legal Stud.* 289, 297.

of plea bargaining's role in reducing crime seem to appreciate. But they are ones with which most who defend waiver rewards based on their role in reducing crime appear to operate. Even on these assumptions, the deterrence defense of such rewards is unpersuasive. Its proponents conceive the alternatives available too narrowly, especially when they assume that providing trials to all individuals charged with crimes is the only viable alternative. Defenders of substantial and variable waiver rewards also ignore the more subtle ways in which such punishment discounts may undermine the authority of legal officials and moral norms against offending.

In the second stage, the social and legal status quo is itself queried. On the assumption that our aim is to reduce genuinely harmful and predatory behavior in society in a cost-effective fashion, many existing criminal prohibitions, the sanctions attaching to their violation, and the distribution of opportunities and other social goods that they enforce might be counterproductive. This will especially be true if too much conduct is criminalized and punished too harshly and destructively, and other, arguably more meaningful, steps to reduce offending are eschewed. At the extreme, in dysfunctional criminal justice systems, the more efficient processing of criminal charges might not be a worthy goal. Granted, substantial waiver rewards might reduce excessive levels of punishment. But they will do so in ways that are highly unsystematic. We might also worry that bartering about punishment is a practice that will undermine many offenders' already weak commitments to the moral norms implicit in the criminal law.

The conclusions all of this points toward are these: We would be better off with fewer criminal prohibitions, ones focused on the reduction of genuinely harmful or threatening conduct. To their violation we should attach sanctions that appear optimal, given a careful weighing of the benefits of legal punishment against its many costs. Once we have such a scheme in place, we should be reluctant to afford the officials charged with overseeing it the discretion to act in ways that undermine the clear, firm, and consistent message that violations of the laws will not be tolerated.

A preliminary point

At the outset, it is worth reminding ourselves that a crime reduction approach to the justification of legal punishment must weigh the benefits of legal punishment, primarily in the form of reduced crime and thus victimization of individuals, against its many costs.[2] Only when its benefits can be expected to exceed its costs, and there are no other, less costly means to achieving comparable benefits, is the resort to legal punishment justified. The costs of legal punishment include the immediate suffering it causes those who must endure it, especially in its harsher forms, as well as

---

[2] A point first emphasized by J. Bentham in *An Introduction to the Principles of Morals and Legislation*, P. Wheelright (ed.) (Garden City NY: Doubleday, Doran, and Company, 1935) chapter 13.

the longer-term diminishment of their life-prospects.[3] The costs also include what are termed the "collateral consequences" of punishment—the losses and burdens on spouses, other family members, and communities when individuals are imprisoned and therefore cannot shoulder their share of financial, childcare, or civic responsibilities.[4] Last but not least, legal punishment is a hugely expensive enterprise, especially when it takes the form of imprisonment.[5] The burdens of supporting it fall mostly on tax-paying citizens, who must also endure its considerable opportunity costs. All of this counsels restraint in the resort to legal punishment, as well as the search for alternative, less costly means of discouraging or controlling behavior that does not respect the lives, bodies, and property of individuals.

To their credit, those who defend robust forms of plea bargaining based on their crime reduction potential recognize the costly and often harmful character of legal punishment. They therefore prefer the use of fines as criminal sanctions, as opposed to imprisonment, because the latter is much more costly socially and its burdens tend to fall on non-offenders.[6] Indeed, they would enjoin the sparing use of fines—preferring the less frequent imposition of very large fines to the recurrent use of smaller ones, especially if the former can be shown to have a similar deterrent impact to the latter. In reality, however, it is acknowledged that many offenders are poor and so unsuitable candidates for paying fines.[7] There is also the concern that draconian, though infrequently administered, fines would have chilling effects. Individuals would be so fearful of being the recipients of such fines that they would refrain from conduct that was perfectly, though perhaps marginally, legal.[8] Hence, most who defend the use of substantial and variable waiver rewards in plea bargaining seem resigned to the current levels and kinds of criminal sanctions.

But from the problems with imposing fines on most offenders or large ones on a few, little follows about the defensibility of current levels or kinds of criminal sanctions. A systematic crime reduction approach to sentencing would require us to scrutinize existing sanctions, to weigh their benefits against their costs. Alternatives would also have to be considered. It is not unreasonable to believe that current sentences in some countries are excessively long and harsh, well past the point of serving any useful deterrent function, and debilitating to the point that offenders are

---

[3] On the long-term effects of imprisonment on offenders' life-prospects, see B. Western, *Punishment and Inequality in America* (New York: Russell Sage Foundation, 2006). The negative psychological effects of imprisonment are documented by Craig Haney, *Reforming Punishment: Psychological Limits to the Pains of Imprisonment* (Washington, DC: American Psychological Association, 2006).

[4] J. Hagan and R. Dinovitzer, "Collateral Consequences of Punishment for Children, Communities, and Prisoners," [1999] 26 *Crime and Justice: A Review of Research* 121.

[5] For one recent estimate of the costs of legal punishment in the United States, see D. A. Anderson, "The Aggregate Burden of Crime," [1999] 42 *J. L. & Econ.* 611. For police protection, corrections, and the prosecution of crimes, Anderson puts the figure at over $100 billion annually.

[6] See Easterbrook (n 1 above) 293. See also G. Becker, "Crime and Punishment: An Economic Approach," [1968] 76 *Journal of Political Economics* 169, and T. J. Miceli, "Plea Bargaining and Deterrence: An Institutional Approach," [1996] 3 *European Journal of Law and Economics* 249.

[7] Easterbrook (n 1 above) 293.   [8] Easterbrook (n 1 above) 293–4.

unlikely to function as law-abiding citizens once they have completed them.[9] No clear-thinking crime reductionist would applaud such a state of affairs. Of course, it is doubtful that we have the empirical information needed to design an optimal crime reduction sentencing scheme, or if we have the computational powers to process that information.[10] But attempting to acquire that information and using it judiciously are what we should aspire to. The fact that those who defend robust waiver rewards seem so little interested in that difficult task and thus content with the status quo is troubling. They thereby make things too easy on themselves when it comes to defending plea bargaining. As we will see, they make things too easy for themselves in other ways as well.

Easterbrook's defense of plea bargaining

Frank Easterbrook has developed what is probably the most sophisticated defense of plea bargaining as a useful crime reduction tool.[11] Easterbrook writes with the United States criminal justice system in mind. Though this might appear to render his analysis of limited value to societies with different legal and criminal justice practices, his defense of plea bargaining is abstract enough that, if successful, it should work in a variety of different contexts. For the most part, Easterbrook takes the legal and social status quo in the United States as a given. Still, it would be a mistake to confuse his implied acceptance of the status quo with something quite different—the claim that it constitutes an optimal crime reduction social and legal scheme. Easterbrook makes no such claim and it seems doubtful he would try to defend it.

These points are noteworthy because my strategy in examining defenses of substantial and variable waiver rewards has so far been to start with the ideal and then to work my way toward the messier reality of things. This chapter departs from that strategy. It begins where Easterbrook does, within a legal and social framework that is more assumed than defended. Nonetheless, some assumptions that Easterbrook does not make are employed in order to focus the analysis on the question of whether large and variable waiver rewards are defensible. Specifically, it is assumed that trial penalties are not in play and that strategic overcharging by prosecutors is absent. Easterbrook defends trial penalties (albeit on retributive grounds) and seems untroubled by strategic overcharging. However, my position has been that neither is

---

[9] For discussion that this is true of the United States, see, among others, E. Currie, *Crime and Punishment in America* (New York: Henry Holt, 1998); M. Tonry, *Thinking about Crime: Sense and Sensibility in American Penal Culture* (Oxford: Oxford University Press, 2004); and Haney (n 3 above).

[10] I question whether we are ever likely to have the empirical information needed to develop an optimal crime reduction sentencing scheme, or the powers of judgment to use that information effectively, in my *Rethinking Imprisonment* (Oxford: Oxford University Press, 2007) 40–50.

[11] Again, see Easterbrook (n 1 above) 308–22, as well as "Plea Bargaining as Compromise," [1992] 101 *Yale L. J.* 1969. There is, it should be noted, a more voluntarist strand to Easterbrook's defense of plea bargaining, one that defends it on contractual grounds rather than instrumental, crime-reductive ones. The contractual defense of plea bargaining is examined in Chapter 7.

defensible; they should therefore not be employed by state officials. What remains for debate is whether robust and variable waiver rewards can be defended as important tools in helping to reduce crime. That brings us to Easterbrook's argument.

Easterbrook begins with the familiar assumption that police and prosecutors must deal with a considerable volume of criminal conduct. They have at their disposal limited resources with which to do so. Prosecutors, in particular, have many more cases than they can possibly seek to adjudicate through criminal trials, especially given the elaborate procedural safeguards that have emerged to protect defendants' rights during trials. Fortunately, prosecutors in the United States are afforded enormous discretion, with regard to both charging decisions and sentencing recommendations. Even if the evidence they have against defendants would likely result in their conviction at trial, prosecutors will often offer waiver rewards in exchange for guilty pleas in order to avoid the toll on their resources that trials would exact. They thereby stretch their resources and are able to increase dramatically the number of cases processed. They also conserve their scarce resources for those few cases which they believe, for one reason or another, should go to trial. Notice that this caseload management rationale for large and variable waiver rewards also would be applicable to the somewhat smaller and less negotiable rewards on offer in other legal systems. Trial avoidance or minimization is on the increase throughout the world and seems without question to be motivated, in part, by the desire of state officials to conserve scarce resources so that a larger volume of criminal cases can be processed.[12]

Of course, state officials are willing to negotiate charges and sentences for another reason besides resource conservation. In some cases, they lack credible and convincing evidence against defendants, though they believe the defendants guilty of some or all the crimes with which they have been charged. In such cases, prosecutors negotiate pleas to gain "half a loaf," that is, to obtain convictions of defendants on some of the charges they have levied against them, or to obtain some punishment of defendants on reduced charges. Since the half-loaf defense of plea bargaining is examined in greater detail in Chapter 8, it is ignored in this chapter. Instead, I focus exclusively on the role of waiver rewards in helping prosecutors extend their resources and thereby expand the scope of legal punishment.

There is, in fact, some reason to believe that increasing the volume of cases processed by legal systems might be a more effective crime reduction tactic than seeing to it that fewer individuals receive the full measure of punishment for their crimes. Empirical studies of the link between sentence severity and marginal deterrence have consistently failed to show that increased sentence lengths are correlated with reductions in offending.[13] Yet empirical studies do demonstrate a link between the certainty

---

[12] See M. Langer, "From Legal Transplants to Legal Translations: The Globalization of Plea Bargaining and the Americanization Thesis in Criminal Procedure," [2004] 45 *Harv. Int'l L. J.* 1.

[13] See A. von Hirsch, A. E. Bottoms, E. Burney, and P. O. Wikstrom, *Criminal Deterrence and Sentence Severity: An Analysis of Recent Research* (Oxford: Hart Publishing, 1999) 47; A. N. Doob and C. M. Webster, "Sentence Severity and Crime: Accepting the Null Hypothesis," [2003] 30 *Crime and*

of punishment, understood as the probability that offenders will be apprehended and punished in some fashion, and marginal deterrence.[14] Thus, the reasoning behind Easterbrook's defense of plea bargaining is plausible—more offenders punished some will reduce crime to a greater extent than fewer offenders punished more severely. Still, we might want to be cautious about this claim, since dramatically reduced punishments could conceivably have the effect of providing weak disincentives to commit crimes, even if such punishments were more broadly dispersed. Easterbrook's deterrence-based argument appears to presuppose that even robust plea bargaining does not make punishment so mild that few are dissuaded from offending by it.

Easterbrook admits that prosecutors' offers might diverge from their estimates of conviction probabilities or from their normal patterns of charge or sentence reduction proffers for a number of reasons. They might offer less attractive discounts for notorious crimes or if they hope to heighten the perceived costs of criminal conduct that has suddenly increased in frequency.[15] The latter tactic fits squarely within the logic of crime reduction; the former less straightforwardly so. Prosecutors might also offer steeper discounts to criminal defendants who can supply useful information about the criminal activities of others. Easterbrook is adamant that it is prosecutors who are in the best position to determine what charge or sentence discounts to offer.[16] They are the state officials who are best apprised of the strengths and weaknesses of the cases against those charged with crimes. They are also in the best position to appreciate the political repercussions of charging and sentencing decisions, or the value of testimony or other evidence that might be supplied by those to whom charge or sentence reductions are offered. Prosecutors are thus well positioned to maximize the number of convictions obtainable with their limited resources. Easterbrook admits that the justice plea bargaining metes out is far from perfect. Yet he is critical of calls for "equity" in sentencing, pointing out the practical infeasibility and substantial costs of efforts to ensure that like offenders are treated alike by the criminal justice system.[17] Plea bargained justice may not be perfect, but it enables prosecutors to process many more cases than they could were trials the norm for all or most defendants.

Collectively, the kinds of relatively unrestrained plea negotiations that are the norm in the United States set the "price" of criminal conduct there—that is, the sentences that offenders can expect to receive for their crimes if they are apprehended and convicted (or more often, if they plead guilty). In this way, plea bargaining operates as a market system, though the buyers and sellers in this case are, as Easterbrook concedes, constrained in ways that normal buyers and sellers in the commercial marketplace are not.[18] Though his argument appears to sleight incapacitation and rehabilitation as

---

Justice: A Review of Research 143; and M. Tonry, "Learning from the Limitations of Deterrence Research," [2008] 37 *Crime and Justice: A Review of Research* 279.

[14] See von Hirsch, et al. (n 13 above) 47.   [15] Easterbrook (n 1 above) 305.
[16] Easterbrook (n 1 above) 299–302.   [17] Easterbrook (n 1 above) 302–5.
[18] For instance, criminal defendants seeking to "purchase" charge or sentence reductions in exchange for their guilty pleas cannot choose from among the prosecutorial "suppliers" of such reductions. See

modes of crime reduction, Easterbrook could conceivably modify his defense of plea bargaining to accommodate them. With regard to incapacitation, he might say that prosecutors should, in crafting plea bargain offers, take into account the past criminal histories of charged defendants or reliable evidence that they are likely to commit further, serious crimes. Presumably, prosecutors would offer more modest charge or sentence discounts to "dangerous" offenders than to those about whom the evidence of continuing criminal proclivities is unavailable or thought unreliable.[19] Indeed, it seems likely that prosecutors who have the authority to do so, already incorporate this kind of information into their plea bargain offers. Similarly, if prosecutors believe that certain defendants are highly amenable to rehabilitation, they can tailor their plea bargain proposals to take this into account. Young or first-time offenders might be offered steeper charge or sentence discounts than older, hardened offenders.

Having to take incapacitation and rehabilitation into account complicates the decisions that prosecutors or other state officials must make. They will have to weigh and balance the costs of going to trial, the probabilities of conviction, and the need to maintain the criminal justice system's deterrent, incapacitation, and rehabilitative purposes. Nonetheless, Easterbrook could argue that prosecutors are in a better position than anyone else in the criminal justice system to perform these complex calculations and thus negotiate appropriate charges and sentences.

Initial problems with Easterbrook's account

Easterbrook's argument for waiver rewards and strong prosecutorial discretion in their deployment relies crucially on the notion that we lack viable alternatives that would enable us to maintain a credible and effective deterrent threat. It might seem that Easterbrook is correct in believing that the elimination of plea bargaining, or the substantial curtailment of it, would so shrink the scope of legal punishment as to jeopardize our ability to keep crime in check. Yet it should be apparent by now that the provision of a trial for each and every criminal defendant not willing to plead guilty is not the sole alternative available to us. Even if it were, it is unlikely that the demand for trials would closely track the number of individuals charged with crimes. As we have seen, the majority of individuals charged with crimes will know that they are, in fact, guilty of them or something close to them.[20] Many of these individuals will be charged with relatively low-level offenses—drug possession, minor property

---

Easterbrook (n 1 above) 291. Easterbrook does suggest, however, that offenders can choose among the jurisdictions in which they commit crimes.

[19] However, the relationship between imprisonment's incapacitation effects and the reduction of crimes in communities is complex, as shown by F. E. Zimring and G. Hawkins, *Incapacitation: Penal Confinement and the Restraint of Crime* (New York: Oxford University Press, 1995), especially 53–9.

[20] Evidence that this is an accurate portrayal of many individuals charged with crimes is provided by M. Heumann in *Plea Bargaining: The Experiences of Prosecutors, Judges, and Defense Attorneys* (Chicago: University of Chicago Press, 1977) 70–1.

crimes, prostitution, public order offenses, and the like. The complete elimination of plea bargaining would be unlikely to spark demands from individuals charged with such crimes to have their days in court.[21] Some would be held on remand, with all of its costs and inconveniences. Others would simply want to avoid the costs and public embarrassment of trials, especially ones that would likely result in their conviction in any event. Pleading guilty would speed up the onset of their criminal sanctions, whatever those might turn out to be. In short, for many criminal defendants, there is little to gain and a lot to lose by stubbornly insisting upon the ritual of a trial.

Obviously, where robust waiver rewards can be obtained, there is something to gain by appearing steadfast in one's insistence upon going to trial. Defendants can hope thereby to win concessions from prosecutors who are eager to avoid depleting their resources. But if there were nothing to gain by such posturing, criminal defendants would face a stark choice: Either plead guilty and get it over with or prolong the inevitable by insisting on a trial. Granted, some would believe or hope that they were not prolonging the inevitable—that a trial might produce an acquittal. But this is also true of some defendants when robust plea bargaining exists. Perhaps more defendants would, in the absence of negotiated charge or sentence discounts, elect to roll the dice on a trial. And perhaps others would suspect that their prospects at trial were dim, but for other reasons (e.g., they are currently free on bail) demand trials if pleading guilty were their only other option. Nonetheless, I am not persuaded that we would be deluged with trials in the absence of negotiated charge and sentence discounts. We would see some increase in the demand for them, though it is hard to say how much of one.

Whatever the increase, I concede that it would strain state officials whose tasks include attempting to process a high volume of criminal cases. For the sake of argument, suppose that the elimination or drastic curtailment of negotiated charge or sentence discounts would result in a 25 percent increase in the demand for trials. How might state officials attempt to cope with this increased demand and what would be the consequences of their actions for the reduction of crime? It seems likely that prosecutors would respond to the increased demand for trials by more often dropping charges in cases of less serious kinds of offenses (thereby conserving their trial resources for crimes that are higher in social costs) or in cases in which the evidence against defendants was not sufficiently probative.[22] The dropping of charges in the

---

[21] As Malcolm Feeley has noted, the process costs of going to trial may rob individuals accused of low-level offenses of their victory, even if they are ultimately acquitted at trial. See his *The Process Is the Punishment: Handling Cases in a Lower Criminal Court* (New York: Russell Sage Foundation, 1992). See also J. Bowers, "Punishing the Innocent," [2008] 156 *U. Pa. L. Rev.* 1117, 1132–40.

[22] It is worth noting that dropped charges in cases in which the evidence against defendants is weak may not constitute pure losses from a crime reduction perspective. In some of those cases, the evidence is weak because defendants are, in fact, innocent. Though their unwarranted punishment might make some marginal contribution to deterrence, the costs to such individuals would very likely outweigh the benefits of punishing them, especially given that those who are actually guilty of the crimes in question would remain free to commit other crimes.

former kinds of cases would, presumably, decrease the disincentives to commit the crimes in question.[23] But we must be careful not to exaggerate the loss of deterrence in such cases. Would-be offenders would still be subject to the embarrassment and inconvenience of arrest and, in some instances, pre-trial detention, at least on the assumption that the police would persist in apprehending those who commit such offenses. The prospect of such unpleasant encounters with the authorities would likely be enough to dissuade some individuals from offending. In response, it might be objected that the police would gradually stop arresting and detaining individuals for offenses once they saw that prosecutors dropped a disproportionately high number of the charges in certain kinds of cases. But prosecutors would not drop the charges in all such cases; nor would all of those charged with such crimes insist on trials, since they would not know whether prosecutors would rise to the challenge and subject them to the cost and embarrassment of a trial. At least some of them would plead guilty in order to get their punishment over with.

The cogency of Easterbrook's argument is further undermined by his sleighting of the alternatives to large and variable waiver rewards. The choice we face is not the simple one between large and variable waiver rewards and providing trials for each and every defendant who refuses to plead guilty. As we have seen, negotiated discounts could exist in any or all of three areas—with respect to charges, sentences, or aid to the authorities in providing evidence or testimony against one's former criminal associates. It is possible to permit negotiations in one or more of these areas without permitting them in all three. Furthermore, there is a range of options concerning the extent to which state officials might be allowed to negotiate in any one of these areas, from more or less complete discretion to negotiate any reduction that it seems likely the courts will accede to, to no discretion to negotiate at all. As we have seen, there could be fixed sentence discounts for defendants who plead guilty to the charges against them or who help the authorities by providing incriminating evidence against others.[24] There are also various possibilities regarding the magnitude of such fixed discounts, ranging from minimal to more substantial ones. Alternatively, we might permit state officials some room to negotiate sentence reductions for guilty pleas or in exchange for providing incriminating evidence, but put a cap on how large such reductions were allowed to become (e.g., no reduction greater than 30 percent of the minimum sentence for conviction on any given charge).[25] It is even possible to have presumptively fixed discounts or caps, ones that prosecutors would be allowed

---

[23] The effects of dropped charges due to weak evidence are less clear. Some of the defendants in question might have been innocent to begin with. Dropped charges might not alter their incentives to break the law on future occasions because they were not inclined to do so in any event. Defendants who were actually guilty might count themselves lucky to have avoided punishment. Whether their escaping punishment would embolden them to commit further crimes or to be more wary of doing so is unclear.

[24] The former alternative, that is fixed discounts for guilty pleas, is suggested by S. Schulhofer in "Plea Bargaining as Disaster," [1992] 101 *Yale L. J.* 1979, 2003–5.

[25] O. Gazal-Ayal discusses caps on sentence discounts in "Partial Ban on Plea Bargains," [2006] 27 *Cardozo L. Rev.* 2295, 2313–17.

to exceed if given permission by judges to do so. In petitioning the courts for such extraordinary discounts, prosecutors would have to provide some explanation of the grounds for their being permitted to grant them.

Also, charge bargaining, which in general appears to have fewer defenders, could be discouraged without being prohibited outright. For instance, prosecutors could be required to provide the courts with a formal explanation of why they were dropping charges (or in some cases, adding charges) after having initially filed them.[26] We could further discourage charge bargaining by permitting the defense greater access to the prosecution's case against the individuals it has charged with offenses, in legal jurisdictions where such access is not guaranteed as a matter of course.[27] In that way, attempts by prosecutors to pressure defendants to plead guilty, by heaping up charges they have no real evidence for or intention to go to trial on, would be more likely to be exposed for the bluffs that they are.

Other possibilities exist as well. In some countries, modest forms of charge or sentence bargaining exist for individuals charged with low-level offenses. However, all of the individuals charged with more serious crimes are given no choice but to proceed to trial.[28] Even full confessions from individuals accused of serious crimes do not preclude trials, though they sometimes shorten them. Since the majority of cases processed in most criminal justice systems are apt to be low-level ones, requiring trials in the more serious cases is unlikely to overburden state officials. Again, there is a plausible case to be made for having greater procedural scrutiny of serious charges than less serious ones, especially if our concerns are to maximize the benefits of legal punishment while minimizing its costs. More serious offenses, typically, carry with them the threat of imprisonment, sometimes for lengthy periods of time. It makes sense, given the enormous and varied costs of imprisonment, to screen more carefully cases in which it is a possible outcome, in order to reduce the chances of its mistaken infliction.

Easterbrook's position appears to be that granting prosecutors wide discretion to negotiate charges and sentences across the entire spectrum of criminal cases enables them to maximize the number of cases processed, given their limited resources, thereby strengthening the deterrent signals sent by the criminal justice system. But it is surely not obvious that limiting prosecutorial discretion to do these things in one or more ways will have anything like the disastrous consequences predicted by defenders of the plea bargaining status quo. Most defendants are unlikely to demand trials, even if pleading guilty for no waiver rewards were the only other option. Fewer still

---

[26] As Y. Ma notes, prosecutorial discretion to add or drop charges is sharply limited in France. See his "Prosecutorial Discretion and Plea Bargaining in the United States, France, Germany, and Italy: A Comparative Perspective," [2002] 12 *International Criminal Justice Review* 22, 33.

[27] Permitting such access is the norm in Germany. See Ma (n 26 above) 38. S. Bibas advocates a more open discovery process in criminal cases in his "Plea Bargaining Outside the Shadow of Trial," [2004] 117 *Harv. L. Rev.* 2463, 2531–2.

[28] See Ma (n 26 above) 31–2. See also R. Adelstein and T. J. Micelli, "Toward a Comparative Economics of Plea Bargaining," [2001] 11 *European Journal of Law and Economics* 47, 60.

would demand them if modest and fixed sentence discounts were available for pleading guilty or helping the authorities solve other crimes. The specter of a criminal
justice system hopelessly clogged with defendants awaiting their day in court is something of a bogeyman that proponents of robust waiver rewards too often drag out
instead of doing the hard work of convincing us that their preferred scheme has the
optimal crime reduction profile.

In fairness to Easterbrook, he has other arguments aimed at convincing us that
limiting prosecutorial discretion in devising and offering waiver rewards is a bad idea.
He contends that asking individuals other than prosecutors to monitor and, if necessary, interfere with negotiations between prosecutors and defendants is unlikely to
produce better outcomes.[29] Why is this? Because prosecutors are in a better position
than other state officials to evaluate the evidence against defendants and determine
how best to allocate the resources at their disposal to process the formidable number
of cases brought to their attention. Even if judges, for instance, could be brought up
to speed with regard to the evidence in a given case, they are apt to be unaware of,
or unsympathetic to, the ways in which interfering with prosecutorial discretion
affects prosecutors' abilities to allocate their resources efficiently. Easterbrook likens
the meddling of other state officials in the plea-negotiation process to politicians'
attempts to regulate the workings of the free market. The latter are, in his view at
least, hardly known for their success; we should not expect the former to turn out
much better.

There is something to this point if what we proposed to do was authorize some state
official, independent of the prosecutor's office, with continuous oversight and correction of the outcomes of plea negotiations. But several of the alternatives to broad
prosecutorial discretion outlined above do not require anything of the sort. Fixed
discounts for guilty pleas do not, and neither would caps on the sentence reductions
that could be offered. Such caps would simply set the boundaries within which negotiations would take place. Efforts to discourage charge bargaining, especially in the
form of making the state's case against defendants fully available to defense attorneys,
would not necessitate judicial oversight of negotiated pleas. Even if we made fixed-
sentence discounts for guilty pleas or discount caps presumptive, subject to prosecutorial appeal before a judge, this would not amount to much of an interference with
the workings of the "free market" in plea negotiations. Presumably, such appeals
would be relatively rare. And it would be prosecutors who initiated them in order to
secure guilty pleas in certain problematic cases, or to reward defendants who provide
crucial help to the state (and who would not provide it without more than the standard discount). Judges would have to evaluate the case made by prosecutors for such
extraordinary discounts, of course, but this is something that they should be capable
of doing if they were asked to do so infrequently.

[29] See Easterbrook (n 1 above) 299 and 301.

The more subtle costs to robust plea bargaining

To this point, I have argued that limiting the discretion of state officials to craft and offer waiver rewards is unlikely to hamper significantly their ability to ensure that the criminal justice system maintains a credible deterrent profile. Even if they cannot engage in charge bargaining, or offer substantial and variable sentence discounts, prosecutors should be able to process enough cases to generate clear signals about the "price" of criminal offending. Would-be offenders who are inclined to weigh the benefits of offending against its costs, and desist from offending if the costs are perceived to be certain and sizable, would receive the prudential incentives they need to conform with the law. But this narrow focus on the adequacy of the deterrent signals sent by the criminal justice system does not do justice to the crime reduction approach to legal punishment's justification. Sophisticated crime reduction theorists have long understood that we are better off if most citizens refrain from criminal offending for reasons that have little to do with the "price" they might have to pay for engaging in it. Not only is legal punishment extraordinarily expensive to the wider public, destructive to the life-prospects of those who directly suffer it, and burdensome to offenders' loved ones and family members, but also the empirical evidence about its crime reduction effects is not terribly encouraging. Easterbrook's focus on the "price" of crime in the form of sanctions is, in other words, pretty thin gruel on which to sustain the criminal justice system's ability to diminish offending.

What other mechanisms, besides the threat of criminal sanctions, will a deeper and more subtle approach to reducing crime call upon? Two stand out, given our concerns. First, it is absolutely crucial that the vast majority of citizens have what H. L. A. Hart termed an "internal point of view" on the moral norms underlying key provisions of the criminal law.[30] This means that citizens must regard things like homicide, assault, and theft in all its varieties as not simply illegal, but as illegitimate ways of acting on or advancing their interests. Individuals who have internalized norms against these forms of conduct will rarely get to the point where they need the threat of criminal sanctions to keep them from offending. Such immoral conduct is, for them, beyond the pale. Alternatively, if they are ever tempted by such conduct, it will be enough for them to remind themselves that electing it is wrong or unacceptable. Importantly, it is plausible to believe that the criminal law, with its explicit prohibitions, complex and authoritative adjudicative procedures, and formidable array of sanctions, plays a vital role in reinforcing such moral norms against harmful and predatory conduct.[31] Such norms may initially be impressed upon citizens by parents, schools, churches, and communities. Indeed, without their influence, the criminal law might be powerless to convince individuals to embrace the moral standards it enforces. But acknowledging that allegiance to these standards has its

---

[30] H. L. A. Hart, *The Concept of Law* (Oxford: Clarendon Press, 1961) 88.
[31] For development of this view, see J. Andenaes, "The General Preventive Effects of Punishment," [1966] 114 *U. Pa. L. Rev.* 949.

origins elsewhere is nonetheless consistent with believing that the criminal law usefully adds to the chorus of social forces that cultivate and sustain it.

Second, individuals sometimes refrain from offending solely because the law prohibits it, quite independently of the sanctions that will be inflicted upon them if they
offend, are apprehended, and convicted. Such desistance is more apt to occur if the
law is seen as having the legitimate authority to require or proscribe actions. [32] In
liberal democratic societies, in particular, the legal authorities might be perceived as
appropriately invested with power, especially if their exercises of it are constrained
by the rule of law. Many citizens in such societies will take the illegality of conduct
as constituting a sufficient reason for avoiding it. In fact, this might be true even if the
legal requirements or prohibitions in question lack other strong moral, religious, or
customary backing.[33] The mere fact that the law speaks makes it worth listening to
and heeding. Still, this motivation to abide by the law may only be presumptive. If
the demands it makes are perceived as unjust or inequitably enforced, citizens might
decide to defy the authorities. But again, the willingness of many citizens to abide by
what the law commands because it commands it limits the need for the state to resort
to the threat of punishment in order to elicit compliance.

Easterbrook could concede these points, but question their relevance to his argument in favor of expansive forms of plea bargaining. To see how they are germane
to that argument, we must engage in some speculation about the ways in which
competing charge-adjudication schemes might perform with respect to reinforcing
moral norms against wrongful conduct and generating allegiance to state authority.
Consider criminal trials, for instance. They can usefully be viewed as highly structured and ritualized morality plays in which state officials present evidence against
the individuals whom they have formally charged with crimes. In doing so, such
officials develop narratives that reveal and implicitly (and often quite explicitly) condemn the wrongdoing alleged. The relevant criminal prohibitions are thus given
forceful formal recognition as the appropriate standards against which to judge the
conduct of the individuals on trial. Also, trials involve calling individuals to account
in very public and potentially (especially assuming they are guilty) embarrassing
ways.[34] When defendants are found guilty, as they often are, prosecutors recommend
sanctions (though defendants' attorneys will typically recommend lesser sanctions)
and judges assign them. The adversary trial system, whatever its faults, is binary and
uncompromising. Defendants are acquitted or they are found guilty and assigned
sentences. There is no haggling about charges or negotiation of sentences. The

---

[32] Here, I borrow from Gordon Hawkins, who is somewhat skeptical of Andenaes' notion that legal
punishment plays a morally educative function. See Hawkins' "Punishment as a Moral Educator," in
R. J. Gerber and P. D. McAnany (eds.), *Contemporary Punishment: Views, Explanations, and Justifications*
(Notre Dame, Ind.: University of Notre Dame Press, 1972) 120.

[33] A point made by Hawkins (n 32 above) 125.

[34] For development of the view that criminal trials involve calling individuals to account for their
actions, see A. Duff, L. Farmer, S. Marshall, and V. Tadros, *The Trial on Trial*, volume 3 (Oxford: Hart
Publishing, 2007) 127–62.

message to the public and to other offenders is clear: If you offend and are convicted, you will be punished. This is not to say that everyone in the public is satisfied with either the verdict or the sentence handed down. For various reasons, they might not be. But there is no obvious sense in which the outcome is a compromise between or among the contending parties.

Furthermore, in criminal trials, both the prosecution and the defense are made to operate according to relatively clear and fixed rules and procedures. Trials are thus solemn undertakings that underscore the extraordinary power of the state. Assuming that state officials act with appropriate seriousness and decorum, the authority of the state is not only vividly on display but typically reinforced.

Criminal trials are, of course, relatively rare and my contention has not been that plea bargaining should be abolished entirely in their favor. But plea bargaining, especially in its more robust forms, seems to convey very different messages to the public, and to would-be offenders, about criminal offending and the state's role in responding to it. First, plea negotiations are typically much less public forms of charge adjudication. They occur behind closed doors, and so outsiders to the process will lack any clear sense of what led to the ultimate disposition of cases.[35] True, defendants who plead guilty have to acknowledge their crimes. But they are not hauled before the court to answer to the charges and evidence against them as they would be forced to do in trials. It is sometimes noted with approval that plea bargaining enables defendants to avoid the expense and embarrassment of trials. What is less often noticed is that this might count against it if the public exposure that trials involve is itself beneficial. Some defendants might be chastened by the full exposure of their criminal conduct at their trials, with the result being a reawakening of their moral consciences and a recommitment to the values underlying the criminal law. By contrast, the more secretive nature of plea bargaining would seem to facilitate continued rationalization about criminal misconduct, denial of it, or self-deception with regard to it.

More significantly, robust forms of plea bargaining might be perceived as suggesting that the state is somewhat fickle or irresolute about the criminal prohibitions that it enacts and enforces. Sure, it adopts numerous criminal prohibitions and attaches sanctions to their violation, sometimes severe ones. But everyone knows that when it comes right down to it, many of those charged with crimes will be offered significantly reduced punishment in exchange for their guilty pleas. Even at the level of general deterrence, this might encourage some would-be offenders to believe that there is room for play in the system's joints—that they will likely not have to endure all of the punishment that is statutorily authorized for their crimes. Veterans of criminal justice systems in which plea bargaining is robust will know that they might not have to serve time for all of their offenses or most of the time for any of them. Beyond

---

[35] In the United States, for instance, only the plea colloquy is public and it might not reveal much of what has been agreed by prosecutors and defendants (or their attorneys) ahead of time.

this, however, are the seemingly corrosive messages that unrestrained plea bargaining sends about the seriousness with which state officials regard the laws they enforce. At the very least, the willingness of such officials to negotiate charges and sentences obscures to some extent the message about crime and its seriousness that we should want the criminal justice system to convey. Morality, religion, custom, and our own consciences tell us that things like murder, assault, and theft are wrong. But then we discover a freewheeling market in which state officials wrangle with criminal defendants (or, more likely, their attorneys) about how the state will officially respond to their acts. It is hard to see how the operations of such a system reinforce the notion that the moral norms underlying significant parts of the criminal law have an unstinting claim on our devotion.

The import of the preceding point should not be exaggerated. Most law-abiding citizens, especially those who are inclined to conform with the criminal law because it enforces legitimate moral norms or because they accept the authority of the state to regulate conduct, will not suddenly change their minds about doing so once apprised of plea bargaining's workings. They might lament its operations and could conceivably lose some respect for the legal officials who are perceived to be bartering with criminal offenders, but they are unlikely to conclude that they too should turn toward lives of crime. However, those citizens who are already offenders or attracted toward offending might draw less desirable conclusions once they see how the charge-adjudication system actually works. Not only might the existence of substantial and variable waiver rewards encourage them to have false hopes about the price of offending, but it could also breed cynicism in them about the strength of society's commitment to the criminal prohibitions that it enacts and enforces. When the "price" of crime is fungible, a different message is sent about the importance of the norms the law enforces to that sent when the "price" is not. Also, those attracted to offending may search more actively for ways to excuse or justify their conduct. Robust forms of plea bargaining seem to offer them more fertile grounds for rationalization.

Furthermore, veterans of the criminal justice system will know or suspect that clever, ruthless, brazen, or well-connected defendants manage to get better deals.[36] It would be naïve to believe that poorer or less well-connected members of the community have no inkling of the ways in which the system is worked by the better off to their advantage. Sure, we say that everyone is equal before the law, but the disadvantaged know or suspect that some citizens fare better than others when they get tangled up with it. Maybe this will not weaken their commitment to abide by its strictures, but it would not be surprising if it did.

Suppose, by contrast, that once prosecutors had filed charges, they had little discretion in bartering them away in exchange for guilty pleas. Suppose also that individuals charged with crimes faced a stark choice—plead guilty in exchange for modest

---

[36] For discussion of the wide variety of factors that ultimately affect plea negotiations, see Bibas (n 27 above) 2463–547.

and fixed sentence discounts, or go to trial and risk receiving the somewhat longer presumptive sentences announced by judges at settlement hearings. The inflexibility of such a system would, it seems, send a very different message about crime and its attendant sanctions. Potential offenders would know that if they committed crimes and were caught and charged with them, there would be little room for negotiation with the authorities. Such a system would send clear, firm, consistent signals that society is serious about the criminal prohibitions it has adopted and which it routinely enforces. This would affirm the importance of the criminal law's underlying moral norms. Individuals tempted to offend would, when confronted with such unwavering enforcement of the norms, have less room to try to convince themselves that no one really takes such standards seriously.

It might be objected that my portrayal of robust waiver-reward schemes is unfair in certain respects. Again, prosecutors or other state officials are more willing to negotiate with those they have charged with crimes when the offenses in question are low-level. Drug crimes, prostitution, public order offenses, and relatively minor forms of theft make up the majority of cases that prosecutors and judges process. Because they are inundated with such cases, state officials cut deals, sometimes generous ones, in order to process cases efficiently. But when the charges against individuals are grave, those same officials are much less inclined to negotiate, or, if they do so, offer handsome charge or sentence discounts.[37] Serious offenders are apt to receive stiff sentences, even if they plead guilty rather than proceed to trial. Neither they nor the public can reasonably infer from negotiated pleas in the other kinds of cases that weighty moral norms are being flouted with regularity by public officials.

Though there is something to this defense of large and variable waiver rewards, I am not convinced that it should completely allay our concerns that such rewards subtly undermine the ability of the criminal law to reinforce moral norms and command the presumptive support of citizens. In the first place, the objection concedes that there will be lots of cases in which prosecutors and judges do cut deals. Their willingness to do so would seem to convey something about the seriousness with which they take the prohibitions in question. Is it that the moral norm-reinforcement function of the criminal law matters less in relation to such prohibitions because the norms underlying them are not all that important? That would seem an unattractive position to defend. We might be better off without the prohibitions altogether than with variable and half-hearted enforcement of them. Also, the willingness of state officials to barter about punishment in low-stakes cases might be taken as a signal by some would-be offenders that those same officials will bargain when it comes to more serious offenses.

To make matters worse, anyone familiar with robust schemes of plea bargaining will suspect that the more robust forms are not strictly confined to the disposition

---

[37] See Bowers (n 21 above) 1154–5. See also W. J. Stuntz, "Plea Bargaining and the Criminal Law's Disappearing Shadow," [2004] 117 *Harv. L. Rev.* 2548, 2563–5.

of lower-level offenses. Sometimes prosecutors do negotiate when the crimes in question are grave, though perhaps less often to conserve scarce resources and more to secure convictions in cases in which the evidence against defendants is weak. Still, the motives of prosecutors might not matter much if what would-be offenders perceive is the continuation of all-too-familiar forms of charge and sentence bargaining.

In short, the availability of large and variable waiver rewards may have more subtle and complex effects on the frequency of criminal offending than proponents envision. True, such rewards might enable prosecutors to process more cases with their limited resources than alternative charge-adjudication schemes. This will increase the intensity of the deterrent signals sent by the criminal justice system. But, at the same time, large and variable waiver rewards might encourage offending by suggesting that the "price" for it is neither high nor uniform nor entirely inescapable. Robust forms of plea bargaining might also weaken the norm reinforcement effects of the criminal law by making offending appear less wrongful than it would appear under less "forgiving" charge-adjudication schemes. And the perception that state officials are not only willing to cut deals about charges and sentences, but also can be manipulated by clever or well-connected defense attorneys into offering better deals, might undermine their authority. Instead of punishment for crimes being determined by a formal, public, and dignified process, it will appear to be assigned, in the words of Robert Scott and William Stuntz, "through what looks like a street bazaar."[38]

Still, it must be conceded that my claims in this section are mostly speculative. In order to evaluate them, we would need more empirical information about the effects of competing charge-adjudication schemes on levels of offending. Cross-cultural criminologists might attempt to gather this kind of information, but it is hard to imagine how they could do so in a reliable fashion. It will not suffice, for instance, to compare the crime rates of countries in which prosecutors are given considerably less discretion to negotiate charges and sentences with those in countries that permit prosecutors much more leeway in this regard. Too many things affect crime rates besides the methods employed by the various criminal justice systems to detect and punish offenses. Indeed, it is not clear how we could devise a study that would hold all of those other factors constant and focus exclusively on charge-adjudication schemes and their effects. The truth is that we may be able to do little more than conjecture about these matters. If nothing else, I hope to have shown that proponents of large and variable waiver rewards have more work to do to convince us that such schemes are optimally crime-reducing.

---

[38] R. E. Scott and W. J. Stuntz, "Plea Bargaining as Contract," [1992] 101 *Yale L. J.* 1909, 1912.

Bringing the background forward: is more punishment always better?

At the outset, I noted that defenders of robust plea bargaining's role in reducing crime mostly take the larger criminal justice system's operations for granted. Again, this is not to say that they fail to express any concerns about the kinds of conduct criminalized or the ways in which such conduct is sanctioned. But they accept enough of the status quo to effectively neutralize it in their analyses of plea bargaining. My aim in this section is to bring forward what has, to this point, been in the background and use it to cast further doubt on the claim that robust plea bargaining's efficiency is a good thing. It might be if it were situated in a broader social and legal context that was well designed to discourage and prevent harmful and predatory conduct. But what if it is situated in a context that seems poorly constructed to perform these tasks? Then what?

My focus will be on the United States. Its legal and social system provides the larger context for Easterbrook's analysis, so it seems fair to subject his defense of plea bargaining to further scrutiny based on a more critical perspective of that context than he offers. We will thereby observe robust plea bargaining in its natural environs, so to speak, and thus discern to what extent it is apt to deliver on its promise to reduce crime. Granted, other societies have eschewed the neoliberal policies of the United States, policies I contend are dysfunctional if our aim is to reduce harmful or predatory conduct.[39] In such societies, the arguments developed so far against Easterbrook's defense of plea bargaining may well suffice. But we can deepen our understanding of the pitfalls of Easterbrook's position on plea bargaining by considering how unbridled forms of it play out in a decidedly non-ideal context. Securing the punishment of more offenders might not serve effectively the aims of crime reduction come what may.

Much of what I have to say about the ways in which the social and criminal justice system in the United States appears misguided in its efforts to reduce harmful conduct at reasonable cost has been said by others, so I will be somewhat brief with the arguments.[40] The US criminalizes too much and sometimes the wrong kinds of conduct. Overcriminalization gives police and prosecutors discretion that they appear to use inequitably, especially in the enforcement of certain kinds of criminal prohibitions. Criminal sanctions have been adopted that there is little reason to believe are optimally crime-reductive and that there is some reason to believe are actually counterproductive. Finally, efforts to control unwanted conduct by the threat of criminal

---

[39] For a useful survey of penal practices in their social and political contexts throughout the world, see M. Cavadino and J. Dignan, *Penal Systems: A Comparative Approach* (London: Sage Publications, 2006).

[40] See, for instance, Currie (n 9 above) and Tonry (n 9 above), as well as F. E. Zimring and G. Hawkins, *Crime Is Not the Problem: Lethal Violence in America* (Oxford: Oxford University Press, 1997).

sanctions often occur in the midst of increasing social and economic inequality, with its apparent tendency to foster offending.

Consider, first, the overcriminalization of conduct. As we noted earlier in relation to a retributive approach to legal punishment, a crime reduction approach to justifying punishment makes more sense if we take the concept of crime with which it operates to be a normative one. No clear-thinking crime reductionist wants to be stuck justifying the punishment of individuals who have committed "crimes" in a society that criminalizes every conceivable kind of behavior, whether it harms or threatens anyone or not.[41] In the main, what crime reductionists should want to punish (and thereby reduce) is behavior that harms or threatens to harm the lives, liberty, or property of others.[42] They may also have to accept the criminalization of conduct violating rules coordinating social behavior or allocating access to scarce resources of various kinds. But crime on such an account of punishment's justification should be understood as wrongful or unjustified conduct (according to some moral or political theory), not simply as conventionally outlawed conduct. If this is correct, then a persuasive case can be made that the overcriminalization of conduct is a pervasive phenomenon in the United States.[43] In particular, there is a tendency to criminalize conduct on hard paternalist grounds or legal moralist grounds, both of which are suspect.[44] There has also been substantial growth in the number of *mala prohibita*, as well as in ancillary or redundant offenses. The moral credentials of some of these prohibitions are suspect, and even in cases where they are not, violations of them are often punished excessively.[45] Ironically, one way to quickly reduce crime and the burdens it creates for police and prosecutors would be to eliminate some of these criminal prohibitions.

Though obvious in certain respects, the preceding point is of considerable relevance to the debate about plea bargaining. It is clear that its emergence, in the United States at least, had much to do with so-called "morals offenses," and plea bargaining's seeming inescapability in the contemporary context is arguably sustained by the continued prohibition of conduct that should not be criminalized at all or to such a significant extent.[46] In the United States, between 20 and 30 percent of those

---

[41] Again, see Bentham (n 2 above) chapter 13.

[42] Cf. D. J. Baker, "Constitutionalizing the Harm Principle," [2008] 27 *Criminal Justice Ethics* 3.

[43] See D. N. Husak, *Overcriminalization: The Limits of the Criminal Law* (New York: Oxford University Press, 2008). See also W. J. Stuntz, "The Pathological Politics of Criminal Law," [2001] 100 *Mich. L. Rev.* 505.

[44] Joel Feinberg exposes the flaws in hard paternalist and legal moralist justifications of criminal prohibitions, respectively, in *Harm to Self* (New York: Oxford University Press, 1986) and *Harmless Wrongdoing* (New York: Oxford University Press, 1990).

[45] See Husak (n 43 above) 103–19.

[46] For discussion of the historical tie between plea bargaining and laws regulating the use and sale of liquor, see G. Fisher, *Plea Bargaining's Triumph: A History of Plea Bargaining in America* (Stanford, Cal.: Stanford University Press, 2003) 19–39.

currently imprisoned are serving time for possessing and trafficking illegal drugs.[47] The burdens of such "crimes" on prosecutors and the courts are much greater than this, of course, since many more individuals are, in other ways, under the purview of the criminal justice system due to such offenses. Importantly, even if no additional resources were devoted to the enforcement of the criminal law, resources could be conserved within the criminal justice system by reducing, if not eliminating, criminal prohibitions which are, at best, tangentially related to the reduction of actions harmful to others.[48] Internal reallocation of such resources might enable prosecutors and the courts to provide more trial adjudication of charges if it turned out that substantial curtailment of plea bargaining appeared advisable on other grounds within an optimal crime reduction scheme.

A further significant aspect of overcriminalization is the discretion it gives police and prosecutors. Again, as William Stuntz has shown persuasively, the criminalization of so much conduct makes it impossible for the authorities to actually arrest and prosecute all of the people who commit crimes. Lots of people use drugs, for instance, but for complicated reasons, the police tend to focus their energies on minorities and the poor in making arrests.[49] Such inequities in policing, I have already suggested, may well be understood by those who are disadvantaged and will likely contribute to their alienation from societal norms in ways that exacerbate their offending. This is bad enough from a crime reduction perspective. But, as we have seen, overcriminalization, with its creation of numerous overlapping and duplicative offenses, empowers prosecutors to engage in charge-stacking.[50] Many legal commentators believe that prosecutors avidly use their charging discretion to put pressure on those arrested for crimes. Faced with multiple counts, the total sentences of which add up to many years of imprisonment, criminal defendants are eager, if not desperate, to strike deals with prosecutors to gain some measure of lenity in exchange for their guilty pleas. Set to one side the concern that this might produce guilty pleas by individuals who are actually innocent of all charges against them. The larger problem is that overcharging, combined with robust and variable waiver rewards, compromises the ability of the criminal justice system to produce sentences that are optimally crime-reductive. Suppose that statutorily authorized sentences have been devised such that, in each case, the sentence range for an offense is based on a weighing of the relevant benefits and costs. Charge-stacking threatens offenders with excessive and therefore

---

[47] See "Drug Use and Dependence, State and Federal Prisoners, 2004," Bureau of Justice Statistics, Special Report (October 2006), at http://bjs.ojp.usdoj.gov/content/pub/pdf/dudsfp04.pdf (accessed July 2, 2011). The report notes that 21 percent of state and 55 percent of federal prisoners are incarcerated for drug crimes (see p. 4).

[48] For a persuasive attempt to show how drug prohibition is, at best, indirectly related to the prevention of harm, see D. N. Husak, "Guns and Drugs: Case Studies on the Principled Limits of the Criminal Sanction," [2004] 23 *Law and Philosophy* 437.

[49] Stuntz (n 43 above) 573–6. See also Stuntz's "Race, Class, and Drugs," [1998] 98 *Colum. L. Rev.* 1795.

[50] Stuntz (n 43 above) 520.

counterproductive sentences. Their harmful conduct (assuming it was harmful) has not changed; all that has changed is the number and kind of charges that prosecutors are empowered to bring against them. Trial penalties work in similar fashion and, when combined with charge-stacking, menace offenders with horrifically long sentences. Robust waiver rewards might work to bring sentences that are artificially elevated in these ways back in line with more optimally crime-reductive ones. But whether or not they will do so is entirely unpredictable. Depending on a range of factors, they could just as easily produce overly short or long sentences. Why any crime reductionist would applaud such a haphazard process for assigning sentences is unclear. Surely we would be more likely to produce optimal sentences if prosecutors were required to charge veridically and recommend sentences from within relevant sentencing ranges that were themselves devised with crime reduction goals firmly in mind.

Perhaps Easterbrook could be convinced by arguments such as these that strategic overcharging and trial penalties should be prohibited or at least strongly discouraged. He might hold out for the negotiation of substantial and variable sentence discounts, but nothing more. However, this brings us to the next problem: There is little reason to believe that current sentencing levels are anything near optimal. Though the debate is complex and contentious, it can be argued that sentencing levels in the United States are counterproductive if the aim is to reduce crime while minimizing the substantial costs legal punishment imposes on all citizens. There has been a gradual ratcheting up of sentences over the last 30 years for all offenses. Perhaps the safest thing to say is that there is little reason to believe that current sentencing schemes have been set with an eye on the evidence about their crime reduction potential, the costs and burdens they create, and their alternatives. Again, the information and calculation requirements for producing an optimal crime reduction sentencing scheme are formidable. Yet numerous authorities who have examined the empirical evidence conclude that there appears to be little relationship between longer sentences and increased deterrence, an uncertain relationship between such sentences and reduced crime via incapacitation, and almost no reason to believe that such sentences rehabilitate offenders.[51] But sentences continue to inch upward in spite of this. In addition, even if the United States could imprison its way to reduced crime levels, there would still be the enormous economic and social costs of attempting to do so, costs that appear insufficiently taken into account by proponents of longer sentences. Again, imprisonment is hugely expensive to the public and has adverse collateral effects on the spouses and dependents of inmates. It is also terrifically damaging to the life-prospects of those made to endure it.[52]

[51] On the lack of correlation between longer sentences and deterrence, see the sources cited in n 13 above. On the tenuous relationship between longer sentences and incapacitation, see Zimring and Hawkins (n 19 above) 60–75.

[52] Again, see Western (n 3 above).

Moreover, the costs of increasingly lengthy punishment have arguably been exacerbated by the emphasis on offenders doing "hard time" while they are imprisoned.
In the United States, rehabilitation programs of all kinds have been cut back, in part,
because the rush to imprison more individuals for longer periods of time has strained
prison budgets.[53] Such programs have also been abandoned because of doubts in
the minds of many politicians and members of the public about whether offenders
deserve any help in turning their lives around or whether they actually benefit from
efforts to provide such help. Yet it seems clear that subjecting inmates to months if
not years of idleness and social isolation, with all of the pathologies they breed, cannot be expected to produce optimal crime reduction outcomes. Most prison inmates
will eventually be released and it is doubtful that current forms of imprisonment do
anything to strengthen inmates' attachment to acceptable moral norms. The United
States would do better, it seems, to adopt the "resocialization" aim of imprisonment
that is the norm in many European countries, according to which prisons are to be
organized and administered to help offenders emerge from them better prepared to
lead productive, law-abiding lives.[54]

Still, shorter sentences and more humane prisons might not reduce crime in the
long term if many offenders return to economically blighted communities that afford
them few opportunities to live meaningful, law-abiding lives. Hence, another way
in which to reduce the burdens on the criminal justice system would be to undertake
broader societal reforms aimed at addressing the social deprivation that seems at the
root of certain kinds of criminal offending. Again, the deeper logic of the crime
reduction approach requires doing more than adopting reforms in the current ways
in which legal punishment is structured and delivered; alternatives to punishment
that might reduce offending more cost-effectively should also be considered.

There is, it must be admitted, debate about the relationship between social deprivation and crime, but I would argue that its worrisome effects from a crime reduction perspective should be conceptualized along three dimensions.[55] First, the
substantially diminished opportunities some citizens have will make certain kinds
of illicit conduct more attractive. Individuals who have few legal avenues along
which they can effectively pursue their interests will turn to illegal ones, especially
if they are lucrative.[56] Second, and as I noted in Chapter 4, severe social deprivation
may undermine the capacities constitutive of responsible citizenship. The children

---

[53] See Currie (n 9 above) 164–5; Haney (n 3 above) 57–90; and D. Garland, *The Culture of Control:
Crime and Social Order in Contemporary Society* (Chicago: University of Chicago Press, 2001) 53–74.

[54] For discussion of "resocialization" as the official aim of imprisonment in Germany, see L. Lazarus,
Contrasting Prisoners' Rights: A Comparative Examination of Germany and England (Oxford: Oxford
University Press, 2004) 37–43.

[55] A good sense of that debate can be gleaned from the essays collected in W. C. Heffernan and
J. Kleinig, *From Social Justice to Criminal Justice: Poverty and the Administration of Criminal Law* (New York:
Oxford University Press, 2000). My claims in this chapter are based, in part, on those developed earlier
in Lippke (n 10 above) 84–98.

[56] See R. B. Freeman, "Why Do So Many Young American Men Commit Crimes and What Might
We Do About It?" [1996] 10 *Journal of Economic Perspectives* 25.

of the severely socially deprived seem most vulnerable in this regard, as they are less likely (for complicated reasons) to be guided and supervised in ways that enable them to avoid stunted or warped moral personalities. Young people, in general, seem prone to irrationally discounting future negative outcomes and amenable to peer pressure.[57] These tendencies may be exacerbated by flawed upbringings that leave them fixated on short-term personal gratification at the expense of the public good. Third, awareness among the socially deprived of their marginalized social and economic status often alienates them from the social order, including many of the law's animating moral norms.[58] Those who do not embrace those norms, but who instead view them as standards serving others' interests, or who regard the law's enforcers as hostile forces, seem more likely, in general, to engage in conduct that is quite properly prohibited. They also might be more prone to offend against legal rules that do not, in any obvious way, protect others' legitimate interests but simply express society's (or some influential portion of its members') disapproval of certain forms of conduct, ones that the poor often find lucrative. Further, we might worry that such cynicism about *mala prohibita* seeps over into *mala in se*.[59]

Viewed in its entirety, the current approach in the United States to reducing conduct that threatens the lives, bodies, or property of others seems poorly designed to achieve its purpose. Conduct is criminalized that does not threaten harm to others at all, or not very directly, and thus requires the authorities to invest scarce resources in pursuing and punishing such conduct. Little is done to diminish the incentives to commit crimes or discourage the development of stunted moral personalities that make people susceptible to seeing offending as a viable option. In lieu of adopting these more fruitful harm reduction strategies, offenders are threatened with longer and harsher sanctions, and prosecutors and the courts are empowered to employ them, with all of their costly and counterproductive effects.

Against this backdrop, we return to the questions of whether, or to what extent, substantial and variable waiver rewards can be defended from within a crime reduction perspective. Suppose that, contrary to what I have argued previously in the chapter, granting prosecutors the authority to offer such rewards would enable them to process significantly more cases than any of the other negotiated settlement schemes available to us. Is it any longer so clear that this increase in punishment output is a

[57] See F. E. Zimring, "Toward a Jurisprudence of Youth Violence," 24 *Crime and Justice: A Review of Research* [1998] 477, 485–90.

[58] For development of the view that social deprivation produces alienation, see J. G. Murphy, "Marxism and Retribution," 2 *Philosophy and Public Affairs* [1973] 217.

[59] There is no use denying that concerted effort to reduce social deprivation, especially by raising the welfare floor, would be costly to those members of society who would have to provide the needed tax revenues. But again, legal punishment in its current forms is also quite costly to those same individuals and seemingly counterproductive, in the longer term, if our aim is to reduce offending. Arguably, we could achieve reduced levels of criminal offending by creating social conditions that enabled more citizens to embrace the norms underlying the criminal law because they had more and better stable opportunities for pursuing their interests and were better equipped (in the sense of having properly developed moral personalities) to do so.

good thing if our aim is to reduce conduct that is genuinely harmful to others? If the increase meant that more serious offenders, whose crimes harmed or threatened their fellow citizens' legitimate interests, were punished with optimally crime reductive sentences, then that would be one thing. Yet increases in the scope of punishment may not often or usually produce outcomes of this sort in circumstances of overcriminalization and excessive sanctions. Instead, robust forms of plea bargaining may simply make it possible for prosecutors to punish more offenders for crimes that should not be crimes in the first place, or punish them in ways that are counterproductive, given what we know or suspect about the kinds of sentences that would reduce offending at reasonable cost.[60] Moreover, given the tendency of social deprivation to generate offending, and the ways in which the exercise of broad police and prosecutorial discretion tends to produce inequities in the arrest and prosecution of minority members and the poor for moral offenses, a disproportionately high number of those who are shoved into the maw of the criminal justice system by plea bargaining will be individuals whose life prospects were bleak to begin with and for whom these will be made bleaker still by their exposure to unjustifiably long and harsh prison sentences. Such an outcome seems unlikely to result in reduced offending levels in the long term.

In short, in the context of a dysfunctional social and criminal justice system, plea bargaining's role as a vital tool that enables prosecutors to keep the punishment machine running smoothly and efficiently appears anything but benign. Heretical as it might seem to say so, perhaps we would be better off with charge-adjudication schemes that clogged up, or at least slowed down, the criminal justice system's ability to manufacture mass punishment, especially if we are unwilling to undertake the broader social and criminal justice reforms that are needed.

It might be objected that by keeping the criminal justice system running smoothly under the current, suboptimal scheme, large and variable waiver rewards play a vital crime reduction role. Since we are unlikely to do anything in the short term about social deprivation, society is better off in two ways by having an efficient mechanism for assigning offenders their sanctions.[61] First, by speeding the assignment of some punishment or other, robust forms of plea bargaining make more vivid the threat that the criminal justice system poses to would-be offenders. By contrast, the overburdened court system that we would have in the absence of robust plea bargaining would give offenders hope. Even if they were apprehended, nothing might come of it. Beleaguered prosecutors would be forced to dismiss charges in lots of cases. Perceiving this, more individuals would risk going forward with their crimes. Second, the harsh sanctions that the criminal justice system currently employs are, in fact, not so suboptimal, given the perverse incentives to commit crimes created by

---

[60] Again, as legal scholars have argued, prosecutors have powerful incentives to pursue serious offenders, even if doing so exacts a toll on their resources. The most likely effect of expanding their resources is that it will enable them to pursue more lower-level offenders. See Stuntz (n 37 above) 2563–4.

[61] Cf. Easterbrook (n 1 above) 309.

social deprivation. Long sentences serve to counteract social deprivation's criminogenic tendencies or, failing that, at least keep offenders locked up for significant periods of time.

Neither of these arguments is terribly convincing. Again, how much of an increase we would see in the demand for trials under more limited waiver-reward schemes is anyone's guess, but they seem unlikely to produce hopelessly overburdened courts. As we have seen, the majority of cases processed by the criminal justice system involve low-level offenses. The "process costs" of trials in such cases make plea deals overwhelmingly attractive to defendants.[62] Even fixed, modest sentence discounts will attract guilty pleas in most of these cases. Also, we should consider how prosecutors, faced with increased demand for trials, might respond. One likely outcome is that they would have to forgo the prosecution of some low-level offenses. Would their doing so be a bad thing if we are mindful of both the need to reduce truly harmful conduct and to do so in ways that are not inordinately costly and, indeed, likely to produce more such conduct? Arguably not, especially if many of the charges dropped were for conduct that should not be criminalized in the first place or punished so harshly as to be counterproductive. Another thing that prosecutors might have to do is drop overlapping or redundant charges against defendants in an effort to induce them to plead guilty to the remaining charges. Since overcharging is apt to produce sentences that are not optimally crime-reductive, this too might produce better overall outcomes.

Furthermore, as we have seen, the evidence about the marginal deterrent effects of harsher sanctions is, at best, unimpressive.[63] There appears to be no strong correlation between marginal increases in the severity of sentences and desistance from crime. There are various hypotheses about why this might be, two of which have direct relevance to the situation of the socially deprived. First, such individuals have less to lose by risking entanglement with the criminal justice system than do citizens who have a stable stake in the social and economic order. Second, in communities in which large numbers of citizens are or have been imprisoned, the stigma of imprisonment may be diminished.[64] Worse than this, it may enhance the social status of citizens who believe themselves unfairly targeted by the authorities or excluded from society's benefits.[65] With regard to punishment's incapacitation effects, matters are more complex. Punishment, especially when it takes the form of imprisonment, does

---

[62] Again, see Feeley (n 21 above) 199–243, and Bowers (n 21 above) 1132–45.

[63] von Hirsch, et al., *Criminal Deterrence and Sentence Severity* (n 13 above) 47. See also Doob and Webster (n 13 above) 143–95.

[64] See D. S. Nagin, "Criminal Deterrence Research at the Outset of the Twenty-First Century," [1998] 23 *Crime and Justice: A Review of Research* 1, 22.

[65] It might be suggested that we could enhance punishment's limited marginal deterrence effects by employing draconian sentences—that perhaps it is relatively small increases in the severity of punishment that account for its unimpressive crime reduction performance. Though it is uncertain whether or not this hypothesis has been tested by criminologists, the logic of crime reduction probably does not support it due to the substantial negative consequences that would result from draconian sentences.

incapacitate offenders. But as we have seen, whether it actually reduces crimes in the communities from whence offenders come depends on a host of factors.[66] Many of the crimes committed by the socially deprived are property and drug offenses. Yet it is precisely those types of offenses that imprisonment is less likely to reduce in communities. Moreover, the costs and burdens of imprisonment, when it is used to punish minor to moderate property offenders or drug offenders, will often swamp the social costs of their offenses.[67]

Still, I would concede that in the context of a poorly designed criminal justice system, the modifications in plea bargaining which I have advocated in previous chapters—involving the substantial curtailment of charge bargaining combined with modest sentence discounts—would not have entirely benign implications for criminal defendants. If we hold most everything else about the status quo constant, modest capped or fixed waiver rewards would tend to produce longer, and hence more costly and destructive, sanctions for many defendants who plead guilty. Indeed, a stronger case for large and variable waiver rewards could be made if their proponents were willing to eschew trial penalties and the use of strategic overcharging by prosecutors. For then no defendants would receive the excessively long sentences that such practices sometimes produce.[68] The question would then be whether we are better off, overall, permitting prosecutors more or less leeway in negotiating sentences, or perhaps no leeway at all. It seems clear that some defendants would wind up better off if prosecutors could offer large waiver rewards than if they could only offer smaller ones, or if modest, fixed discounts were the only ones available. This is a point in favor of allowing prosecutors greater discretion. However, as we have seen, the more freewheeling kinds of plea bargaining may undermine the ability of the criminal justice system to send clear, firm, consistent messages about the wrongfulness of certain kinds of conduct. That might reduce their overall effectiveness when compared with adjudication schemes that afford prosecutors less scope to barter.[69]

---

[66] Zimring and Hawkins (n 19 above) 53–6.

[67] Though this will not be true for "high-rate" offenders. See D. S. Nagin, "Deterrence and Incapacitation," in M. Tonry (ed.), *The Handbook of Crime and Punishment* (New York: Oxford University Press, 1998) 345, 362–4.

[68] As occurred, notoriously, in *Bordenkircher v. Hayes*, 434 US 357 (1978).

[69] Michael O'Hear has argued persuasively that part of what determines how those convicted of crimes react to their punishment is their perception of the procedural justice of their convictions. Defendants who believe that the authorities have at least listened to their side of the story and have treated them respectfully throughout the plea adjudication process are more likely to accept the fairness of their punishment. Importantly, there is evidence suggesting that offenders who are more accepting of their punishment are more amenable to rehabilitation and likely to refrain from future offending. Of course, there is no guarantee that under a charge-adjudication system in which waiver rewards are modest, prosecutors will do a better job of listening to defendants or treating them respectfully than they would under a scheme in which such rewards are more generous. But the powers currently granted to prosecutors go well beyond permitting them to negotiate large and variable waiver rewards, encompassing charge-stacking and threats of trial penalties. These tactics are routinely employed to put overwhelming pressure on defendants to plead guilty. It would not be surprising to find that many defendants resent being pressured in these ways, and that this undermines their sense that they have been treated fairly by the authorities. Though it is possible to defend robust waiver rewards while rejecting

A larger, more disturbing point is this: Neither scheme of charge adjudication is apt to have more than marginal impact on our ability to reduce harmful conduct, especially within a larger social and criminal justice system that is badly designed to prevent such conduct. If what we want to do is minimize harmful behavior in society, we would do better, arguably, to focus on decreasing social deprivation, eliminating criminal prohibitions that are only tangentially related to the prevention of harm but which expose citizens to damaging forms of punishment, and rethinking our approach to punishment, resorting less often to imprisonment, and to more humane and rehabilitative forms when we do employ it.

Concluding remarks

The conclusions reached in this chapter can be summarized as follows: There seems little reason to believe that more robust forms of plea bargaining have superior crime reduction credentials when compared with more limited forms if the social and legal status quo is taken as a given. Limiting prosecutorial discretion to engage in charge or sentence bargaining is unlikely to produce significant increases in the demand for trials. Moreover, doing so might lessen the damaging perception that society is not entirely serious about the criminal prohibitions that it enacts, or fair in its enforcement of them. Once a critical perspective on the social and legal status quo is introduced, the vaunted ability of robust plea bargaining to amass convictions appears a mixed blessing. The criminal law and the institutions that serve it may not be protecting us from truly harmful conduct in ways that are reliable or do more good than harm. Nonetheless, modifications in plea bargaining, all by themselves, will do little to help matters. We would likely achieve better outcomes by reducing overcriminalization in all of its forms and improving the social and economic lot of the disadvantaged.

With respect to the larger themes of this book, the lesson of this chapter is that the logic of crime reduction offers little support for large and variable waiver rewards, awarded at the discretion of prosecutors and the courts. The claims that such rewards are necessary for keeping an overburdened criminal justice system afloat, and therefore useful in combating crime, are more often casually asserted than carefully defended.

---

charge-stacking and threats of trial penalties, it is important to note the way in which the powers currently granted to prosecutors may work against the goal of crime reduction. For O'Hear's discussion, see his "Plea Bargaining and Procedural Justice," [2008] 42 *Ga. L. Rev.* 407.

6

Rewarding Cooperation

Some of the individuals who are formally accused of crimes will encounter the unpleasant prospect that should they insist on going to trial, they will have to endure damaging testimony from other individuals with whom they (allegedly, we should say) criminally associated. This incriminating evidence might have been procured by state officials through promises of charge or sentence reductions for the accomplices in question. To this point, we have focused on reductions in the punishment assigned offenders in exchange for their admissions of guilt—reductions that I have termed "waiver rewards." Yet punishment reductions are also made available for defendants who cooperate in testifying or otherwise providing evidence against their accomplices in crime. The two kinds of punishment reductions often go hand-in-hand, of course, but for analytic purposes we can separate them. My focus in this chapter will be on the second kind of reduction, which I term "cooperation rewards."

Cooperation rewards have become a fixture of plea bargaining in the United States. So familiar and seemingly inevitable is this form of plea negotiation by prosecutors and charged defendants that even one of plea bargaining's most persistent critics at one point defended it, suggesting that it did not really amount to plea bargaining proper.[1] Gaining such rewards has assumed special urgency in an era of mandatory minimum sentencing and Federal Sentencing Guidelines.[2] Criminal defendants who face formidable sentences and have few prospects for leniency otherwise are eager, perhaps desperate, to offer the authorities "substantial assistance" and thereby reduce the time they will wind up spending behind bars. Defendants who earn both waiver and cooperation rewards could see substantial reductions in the sentences they serve for their crimes. It might be hoped that the practice of offering cooperation rewards is one that will remain peculiar to the United States, with its unrestrained forms of plea bargaining. But the practice appears to be spreading. Since 2005, under the auspices of the Serious Organized Crime and Police Act, British prosecutors have been authorized to enter into cooperation agreements with defendants which might earn the latter substantial charge or sentencing leniency.[3] It might be too early to tell how

[1] A. W. Alschuler, "Plea Bargaining and Its History," [1979] 79 *Colum. L. Rev.* 1, 4.

[2] J. Standen, "Plea Bargaining in the Shadow of the Guidelines," [1993] 81 *Cal. L. Rev.* 1471, and C. K. Y. Lee, "Prosecutorial Discretion, Substantial Assistance, and the Federal Sentencing Guidelines," [1994] 42 *UCLA L. Rev.* 105.

[3] See N. Vamos, "Please Don't Call it 'Plea Bargaining'," [2009] 2009 *Crim. L. Rev.* 617, 627.

widespread the use of cooperation rewards will become in England and Wales. But the challenges state officials face in detecting or gathering sufficient evidence concerning certain kinds of crimes will make the use of such rewards enticing.

There are numerous potent objections to the practice of offering cooperation rewards. First, it appears to promote absolute injustice by enabling individuals who have committed numerous crimes to evade punishment for some of them and proportionate punishment for some or all of them. As such, cooperation rewards seem at odds with retributive accounts of sentencing, according to which individuals should have to endure sanctions proportional with the seriousness of (all of) their crimes.[4] Moreover, there is something troubling about rewarding individuals for fulfilling what might appear to be obligations on their part. Consider cases in which individuals have committed crimes that involve serious moral wrongs such as rape or murder. In such cases, individuals arguably have a moral duty to admit their crimes when confronted by the authorities and provide incriminating evidence against others with whom they acted. Though we expect people to meet their obligations, and might be prepared to penalize them if they do not, we usually do not reward them for doing so. Yet charge or sentence concessions appear to do just that.

Second, cooperation rewards appear to promote comparative injustice.[5] If S and T have committed crimes of equal seriousness, and the only reason S receives a reduced sentence is because S agreed first to provide incriminating evidence against T, nothing about S's readiness to cooperate changes the essential nature of the crimes S committed. Why, then, should S be punished any differently from T?

Third, cooperation rewards seem likely to yield unreliable evidence. Those prepared or eager to cooperate with authorities might be expected to downplay their own culpability regarding their crimes, while distorting or exaggerating that of their accomplices, in order to secure the best possible deals for themselves.[6] Concerns about the reliability of such evidence are heightened when the plea agreements are contingent upon individuals doing more than fully and accurately revealing what they know, but rather upon helping prosecutors successfully secure convictions of additional suspects.[7] In cases in which charge or sentence reductions are made contingent

---

[4] It is also not apparent how well substantial charge or sentence reductions comport with the deterrent or incapacitation aims of legal punishment. However, I focus, for the most part, on the relationship between cooperation rewards and deserved punishment.

[5] D. C. Richman, "Cooperating Defendants: The Costs and Benefits of Purchasing Information from Scoundrels," [1996] 8 *Federal Sentencing Reporter* 292, and I. Weinstein, "Regulating the Market for Snitches," [1999] 47 *Buff. L. Rev.* 563.

[6] It has sometimes been claimed that cooperation rewards are suspect because they are tantamount to bribery by prosecutors. See the discussion in G. C. Harris, "Testimony for Sale: The Law and Ethics of Snitches and Experts," [2000] 28 *Pepp. L. Rev.* 1, 9. But bribery is wrong because it attempts to induce individuals to ignore wrongdoing or illegality, which it is their responsibility to police or regulate, or because it tempts individuals to engage in wrongdoing or illegality. Cooperation rewards need not do either of these, at least if those to whom they are given testify truthfully about what they know (either pre-trial or during a trial).

[7] See Y. A. Beeman, "Note: Accomplice Testimony Under Contingent Plea Agreements," [1987] 72 *Cornell L. Rev.* 799.

upon prosecutorial success at convicting others, as they sometimes are in the United States, cooperators must worry that truthful testimony that does not sufficiently incriminate others will lead prosecutors to renege on their promises of cooperation rewards. Given the enormous discretion that prosecutors possess in determining who will receive cooperation rewards, defendants have powerful incentives to please prosecutors at some predictable cost to their truthfulness in revealing what they and their accomplices have done.[8] Furthermore, plea bargains in exchange for accomplice testimony reduce the incentives that police investigators and prosecutors have to develop or pursue other, more reliable sources of evidence.

Fourth, cooperation rewards encourage individuals to betray their former friends or associates. Yet betrayal is usually considered ignoble, and the term "snitch," used to characterize those who turn against their accomplices, is an epithet of near universal scorn. If loyalty is a good thing, and betrayal a bad one, is there not some cost to plea bargaining practices that penalize the former and encourage the latter?[9]

Though some of the preceding problems with cooperation rewards can be shown to be more apparent than real, or minimized if we adopt limits on the magnitude of such rewards and reduce the unilateral control prosecutors have over their allocation, I contend that the practice remains a morally troublesome one. In analyzing and evaluating cooperation rewards, it is crucial, once again, to distinguish what we might say about them under certain ideal conditions from what we might say about them if we adopt a critical perspective on current social and criminal justice practices. It is one thing to analyze cooperation rewards on the following assumptions: We live in a reasonably just society that affords all citizens opportunities to pursue their interests within legitimate moral bounds; those charged with crimes are not targeted, in part, because they are socially disadvantaged, rather they are charged with violating criminal prohibitions that any decent society must enact and enforce, and face sanctions proportionate with the seriousness of their offenses. It is quite another if some or all of these assumptions are routinely not satisfied. Yet, as we have seen in previous chapters, overcriminalization, policing inequities, and severe social deprivation compromise the ability of the criminal justice system to produce reasonable and just outcomes.

Cooperation rewards are troubling enough in criminal justice systems that are just in their operations. They are more troubling still in the context of criminal justice systems that have gone off the rails in significant respects. I am not convinced that we can fix the problems with cooperation rewards by limiting their size or the discretion prosecutors have over them, though I agree that doing both of these things is a good idea. There are circumstances in which prosecutors appear to have few viable options but to employ cooperation rewards. If the crimes they can thereby effect punishment

---

[8] There is considerable debate about the wisdom of such prosecutorial discretion. See Lee (n 2 above) 149–74, and Weinstein (n 5 above) 601–25.
[9] Cf. Weinstein (n 5 above) 621–5.

of are serious enough and significant in number, and no other viable options for resolving them exist, then prosecutors, perhaps with the aid and oversight of the courts, might be permitted to use cooperation rewards. The problem is that such special conditions do not always exist and, increasingly perhaps, tend not to.

Rewarding betrayal, penalizing loyalty

The concern that cooperation rewards encourage betrayal, and thereby undermine the value of loyalty, might seem the one that is most easily addressed. For even if loyalty is a good thing, *ceteris paribus*, arguably it is not a good thing when shown toward groups engaged in nefarious activities. Especially in cases in which the criminal activities under investigation have resulted in serious harms to innocent citizens, we might very much want the individuals involved to betray their former associates so that they can be brought to justice. Still, is there not some taint to a person's character in the betrayal of his or her criminal confederates? Part of the reason why loyalty is prized is because it motivates individuals to delay their own gratification, or perhaps sacrifice it altogether, in cooperative efforts with others aimed at achieving common goals. The betrayals that charge or sentence concessions induce are doubly shocking—not only are commitments to a common enterprise abandoned, but narrow self-interest reasserts itself in the guise of efforts by those who betray to save their own skins. It is possible, of course, that cooperators have undergone genuine changes of heart, such that they now recognize the dubious character of their former criminal activities. If so, we might have more respect for them if they publicly renounced their offending, supplied the authorities with whatever incriminating evidence they had, and embraced the full measure of punishment for their misconduct. The willingness to take concessions, or worse to seek them out, suggests that they are attempting to evade some responsibility for their former activities. By contrast, there is something almost honorable about the offender who, in word or in deed, says "I am no better than any of my former associates and should be punished like them."

It might be thought that there is some residual disvalue to the induced betrayal of former criminal associates if loyalty is a virtue that the government should encourage, or at least not seek to discourage. Whatever good purposes are served by such betrayals, they nonetheless might be thought to marginally diminish the ability or willingness of individuals to trust and work together with their fellow citizens.[10] In doing so, such betrayals make some contribution to a general climate of suspicion or distrust, one that is antithetical to the formation of bonds of loyalty. This concern about induced accomplice testimony might be bolstered by noting that not all of the groups betrayed will have been formed specifically for the purpose of engaging in criminal activities. Sometimes organizations whose primary purposes are entirely legitimate, even laudatory, gradually drift over into illicit activities. And

---

[10] Weinstein makes this point as well (n 5 above) 624–5.

some groups, a substantial portion of whose activities are criminal, also fulfill other important functions for their members, such as providing social or economic support, or serving to bolster the self-esteem of otherwise socially marginalized individuals. Hence, official inducements to betrayal would seem to subtly discourage the formation of social bonds of quite diverse and not altogether deleterious kinds.

It seems doubtful, however, that cooperation rewards offered in exchange for accomplice testimony will have significant repercussions for the willingness of individuals to form social bonds with others. R. E. Ewin argues persuasively that our tendency to forge such bonds is deeply ingrained in our social natures.[11] Indeed, Ewin goes so far as to argue that loyalty is not really a virtue, but instead the "raw material" for the exercise of the virtues (and vices) through its creation of social networks within which individuals must then make the problematic choices with which the virtues are centrally concerned.[12] Even if we do not go this far with Ewin, he is probably correct in suggesting that humans cannot be easily discouraged from forming social bonds. The key, as Ewin notes, is to encourage them to be more discriminating in doing so. But there seems little reason to believe that we will sow the seeds of social mistrust in any general or significant way if we occasionally induce individuals to abandon dysfunctional or harmful social groups.

The idea that certain types of loyalty are misplaced and so justifiably undermined might seem to dispose entirely of the objection that cooperation rewards have some taint because they induce betrayal. However, there are complications here that should not go unnoticed. For one thing, we seem unwilling to take some of the steps necessary to discourage the formation of groups, some or all of whose activities involve criminality. As Ewin notes, if loyalty is natural to people, we should expect them to form bad loyalties if they are socially marginalized and excluded from good ones.[13] Those deprived of other viable options for advancing their interests may be drawn toward associations that involve, to a greater or lesser extent, criminality. That is bad enough if we are at all concerned about the social conditions in which legal punishment can be justifiably inflicted.[14] What seems worse is the expectation that such individuals should, when arrested and charged with crimes, betray their confederates in the interests of loyalty to a larger community which does not do enough to protect their rights or advance their welfare. Granted, if the crimes that the socially deprived are involved in are grave enough, we might act reasonably in prodding them to betray their associates. But sometimes their illicit activities will be ones that arguably should not be proscribed in the first place, or, though they should be proscribed, should be punished less harshly than the law requires, or are crimes engaged in by many

---

[11] R. E. Ewin, "Loyalty and Virtues," [1992] 42 *Philosophical Quarterly* 403, 413. See also his "Loyalties, and Why Loyalty Should be Ignored," [1993] 12 *Criminal Justice Ethics* 6.

[12] Ewin, "Loyalty and Virtues" (n 11 above) 419.

[13] Ewin, "Loyalties, and Why Loyalty Should be Ignored" (note 11 above) 41.

[14] Cf. J. G. Murphy, "Marxism and Retribution," [1973] 2 *Philosophy and Public Affairs* 217.

others in society who are less frequently arrested or charged by the authorities.[15] It is probably no coincidence that the economically downtrodden are drawn to lucrative crimes such as trafficking in drugs and sex. Nor is their resentment at being disproportionately singled out for prosecution by the authorities entirely groundless.[16] We should not be surprised if such individuals do not react with remorse when charged with or convicted of such crimes, or if they respond with ambivalence to prosecutorial efforts to induce the betrayal of their former associates. It may be too much to ask or expect prosecutors to not offer cooperation rewards in such cases. Their duty is to enforce the law as they find it, not as they might hope it to be. But this does not excuse the rest of us (and maybe not even prosecutors themselves) from ignoring the ways and extent to which inducing betrayal as a means of enforcing the law is, in some cases, a morally ambiguous business. We should, it seems, have qualms about pressuring individuals to abandon associations to which, in some cases, we leave them few alternatives, especially when we do so in the name of punishing acts that it is not clear should be crimes or punished so harshly as crimes.

Absolute injustice and the duty to cooperate

There are well-known difficulties with the notion of absolute or non-comparative proportionality, mostly borne of uncertainties about how to anchor the sanction scale for the vast array of criminal offenses.[17] But at an intuitive level, it is not hard to conceive of cases in which our sense that an absolute justice has occurred will be vivid. Suppose that S, T, and U have all equally been involved in committing some fairly serious crime. S is apprehended first and the prosecutor cuts a deal with S to testify against T and U at their trials. As a result of agreeing to cooperate, S receives a very mild sentence for her role in the crime. Leave to one side, for the time being, the comparative injustice that results if T and U receive much longer sentences. Independently of that, S's cooperation reward yields a sentencing outcome in S's case that does not seem to match her crime. The absolute injustice of this may be compounded in cases in which S was involved in the commission of more than one serious offense but the cooperation reward she receives involves the dropping of most of the charges against her and the recommendation of a generous sentence reduction for the charge to which S agrees to plead. Of course, prosecutors may not often be so generous in doling out cooperation rewards, unless the crimes that they can thereby

---

[15] For discussion of the indefensibility of current forms of drug prohibition, see D. Husak and P. de Marneffe, *The Legalization of Drugs* (Cambridge: Cambridge University Press 2005). Though Husak and de Marneffe disagree on whether we should continue to prohibit drugs of certain kinds, they agree that current sentences for drug crimes often do more harm than the harms they are designed to prevent or punish.

[16] See Jennifer Hochschild's characterization of the "estranged poor" in "The Politics of the Estranged Poor," [1991] 101 *Ethics* 560.

[17] See A. von Hirsch, *Censure and Sanctions* (Oxford: Clarendon Press, 1993) 36–46.

resolve are serious and large in number, and the evidence they are otherwise able to amass against the cooperator's accomplices is nowhere near what they would need to obtain to convict them at trial.

There is, it must be admitted, something to be said for tolerating the absolute injustices that substantial cooperation rewards create if we can thereby effect the punishment of a significant number of offenders whose crimes are quite serious. Prosecutors, it might be claimed, are in the business of seeking to maximize the number of serious offenders who receive the punishment they deserve, even if this means, on some occasions, they must grant cooperation rewards that result in some offenders not getting all the punishment they deserve. In a perfect world, all offenders would admit their crimes and accept their just punishment. In a slightly less perfect world, prosecutors would be able to acquire sufficient evidence against offenders without offering cooperation rewards to one or more of their accomplices. But we do not live in either of these worlds, so prosecutors with finite resources at their disposal and insufficient evidence must reluctantly, we should assume, accept some trade-offs.

Before we can accept the logic of this trade-off argument, we need to address a further concern about granting cooperation rewards to individuals who are guilty of serious offenses. Such rewards appear to compensate them, sometimes quite handsomely, for fulfilling their obligations. Though we expect people to fulfill their obligations, and sometimes punish them if they fail to do so, we do not usually think it appropriate to reward them for it. Individuals whose crimes involve grave moral wrongs against other individuals should, it might be argued, not only confess to their crimes but willingly help the authorities to apprehend and punish their accomplices. Not only is it unseemly for serious wrongdoers to attempt to parlay what they know into getting better deals for themselves, the authorities should neither encourage nor reward them for doing so.

It is instructive in this context to contrast cooperation rewards with our usual attitudes toward, and treatment of, non-offenders who possess evidence pertinent to a criminal trial or investigation. Witnesses to crimes, or citizens who have incriminating testimony to offer against criminal defendants on trial, are routinely subpoenaed by the prosecution and therefore legally bound to appear before the court to testify. Also, the Sixth Amendment to the United States Constitution requires the authorities to compel witnesses to appear in court when defendants (or their attorneys) believe that they can provide evidence relevant to the putative innocence of those on trial. Subpoenaed witnesses who fail to appear, or who do appear but refuse to testify or otherwise cooperate while on the stand (setting aside those who take the Fifth), are subject to contempt citations. The typical penalty for contempt in such cases is confinement of the witness to jail for the duration of the trial.[18] In most instances, this will amount to a few days of incarceration.

---

[18]   See L. S. Beres, "Civil Contempt and the Rational Contemnor," [1994] 69 *Indiana L. J.* 722, 726.

Moreover, witnesses who do appear and cooperate with the court are not rewarded for doing so, though some are provided with modest compensation if they incur substantial costs in appearing, and a few are afforded forms of witness protection. All of this makes sense if it is assumed that witnesses with probative evidence one way or the other have legal and moral duties to provide it to the court (and perhaps to other authorities prior to trial). Yet this makes more pressing the question of why those directly involved in criminal activities are thought worthy of compensation for their cooperation.

Admittedly, there are instances in which it appears that people are rewarded for fulfilling their moral responsibilities. Consider the common practice of posting rewards for information leading to the apprehension and conviction of offenders, or for information that may help the authorities to solve crimes. It could plausibly be claimed that members of the public who have information relevant to the successful prosecution of criminal offenses have moral obligations to provide it to the authorities independently of any rewards they might receive for doing so. Yet we do not think it anomalous to give them the proffered rewards when they do come forward (though, importantly, we would think it inappropriate to give such rewards to any of the individuals directly involved in the crime who come forward with relevant information).

However, I do not believe that this practice necessarily shows that it is appropriate to reward wrongdoers for fulfilling their moral obligations. Consider, for instance, what we would think about someone who had incriminating evidence that would enable the authorities to solve a serious crime but who refused to come forward with it until a substantial reward was offered in the case. My sense is that we would condemn such an individual if we could show that he had the evidence and knew that he had it, but waited until he could get something for it. We would believe, in other words, that there was something improper about his calculated and self-interested use of that information. Of course, he might not have realized that he had the relevant evidence or that the authorities needed it to solve the crime. One of the functions of posting rewards is to put the public on notice with regard to serious crimes that have not been solved. The posting of rewards is a way of heightening and focusing public awareness on specific criminal events, thereby generating leads that members of the public may not know they possess. It is also a way of encouraging the public to be on the lookout for specific individuals. And it may provide a crucial incentive to get individuals to come forward who are reluctant to reveal what they know because they face some danger in doing so or are concerned about the subsequent burdens (e.g., of testimony at a trial) that they will have to shoulder. In these cases, we offer a "reward" to such individuals in recognition of their having to do more than the ordinary duties required of citizenship. In similar ways, we recognize or reward individuals who must undertake unusual burdens or make extraordinary sacrifices to fulfill their moral obligations. For instance, we praise the parents of disabled children who invest extra effort in seeing to it that their offspring receive the very best health care treatment or educational opportunities. Sure, such efforts are, in a way, obligatory, but that does not preclude us from acknowledging that their fulfillment is sometimes exceedingly difficult.

It might be suggested that we reward offenders for providing evidence against their accomplices in recognition of the dangers of retaliation they face in cooperating with the authorities. These dangers are very real in cases in which the cooperator betrays an entrenched criminal organization, with members both in and outside prison who have the means at their disposal to exact vengeance against snitches. Furthermore, perhaps we do recognize implicitly the strong human disinclination to betray friends and associates with whom individuals have developed ties of loyalty. In order to overcome that disinclination, the authorities provide an inducement in the form of cooperation rewards. Though plausible, we still might not find these considerations on behalf of cooperation rewards fully persuasive.

Why not? Because criminal offenders, unlike members of the general public, argu-ably have more stringent obligations to repair the wrongs in which they have been involved. It seems appropriate to say of crime participants that "they helped create the mess, now they can help clean it up." What do their more stringent obligations require of them? First, they can reasonably be expected to make more sacrifices in helping to bring their fellow wrongdoers to justice. If this means that they have to supply incriminating testimony on numerous occasions, at some expense to them-selves in terms of travel or time off from work, then so be it. Or, if witness protec-tion programs require them to change their lives in substantial ways, then change them they must. By contrast, we might be more reluctant to require such sacrifices of ordinary citizens who just happened to be witnesses to crimes. Second, those involved in crimes might reasonably be expected to take more risks to see to it that their fellow wrongdoers are brought to justice. The individuals they betray might be determined to retaliate against them. We may owe protection to all witnesses who provide incriminating evidence if we believe that the individuals against whom they testify will subsequently seek reprisals. But such protection is never perfect, so we might be more hesitant to expose ordinary citizens to the risks engendered by their testimony. However, those directly involved in the wrongdoing might be thought to have a stronger duty to take the relevant risks. Hence, having to do or risk more is precisely what we should demand and expect of criminal wrongdoers, and not some-thing for which they should be rewarded.

Still, the claim that offenders have a moral duty to admit their wrongdoing and help the authorities track down and punish their criminal cohorts will be resisted on the grounds that it is inconsistent with the Fifth Amendment guarantee of the right against self-incrimination. Those suspected or charged with crimes, so the argument goes, have a legal right to remain silent in the face of official interrogation. They also have a legal right that the authorities not employ measures such as torture, threats of physical violence, deceptive manipulation, or severe forms of psychological pressure or stress to break their silence, or threaten to hold them in contempt of court should they be put on the stand and refuse to tell what they know.[19] True enough, but all of this is consistent with criminal wrongdoers nevertheless having a moral duty to admit their crimes and help the authorities. The Fifth Amendment limits the means that the state can permissibly employ to get suspects to do what, morally speaking, they ought to do. Yet, arguably, it does not stand for the proposition that those who have committed serious crimes have a moral right to conceal them or refuse reasonable requests from the authorities for assistance in solving them. Indeed, it is very difficult to conceive of the moral theory according to which individuals would be justified in refusing to respond to official inquiries into their actions, especially on the assumptions that (a) the authorities have reasonable grounds for regarding them as suspects in a criminal case, and (b) the crimes in question involve serious moral wrongs.[20]

It might be claimed that criminal suspects should not be expected to aid the authorities in bringing about their own punishment—that individuals have an inviolable privacy interest in controlling to whom they reveal their moral transgressions and under what conditions.[21] Alternatively, it might be claimed that punishment is such a terrible thing that we would be asking too much of individuals to require them to aid the authorities in bringing it upon themselves.[22] But neither of these arguments seems convincing. The criminal law already forces individuals suspected of crimes to provide evidence against themselves in myriad ways, in the form of fingerprints, blood samples, financial records, and the like. Individuals required to furnish the authorities with evidence of these kinds might fervently wish not to cooperate, but the law does not respect their wishes, though their cooperation will, in many cases, result in their having to endure criminal sanctions.

A more persuasive argument that some of those guilty of crimes do not have a moral obligation to admit them, or aid the authorities in rounding up and convicting their accomplices, can be made, however, if we return to the problems raised by overcriminalization. Some criminal defendants who are technically guilty of one or more crimes may have been overcharged by prosecutors hoping to pressure them into pleading guilty or cooperating. Such defendants arguably do not have a

---

[19] Courts in the United States have held that the Fifth Amendment does more than this; in particular it precludes the prosecution from citing defendants' refusals to testify at their own trials as evidence of their guilt. But this additional element is controversial. See, for instance, A. W. Alschuler, "A Peculiar Privilege in Historical Perspective," in R. H. Helmholz, et al., *The Privilege Against Self-Incrimination: Its Origins and Development* (Chicago: University of Chicago Press, 1997) 181, and L. Laudan, *Truth, Error, and Criminal Law* (Cambridge: Cambridge University Press, 2006) 150–4. Stephen Schulhofer defends the prohibition on the state's citing the defendant's refusal to testify in "Some Kind Words for the Privilege Against Self-Incrimination," [1991] 26 *Val. U. L. Rev.* 311, 334.

[20] Cf. R. Bronaugh, "Is There a Duty to Confess?" [1998] 98 *American Philosophical Association Newsletter on Philosophy and Law* 86.

[21] See R. S. Gerstein, "Privacy and Self-Incrimination," [1970] 80 *Ethics* 87.

[22] David Dolinko develops and critiques this argument in his "Is There a Rationale for the Privilege Against Self-Incrimination?" [1986] 33 *UCLA L. Rev.* 1063, 1090. He also argues persuasively against Gerstein's privacy defense of the privilege against self-incrimination, at 1122–37.

moral obligation to admit their "guilt" or cooperate with the authorities if doing so will result in their being punished on duplicative or otherwise excessive charges. Similarly, we might reasonably doubt that defendants have a moral obligation to confess and cooperate with the authorities if they are charged with violating dubious or indefensible criminal prohibitions, or face clearly disproportionate sentences for having violated defensible ones, or have been unfairly singled out by the authorities for violating prohibitions that many other citizens violate with relative impunity.

Admittedly, all of these claims about indefensible laws, overcharged defendants, inequitably enforced criminal prohibitions, and disproportionate sentences are controversial, both at the level of theory and in their application to existing laws and practices. Again, many observers of the criminal law in the United States believe that some or all of these kinds of defects increasingly undermine its ability to produce substantively just outcomes, though they disagree on some of the details about when or how this is so.[23] If they are at all correct in their analyses, the implication is that many of the individuals charged with crimes are to some extent themselves victims of a criminal justice system that overreaches. Such unfortunate criminal defendants may be morally entitled to remain silent and uncooperative in the face of the state's unjustifiably harsh or unequal treatment of them. We might even be tempted to view the offer of cooperation rewards to such defendants with less concern since, if nothing else, they afford them some measure of lenity in an otherwise unjustifiably harsh and sometimes arbitrary system. Of course, it will be a most unsystematic form of lenity—offered to a select few, more or less at the prosecutor's discretion—and one that will come at some personal cost to defendants who must betray their former associates. Furthermore, we must be careful not to extend what we think and say about such defendants to those who are guilty as (appropriately) charged of serious offenses and face proportional sanctions for their crimes. Crimes such as murder, rape, aggravated assault, and theft, whether conducted by individuals or organizations, are rightly prohibited and punished severely. Individuals who commit or are involved in them appear to have no moral legs on which to stand in remaining silent and uncooperative in the face of official accusation, even if the law makes it possible for them to do so.

Given the wide variety of criminal defendants, there may be few general conclusions that we can safely draw about the absolute justice or injustice of cooperation rewards. Even if we believe that overcriminalization produces too many defendants charged with too many crimes and threatened with too much punishment, prosecutors can, at most, be faulted for only some of these defects. They must take the criminal law as it is given to them and attempt to enforce it (though this does not preclude their doing so in ways that minimize substantive injustices). But one implication

---

[23] See, among others, M. Tonry, *Thinking About Crime: Sense and Sensibility in American Penal Culture* (Oxford: Oxford University Press, 2004); D. Husak, *Overcriminalization: The Limits of the Criminal Law* (Oxford: Oxford University Press, 2008); and W. J. Stuntz, "The Pathological Politics of Criminal Law," [2001] 100 *Mich. L. Rev.* 505.

of the discussion in this section would seem to be that, when they are employed, cooperation rewards should be kept modest. If the crimes that can be successfully prosecuted by employing them are both serious and significant in number, and no other viable options for prosecuting them exist, then state officials may well be justified in providing cooperating defendants with some additional incentive to do what, morally speaking, they should do. The incentives should not be allowed to become too large, however, or the paradox of rewarding individuals for fulfilling their moral obligations will become intolerable. In general, sentence reductions in the range of, say, 10 to 20 percent for cooperators should be the rule. Larger rewards, in the form of charge reductions or more substantial sentence reductions, should be the exception and might reasonably be subject to more oversight by presiding sentencing judges.

Moreover, what holds for individuals involved in serious *mala in se* offenses would seem to hold for all of the other types of offenders to whom prosecutors might be tempted to offer cooperation rewards—namely, such rewards should be kept modest. It would be odd for prosecutors themselves to attempt to justify larger rewards for mid- to low-level offenses on the grounds of overcriminalization. That would lead us to question what they are doing in the first place by prosecuting such offenses. In any event, the solutions to overcriminalization must be more systematic—the elimination of overlapping or duplicative criminal prohibitions and overall sentence reductions, among them. Cooperation rewards will always and only promote absolute justice much too haphazardly.

Comparative justice

Whether or not those who receive cooperation rewards get what they deserve in some absolute sense, it would seem that such rewards have a tendency to create comparative injustices. Defendants who cooperate with authorities in revealing incriminating evidence against their former associates may be convicted of fewer crimes or punished less harshly than their former associates, sometimes in spite of scant differences in the crimes committed by cooperators and those they betray. The comparative injustices will be compounded in cases in which the rewards for incriminating evidence go to those defendants who police first happen to apprehend, or prosecutors first happen to make plea bargain offers to or reach plea agreements with. For why should such contingent and seemingly arbitrary factors of temporal order be permitted to affect the sentences defendants receive? There seems a deep tension between the practice of rewarding criminal defendants who betray their associates and the important value of preserving what is known as ordinal proportionality in punishments.[24]

It is sometimes contended that criminal defendants who plead guilty and cooperate with the authorities are properly rewarded because of their evident remorse for their crimes. Though we have rejected the remorse argument as a defense of charge

---

[24] Again, the notion of ordinal proportionality is discussed by von Hirsch (n 17 above) 18.

or sentence discounts for defendants who waive the right to trial, it might briefly be reprised in the current context to defend discounts for defendants who provide incriminating evidence against their former accomplices. Such defendants, so the argument goes, demonstrate their remorsefulness for their crimes by their willingness to cooperate with the authorities in bringing their former associates to justice. Not only are the more remorseful appropriately liable to reduced criminal sanctions, they are also more likely to turn themselves in to the police or seek out prosecutors in order to provide them with incriminating evidence. Hence, the fact that those who are arrested or plead guilty first receive charge or sentence reductions in exchange for the evidence they provide, while those they incriminate do not, is not always as arbitrary as it appears. Those who cooperate with the authorities are often the ones who acknowledge the wrongfulness of their earlier conduct and act appropriately in helping the authorities to apprehend and prosecute their accomplices. Given these differences between cooperators and those they implicate, there is no comparative injustice if the former receive less punishment than the latter.

The flimsy logic of the remorse argument is not improved by its recasting in the present context. The conjecture that those who agree to incriminate their former associates are genuinely remorseful for their crimes, as opposed to quicker at grasping what is in their self-interest, or desperate to do so given the charges and sanctions that they otherwise face, likely cannot be sustained in the majority of cases. There is, in addition to this, the somewhat embarrassing point that those who are genuinely remorseful should not really be shopping for charge or sentence reductions, but should embrace the full measure of their just punishment.

Nonetheless, the comparative injustice argument against cooperation rewards may not be as persuasive as it initially seems. Prosecutors will invariably find themselves with limited resources at their disposal. Suppose that they use cooperation rewards in an effort to expand the scope of criminal justice—to obtain more convictions than they otherwise would obtain in the absence of such rewards. Initially, it does seem objectionable, on grounds of comparative justice, for them to operate in this fashion. Consider a simple case: Suppose that S and T are both guilty, and equally guilty, of having committed a crime for which the proportionate punishment is ten years' imprisonment. Yet the evidence against S's guilt is much stronger, especially in the absence of S's cooperation in implicating T, than is the evidence for T's guilt. The prosecutor therefore offers S the recommendation of a substantial sentence discount if S will cooperate in providing evidence against T. S pleads guilty, cooperates, and receives a five-year sentence. T is found guilty, or perhaps pleads guilty when it becomes clear that S is going to cooperate, but receives a comparably longer sentence, say ten years if T is convicted at trial, or eight if T agrees to plead guilty. The prosecutor has used cooperation rewards to increase the number of convictions she would otherwise be able to obtain, and she has done so at some substantial cost to comparative justice—S and T were not relevantly different and yet they received very different sentences. This would seem to count against what the prosecutor has done.

If we focus narrowly on the sentences that S and T ultimately receive, the preceding argument seems convincing. But notice what might have occurred had the prosecutor not been allowed to offer S the cooperation reward. Since the evidence against S was strong, S was likely to have been convicted and punished in any case. Without S's help, T might have escaped all punishment, though, by hypothesis, T was just as guilty as S of the crime. Yet where is the comparative justice in S's receiving a ten- or eight-year sentence (the latter, if S pleads guilty) and T's receiving no sentence at all? By any plausible measure, it would appear that S's receiving an eight-year sentence and T's receiving none is comparatively more unjust than S's receiving a five-year sentence and T's receiving an eight- or ten-year sentence. It might be objected that the comparative injustice in the latter case, produced by the prosecutor's use of a cooperation reward, is brought about more directly by her actions, whereas the former, seemingly greater comparative injustice is not. If the prosecutor has the goods on S but not on T, then the comparative injustice that results if S is convicted and T is not "flows from the nature of the case" rather than from the prosecutor's actions (at least assuming that the prosecutor has done everything in her power, short of offering a cooperation reward to S to gain evidence against T). But this objection is unpersuasive, since it would seem that the greater comparative injustice in that case is produced directly by the prosecutor's failure to offer S a cooperation reward.

Granted, I have described only one case and there will be lots of other and different kinds of cases in which cooperation rewards will be utilized by prosecutors. Nonetheless, the case described is apt to be fairly representative of those in which cooperation rewards are employed and so does suggest that the comparative injustice argument against cooperation rewards is less telling than it seemed initially. In evaluating that argument, we should not only focus narrowly on the punishment like offenders receive as a result of the deployment of such rewards, but also on what punishment offenders would have received in the absence of their deployment. Perhaps prosecutors should be encouraged to keep cooperation rewards modest, to prevent disparities in the sentencing of like offenders from growing too large. If S is given a huge cooperation reward, one that reduces S's sentence to two years' imprisonment, then on overall comparative justice grounds, the distribution of punishment that results is not much different from the one that would have occurred in the absence of the cooperation reward. T should not get all or most of the punishment and S very little of it, since both are equally culpable. Yet some sentencing disparities between those who cooperate and those who do not, seem defensible, especially if they effect punishment of more of the individuals involved in crimes than would otherwise have resulted and some punishment for all of them.

One commonly expressed concern about cooperation rewards has been that they will tend to go to individuals who are higher up in criminal organizations rather than to low-level members.[25] Those higher up may know more about the operations

---

[25] See Weinstein (n 5 above) 611–17, and Richman (n 5 above) 292.

of such organizations and thus be more useful to police and prosecutors who are attempting to dismantle them by charging and convicting their members. Yet those higher up are thought to be more culpable for an organization's criminal activities, so it seems comparatively unjust that they should receive less punishment than those beneath them on whom they snitch and who may not receive cooperation rewards. It is, it should be noted, an empirical question whether cooperation rewards are granted disproportionately to those higher up.[26] But suppose that they are. Again, it does not necessarily follow that the comparative injustices that such a practice produces are greater than those that would exist in their absence. If, by offering such rewards, prosecutors can charge and convict middle- and lower-level members of the criminal organization, then those individuals will receive at least some of the punishment that is their due. True, those who betray them might not receive the proportionally worse punishments that they deserve (though they are apt, in many cases, to receive fairly high levels of punishment, assuming that they are the prime movers in the organization). Though there is some comparative injustice produced by cooperation rewards in such cases, notice that, in their absence, those higher up alone would be punished, while those beneath them would receive none or considerably less of the punishment their crimes merit. That, too, seems comparatively unjust. Again, the key in such cases might be to prevent the cooperation rewards given to those higher up from becoming so large that the comparative injustices thereby generated swamp the gains in comparative justice produced by employing them.

The contention that cooperation rewards, if employed judiciously, might actually help us achieve more overall comparative justice than would be achieved in their absence may be resisted for another reason: We do not always believe that extending the scope of legal punishment is a good thing. Again, some current criminal prohibitions may be indefensible, some defensible ones might have disproportionate sanctions attached to their violation, and poorer citizens may be targeted disproportionately by the authorities for the violation of certain kinds of prohibitions. The former two kinds of defects yield absolute injustices, even assuming that defendants have not been overcharged by prosecutors bent on gaining their cooperation or inducing them to plead guilty. Unequal enforcement of criminal prohibitions may yield both absolute and comparative injustices—the former if the prohibitions are dubious to begin with, the latter if other citizens who commit similar kinds of offenses tend to escape the scrutiny of the criminal justice system. In short, to the extent that cooperation rewards are employed to sweep the socially deprived into the criminal justice system for conduct that should not be criminalized at all or not as much, we might be unimpressed by the argument that they may actually reduce comparative injustices in certain kinds of cases. Instead, we might prefer that

---

[26] A useful summary of the evidence is presented by L. D. Maxfield and J. H. Kramer, "Substantial Assistance: An Empirical Yardstick Gauging Equity in Current Federal Policy and Practice," [1998] 11 *Federal Sentencing Reporter* 6.

prosecutors employ cooperation rewards parsimoniously, to the extent necessary (though no more than this) to secure punishment of those whose conduct is clearly intolerable in civilized society and who face proportionate punishment for such conduct. Unfortunately, there may be little reason to believe that prosecutors so confine their use of cooperation rewards.

Cooperating witness reliability

The value of cooperating witnesses depends, in part, on their truthfulness in revealing what they know, that is, on their accurately and fully recounting the events under investigation. It also depends on the extent to which the evidence they provide enables prosecutors successfully to pursue charges against others involved in criminal activity. The extent to which the evidence witnesses provide will help prosecutors cannot be easily determined in advance. Thus, prosecutors are naturally reluctant to make firm commitments on cooperation rewards until they have some sense of what witnesses have to offer and, beyond this, until cooperating witnesses have actually testified at their accomplices' trials, should that turn out to be necessary.

There are two reasons to be concerned about the reliability of cooperating witnesses. First, defendants who cooperate may seek to conceal or downplay their own crimes, and thus shift responsibility for criminal acts onto others, for reasons that are entirely independent of minimizing their exposure to punishment. By making themselves appear less bad, cooperating witnesses might thereby be better able to salvage their own self-respect and reduce the social disapproval apt to come their way because of their criminal misconduct. Granted, this tendency of cooperators to disguise or minimize their crimes at the expense of others will sometimes be counteracted by a residual sense of loyalty to those with whom they formerly associated, or fear of retaliation from them. But the desire of all of us to appear less bad to ourselves and others is powerful enough that it arguably gives us some reason for keeping cooperation rewards modest. We might, in other words, presume that cooperators have behaved worse than they are willing to admit and that those they provide evidence against have not behaved as badly as cooperators claim. If this is at least generally true, then sentencing disparities between cooperators and those they cooperate against should be minimized unless it is clear that the crimes that the two have committed are different in degree or kind.

Second, since the sentencing fate of cooperating witnesses rests largely in the hands of prosecutors, the incentives such individuals have to give prosecutors what they want and need to successfully charge and convict accomplices are worrisome. In particular, when the crimes in question are punished harshly by the criminal law (whether justifiably or not), potential cooperators will be highly motivated to seek sentence concessions, even at some expense to the truth about their own and others' actions. Moreover, prosecutors might not be as bothered as they should be about cooperating witness testimony which they have some reason to believe is wholly or partially false—indeed, with testimony that prosecutors know is untruthful—if it helps them to secure the convictions of other individuals whom they believe are guilty of serious crimes. Again, these concerns about cooperators will be intensified when the rewards they might receive are made contingent not only upon their testifying fully and truthfully, but upon helping prosecutors actually gain convictions of others. Yvette Beeman argues that the latter sorts of agreements, wherein defendants receive charge or sentence concessions only if they meet some vaguely specified standard of "useful" testimony against their accomplices as determined by prosecutors, should be prohibited.[27] She contends that such agreements give defendants powerful incentives to please prosecutors by supplying them with incriminating, yet unreliable, evidence against their former accomplices. The risk that truthful testimony that is not sufficiently incriminating will fail to satisfy prosecutors in such cases is simply too great. Beeman sees fewer problems with non-contingent plea agreements, though such agreements typically allow prosecutors to withhold charge or sentence concessions if they believe that the cooperating defendants have not revealed all they know (that is, have not cooperated fully). Still, defendants in the non-contingent cooperation agreement cases might have concerns similar to those of their counterparts who agree to testify under contingent agreements. For what prevents prosecutors in the non-contingent cases from deciding that defendants have not been fully truthful when they fail to provide what prosecutors believe is evidence sufficient to ensure the convictions of accomplices? Contingent agreements may heighten the incentives to exaggerate or otherwise distort the culpability of co-offenders, but they do not appear to create incentives that are different in kind.

Perhaps it is not the nature of the cooperation agreement that matters, but the magnitude of the rewards offered for cooperation and, more importantly, the possibility that prosecutors might have largely unfettered discretion in determining whether defendants have or have not been cooperative enough to merit them. As the literature on "substantial assistance" waivers under the US Federal Sentencing Guidelines demonstrates, it will not be easy to figure out ways to limit the discretion of prosecutors to determine who should receive cooperation rewards.[28] Under the Guidelines, prosecutors have the exclusive authority to initiate cooperation rewards and determine whether witnesses have been fully cooperative. Judges cannot intervene on behalf of witnesses who contend that they have cooperated fully but have not been granted the charge or sentence concessions they believe are their due. Most commentators who examine this state of affairs lament the power that this grants prosecutors, but struggle to find solutions that both acknowledge the superior epistemic credentials of prosecutors in such cases—they likely have a better sense than anyone else whether

---

[27] Beeman (n 7 above) 802.
[28] See Weinstein (n 5 above) 625–32, and C. K. Y. Lee, "From Gatekeepers to Concierge: Reigning in the Federal Prosecutor's Expanding Power Over Substantial Assistance Departures," [1997] 50 *Rutgers L. Rev.* 199.

a witness has cooperated fully—and effectively limit prosecutorial control over the allocation of cooperation rewards.

One suggestion is that we cap the absolute number of cooperation rewards that prosecutors are permitted to hand out in a given time period.[29] By reducing the frequency of their use we might encourage prosecutors to use them more judiciously. Yet such a cap does little, by itself, to ensure the reliability of cooperating witnesses in the cases in which they are used. Nor does it help with the problem of prosecutors arbitrarily withholding cooperation rewards from witnesses whom prosecutors deem less than fully cooperative, or fully cooperative but not ultimately helpful enough in enabling prosecutors to secure convictions of their accomplices. Others have suggested the adoption of guidelines for prosecutors (initially, for Federal prosecutors, though we might eventually extend their application to all of them) that would regularize the use of cooperation rewards.[30] If nothing else, such guidelines might reduce some of the inconsistencies that exist in the practice across jurisdictions. Still, we might wonder about the effectiveness of such guidelines in the absence of an external enforcement mechanism of some kind. If the guidelines are overseen and enforced by other prosecutors whose sympathies can be expected to lie with those who, like them, fill difficult and demanding roles in the criminal justice system, we might reasonably worry that the guidelines will have little practical effect. And again, regularizing their use might do little to address the problems with the reliability of cooperating witnesses.

One partial solution to the problems with reliability would be to have the courts play a more active role in vetting cooperating witnesses who are scheduled to testify at their accomplices' trials, examining what George Harris terms "indicia of reliability" in relation to such witnesses prior to their actually providing testimony in court.[31] Harris makes various recommendations about how to enhance the reliability of cooperating witnesses and reduce the advantages prosecutors have in discovering and employing them.[32] If the courts performed some preliminary evaluation of the reliability of such cooperating witnesses, to determine whether there are prima facie grounds for allowing them to testify, that might discourage the most egregious abuses of the prosecutor's power to unilaterally allocate cooperation rewards (e.g., in the United States, the use of jailhouse snitches).

Another way in which we might marginally enhance the reliability of cooperating witness testimony is by keeping cooperation rewards modest. We have seen other reasons in support of such an approach, one that limits such rewards to something in the range of a 10 to 20 percent sentence reduction. In this context, the argument for doing so is straightforward: With less to gain by implicating their former associates, defendants, we might hope, would be less susceptible to prosecutorial pressures to shade the truth about their own or others' conduct. The difficulty, admittedly, will be

---

[29] Weinstein (n 5 above) 630–1.   [30] Lee (n 28 above) 245–51.   [31] Harris (n 6 above) 62–4.
[32] Harris (n 6 above) 62–8.

to prevent prosecutors from circumventing a policy of modest cooperation rewards by adjusting the charges against cooperating witnesses. Even if we believe that smaller sentence reductions would give cooperators less incentive to distort the truth, prosecutors could provide cooperators with larger rewards by reducing or eliminating charges against them. In previous chapters we have examined the arguments against robust forms of charge bargaining. It is tempting at this point, therefore, to simply stipulate that prosecutors will not be permitted to resort to charge bargaining. But the practical problems with detecting and discouraging charge bargaining have also been noted. One solution in the current context would be to require prosecutors not only to identify cooperating witnesses at their plea hearings but also furnish a record of all charges filed against them to sentencing judges. In that way judges could learn about charge reductions and insist that prosecutors explain and justify them.[33] There might be cases in which prosecutors could argue convincingly that something more than a modest reward was needed to induce a witness to cooperate. Some witnesses might be fiercely loyal to or fearful of their former associates, and yet be in the possession of valuable evidence that would enable prosecutors to pursue successfully serious charges against them. We might be hesitant to deprive prosecutors of the resources they need to proceed in such cases, even if we believe that substantial cooperation rewards should more often be the exception rather than the rule. Requiring prosecutors to at least explain and justify larger than normal cooperation rewards might discourage them from resorting to them too often. If it did not, then we might have to consider asking judges to take more controversial steps to rein in prosecutorial abuse of their discretion in handing out cooperation rewards.[34]

Under the Sentencing Guidelines, only prosecutors can initiate grants of substantial assistance awards. Witnesses who have cooperated fully, or who believe that they have done so, have little recourse if the prosecutor does not agree that their efforts merit charge or sentence concessions. This seems a curious state of affairs, even if we grant that prosecutors will typically be in the best position to judge whether witnesses have fully cooperated. Permitting witnesses who believe that they have cooperated fully to contest a prosecutor's refusal to support a substantial assistance award to the presiding judge seems advisable as a matter of fairness and as a way to enhance witness reliability. After all, what we presumably want cooperating witnesses to do is reveal all that they know, not embellish the facts in order to please prosecutors. Yet if such

---

[33] Granted, this procedure may work to discourage prosecutors from handing out large cooperation rewards only if there is no "pre-charge bargaining" between them and cooperating witnesses. By pre-charge bargaining, I mean negotiations over which charges will be filed initially by prosecutors in relation to cooperating witnesses. Such bargaining, if it occurred, would likely leave no written record which the judge could use to determine whether unusually generous cooperation rewards were being granted by prosecutors.

[34] For instance, it is more difficult in some countries than it is in the United States to drop charges once they are initially filed. See Y. Ma, "Prosecutorial Discretion and Plea Bargaining in the United States, France, Germany, and Italy: A Comparative Perspective," [2002] 12 *International Criminal Justice Review* 22, 33.

witnesses know that fully revealing what they know might not gain them the recommendation of a cooperation reward from prosecutors and they have no recourse in that event, it seems plausible to think that witnesses will be tempted to try to give prosecutors what they want, whether it is veridical testimony or not. Of course, prosecutors should be given the opportunity to explain their side of the story to judges, and perhaps judges should be inclined to give them the benefit of the doubt. But the edge prosecutors would have in any such hearing would be presumptive and therefore rebuttable, given a sufficiently compelling case for a sentence concession made by the cooperating witness.

It might be objected that my concerns about cooperating witness reliability are exaggerated, since any evidence that they provide against their accomplices can be contested at trial.[35] Also, since any plea agreements that prosecutors have worked out with accomplice defendants have to be revealed during the trials of those against whom they testify, jurors will be in a position to evaluate such testimony with a healthy dose of skepticism. Yet, as Harris argues at length, jurors in criminal trials will typically be unaware of all of the stage-setting that goes into the production of cooperative witness testimony.[36] Jurors may not realize the extensive coaching that such witnesses receive or the ways in which it may make the defendants on trial look more culpable than they actually are (and the cooperating witness look less culpable than he actually is). Harris also points out that prosecutors never offer cooperation rewards to individuals who might provide exculpatory evidence against the defendants on trial, though presumably in their position as officers of the court charged with the pursuit of justice, they should be prepared to do so.[37]

In fact, the problems with cooperating witness reliability go deeper than Harris's analysis recognizes. He appears to take for granted the fact that, at some point, there will actually be trials at which such witnesses will testify, and therefore an opportunity for defense attorneys to contest what they say. Yet this ignores the likelihood that many individuals implicated by their former associates will find it in their best interest to reach their own plea agreements with state officials. This means that accomplice testimony against them will never be challenged at trial; neither will the suspect motives of those who provide it be taken into account by jurors. It will not do to respond to this by noting that the accomplice testimony must be, in such cases, reliable, or else the defendants against whom it is directed would not seek to negotiate plea agreements themselves. For it could be that individuals falsely incriminated by their former associates will decide it is in their best interest to plead to something rather than risk trials and possibly harsher sentences. Or, it may be that the individuals against whom the testimony is offered are guilty of some criminal wrongdoing, just not the wrongdoing for which their accomplices find it in their interest to implicate them. Knowing that they are guilty of some criminal wrongdoing, such individuals may attempt to negotiate pleas even if they believe themselves innocent of some or all

---

[35] Alschuler (n 1 above) 4.   [36] Harris (n 6 above) 53–4.   [37] Harris (n 6 above) 50.

of the charges concerning which their former accomplices have supplied prosecutors with "evidence." In either case, the unreliability of such evidence is not contested and is permitted to work inappropriately against individuals.[38]

Concluding remarks

My discussion has made no attempt to produce an algorithm that prosecutors and the rest of us might employ to determine when cooperation rewards are granted justifiably. I have suggested that we might be more confident about their use when the crimes that can thereby be resolved are serious *mala in se*, significant in number, and the rewards are kept modest. Large cooperation rewards will often be absolutely unjust and sometimes comparatively unjust, and may exacerbate problems with the reliability of cooperating witness testimony, especially if prosecutors have sole discretion in determining who receives them. The claim that sometimes prosecutors are justified in offering compensation rewards has considerable plausibility. They have limited resources, as do the police who assist them. Many serious kinds of criminal activity might go unpunished if we deny them the use of such rewards.

Still, cooperation rewards will sometimes be employed in the service of flawed criminal prohibitions—ones that criminalize conduct that is harmless or only marginally harmful, or sanction too harshly conduct that should be criminalized. Further, some criminal justice systems are situated in broader social contexts that fail in important respects to ensure that all citizens enjoy the conditions supportive of responsible conduct, thereby encouraging and facilitating the development of appropriate loyalties. For all of these reasons, we might view cooperation rewards with some ambivalence. Their use is not, and at present cannot be, confined to cases in which they are a vital weapon in the fight against conduct that no civilized society can tolerate. Instead, they are often used in the promotion of ends that no civilized society should be proud of.

---

[38] Granted, some of Harris's recommendations—allowing defense attorneys to have access to cooperating witnesses prior to trial, for instance—might help address the problem with incriminating evidence that is never properly contested. We could also imagine that, even in the absence of a trial, judges could be asked to perform some preliminary evaluation of the credibility of cooperating witnesses. In that way, defense attorneys might be able to eliminate some witnesses against their clients, or at least be in a better position to advise them about their prospects should they insist on going to trial.

7

Plea Bargains as Contracts

To this point, defense of waiver rewards which are the staple of negotiated criminal settlements has proceeded along lines familiar to anyone conversant with the philosophical literature on the justification of legal punishment. Such rewards have been supported on the grounds that they enable prosecutors to expand deserved punishment, enhance the crime reduction profile of the criminal justice system, and reduce the punishment of genuinely remorseful offenders. Even defenses of the cooperation rewards discussed in Chapter 6 were premised on their role in enabling state officials to punish more rather than less of the individuals guilty of crimes. In short, plea bargaining rewards have been linked to the promotion of one or more of the aims of legal punishment.

In this chapter, we turn to an account of plea bargaining, one implication of which appears to be that we should detach defense of it from the aims of legal punishment. According to this account, negotiated plea settlements should be conceived as contracts between criminal defendants and the prosecutors (or other state officials) whose role it is to file and pursue charges against them.[1] In exchange for promised charge or sentence concessions from prosecutors, defendants agree to plead guilty and waive their legal right to trial. Defendants thus exchange something that is uncertain (acquittal at trial) for something that is rather more certain (some diminishment of the sanctions meted out to them).[2] Likewise, state officials are assured convictions, though they may have to forgo some charges and accede to sentence recommendations that they know or suspect may not give offenders what they deserve, given their criminal acts. As with any kind of agreement, there are important ethical concerns about whether the parties, and especially criminal defendants, have voluntarily entered into them or fully understood their terms. Assuming that they have done so, proponents of the contract view of plea bargaining contend that negotiated criminal

---

[1] Prominent defenders of the view include T. W. Church, Jr., "In Defense of 'Bargain Justice'," [1979] 13 *Law & Soc'y Rev.* 509; F. H. Easterbrook, "Criminal Procedure as a Market System," [1983] 12 *J. Legal Stud.* 289, and "Plea Bargaining as Compromise," [1992] 101 *Yale L. J.* 1969; and R. E. Scott and W. J. Stuntz, "Plea Bargaining as Contract," [1992] 101 *Yale L. J.* 1909. Prominent critics of the view include A. W. Alschuler, "The Changing Plea Bargaining Debate," [1981] 69 *Cal. L. Rev.* 652, and S. J. Schulhofer, "Plea Bargaining as Disaster," [1992] 101 *Yale L. J.* 1979.

[2] Plea agreements might not yield certain outcomes for defendants if they are entered into by prosecutors but must be ratified by judges.

settlements are presumptive goods that deserve society's respect and enforcement.[3] Moreover, if all the parties to the exchange are happy with its terms, then there would appear to be few grounds for requiring its revision or circumscribing it in advance. The contract view will therefore support variable and substantial waiver rewards, if that is what the contracting parties agree on.

The suggestion that the disposition of charges in criminal cases should be subject to straightforward negotiation between state officials and criminal defendants (or their attorneys) will be regarded by some as making a mockery of procedural and substantive justice in the enforcement of the criminal law. It will seem that such a view could only be put forward in countries that elevate free-market ideology to an unreasonably high level.[4] Perhaps it goes without saying that the contract view has been advanced most spiritedly by legal scholars contemplating the freewheeling forms of plea bargaining that exist in the United States. It does not follow from any of this that it is a view without merit. I shall treat it as a serious proposal, though one that must be subjected to close scrutiny.

Proponents of the contract view acknowledge various complications with it, mostly borne of the facts that prosecutors are not fully autonomous agents and defendants are typically represented by attorneys who do most of the negotiating. Prosecutors presumably are not supposed to enter into these contracts with an eye toward advancing their own personal interests, especially if these are conceived as different from those of the public whom they are sworn to represent. This is a point to which we shall return, since it casts considerable doubt on the notion that plea agreements should be regarded as independent goods—that is, as valuable independently of their serving the larger aims of the criminal justice system. But, for the time being, it will be useful to ignore this and state the contract view in undiluted form. Defense attorneys, too, have responsibilities to their clients, ones that require them to keep their own interests (in their reputations or in the efficient resolution of cases) in the background and work on behalf of their clients. In short, prosecutors are agents of the public, and defense attorneys are agents of their clients. Hence, those who would convince us that plea bargains are usefully conceived as contracts are forced to confront the problems with ensuring that the interests of the agents involved are maximally made to conform to those of their principals. Yet these agency problems are familiar from other

---

[3] See Easterbrook, "Plea Bargain as Compromise" (n 1 above) 1976–77, for a clear statement that defendants, in particular, should be able to strike such agreements on their own behalf. See also Scott and Stuntz (n 1 above) 1913–14.

[4] M. Langer neatly characterizes that underlying logic of the contract view as one in which criminal procedure governs a "dispute between two parties (prosecution and defense) before a passive decision-maker (the judge and/or jury)..." in "From Legal Transplants to Legal Translations: The Globalization of Plea Bargaining and the Americanization Thesis in Criminal Procedure," [2004] 45 *Harv. Int'l L. J.* 1, 4. See also T. Weigend, "Is the Criminal Process About Truth?: A German Perspective," [2003] 26 *Harv. J. L. & Public Pol'y* 157.

contexts and are rarely thought to be so grave as to threaten the contract account of plea bargaining.[5]

It is worth noting, if it is not already apparent, that the contract view is normative in character. It is not simply the view that so conceiving of plea bargains helps us to make sense of them—though it surely is supposed to do at least that. It is also the view that plea agreements have value in their own right, as exercises of the legitimate discretion of the parties involved to act in the public's best interests, in the case of prosecutors, or in their own interests, in the case of criminal defendants. In the words of Robert Scott and William Stuntz: "Parties who are denied either freedom to contract or freedom to exchange entitlements suffer unnecessary constraints on their choices, constraints that undermine the value of the entitlements themselves."[6] Indeed, proponents of the contract view are prepared to criticize court or legislative efforts to stifle or prohibit negotiated plea settlement on the grounds that doing so is not sufficiently respectful of the autonomy of defendants and unduly meddlesome in decisions that properly belong to prosecutors.[7]

To elaborate the preceding point, compare negotiated criminal settlements with commercial transactions. The parties to commercial transactions are generally deemed capable of best appreciating and acting on their own interests. Contract law provides a framework within which parties who desire to effect commercial exchanges can do so efficiently and reliably. If Jones has widgets to sell and Smith desires to purchase widgets, then it may be possible for them to reach an agreed-upon price and complete a transaction. Assuming no force or fraud, and assuming that the widgets are Jones' to sell and the proceeds Smith uses to purchase them are hers to disburse, then the agreements they enter into are plausibly cast as expressions of their autonomy. Moreover, shrewd dealing in such contexts is not only rewarded but admired. Jones might have the market more or less cornered on widgets and so be able to command a high price for them. Or Smith might be a prodigious user of widgets such that Smith can negotiate much lower prices for them than Smith's competitors by threatening to take her business elsewhere if Jones will not meet her price demands.

There is, it should be noted, a long-standing debate about the appropriate background conditions that must be satisfied for such commercial transactions to be efficient or in other ways socially beneficial.[8] This debate concerns such things as whether, and to what extent, the government should intervene in the operations of otherwise free markets to prevent the emergence of monopolies or oligopolies, whether minimum wages should be enforced in labor markets, unemployed workers

---

[5] See Easterbrook, "Plea Bargaining as Compromise" (n 1 above) 1975, where he notes that there are numerous other contexts in which agents are imperfect representatives of their clients.

[6] Scott and Stuntz (n 1 above) 1913.

[7] Easterbrook pointedly suggests that prohibiting plea bargaining to protect defendants smacks of paternalism. See "Plea Bargaining as Compromise" (n 1 above) 1976–77.

[8] See J. Rawls, "A Kantian Conception of Equality," in S. Freeman (ed.), *John Rawls: Collected Papers* (Cambridge, Mass.: Harvard University Press, 1999) 257.

should be supported by the state or the companies that have recently let them go, and whether the state should maintain a welfare floor. The absence of the requisite background conditions might be taken to undermine the voluntary character of contracts, their social value, or both. Political theorists have also disagreed profoundly about how to characterize just initial entitlements, such that subsequent exchanges can be meaningfully regarded as ones which the contracting agents are entitled to effect.[9] No one is prepared to honor agreements between thieves and their fences even if they are informed and voluntary. But assuming that the appropriate background conditions are in place and the parties to agreements are entitled to the things they seek to exchange, then commercial transactions which are free of force or fraud are not otherwise subject to much in the way of further scrutiny. They are honored and enforced because they have been freely entered into, even if we believe that one or more of the parties to them should have bargained for better terms or should not have contracted at all.

Though illuminating in certain respects, my contention is that the analogy with commercial transactions is apt to mislead us in the context of negotiated criminal settlements. For one thing, such settlements are not easily detachable from the independent normative standards provided by an account of legal punishment's justifying aims. To the extent that negotiated criminal settlements fail to serve the aims of retribution, crime reduction, or perhaps some combination of the two, they are appropriately subject to scrutiny and criticism even if they are entered into freely and informedly. More than this, proponents of the contract view have failed to analyze carefully or fully the requisite background conditions that must be satisfied if negotiated criminal settlements are to be regarded as respectable agreements. In particular, they have not been clear enough about insisting that the criminal prohibitions enforced must themselves be defensible and attended with sanctions that are proportionate. Proponents of the contract view have also at times failed to notice the ways in which the behavior of prosecutors or criminal defendants is coercive or involves the exchange of things to which they are dubiously entitled.

I do not conclude that negotiated plea settlements are never usefully viewed as contracts which the parties are entitled to forge and have ratified. Instead, I suggest that there are many more conditions that have to be satisfied before such settlements are worthy of our respect than proponents of the contract view acknowledge. I also show that those conditions shape the kinds of negotiated settlements that are worthy of our respect in ways and to a degree such that the element of free agreement, so important in commercial settings, recedes into the background. Negotiated criminal settlements rarely have free-standing value; they are not goods "simply because" they have been freely entered into, at least not in the ways in which commercial transactions will often have such value.

---

[9] Even Robert Nozick, an ardent supporter of free exchanges in *Anarchy, State, and Utopia* (New York: Basic Books, 1974), notes that there must be justice in initial entitlements (p. 150).

Initial doubts

Two initial difficulties might be raised with the admonition to view negotiated criminal settlements as we view commercial transactions. First, as some defenders of the contract view acknowledge, prosecutors (and judges) are government-instituted monopolists. Not only is there no one else to whom defendants can turn if they cannot reach a satisfactory pre-trial settlement with state officials, there are no potential law enforcement entrepreneurs on the horizon.[10] Such monopoly power is widely seen as problematic in the commercial sphere where, if it exists, it is typically subject to independent regulation. Yet prosecutors in the United States, at least, have by custom and law enormous discretion which is largely unchecked by other institutional actors.[11]

Frank Easterbrook dismisses the problem posed by such a government-instituted monopoly with the somewhat fanciful notion that criminal defendants are free to shop among prosecutors or judges ahead of time, by choosing the jurisdiction in which they commit their (alleged, we should say) crimes.[12] Not only does this response ignore the relative impoverishment of many criminal offenders, such that their abilities to "shop" will be sorely limited, it also seems doubtful that they will find much variety among state officials. There may be some variation among prosecutors in different jurisdictions with respect to the crimes they prosecute or the deals they are willing to offer, but it seems unlikely to be substantial. Potential offenders who do "shop" are apt to find themselves choosing among similar "punishment suppliers" who vary only by geographical location, unless they can locate prosecutors or judges who are so incompetent, corrupt, or overburdened by their caseloads as to be desperate to resolve cases on terms highly favorable to criminal defendants. If state officials of these kinds exist, and they might, of course, it seems doubtful that we should welcome them because they effectively loosen the state's monopoly on criminal prosecutions.

A more promising argument points to the fact that criminal defendants are also monopolists of a sort.[13] As Scott and Stuntz note, defendants retain some bargaining power in the face of prosecutorial monopoly due to the "call" that each of them has on the prosecutor's or judge's time.[14] If state officials attempt to drive too hard a bargain, defendants can demand trials. Trials are tremendously burdensome to state

---

[10] See Easterbrook, "Criminal Procedure as a Market System" (n 1 above) 291. In "Plea Bargaining as Compromise" (n 1 above), Easterbrook points to other ways in which plea agreements are unlike commercial transactions (at p. 1975). He then employs the language of "compromise" to characterize such agreements rather than "contract," though he continues to defend them as agreements into which defendants and prosecutors should be allowed to enter.

[11] Easterbrook is a forceful defender of this discretion in "Criminal Procedure as a Market System" (n 1 above) 299–308, as well as in other places throughout his essay.

[12] Easterbrook, "Criminal Procedure as a Market System" (n 1 above) 291.

[13] Easterbrook notes this in "Plea Bargaining as Compromise" (n 1 above) 1975, calling prosecutors and defendants "bilateral monopolists."

[14] Scott and Stuntz (n 1 above) 1924.

officials and in most cases they strongly desire to avoid them. The problem with this argument, which Scott and Stuntz see only partially, is that state officials are at times given the ability by courts and democratically elected legislators to demand exorbitant "prices" in exchange for guilty pleas.[15] Courts in the United States, for instance, have done little to curb the threat of trial penalties, as I earlier characterized them, and indeed seem to construe them as quite reasonable measures for prosecutors or judges to employ.[16] In addition, US legislators, as Stuntz has shown so eloquently, have enacted overlapping and redundant criminal statutes that empower prosecutors to charge individuals with numerous offenses covering a single criminal event or connected series of them.[17] The result is that even in the absence of trial penalties, defendants face fearsome sentences if convicted at trial on all charges, especially in jurisdictions without concurrent sentencing policies. Add to this the tendency of legislators to enact disproportionate sentences for certain kinds of offenses—sentences that they may not, as Stuntz has shown, really want prosecutors to inflict in most cases—the result is that the tools given prosecutors to exact high "costs" on defendants who refuse to plead guilty make them monopolists of a distinctively threatening sort. These are points that I shall come back to later in the chapter.

Defenders of the contract view might plausibly argue that it is the pressure tactics employed by state officials in some countries that constitute the problem, not the mere fact that those officials are monopoly providers. If prosecutors charge defendants veridically, and if they and judges refrain from threatening trial penalties, then their status as monopolists should not trouble us. After all, criminal defendants cannot reasonably complain about the lack of alternative suppliers of punishment if state officials base the charges they bring, and the sanctions they impose, on convincing evidence about the crimes individuals have committed.

Assuming that proponents of the contract view are thereby able to parry the monopoly objection, they must confront a second one: Transactions between prosecutors and criminal defendants (or their attorneys) are decidedly different from commercial transactions because some defendants are confined under lock and key until their cases are resolved, whether through negotiated settlements or trials. This seems an important difference, and one that might, all by itself, call into question the voluntary character of settlements reached in quite a few criminal cases. Of course, not all criminal defendants are remanded until their trials, and many of them will be veterans of confinement such that they are not especially terrified at its prospect. Moreover, those defendants unnerved by pre-trial confinement seem unlikely to agree to plea

---

[15] Scott and Stuntz recognize that the ability of prosecutors to "manipulate post-trial sentences" by overcharging has coercive potential (n 1 above) 1962. Stuntz, in "Plea Bargaining and Criminal Law's Disappearing Shadow," [2004] 117 *Harv. L. Rev.* 2548, elaborates this point forcefully.

[16] Church, as we will see, recognizes the coercive potential of trial penalties, calling them an "unconstitutional burden on the right to trial..." (n 1 above) 520.

[17] Stuntz (n 15 above) 2558, and especially in "The Pathological Politics of Criminal Law," [2001] 100 *Mich. L. Rev.* 505, 507, and 512–23.

deals involving substantial prison sentences in the rare cases where they are actually innocent of the charges against them, since such negotiated settlements will not result in their release from confinement but, in fact, its prolongation. The worrisome cases, as others have noted, are those involving defendants held on remand who are innocent of the charges against them, but who might be induced to plead guilty by proffers of non-custodial sentences or sentences involving time already served awaiting the final disposition of their cases.[18] Concern about such cases should be greater when the individuals in question are novices to penal confinement. The practical problem, of course, is that we are unable to distinguish such innocent defendants from the vast majority who are guilty. Hence, we may have little recourse but to affirm plea agreements reached between prosecutors and defendants held on remand, though we might worry that the voluntariness of some of those agreements is compromised by the fact that one of the parties is held captive. Fortunately, we can reasonably hope that the number of agreements that suffer from this flaw is small.

Background conditions

Criminal statutes on the books and the sanctions attaching to their violation provide the legal framework within which prosecutors operate, though it is apparent that prosecutors have considerable discretion in determining which statutes they will enforce and against whom.[19] Defenders of the contract view of plea bargaining seem for the most part to take existing criminal prohibitions and sentencing schemes for granted, though it is not clear that they would have to do so.[20] There seems no reason why they could not criticize the ways and extent to which the conduct of individuals is criminalized in any given society. Of course, their doing so would require them to develop and defend substantive theories of criminalization and sentencing, normative projects which they might regard as separate matters and, as such, beyond their remit in discussing plea bargaining. Still, it is important to appreciate how unjust background conditions—in the form of dubious criminal prohibitions or disproportionately harsh sentences—might undermine our willingness to regard negotiated criminal settlements as exemplary voluntary agreements. Granted, claims that specific criminal prohibitions are unjustified or punished disproportionately will inevitably prove controversial. We can sidestep those controversies and develop the points worth making by focusing on cases of undeniable state overreaching. How far, or in

---

[18] See A. W. Alschuler, "The Prosecutor's Role in Plea Bargaining," [1968] 36 *U. Chi. L. Rev.* 50, 62. For discussion of the ways in which generous prosecutorial offers in weak cases are apt to persuade the innocent to plead guilty, see O. Gazal-Ayal, "Partial Ban on Plea Bargains," [2006] 27 *Cardozo L. Rev.* 2295.

[19] Stuntz emphasizes this discretion (n 17 above) 519–22, and (n 15 above) 2549.

[20] In fairness, Scott and Stuntz are aware that sentencing schemes are crucial in determining prosecutors' bargaining powers and that disproportionately harsh schemes enhance that power (n 1 above) 1962.

what ways, existing criminal prohibitions in any society involve such overreaching, admittedly, will be matters for further analysis and debate.

Consider, first, societies that pass laws enforcing invidious racial discrimination—laws prohibiting individuals of certain races from traveling or living in specified areas, or holding specified jobs. Individuals arrested and charged with violating such manifestly unjust laws might be offered plea settlements that reduce their punishment in exchange for waiving their rights to trial. There should be no disputing that the outcomes of such settlements are substantively unjust. The state has exceeded its rightful authority in passing and enforcing such laws. Those guilty of violating them are punished unjustly, however their guilt is determined, and their acceding to plea agreements in no way alters this. But the question is how we should view such plea agreements if and when they occur. Assume that prosecutors in such cases charge individuals pursuant to the law and their rightful authority. As such, they do not appear like gunmen who act with no palpable state imprimatur. Defendants, for their part, make the same calculations that defendants charged under legitimate criminal prohibitions make—whether to plead guilty in exchange for some waiver reward or go to trial and risk sentences that may turn out to be substantially longer. Appreciating the odds against their prevailing at trial, many will accept plea agreements.

I concede that we should probably accede to and enforce such agreements *in the circumstances*. But surely we should not be tempted to regard them as anything other than highly qualified goods. Imagine that sometime after prosecutors and those charged with such crimes reached their agreements, the society in question suddenly came to its senses and repealed the repulsive laws that occasioned them and declared all prior convictions under the laws to be null and void. Would proponents of the contract view suggest that those citizens convicted pursuant to the now repudiated laws serve the remainder of their sentences because, after all, they *agreed* to them? It seems preposterous to think that they would. Instead, they would properly regard such prior agreements as little different from the "agreements" of mugging victims to hand over their wallets—as actions forced on them by the predicament that they (unjustly) found themselves in. It might be protested that prosecutors are not muggers, even when they enforce morally dubious laws. They are elected officials in democratic (or perhaps semi-democratic) regimes with specific and proscribed responsibilities. They are not outlaws. But though they do not intend to be outlaws and no doubt do not view themselves as such, it is not apparent why their intentions, self-understandings, or social status matter if the laws that they enforce exceed a political regime's legitimate authority. As we shall see, prosecutors who threaten trial penalties or engage strategically in charge-stacking against defendants in order to pressure them into guilty pleas also act pursuant to their legal authority in some countries and likely do not regard themselves as doing anything wrong. Yet that does not shield them or their actions from scrutiny. The law can give prosecutors or other state officials legal warrants to act in ways that are unjustified. Armed with such warrants, state officials can put citizens in choice situations that are exceedingly difficult. The officials will look like they are just doing their jobs. No overt coercion will be present or needed. Yet the officials will have been given legal entitlements to exchange to which, we are supposing, they are not morally entitled. In a similar way, feudal lords might have had the legal authority to simply confiscate some of the property of those under their dominion. If they offered to seize less than they were legally entitled to in exchange for reduced levels of protest and unrest from the unfortunates upon whom they preyed, it seems doubtful that contract theorists would laud such settlements as paradigms of voluntary exchanges. Yet it is hard to see how the negotiated settlements of those prosecuted pursuant to unjust laws can be viewed any differently.

It does no good to point out, as proponents of the contract view often do, that the option of going to trial would be unlikely to improve things for citizens charged with violating laws whose moral credentials are questionable. Obviously, those prosecuted (or should we say "persecuted?") pursuant to such laws might wind up worse off if they insist on their day in court. But, by the same token, mugging victims who do not accede to their attackers' demands will also wind up worse off in most instances, or at least so we should assume.[21]

Similar considerations apply to the enforcement of criminal prohibitions that are fully justified but are attended with sanctions that punish the associated wrongdoing out of all proportion to its gravity. Suppose that a society got so caught up in the logic of deterrence that it adopted draconian sanctions—20-year minimum prison sentences under very harsh conditions—for even the most minor kinds of offenses.[22] Individuals arrested and charged with such crimes would be terrified at the prospect of the sentences they faced and thus keen to gain some measure of lenity from the authorities. But any negotiated settlements that such defendants "agreed" to would hardly seem the sorts of contracts that we would hail as expressions of their autonomy. Again, prosecutors will in these circumstances have been given legal warrants to which they are not morally entitled. Sure, they can exchange those warrants, and the threats they pose, for guilty pleas, but they should not be provided with them in

---

[21] Consider what a civil law analogous to such indefensible criminal prohibitions would look like. Imagine that social attitudes and practices in a given society resulted in civil plaintiffs more or less inevitably prevailing at trial regardless of the merits of their cases. Suppose that social animus toward certain individuals or organizations is so intense that almost any claim of negligently inflicted injury by them will result in substantial compensation for plaintiffs in cases that go to trial. In such circumstances, the socially scorned defendants would be eager to arrange pre-trial settlements, knowing the low probability of their winning at trial. Yet it seems doubtful that anyone would claim that their decisions to settle out of court were paradigmatic cases of voluntary agreements, though the force in question would be provided by widespread social attitudes rather than tort plaintiffs themselves. It might be objected that tort plaintiffs in such cases would be unlike prosecutors tasked with enforcing unjust laws. The latter should be presumed to act in good faith, whereas the former must know that they are perpetrating frauds. No doubt some tort plaintiffs would know or suspect this. But others might have, and pursue, genuine claims against the despised defendants. Yet they, too, would benefit from the social practices that made the relevant defendants desperate to settle out of court.

[22] As any crime reduction theorist would be quick to point out, such a draconian sentencing scheme would be very bad policy because it ignores the terrific costs for offenders, their loved ones, and society as a whole of long prison sentences for crimes that are apt to be relatively low in social costs.

the first place. Disproportionate sanctions operate just like threats of trial penalties. The only difference is that they will have been supplied to prosecutors by legislators rather than devised by prosecutors themselves.[23]

Admittedly, if disproportionate sanctions are not modified so that they are brought in line with what fairness or optimal crime reduction requires, we may have little choice but to honor the negotiated settlements worked out between prosecutors and defendants. Insisting that defendants plead guilty or go to trial and take their chances will not improve their options. But again, if lawmakers suddenly came to their senses, repealed the draconian sentences, and required all individuals convicted under the former sentencing scheme to have their sentences recalibrated downwards, can we seriously imagine any contract theorist insisting that the prior agreements reached should be respected and enforced? If not, then this suggests how little normative weight such agreements carry simply on the grounds that they were acceded to by criminal defendants who had bleak choices foisted upon them by the law.

Proponents of the contract view of plea bargaining could, I suppose, readily accept the points just made. Maybe they would even regard them as too obvious to insist upon. If so, fine, but the fact is that plea agreements in existing societies may be rendered somewhat problematic due to unjust laws and disproportionate sanction schemes. It is important to call attention to that fact in ways that defenders of the contract view have not always been careful about doing. Negotiated criminal settlements that are devoid of overt coercion may nonetheless fall short of paradigmatic free agreements if crucial background conditions are not satisfied.

Dubious prosecutorial tactics

Prosecutors have complex responsibilities in most legal systems and they are rarely given anything close to the resources they need to conduct trials for the numerous criminal cases that they must attempt to resolve. It is understandable, though lamentable, that they sometimes come to value the efficient processing of their caseloads over other things, including their duty to pursue both procedural and substantive justice. Proponents of the contract view of plea bargaining are not entirely insensitive to the ways in which prosecutors employ tactics that are in some cases indistinguishable from unjustified threats. What they have not discerned clearly enough, however, is the extent to which the entire array of powers that prosecutors might be granted by the courts and lawmakers pose serious problems for the notion that negotiated

---

[23] Someone might be tempted to suggest that there is nothing untoward about threatening defendants with disproportionate sanctions because, after all, they will have had advance warning that such sanctions exist. Setting aside the cogency of this argument in relation to innocents charged with crimes, it is not persuasive even in relation to guilty defendants. A threat to do something indefensibly harsh to someone if they do not comply with one's wishes does not, all by itself, make it appropriate to carry out the threat in the event of non-compliance. Advance warning is a necessary but not sufficient condition of just punishment. See, for instance, A. H. Goldman, "The Paradox of Punishment," [1979] 9 *Philosophy and Public Affairs* 42, 54–5.

criminal settlements are voluntary agreements. Again, the United States serves as a poster child for the over-empowerment of state officials when it comes to creating plea agreements.

Recall that Scott and Stuntz argue that prosecutorial monopoly is not a problem because defendants have a valuable bargaining chip at their disposal—their "call" on the prosecutor's resources should pre-trial negotiations fail. In response, I suggested that Scott and Stuntz's argument was flawed because a defendant's "call" on the prosecutor's resources is fraught with peril. Chapter 2 was devoted to showing that trial penalties, as I defined them, are indefensible. Again, trial penalties are longer sentences recommended or assigned to defendants over and above the ones they would receive if they exercised their right to trial, were found guilty, and received their presumptive sentences—the sentences they should receive given the severity of their crimes. Trial penalties are attempts to punish defendants specifically for having elected trial adjudication. If my arguments against trial penalties are persuasive, then it follows that the implicit or explicit threat of them by prosecutors is not justified and is arguably tantamount to putting criminal defendants under duress. The threat of longer sentences often will be psychologically compelling to criminal defendants, and no plausible moral defense of wielding such threats exists.[24] State officials who threaten or exact trial penalties are not simply doing their jobs, not if their jobs are understood to be charging defendants according to the evidence and recommending sentences that reflect the gravity of their crimes.

Someone might argue that the threat of a trial penalty is not coercive because it does not put criminal defendants in as dire a position as that of victims threatened by muggers. Mugging victims face grave harms that criminal defendants rarely encounter, even when their crimes are serious ones. But I doubt that this objection can be sustained. Suppose, for instance, that a defendant is charged with a crime for which the judge at a settlement hearing sets the presumptive sentence as one year's imprisonment. The prosecutor offers her probation if she will plead guilty, but threatens her with a sentence of two years if she proceeds to trial and is convicted. The extra year of imprisonment is the trial penalty in this case. Of course, we might hope that the judge in the case will refuse to go along with the prosecutor in attempting to exact such a penalty. But set that to one side and consider the following question: Is it true that a threat of "probation or (the risk of) two years in prison" is not coercive in the way that the threat of "your money or (the risk of) your life" is? I do not see how that could be so. Suppose that muggers threatened to lock their victims in prison for some period of time, rather than harm them physically, if they did not hand over their money. It seems unlikely that we would be prepared to look the other way when muggings occurred. Neither would we do so if they could only lock up their victims for a year or six months or three days. True, there might come a point at which the trial

---

[24] For discussion of the "psychological" and "moral" elements of duress, see A. Wertheimer, "The Prosecutor and the Gunman," [1979] 89 *Ethics* 269, 271.

penalties threatened by state officials become so meager that they no longer constitute coercion. But, by the same token, meek or ineffectual muggers might threaten such mild harms so that their actions, too, would no longer be coercive. Trial penalty threats, if and when they occur, are unlikely to be so benign.

Proponents of the contract view disagree about the moral status of trial penalties. Thomas Church regards them as inappropriate. He calls them a "surcharge for refusal to plead guilty," and concedes that they "very probably constitute the unconstitutional burden on the right to trial that, critics charge, inheres in all plea bargaining."[25] He therefore recommends reforms that would discourage, if not eliminate, the practice, including doing away with prosecutorial sentence recommendations altogether and having separate judges oversee plea bargaining and trials. Implementation of the latter recommendation would mean that defendants who failed to reach plea deals under the auspices of one judge would not then have to turn around and have trials presided over by the same judge, who would have some motive for retaliating against defendants' earlier refusals to enter guilty pleas.

In contrast, Frank Easterbrook defends trial penalties. He argues that most defendants who go to trial will likely perjure themselves when they take the witness stand.[26] Thus, judges will act appropriately by imposing some extra measure of punishment on them if they are convicted, though it is an extra measure of punishment that has little bearing on the actual charges for which they are on trial. This rationale for trial penalties is badly flawed. First, some defendants will not take the witness stand at all. Why, then, should they suffer trial penalties? Second, some will take the witness stand, tell the truth, or at least not lie, and still be convicted. Again, why should such defendants suffer trial penalties? Since we cannot assume that all defendants who testify and are convicted have perjured themselves, it would seem that state authorities should have to show, beyond a reasonable doubt, which of them has done so. Yet this would require a further trial. If the state successfully proved perjury at one of these additional trials, then the sentence imposed for perjury would not actually constitute a trial penalty. Defendants would have committed a further crime and been shown to have done so. Easterbrook's argument, in effect, licenses judges to presume and punish perjury without having to offer one shred of evidence for it beyond their own intuitions about the veracity of defendants.

Scott and Stuntz do not distinguish waiver rewards from trial penalties. This is shown most clearly in their response to the charge that plea bargaining involves an "improper threat" that makes it tantamount to duress, because defendants face a significant pre- and post-trial sentence differential.[27] Scott and Stuntz remark that "the argument about the size of the sentencing differential reduces to the claim that

---

[25] Church (n 1 above) 520.

[26] Easterbrook, "Criminal Procedure as a Market System" (n 1 above) 315, though Easterbrook does not distinguish the contributions that waiver rewards and trial penalties make to the longer sentences assigned defendants convicted after trials.

[27] Scott and Stuntz (n 1 above) 1919.

the choice to plead guilty is too generous to the defendant, an odd claim to make alongside the general claim that the system treats the defendant unfairly."[28] But this response only makes sense in relation to waiver rewards that reduce defendants' sentences below their presumptively deserved ones, for it is only such sentences that can be plausibly thought to treat them "too generously." The mere fact of a pre- and post-trial sentencing differential is not the issue, since such a differential exists even if prosecutors offer only waiver rewards. Even a significant sentencing differential may not, in and of itself, be coercive, especially if it is the product of a very generous waiver-reward offer. Only if it is partly the product of a post-trial sentence recommendation that is more severe for no reason other than to penalize the defendant for having elected trial adjudication does such a differential depend, in part, upon a trial penalty. Since Scott and Stuntz do not distinguish the different bases for sentence differentials, they fail to address the problem raised by trial penalties.[29] Yet if trial penalties are ubiquitous in plea bargaining in countries like the United States, then many negotiated criminal settlements may turn out to be something other than laudable free agreements.

Granted, defenders of the contract view are correct when they argue that we would not be doing any favors to criminal defendants who face trial penalties if we refused to accept their plea agreements and insisted, instead, that they should proceed with trials. The outcomes of trials, assuming conviction, would usually be longer sentences, sometimes significantly longer because they would include the trial penalty surcharge. But the attempt to vindicate negotiated settlements in this way is convincing only if we continue to permit prosecutors (or judges) to wield trial penalty threats. By the same token, if we permitted gunmen to threaten people with impunity, then it would be preposterous of us to insist that the hapless victims of such coercion ought to refuse to hand over their wallets. Individuals faced with bleak alternatives, and unjustifiably bleak ones, will "agree" to do things that otherwise they would scorn. But we should not dignify such agreements with the appellations "free" or "voluntary."

Though Scott and Stuntz may not appreciate the coercive potential of trial penalties, they are troubled by the prosecutorial practice of overcharging or charge-stacking, especially when it consists of little more than attempts by prosecutors to pressure defendants into pleading guilty. As we have seen, overcharging can take different forms. In some cases, prosecutors charge individuals with crimes that are more serious than the evidence warrants, hoping that they can thereby convince defendants to plead guilty to some lesser charge.[30] But the more common type of overcharging consists of prosecutors levying numerous duplicative or overlapping charges against defendants for a single criminal act or episode. In either case, overcharging appears

---

[28] Scott and Stuntz (n 1 above) 1920.

[29] Subsequently, Scott and Stuntz (note 1 above) at 1961–6, do worry about the possibility that post-trial sentences will be manipulated by prosecutors, but their focus is on overcharging and habitual offender statutes, and the contributions they make to sentences, rather than trial penalties.

[30] This is what Alschuler refers to as "vertical" overcharging (n 18 above) 86.

to be a deliberate strategy by prosecutors to effect guilty pleas, rather than an honest mistake or disagreement with the defense about what the evidence shows.[31]

When such strategic overcharging is present, Scott and Stuntz speak of post-trial sentences having been "manipulated by the prosecutor," and suggest that they have coercive potential.[32] In his subsequent work, Stuntz has shown in some detail how overbroad and overlapping criminal statutes give prosecutors enormous and largely unfettered discretion to threaten criminal defendants with sentences that bear only a tenuous relationship with the seriousness of their crimes.[33] Stuntz argues that the state legislators who write the majority of criminal statutes have political motives to define crimes expansively and attach sentences to them that are harsher than those they really want prosecutors to impose in most cases. Sweeping statutes ensure that all possible instances of criminal activity are covered, and overlapping and duplicative statutes empower prosecutors to charge and gain plea agreements even with individuals against whom the evidence of criminal conduct is relatively weak. Add to that the credible threat of draconian sentences, and "prosecutors are often in the position to dictate outcomes..."[34]. Stuntz writes: "Charge-stacking, the process of charging defendants with several crimes for a single criminal episode, likewise induces guilty pleas, not by raising the odds of conviction at trial, but by raising the threatened sentence."[35]

Again, prosecutors do nothing improper, in my view, if they charge individuals with crimes that accurately reflect or capture the illegal conduct in which those individuals have engaged, and seek to have sentences imposed that reflect the gravity of their criminal conduct. But matters are different if they use their charging discretion to menace defendants with sentences that are disproportionate. They then employ threats that appear indistinguishable from those of trial penalties. Any "agreements" that result from such threats are rather implausibly described as "voluntary," at least from the defendant's perspective.

It might be objected that whatever we say about the morality of overcharging as a settlement-creating tactic, it is one to which prosecutors are legally entitled. Since it is the legal entitlements of the parties that we should scrutinize, criminal plea settlements that result from deliberate overcharging by prosecutors are worthy of our respect and should be enforced. But it is hard to see how this position can be maintained with a straight face. As we have already seen, contract theorists are sometimes prepared to criticize the legal powers that prosecutors have been handed. Church rejects trial penalties, though it seems clear that they are a tolerated practice, at least

---

[31] Another possibility that should be noted is that prosecutors may initially file numerous charges, believing that they have plausible evidence for all of them only to subsequently have some of that evidence ruled inadmissible. This is not strategic overcharging as I understand it.

[32] Scott and Stuntz (n 1 above) 1920. See also 1921 and 1965.

[33] Stuntz (n 17 above) 512–23, (n 15 above) 2554–62. As his views about prosecutorial discretion have evolved, Stuntz has employed language to characterize prosecutors' plea bargaining strategies that suggests they are coercive.

[34] Stuntz (n 15 above) 2558.   [35] Stuntz (n 17 above) 520.

under United States law. He also recommends that criminal defendants be given more access to the state's case against them, though this is contrary to common practice and would, in some cases, make it harder for prosecutors to gain plea agreements. Stuntz is harshly critical of overcharging, though it is perfectly legal and, in fact, common practice in the United States. In short, contract theorists appear unwilling to take legal entitlements, as they are currently constituted, as the unproblematic background against which negotiated criminal settlements are to be evaluated. Neither could they do so plausibly, since it is easy to find or conceive of legal regimes in which outright coercion or theft of property by some citizens against others is permitted; no contract theorist would be prepared to validate such "exchanges."

Granted, given the practical problems in detecting and discouraging overcharging, we may have little choice but to accept negotiated settlements that we suspect are partly the product of threats to which prosecutors are not entitled. Again, enforcing them may be the lesser of two evils, if the only other option is to force overcharged defendants to go to trial. But it is no better than that. We could blunt the impact of overcharging by adopting concurrent sentencing schemes for all offenders, or by authorizing judges to assign sentences that reflect the criminally culpable conduct of individuals, independently of the charges to which they pleaded or were found guilty.[36] Yet in the absence of these reforms or others like them, we may have to enforce many negotiated plea settlements which we know or suspect are partly a consequence of sharp tactics by prosecutors.

Waiver rewards and the aims of punishment

Suppose that the laws enforced are reasonably just, the sanctions attaching to their violation are proportionate or at least not clearly disproportionate, and that prosecutors refrain from strategic overcharging and threatening trial penalties. Might we then conclude that negotiated settlements, premised on the offer and acceptance of waiver rewards by defendants, are presumptively valid and enforceable free-standing agreements? Not if the arguments in previous chapters challenging robust waiver rewards are convincing. Those arguments have coalesced around the notion that, to be defensible, waiver rewards should be fixed and modest. If they are not, then prosecutors or judges, in pursuing and finalizing plea agreements, are dealing in counterfeit currency. Jurisdictions that permit state officials to offer those charged with crimes substantial waiver rewards (whether variable or fixed) operate with legal warrants that cannot be given a persuasive normative justification.

Granted, the arguments in previous chapters have all presupposed that the evaluation of plea bargaining cannot be detached from the aims of legal punishment. Large and variable waiver rewards have been found wanting because of their tenuous relationship to the optimal reduction of crime or the punishment of offenders in

---

[36] The latter strategy is defended by Stuntz (n 17 above) 594–6.

accordance with their just deserts. Proponents of the contract view might not concede the necessity of a connection between negotiated criminal settlements and the aims of legal punishment. Instead, they might argue that negotiated criminal settlements, like commercial transactions, are presumptively to be enforced so long as the parties to them reach an informed agreement as to their terms. The crucial question is not whether such agreements can plausibly be thought to advance the larger aims of the criminal justice system, but simply whether all of the parties to them are happy.[37] If they are, then the settlements have free-standing value.

In fact, however, proponents of the contract view seem disinclined to take such a radical tack. They routinely cast plea agreements as instrumentally valuable in serving the larger aims of the criminal justice system. As we saw in Chapter 5, Easterbrook notes our desire to "get the maximum deterrent punch out of whatever resources are committed to crime control."[38] He cites with approval prosecutors' strong interests in reaching plea agreements so that "they may put the released resources to use in other cases, thus increasing deterrence."[39] Likewise, Church defends plea bargaining against charges that "it is necessarily irrational or otherwise detrimental to the deterrent function of the criminal law ... "[40] He takes that function to be part of the assumed background of negotiated pleas and hopes to show that they are fully consistent with it. More than this, he argues that the increased number of sure convictions that plea bargaining yields is at least as plausible a route to the "effective deterrence of criminal behavior" as fewer convictions accompanied by longer sentences would be.[41] Scott and Stuntz claim that "plea bargaining provides a means by which prosecutors can obtain a larger net return from criminal convictions, holding resources constant."[42] This claim is ambiguous, depending on what Scott and Stuntz mean by "larger net return." But they subsequently offer a clue to their meaning in a discussion of proposals to have judges oversee plea agreements: "The premise that judges are better than prosecutors at internalizing social interest in deterrence and retribution seems to us implausible on its face."[43] They appear to be saying, in other words, that prosecutors are in a better position than judges to determine whether and when negotiated settlements will promote the traditional aims of legal punishment.

Of course, proponents of the contract view might admit that the evaluation of negotiated criminal settlements cannot easily be detached from the overarching aims of the criminal justice system, but argue that this does not entail that each and every settlement reached by state officials must be guided by those aims. It is enough if the sentencing scheme is set up to, in general, advance those aims,

---

[37] Here I borrow, in slightly altered form, Alschuler's quip about the contract view (n 1 above) 683, which he, in turn, borrows from the late entertainer Ted Lewis.

[38] Easterbrook, "Criminal Procedure as a Market System" (n 1 above) 290. On the other hand, Easterbrook is harshly critical of efforts to ensure that criminal justice outcomes accord with offenders' deserts (pp. 302–5).

[39] Easterbrook, "Criminal Procedure as a Market System" (n 1 above) 309.

[40] Church (n 1 above) 519.   [41] Church (n 1 above) 519.

[42] Scott and Stuntz (n 1 above) 1915.   [43] Scott and Stuntz (n 1 above) 1955.

and if the rules governing negotiated settlements do not thwart or undermine the sentencing scheme. With the proper constraints in place, state officials will have discretion to resolve cases as they see fit without having to make constant reference to the system's governing aims. On this point, I would agree. But the crucial debate then concerns the appropriate constraints and I have attempted to show that they should be substantially more confining than those to which prosecutors (and judges) in the United States have grown accustomed. If my arguments for those constraints are persuasive, then negotiated settlements that violate them are unworthy of our support and enforcement, even if they are mutually agreed to by state officials and those charged with crimes.

Defendants' entitlements

In thinking about whether, and to what extent, negotiated criminal settlements are informed, free agreements worthy of our respect, it is not only the behavior of state officials that must be examined. Those charged with crimes can also attempt to exchange, for their benefit, goods to which they are legally but not morally entitled. Or so I shall argue. Proponents of the contract view assume that criminal defendants act appropriately in attempting to evade or minimize their punishment. To see how troublesome that assumption is in some instances, consider the following case.

Suppose that an individual, call him "McGurk," has committed a serious *mala in se* offense, involving the brutal rape of a woman. Though McGurk was careful not to let the victim see him and wore a condom during the attack to minimize the chances of being betrayed by his DNA, the police have nonetheless arrested him for the crime and the prosecutor has charged him with it. McGurk is guilty and he knows it. There is no credible defense to the charge that he could offer at a trial. He has not been overcharged and the sentence he faces for his crime is fitting, given the gravity of his offense and his culpability in committing it. Fortunately for McGurk, his attorney informs him that the prosecution's evidence for the charges is short of conclusive. He therefore tells McGurk that if he insists on exercising his legal right to a trial, the prosecutor will surely offer him a plea bargain to a substantially reduced charge. McGurk smiles and tells his attorney to inform the prosecutor that he intends to exercise his legal right to a trial.

McGurk's attorney appears to be giving him impeccable legal advice. And from a completely amoral perspective, McGurk should do precisely what his attorney says. The problem is that many of us do not subscribe to such a completely amoral perspective on these things. If the facts of the case are as described, we probably think that McGurk should admit his guilt and accept his punishment. The proper attitude toward one's serious wrongdoing is not to deny it—or, worse, to exploit deficiencies in the evidence that one has engaged in it to one's advantage—but to acknowledge one's misconduct, feel remorse about it, and embrace one's punishment as a justified response by the community to what one has done. McGurk appears to be the antithesis of the genuinely remorseful offender discussed in Chapter 4.

Would proponents of the contract view applaud the suggestion that McGurk view his situation amorally? They could not, it seems clear, consistently urge an amoral perspective on the law. Doing so would conflict with their normative view that the law ought to enforce free agreements. Neither could they defend an encapsulated amoralism—one appropriate to those charged with crimes but not appropriate more generally. For that would leave them in the untenable position of defending McGurk if he attempted to kill the eyewitness who put him at the scene of the crime, bribed the prosecutor or judge, or broke into the police lab, stole, and destroyed the incriminating evidence against him (or had others do so). Yet viewed amorally, these are precisely the things that McGurk should do to enhance his bargaining position. And once he has done them, he should attempt to ensure that any evidence implicating him for these additional crimes is destroyed or otherwise negated, to better his bargaining position should he be charged with them. Indeed, viewed amorally, there is nothing McGurk should stop at to minimize his exposure to the risk of criminal sanctions.

It might be objected that though McGurk is legally entitled to a trial, he is not legally permitted to destroy evidence, kill witnesses, or bribe officials. True enough, but that just pushes the argument back a step. Presumably McGurk is not legally entitled to do the latter sorts of things because he would be unjustified in so acting. If that is the case, then proponents of the contract view must convince us that McGurk does not act wrongly in demanding a trial, the likely outcome of which is that he will evade all punishment for his crime. As we have seen, it does not suffice to suggest that the law defines what McGurk is entitled to do in the process of effecting negotiated settlements. Proponents of the contract approach are, in other contexts, prepared to question what the law permits, especially when they see it as thwarting or failing to protect freely negotiated criminal settlements. They must therefore provide us with a normative defense of McGurk's attempt to exploit his "call" on the prosecutor's time and resources.

McGurk's leverage in brokering a deal is based on two factors in addition to his legal right to demand a trial. First, the evidence against him is weak, in part because of his own successful attempts to cover up his crime. Yet it is hard to see how the fruits of his cover-up are things to which he is morally entitled. They may be his good fortune to have, but he would surely have no legitimate complaint if his attempts to conceal his crime were thwarted by the authorities. Even if he had not attempted to cover up his crime, and the failings in the state's case against him were solely the result of the inability of the authorities to find the damning evidence against him, it does not seem that McGurk would be entitled to his good fortune. Again, he would have no legitimate complaint if the authorities managed to track down the incriminating evidence and were prepared to use it against him.

Second, McGurk has the legal right against self-incrimination, and this might be exploited by him in his efforts to negotiate a settlement. This right entails that the authorities cannot use compulsion in any of its forms to extract a confession from him, or force him to testify at his trial. Whether his decision not to testify at his trial can be cited by state officials as evidence implicating him varies from country to country. Albert Alschuler has argued, convincingly it seems to me, that suspects and defendants should be protected from state efforts to compel confessions from them—indeed, they should be protected much more vigorously than they currently are—but that their failure to testify at their trials ought to be something to which prosecutors can allude as incriminating them.[44] Nonetheless, whether or not we permit the state to cite a defendant's refusal to testify may not matter much, practically speaking. Jurors (or judges, in the case of a bench trial) may well draw their own inferences when defendants refuse to testify at their trials, whether encouraged by prosecutors to do so or not. Jurors will very much want to hear from defendants and might not look kindly upon defendants who remain silent.[45] Still, we can imagine cases in which defendants like McGurk do take the stand and simply deny their involvement in the crime of which they are accused.[46] In those kinds of cases, guilty defendants may not derive much of their negotiating leverage from the right against self-incrimination. It is the paucity of the evidence against them, combined with the high standard of proof the prosecution must meet, that is decisive.

Since it is doubtful that McGurk is morally entitled to exploit the paucity of evidence against him in his efforts to negotiate reduced punishment for himself, the case for his doing so depends primarily on the defensibility of his exercising his right to trial. It is undeniable that McGurk has a legal right to a trial and I conceded in Chapter 2 that the legal right to trial has firm moral grounding. There are numerous private and public goods that trials produce, even trials of individuals who are, in fact, guilty of the crimes with which they have been charged. Moreover, since the moral rights of individuals carry with them presumptions against their infringement by state officials, it makes sense to saddle those officials with the burden of proof in overcoming those presumptions. However, I also allowed that, at times, it makes perfectly good sense to say of defendants that though they have a moral right to a trial, it is a right that it would be wrong for them to exercise.[47] Some exercises of the right

---

[44] A. Alshuler, "A Peculiar Privilege in Historical Perspective," in R. H. Helmholz, et al., *The Privilege Against Self-Incrimination: Its Origins and Development* (Chicago: University of Chicago Press, 1997) 202–4.

[45] See, for instance, D. Dolinko, "Is There a Rationale for the Privilege Against Self-Incrimination?" [1986] 33 *UCLA L. Rev.* 1075.

[46] There is, of course, the complication here that some defendants who take the stand will have past criminal records that the prosecution can cite in attempts to impeach them.

[47] Again, the notion that individuals can have moral rights that it is nonetheless wrong of them to exercise in some circumstances is developed by J. Waldron, "A Right to Do Wrong," [1981] 92 *Ethics* 21, 29.

to trial will not produce any private goods to which defendants are entitled, precisely because they are guilty as charged. And some trials will produce few, if any, public goods. They will not expose any official misconduct by police or other authorities that would otherwise not have been brought to light. Neither will they enable guilty defendants to protest laws that they sincerely believe are unjust or pernicious or that set too harsh a punishment.

It could be argued that any trial will serve an educative purpose, reaffirming the values of due process, the presumption of innocence, and the heavy burden of proof on the state. Indeed, if we are to defend McGurk's exercise of his moral right to a trial, it will have to be on such a slender basis. Again, we are assuming that he is guilty as charged, faces proportionate punishment for his crime, and the authorities have done nothing wrong in arresting and charging him. Even if we grant that McGurk's trial would make a modest contribution toward educating the public, this seems an unimpressive argument to muster on his behalf. He is no public benefactor, as he is obviously not motivated by anything other than the protection of his own interests. If he were to prevail at trial, the substantive injustice thereby produced would be grave. If he takes advantage of the threat to go to trial to gain significantly reduced punishment, the substantive injustice is only somewhat less grave. The balance of values appears to clearly weigh against his doing what he is entitled to do. That is why few of us would be inclined to clap him on the back and congratulate him on his shrewd dealing if he managed to finagle an undeservedly light sentence from state officials. McGurk trades on goods to which criminal defendants may, in general, be entitled, but which he arguably should not exploit given the circumstances of his case.[48]

Suppose that the preceding line of argument is rejected and McGurk's dealings are viewed as eminently defensible. Still, the outcome, if it involves getting state officials to agree to less than his deserved punishment, is one most of us would rightly lament. We are reluctant to divorce the evaluation of negotiated criminal settlements from the moral norms of justice or crime reduction, in spite of assurances that they were agreements freely reached. Part of what is so disconcerting about the contract view of plea bargaining is that, at times, it seems to tolerate, if not encourage, detachment from such moral norms. There is no suggestion by proponents of the view that defendants who are guilty of quite serious offenses do anything improper in attempting to get the best deals that they can for themselves, even if this means that they wind up receiving much less punishment than their criminal acts merit. This makes a kind of bizarre sense if we view negotiated criminal settlements as we view commercial transactions, where shrewd bargaining and the exploitation of every legally

---

[48] However, as I have noted previously, it does not follow that McGurk should be punished specifically for wrongly exercising his right to trial. That is the import of retaining the claim that he has a moral right to act as he does, though he acts in a way that is decidedly less than admirable.

available advantage is expected and encouraged. Yet shrewd bargaining by individu-als guilty of, and charged with, heinous offenses is not something to be celebrated. It is, in a way, insulting to honest business people to analogize McGurk's dealings with theirs. And notice this, it is not just McGurk's actions that are subject to evaluation by the independent norms of justice or crime reduction. The prosecutor's conduct also would be appropriately scrutinized if she offered McGurk reduced charges or pun-ishment simply to free up time or other resources for herself. Serious crimes demand her attention and efforts in ways that minor ones do not. We might have to accept the prosecutor's reaching a plea agreement with McGurk if the alternative is to risk his acquittal. But we would rightly reject such trade-offs for less compelling reasons.

It might be objected that any discomfort we have with McGurk's deal-making derives mostly from the assumption that he is guilty. But that, the objection con-tinues, is something we will not know about most individuals charged with seri-ous crimes. Some of them might be innocent but unable to prove themselves so. Perhaps it is those defendants that proponents of the contract view would have us focus on. Their negotiated settlements do not seem affronts to morality in the ways that McGurk's does. True enough, yet many, if not most, of the individuals charged with serious crimes will be guilty of them, and some will find themselves in situations like McGurk's. The state lacks conclusive evidence of their guilt, in part because they have taken pains to cover up or destroy the evidence of their crimes. Such defendants do not act appropriately in contriving deals for themselves, and yet the contract view appears to suggest otherwise.

If the preceding conclusion seems too harsh, it might be because we are prone to thinking of criminal defendants of very different kinds. Some will be reluctant to admit their guilt for quite understandable reasons—because they have been badly overcharged by prosecutors or face disproportionate sanctions given the character of their conduct. Other defendants will be alienated from the criminal law because it criminalizes conduct that arguably it should not, or because they know that legiti-mate criminal prohibitions are inequitably enforced.[49] And still other defendants will have little use for many of the moral norms expressed and enforced by the crimi-nal law because they will feel that society has afforded them few legitimate opportu-nities. I concede that many of these other kinds of defendants may be on more solid moral ground in threatening to go to trial, and therefore in attempting to reach some sort of negotiated settlement which reduces their (arguably unjust) punishment. Such defendants are more appropriately conceived as rational contractors focused narrowly on the protection of their own legitimate interests, and thus are very different from the McGurks of this world. Nonetheless, there are costs to widespread detachment from the criminal law that proponents of the contract view of plea bargaining do not seem to countenance. It is not a good thing if a significant number of citizens view

---

[49] On the latter point, see W. J. Stuntz, "Race, Class, and Drugs," [1998] 98 *Colum. L. Rev.* 1795.

the criminal law as a rigged or oppressive system which they must circumvent or manipulate. Not only will this more or less inevitably produce more offending, with all of its costs, it will also require the state to invest more resources in enforcement of the law and punishment of offenders.

Detachment from the criminal law seems, as it were, officially incorporated into the contract view of plea bargaining. Those charged with crimes are not seen as doing anything worrisome if they negotiate about their punishment. This is, I have argued, a repulsive notion in relation to defendants like McGurk. In relation to other kinds of defendants, it may not be quite so bad, but it is not exactly something to cheer about. To the extent that a willingness to negotiate signifies detachment from the criminal law, it may be a sign that the social or criminal justice system is dysfunctional in certain respects. We would be much better off if criminal prohibitions had the allegiance of most citizens, such that if and when they disobeyed them, and were caught doing so, they admitted their guilt and accepted their just punishment.

Honorable negotiated settlements

There are, I concede, negotiated plea settlements that involve no wrongful conduct on the part of either state officials or criminal defendants, or that do not involve the exchange of things to which one or both of the parties is not entitled or of which they should not avail themselves. There is a substantial plea bargaining literature that describes instances of plea negotiations in which both sides act in good faith in attempting to fix charges that properly reflect defendants' criminal conduct and arrive at sanctions that are proportionate given that conduct.[50] Importantly, the defendants described in that literature are mostly resigned to pleading guilty. They know that they have broken the law and are willing to admit having done so in exchange for some modest charge or sentencing lenity from the prosecutor. Prosecutors, for their part, are not depicted as ruthlessly bent on extracting pleas or imposing the harshest sentences allowed by law. Indeed, they are often portrayed as attempting to evade the sentencing constraints statutorily imposed on them in the interest of making recommendations that are fairer to defendants or less destructive of their future prospects. But notice that part of what makes these kinds of plea agreements appear so benign is that the two sides do not treat them as commercial transactions in which they are each concerned to drive the hardest bargains they can, employing whatever means are available to them under the law. Instead, defendants are, if not genuinely remorseful, at least willing to admit their guilt. And prosecutors are not attempting to extract

---

[50] See M. Heumann, *Plea Bargaining: the Experiences of Prosecutors, Judges, and Defense Attorneys* (Chicago: University of Chicago Press, 1977); C. McCoy, *Politics and Plea Bargaining: Victims' Rights in California* (Philadelphia: University of Pennsylvania Press, 1993) 49–74; and L. M. Mather, *Plea Bargaining or Trial? The Process of Criminal Case Disposition* (Lexington, Mass.: Lexington Books, 1979).

every last pound of flesh from defendants, or prone to threatening that they will do so. The negotiations are motivated and informed on both sides, we might say, by the desire to reach reasonable outcomes, given the agreed-upon fact that some crime has occurred. It helps, of course, if the crimes in question are ones which a defensible theory of criminalization would treat as legitimate.

Put differently, such negotiated settlements seem worthy of our respect because they occur within a legal context that is, for the most part, properly structured to achieve the aims of legal punishment, with the parties to them conducting themselves in ways consonant with those aims. But this suggests that it is not the mere fact of agreement between the parties that is doing most of the normative work. Instead, their agreements merit our respect and confidence because they concern bona fide cases of criminal conduct, are reached within the context of a defensible sentencing scheme, and involve no evasion of responsibility by the guilty for their actions or use of questionable pressure tactics by prosecutors. It is, in other words, the justice of the outcomes that matters (or, if one prefers, its conduciveness to optimal crime reduction) as much as, if not more than, the fact that they were agreed to. As we have seen, settlements forged outside of these constraints may have to be accepted and enforced unless or until proper negotiation frameworks are implemented. But such settlements are not immune to evaluation by reference to independent moral norms of justice or crime reduction.

Similarly, in other kinds of negotiated criminal plea settlements, it is the broader context in which they occur, along with the attitudes and motivations of the parties, which plays a crucial role in our evaluation of them. There are cases of genuine disputes between prosecutors and those they have charged with crimes. Defendants (or their attorneys) and prosecutors might honestly disagree about which charges accurately capture the particular crime (or crimes) defendants have committed, whether they have committed crimes at all, or what constitutes appropriate punishment for the crimes that defendants admit they have committed. In these kinds of cases, some sort of compromise worked out between the contending parties might be entitled to our more or less unqualified respect. But again, this will likely be true only if such agreements are struck in the right kind of context, one marked by defensible laws and sentencing schemes, and in which defendants are not attempting to evade responsibility for their crimes and prosecutors are not pressuring them unduly to admit their guilt. In these circumstances, negotiated settlements that split the differences, so to speak, might produce better outcomes than trials, with their greater tendencies to yield victory for one side at the expense of the other.

Not all negotiated criminal settlements involve wrongdoing by one or both of the parties. Some involve no wrongdoing at all; some involve wrongdoing by only one of the parties. The former are appropriately deemed good and honorable; the latter are bad but, as things are, may have to be acceded to. When there is wrongdoing on both sides, negotiated settlements are ugly. We may have to accept such settlements because, in the absence of legal reforms or the ability to prove wrongdoing, we have little choice. The contract view of plea bargaining invites us to gloss over the important differences in the kinds of negotiated settlements that are reached in existing criminal justice systems, suggesting that all of them have the sheen of respectability that comes from their being free agreements between parties who exchange things to which they are entitled. That is an invitation that we should resist; it obfuscates more than it clarifies.

8

Principled Criminal Prosecution and Half-Loaves

State officials do not engage in plea bargaining solely to conserve their resources. They also offer criminal defendants charge and sentence concessions in exchange for guilty pleas because they suspect that the evidence they have falls short of meeting the rigorous standard of proof required by the criminal law. When the evidence they have is not conclusive beyond reasonable doubt, state officials might, more or less reluctantly, elect to compromise. The outcomes in such cases will often be at considerable variance with the ones which factually guilty defendants deserve, given the nature of their crimes. Though the officials involved and the rest of us presumably know this, the idea is that we should accept substantial waiver rewards in such cases as the price of getting "half a loaf"—that is, of effecting at least some punishment of the offenders in question.[1] The alternative is to go to trial on the charges, risk acquittals, and thus lose everything. Such an outcome, it is alleged by defenders of half-loaf plea bargaining, is worse than agreeing to reduced punishment, even dramatically reduced punishment.

In practice, of course, it will be difficult to tell whether, and to what extent, the half-loaf justification of substantial waiver rewards, as opposed to the resource conservation one, is operative in a given case. In some cases, both will be present. Prosecutors with less than conclusive evidence against defendants will be loath to expend their scarce resources on trial adjudication of the relevant charges.[2] But in theory, at least, it is possible to separate the two rationales. We can easily imagine that there is a set of cases that prosecutors would be willing to take to trial, assuming that defendants cannot be persuaded to plead guilty in exchange for modest waiver rewards, but for the very real possibility that the trials would produce outright acquittals. Often such cases will involve the more serious kinds of offenses, ones for which, as we have already noted, state officials have powerful motivations to try and see to it that offenders are punished. In any event, the assumption in this chapter will be that

---

[1] I am uncertain about the origins of the phrase "half a loaf". I first ran across it in Albert Alschuler's article, "The Prosecutor's Role in Plea Bargaining," [1968] 36 *U. Chi. L. Rev.* 50, 60.

[2] See A. Duff, L. Farmer, S. Marshall, and V. Tadros, *The Trial on Trial, Vol. 3: Towards a Normative Theory of the Criminal Trial* (Oxford: Hart Publishing, 2007) 176. However, it is not clear how two weak rationales for more-than-modest waiver rewards taken together produce a strong case for them.

the state officials who offer waiver rewards do so because they fear trial adjudication will result in what they regard as the mistaken acquittal of offenders.

One question that immediately comes to the forefront, given our conclusions in previous chapters, is whether veridical charging requirements (with no real bargaining about charges permitted) and modest, fixed waiver rewards would unduly hamstring state officials in the half-loaf cases. The literature on these cases certainly suggests that such limitations on state officials would be deleterious. It is assumed that the weakness of the evidence in these cases is apparent to defendants and their attorneys, as well as to prosecutors. As a result, defendants will insist on generous waiver rewards as the price of forgoing the trials that offer them realistic chances of acquittal. Prosecutors, too, will apprehend the logic of the situation and bargain accordingly. As Albert Alschuler puts it, it is not unusual to find prosecutors "bargaining hardest when the case is weakest…"[3] Since prosecutors want to amass convictions, they will be reluctant to drop charges even when the evidence supporting them is thin. They will instead try to salvage something from such cases, even if it means they must agree to charges that do not really reflect the crimes individuals have committed or sanctions that are disproportionate with the severity of their offenses.

In addressing the issues raised by half-loaf plea bargaining, I elaborate the notion of the "principled prosecution" of cases. State officials who are committed to the principled prosecution of cases understand and embrace the complex role that they have in the criminal justice system—one that requires them to vigorously pursue the appropriate punishment of criminal offenders while acting in accordance with the constraints of procedural justice. I contend that officials committed to principled prosecution would be reluctant to engage in half-loaf plea bargaining. In most cases, they would see it as producing substantively unjust outcomes and, equally importantly, contrary to the deeper values that ground the commitment to procedural justice. The two most convincing arguments for such bargaining—getting potentially dangerous offenders off the streets for some period of time or giving offenders at least some of what they deserve for their crimes—do not, for the most part, support the wholesale reduction of charges and sentences that occurs in the half-loaf cases. If my arguments are convincing, then it turns out that "getting something rather than nothing" is not a very powerful justification for state officials agreeing to substantial waiver rewards in these kinds of cases.

It will not be denied that state officials in general, and prosecutors in particular, face some very difficult dilemmas in the half-loaf cases. This will especially be true when they have incriminating evidence against defendants which, for one reason or another, they know or suspect will be unavailable to them should such cases go to trial. Yet even in these troubling cases, it is far from clear that the resort to substantial waiver rewards is justified.

---

[3] Alschuler (n 1 above) 60.

Some preliminary points

To begin, it is useful to divide the criminal cases that state officials confront into three rough categories. The majority of cases will involve low-level offenses, encompassing drug crimes, relatively minor property crimes, public disturbance offenses, simple assaults, and the like. As the literature on plea bargaining makes abundantly clear, almost no one in the criminal justice system wants such cases to go to trial.[4] Prosecutors certainly do not want to waste their finite resources on the trial adjudication of charges like these. Likewise, judges do not want to have to try them. Surprisingly perhaps, those charged with such offenses quite often do not want to have their day in court, especially if they can plead guilty and receive a substantial measure of lenity in return. This is especially true if those charged with such crimes already have criminal records. For them, another mark on their records is not something to be terribly concerned about, whereas avoiding prolonged pre-trial detention or a jail or prison term for the latest offense is.[5] Even defendants who are entirely innocent will have powerful incentives to plead guilty if by doing so they can avoid harsh (or harsher) punishment. This is a point we come back to. The important thing to note at this juncture is this: It seems likely that the main motivation of state officials in attempting to resolve these kinds of cases through plea bargaining almost always will be the conservation of their resources, not the obtaining of half-loaves. For one thing, there are unlikely to be victims clamoring at all or very loudly for justice in these kinds of cases. For another, the offenders in these kinds of cases probably will not appear to state officials as being terribly dangerous, such that getting them off the streets for some period of time or punishing them severely assumes great importance.

Beyond these two points, there is another: There is simply an embarrassment of riches for prosecutors when it comes to low-level offenses. There are innumerable cases for them to choose among—so many that they cannot possibly see to the prosecution of all of them.[6] This gives them the luxury of dropping charges in cases in which the evidence is weak. There are lots of other cases, after all, that will enable them quickly and more easily to burnish their conviction resumés. This is not to say, of course, that there are no low-level crimes that might be resolved by generous waiver-reward offers, because prosecutors would prefer to gain half a loaf rather than risk getting none at all. There will be some, but as will subsequently become clear, they do not provide very persuasive reasons for accepting half-loaf plea bargains.

---

[4] For the classic statement of this view, see M. Heumann, *Plea Bargaining: The Experiences of Prosecutors, Judges, and Defense Attorneys* (Chicago: University of Chicago Press, 1977). For a recent statement of it, see J. Bowers, "Punishing the Innocent," [2008] 156 *U. Pa. L. Rev.* 1117, 1141–2. See also the high rate of guilty pleas (estimated at over 90 percent) in Magistrates' Courts in England and Wales, in A. Ashworth and M. Redmayne, *The Criminal Process*, 4th edition (Oxford: Oxford University Press, 2010) 293.

[5] On this, see Heumann (n 4 above) 69–70.

[6] This is a point stressed by William Stuntz in "Plea Bargaining and the Criminal Law's Disappearing Shadow," [2004] 117 *Harv. L. Rev.* 2548, 2564.

At the other extreme are serious criminal offenses, crimes such as homicide, aggravated assault, rape, child molestation, armed robbery, or theft of substantial amounts of property. Generally, state officials will have less leeway to offer substantial waiver rewards in such cases.[7] There will be victims (or their loved ones) looking over their shoulders, demanding stout punishment of those believed guilty of having committed such crimes. There will also be more public interest in the outcomes of these cases. Citizens very much want serious offenders to be punished. They also want dangerous ones to be incapacitated by imprisonment. State officials also may believe fervently in securing the punishment of serious offenders, quite independently of concerns they have about how failure to do so might hurt their political standing or career ambitions. Prosecutors in such cases might have little choice but to go to trial if defendants refuse modest waiver rewards for pleading guilty. And they may have to conduct trials even if the evidence they have is short of conclusive. The victims of serious crimes and the public more generally will be less tolerant of generous plea bargains. Indeed, some might rather have prosecutors go for broke and risk acquittals than bargain with such offenders. Again, however, this does not mean that no serious cases could be resolved through half-loaf bargaining. Some might be, and the issues they raise will occupy us in later sections of this chapter.

A third group of crimes consists of mid-level offenses—breaking and entering, robbery, forgery, counterfeiting, racketeering, and many white-collar crimes, among them. State officials in these mid-level cases will not have the amount of discretion they have in making decisions about whether or how to prosecute low-level offenses, but their decisions will not be as constrained as they are with the more serious offenses. Though there will often be victims of these crimes, typically they will not have been harmed or traumatized to such an extent that they demand exacting punishment of offenders. Also, the dangerousness of such offenders will not be as patent, which is not to say that concerns about it will exert no influence over prosecutors. My sense is that half-loaf bargaining is apt to be most common in the mid-level cases. Prosecutors will have to take the crimes involved seriously, but not so seriously that they will feel compelled to go to trial in cases in which the evidence is not sufficiently strong.

This brings me to a second point: So far, I have loosely characterized the half-loaf cases as ones in which the evidence against defendants is short of conclusive beyond reasonable doubt. There is, it must be admitted, no entirely precise way to judge the strength of the evidence against a given defendant. With enough experience, prosecutors will, we should assume, become quite adept at evaluating the probative value of the evidence they have at their disposal. But even they may not be able to say in any very rigorous way how close to meeting the standard of proof the evidence is in a given case, especially in advance of their having tried it. Still, it would be a mistake to operate with the assumption that all cases in which the state's evidence is slightly short

---

[7] Stuntz (n 6 above) 2563.

of conclusive constitute genuine half-loaf cases. Why is this? Because it is plausible to believe that prosecutors will win a majority, and maybe a substantial majority, of the cases in which the evidence they have is strong but not decisive. For instance, it is estimated that the prosecution wins 80 percent of the felony cases that go to trial in the United States, the country in which half-loaf plea bargaining is most common.[8] Very probably, not all of these were cases in which the state's evidence was conclusive. Yet the state still won most of them. It does so for a variety of reasons which it will be useful to review, if only briefly.[9]

First, prosecutors tend to have more resources at their disposal than do most criminal defendants. They have the police to help them investigate crimes and paid staff to help them compile and sort through evidence. Many criminal defendants, by contrast, are indigent. How well they will be represented by legal counsel varies from country to country. In the United States, it is generally agreed that the quality of indigent defense is scandalous.[10] In England and Wales, it appears to be considerably better.[11] Yet even where it is respectable, state officials are likely to retain significant advantages in the resources they can deploy to investigate and convict people of crimes.

Second, prosecutors act and, more importantly, are perceived by the public (including members of the jury pool) as acting on behalf of the interests of all citizens. Their status as representatives and protectors of the public welfare gives them a powerful persuasive edge in the courtroom, especially since they will be pitted against what many citizens regard as little more than "hired guns" in the form of defense attorneys.

Third, the mere fact of public accusation of crimes is highly stigmatizing. In spite of the official stance and rhetoric of procedural criminal law—that criminal defendants are entitled to the presumption of innocence—there is disturbing evidence that suggests that jurors will sometimes believe otherwise.[12] Some of them may even believe that individuals on trial are guilty until proven innocent and expect defendants to convince them of their innocence.

---

[8] See W. J. Stuntz, "The Pathological Politics of Criminal Law," [2001] 100 *Mich. L. Rev.* 505, 570. However, it is worth noting that the state's success in jury trials is not always so high. Ashworth and Redmayne report acquittal rates in the 50–60 percent range in the Crown Courts of England and Wales (n 4 above) 294.

[9] I offer a more elaborate account of the advantages that the state has in prosecuting individuals in "Punishing the Guilty, Not Punishing the Innocent," [2010] 7 *Journal of Moral Philosophy* 462, 477–81.

[10] For commentary on indigent defense in the United States, see N. Lefstein, "In Search of Gideon's Promise: Lessons from England and the Need for Federal Help," [2004] 55 *Hastings L. J.* 835; S. Schulhofer, "Plea Bargaining as Disaster," [1992] 101 *Yale L. J.* 1979, 1988–89; and S. Bibas, "Plea Bargaining Outside the Shadow of Trial," [2004] 117 *Harv. L. Rev.* 2463, 2476–82.

[11] See Lefstein (n 10 above) 861–900.

[12] See M. J. Frank and D. Borschard, "The Silent Criminal Defendant and the Presumption of Innocence: In the Hands of Real Jurors, is Either of Them Safe?" [2006] 10 *Lewis & Clark L. Rev.* 237, 249–51, and K. A. Findley and M. S. Scott, "The Multiple Dimensions of Tunnel Vision in Criminal Cases," [2006] 2006 *Wis. L. Rev.* 291, 340–1.

The reason that all of this matters for our purposes is that it seems plausible to believe that the genuine half-loaf cases, those on which we should focus our attention, will be ones in which the state's evidence is significantly less than conclusive. The state will likely win the vast majority of cases in which the evidence is conclusive or even close to it, and prosecutors presumably know that. The cases that should give prosecutors the most pause will be ones in which the evidence comes up considerably short of proving guilt beyond reasonable doubt. These are the cases in which state officials will be most sorely tempted to settle for half a loaf and ones in which they might appear justified in doing so.

A further point involves noting, once again, the crucial distinction between the analysis of plea bargaining in ideal versus non-ideal contexts. We might be more sanguine about half-loaf plea bargaining in settings where overcriminalization is the norm. If the state prohibits actions that arguably it should not, or over-punishes actions that it should prohibit, we might not lament and might even welcome half-loaf bargains with their tendency to produce dramatically reduced sentences. Similarly, if prosecutors routinely threaten trial penalties or engage in strategic overcharging in order to put pressure on defendants to plead guilty, then we might be more accepting of prosecutors acquiescing in significant charge or sentence reductions in order to forge deals.

However, my strategy will be to analyze half-loaf plea bargaining in a different context, one purged of many of the pathologies that infect some existing criminal justice systems. Doing so will enable us to focus squarely on the logic of such bargaining. It is a mistake, it seems to me, to tolerate half-loaf plea bargaining because there are other problems with the criminal justice system that it helps to ameliorate. The question we should ask is whether such bargaining is acceptable when the criminal law does not overreach. This is a question, I suggest, that cannot be answered without careful consideration of the functions of criminal prosecutions. It also cannot be answered without scrutinizing the logic of half-loaf reasoning. I contend that such reasoning is sufficiently problematic that we should be wary of having state officials employ it.

Criminal prosecution and principled state actors

Albert Alschuler once claimed that the half-loaf cases were precisely the ones which, on the most basic assumptions of our legal system, ought to go to trial. As he put it: "If trials ever serve a purpose, their utility is presumably greatest when the outcome is in doubt."[13] When the state's case appears less than conclusive, it really should be tested in the crucible of a trial. And yet, Alschuler lamented, prosecutors in the United States respond to the weakness of the evidence in such cases by offering more generous waiver rewards so as to salvage some sort of conviction from them. Worse

---

[13] Alschuler (n 1 above) 64.

than this, they strategically overcharge defendants and threaten them with trial penalties. Doing so enables them to open up formidable sentencing differentials between plea bargained and trial outcomes, thus putting terrific pressure on defendants, even wholly innocent ones, to accede to guilty pleas. Moreover, the possibility of manipulating sentencing differentials in these ways encourages prosecutors to pursue charges in cases in which the evidence against individuals is quite weak, knowing that some sort of conviction can, no doubt, be gleaned from them.[14] Hence, though the half-loaf cases ought to be tried, prosecutors have been given extraordinary abilities to discourage defendants from daring to insist upon it.

Setting to one side, for the time being, the problems raised by unrestrained plea bargaining and rapacious prosecutors, it is useful to remind ourselves why Alschuler's claim about the half-loaf cases makes abundant good sense. As we saw in Chapter 2, trials serve a vital purpose in the legal system, given the fact that the state officials who initiate investigations into crimes and charge individuals with them should not be allowed to make authoritative decisions concerning whether those whom they suspect of crimes are actually guilty of them. Given the abundant opportunities for error by state officials, if not for dishonest or malicious conduct in prosecuting people for crimes, trials structured to give criminal defendants the presumption of innocence and the state a heavy burden of proof to shoulder are our most reliable (albeit imperfect) means for avoiding errors—especially errors that consist in the unjust punishment of individuals. There is room for debate about how strong our preference should be for permitting the guilty to go unpunished rather than having the innocent punished.[15] But some degree of preference for the former over the latter is surely defensible and is part of what undergirds our placing obstacles in the state's path when it seeks to impose legal sanctions on those individuals whom its officials suspect of crimes. After all, when the innocent are punished, two injustices occur—the wrong persons have criminal sanctions inflicted upon them and the persons actually guilty of crimes go unpunished. Whether one favors a retributive or crime reduction rationale for punishment, such outcomes are highly undesirable.

There is also room for debate about the kinds of trials that best serve as checks on the unwitting or deliberate abuse of the state power to accuse and punish. But that those accused of crimes have a right to hear the evidence against them, to challenge it, to put on a defense against the charges, and to have the cogency of the state's case against them evaluated by an impartial agent or group of agents seems incontrovertible. Admittedly, defendants who know that they are guilty as charged and are willing to admit it, whether or not the state has managed to amass conclusive evidence against them, may not need or desire to go forward with such elaborate forms of

---

[14] See A. W. Alschuler, "The Changing Plea Bargaining Debate," [1981] 69 *Cal. L. Rev.* 652, 688.

[15] See Lippke (n 9 above) 465–73. There I argue that the oft-cited figure, from William Blackstone, that we should prefer to let ten guilty individuals go free to punishing one innocent one, cannot be defended on any plausible account of legal punishment's role in society. However, I suggest that some lesser degree of preference is likely to be defensible.

official inquiry. Yet the option of doing so should be available to them. Moreover, as I argued previously, they should not be penalized for exercising it.

Importantly, the notion that legal punishment is such a prima facie evil that limits on the state's power to inflict it should not be resented or resisted but instead faithfully adhered to is something that prosecutors, judges, and even the police should be capable of appreciating. To simplify things, my primary focus in what follows is on prosecutors and criminal court judges. But other state actors, police officers and criminal investigators foremost among them, should also be judged against the standards of principled prosecution.

Prosecutors in some countries (e.g., the United States) appear to have become "conviction maximizers."[16] Once the decision is made to charge individuals with one or more crimes, prosecutors appear deeply reluctant to forgo all punishment of them, though they are quite willing to compromise on the amount of punishment to be assigned. Yet various prosecutorial codes of conduct suggest that prosecutors' responsibilities are more complex than simply amassing convictions. The American Bar Association standards for prosecutors state that the prosecutor "is an administrator of justice, an advocate, and an officer of the court."[17] More pointedly, the same standards note that "the duty of the prosecutor is to seek justice, not merely to convict."[18] In England and Wales, *The Code for Crown Prosecutors*, Principle 2.3, states unequivocally that "Crown Prosecutors must always act in the interests of justice and not solely for the purpose of obtaining a conviction."[19]

The meaning of these high-sounding phrases is far from self-evident and cynics might claim that they are little more than platitudes.[20] However, Bennett Gershman helpfully suggests that prosecutors have three primary constituencies—victims, the general public, and the accused.[21] This "tripartite responsibility" requires prosecutors to skillfully balance the legitimate interests of these groups, interests that sometimes, although not invariably, compete against one another. Arguably, prosecutors will achieve the correct balance if they vigorously pursue conviction of those whom they reasonably suspect are guilty of crimes, while at the same time upholding standards of both procedural and substantive justice.[22] The duty to ensure procedural justice requires them to pursue convictions in ways that respect the due process rights of the accused. No one's legitimate interests are served by punishment of the innocent or disproportional punishment of the guilty. This is obviously true of the individuals who are suspected of crimes, but it is equally true of victims, who can justifiably

---

[16]   See, for instance, Bowers (n 4 above) 1128, and S. Z. Fisher, "In Search of the Virtuous Prosecutor: A Conceptual Framework," [1987–88] 15 *Am. J. Crim. L.* 197, 198–200.

[17]   American Bar Association, *Criminal Justice Section Standards*, Standard 3–1.2 (b).

[18]   American Bar Association, *Criminal Justice Section Standards*, Standard 3–1.2 (c).

[19]   Crown Prosecution Service, *The Code for Crown Prosecutors* 2004.   [20]   Fisher (n 16 above) 220.

[21]   B. L. Gershman, "Prosecutorial Ethics and Victims' Rights: The Prosecutor's Duty of Neutrality," [2001] 14 *Geo. J. Legal Ethics* 559, 561.

[22]   See Fisher (n 16 above) 236–7. See also B. A. Green, "Why Should Prosecutors Seek Justice?" [1999] 26 *Fordham Urb. L. J.* 607, 634.

demand only proportional punishment of the guilty, and the general public, who must bear the burdens of unjust punishment. Prosecutors must therefore scrupulously avoid thwarting or undermining the vital screening function that defendants' procedural rights are designed to play.[23] And they should keep the gravity of the offenses that individuals are suspected of committing ever in view in making charging decisions and sentencing recommendations. Only then can they ensure that, whatever the law might technically permit, the sanctions imposed on those who plead or are found guilty are appropriate given their crimes.[24]

How might prosecutors who take seriously their complex responsibilities, ones imposed on them by both the law and the underlying political morality of the criminal justice system, proceed when they confront genuine half-loaf cases? For brevity's sake, I shall refer to prosecutors who view their role as more multifaceted than that of amassing convictions as "principled prosecutors." Principled prosecutors fully accept the right of the accused to a fair hearing before an impartial adjudicative body. They are not grudging or cynical about the rights of the accused, because they recognize the fallibility of the process that has produced charges against those accused. Principled prosecutors, while not deaf to the cries from some in the press and public for harsh punishment of offenders, nonetheless are steadfastly committed to justice in the sentencing of the guilty. Further, principled prosecutors will recognize the perils of the half-loaf cases. They understand that such cases contain a disproportionate number of innocent defendants or defendants who have been charged inappropriately.[25] This gives principled prosecutors pause when they encounter such cases. They will also be aware of the very real possibility that sometimes there is a paucity of evidence against defendants because police or investigators have jumped to conclusions too quickly about the identities of those involved in crimes. What some have termed "usual suspects" policing occurs more often than we would like to admit.[26] So do efforts by the police or investigators to manipulate the identification of suspects by rigging line-ups or repeatedly showing eyewitnesses photos of individuals whom police regard as likely candidates for having committed the crimes under investigation. Such tactics encourage (whether intentionally or not) the mistaken identification of innocent individuals as the perpetrators of crimes.[27] Prosecutors are highly dependent upon the police and other investigators in building cases against those suspected of crimes, and so must cultivate and maintain good working relationships with such officials.[28] Nevertheless, principled prosecutors know that the police sometimes make honest mistakes and occasionally make not-so-honest ones.

[23] Similarly, Ashworth and Redmayne argue that prosecutors should serve as "ministers of justice" (n 4 above) 65.

[24] Cf. Stuntz (n 8 above) 594–6, where he argues that judges may need to assert their authority to ensure that sentencing outcomes are proportionate, whatever the law technically permits.

[25] See O. Gazal-Ayal, "Partial Ban on Plea Bargains," [2006] 27 *Cardozo L. Rev.* 2295, 2309–13.

[26] Bowers (n 4 above) 1125–6. See also R. O. Lempert, S. R. Gross, and J. S Liebman, *A Modern Approach to Evidence Law*, 3rd edition (St Paul, Minn.: West, 2000) 327–8.

[27] See Bowers (n 4 above) 1126.   [28] Bowers (n 4 above) 1126–7.

In the half-loaf cases, in particular, these concerns should loom somewhat larger in the minds of prosecutors as they make decisions about how to proceed.

An additional argument against permitting the kinds of waiver rewards that facilitate half-loaf plea bargains is this: Such plea agreements are contrary to the central purpose or purposes of any defensible sentencing scheme. Whether one is a retributivist, crime reductionist, some combination of the two, or supports an altogether different rationale for sentencing, one will want sentences to be determined by the character of the crimes being punished, not by the strength of the evidence against defendants. Yet it is commonplace for those who defend half-loaf plea bargaining to suggest that sentences in such cases should be determined by discounting the normally assigned sentence by the probability of trial conviction.[29] If, for instance, a prosecutor would normally recommend a ten-year sentence for someone believed guilty of a crime of a certain type, but the probability of conviction in a given case is only 60 percent, then the prosecutor should offer a six-year sentence recommendation to the defendant in the case. In the words of the authors of a *Yale Law Journal* article published nearly 40 years ago, sentences in half-loaf cases are thus determined by factors which "are totally devoid of genuine penological significance."[30] It is not apparent why principled prosecutors would participate in the deliberate subversion of a sentencing scheme in this fashion. Neither is it clear why trial judges who take their responsibilities seriously would do so, permitting what they know or believe to be the assignment of significantly reduced sentences to individuals for reasons unrelated to the harm they have done or the culpability with which they acted.

My contention is not that principled prosecutors should quickly throw up their hands and give in when confronted by half-loaf cases, dropping any and all charges that the evidence is not adequate to support. Instead, they would strongly and probably correctly suspect that many of the defendants in such cases are, in fact, guilty. They might also believe that if they seem determined to forge ahead in such cases, some defendants will cave in and agree to plead guilty for the kinds of modest and fixed sentence discounts that I have previously argued are defensible. Nonetheless, many such defendants will not admit their guilt. They or their attorneys will recognize the dubious nature of the state's evidence against them and demand more in the way of concessions from prosecutors. If such concessions are not available, then defendants will insist on their day in court. Even so, principled prosecutors, for reasons we have already noted, will be strongly disinclined to simply drop the charges in some of these cases. If the crimes in question are serious enough, principled prosecutors might believe that they have few options but to proceed to trial and attempt to win convictions. Better to do that than to concede to charges or sentences that they believe do not match in any very close way the crimes individuals have committed.

---

[29] See, for instance, F. Easterbrook, "Criminal Procedure as a Market System," [1983] 12 *J. Legal Stud.* 289, 292.

[30] "Note: Restructuring the Plea Bargain," [1972] 82 *Yale L. J.* 286, 291.

In some cases, however, the only viable option will be for principled prosecutors to drop charges which the evidence does not adequately support. They will recognize that they have the option of dropping the charges for the time being and hoping that more evidence will eventually emerge. If it does, then they can, in good conscience, reinstate the charges and press them through the courts if defendants will not come to heel in exchange for modest sentence discounts. Of course, additional evidence may never surface. But leaving off prosecution for the time being does not foreclose it altogether.

It might be objected that the preceding argument rushes too quickly to its conclusion. The argument assumes that prosecutors have an obligation to evaluate the sufficiency of the evidence against defendants. If that evidence appears significantly short of conclusive and defendants are unwilling to enter guilty pleas in exchange for receiving modest waiver rewards, then the responsible thing to do in some cases will be for prosecutors to drop charges. But it could be claimed that prosecutors are justified in pressing forward with charges so long as a trial is "more likely than not to convict the defendant of the charge alleged."[31] Prosecutors should not be put in a position in which they are tasked with determining whether the evidence is at or near the standard of proof required in criminal cases. To do so would be to require "a new subtrial, informal and often ex parte, interposed between the determinations of the accusing and judging authorities."[32] Specifically, prosecutors should not be asked to evaluate the sufficiency of evidence that they have never seen fully challenged by defense counsel in the formal setting of a trial. Further, they should not be expected unilaterally to resolve technical legal matters (e.g., a defendant's claim that he acted in reasonable self-defense) concerning which it seems important to bring in broader community judgments, in the form of jury verdicts.[33] Therefore prosecutors, even principled ones, should not drop charges as long as the evidence in a case meets the much weaker standard of being more likely than not to yield trial convictions.[34]

We might agree with all of this on the assumption that most half-loaf cases will ultimately go to trial.[35] Trials do serve as vital checks on the power of state officials unilaterally to accuse individuals of crimes and impose sanctions on them. Indeed,

---

[31] This is the standard in the Code for Crown Prosecutors in England and Wales, quoted in R. Young and A. Sanders, "The Ethics of Prosecution Lawyers," [2004] 7 *Legal Ethics* 190, 200.

[32] H. R. Uviller, "The Virtuous Prosecutor in Quest of an Ethical Standard: Guidance from the ABA," [1973] 71 *Mich. L. Rev.* 1145, 1157.

[33] See Young and Sanders (n 31 above) 201.

[34] Bennett Gershman argues forcefully against the claim that prosecutors should turn over the responsibility to assess the evidence against defendants to jurors. He notes that prosecutors are much more experienced in evaluating evidence than jurors and have a fuller appreciation of how the evidence in a given case was developed. They are thus in the best position to know whether that evidence is convincing beyond reasonable doubt. See his "The Prosecutor's Duty to Truth," [2001] 14 *Geo. J. Legal Ethics* 309.

[35] Young and Sanders appear to recognize that plea bargaining raises problems with their defense of the notion that prosecutors should proceed with cases in which conviction at trial is "more probable than not" (n 31 above) 208.

I have conceded that there will be some cases, especially those involving serious crimes, in which prosecutors do nothing improper by proceeding to trial if defendants refuse to plead guilty, and this in spite of the shortcomings in the evidence prosecutors are able to muster. Trials will, in such instances, presumably work in their normal, albeit imperfect, ways to ensure defendants' procedural rights. But the crucial question concerns whether prosecutors in the half-loaf cases should be permitted to offer defendants more than modest waiver rewards (or, worse, overcharge them or threaten them with trial penalties) when defendants refuse to plead guilty. If they are permitted to do so and the inducements provided become substantial enough, then the likely outcome will be that many defendants in such cases will come around to pleading guilty. It would seem that prosecutors will then have acted not only as accusers but as the kinds of unilateral judges of cases that the argument insists they should not be. It does no good to argue that prosecutors act properly by offering such inducements (or threats) because the evidence in the cases in question is strong enough for them to accuse and press charges against defendants in the first place. Though that is correct, the fact remains that the evidence falls significantly short of being convincing beyond reasonable doubt. And the whole point of increasing the size of waiver rewards is to free prosecutors from having to face the dilemma they would otherwise confront—whether to go to trial or drop the charges in such cases for the time being. Principled prosecutors will not attempt to evade that dilemma by ramping up the pressure on defendants to accept guilty pleas.

It might be objected that even modest waiver rewards put some pressure on half-loaf defendants to plead guilty. In addition, process costs might increase this pressure, especially in cases in which individuals are charged with low-level offenses.[36] There is some truth to these claims, but I do not see how it carries us all the way to permitting prosecutors, or judges, to offer more substantial and variable waiver rewards in half-loaf cases. There might be little we can do to fully eliminate process costs, though there are surely ways to reduce them.[37] Waiver rewards, especially large and variable ones, are not so inevitable. If we permit them, then we are deliberately giving state officials the tools to pressure defendants in half-loaf cases, in spite of the fact that the evidence they have might only make it more probable than not that those accused of crimes are guilty. We could reject waiver rewards in their entirety and thus reduce the incentives that innocent half-loaf defendants have for pleading guilty. We would not eliminate such incentives completely, though, since process costs might persist in spite of our efforts to diminish them, and they will exert some influence over defendants' decisions. But my sense is that the combination of modest waiver rewards and whatever process costs are ineliminable will not induce many innocent half-loaf defendants in moderate to serious cases to plead guilty. Moreover, it seems

[36] See M. M. Feeley, *The Process is the Punishment: Handling Cases in a Lower Criminal Court* (New York: Russell Sage Foundation, 1992) 199–243.

[37] Feeley briefly surveys some suggested reforms, though he is mostly skeptical of our ability to reduce process costs (n 36 above) 278–97.

dubious logic to argue that because the combination will convince a few defendants to plead guilty, we should therefore equip state officials with the means to persuade more of them to do so.

Principled prosecutors should be wary of proposals to expand their already formidable leverage. They will accept the proposition that it is better to let the guilty go unpunished than effect punishment of the innocent, and believe that the presumption of innocence, the burden of proof on the state, and the high standard of proof it must meet are appropriate institutional expressions of that proposition. Though they will pursue aggressively those whom they suspect of crimes, they will be reluctant to circumvent defendants' procedural rights to obtain more convictions. If they, the police, or investigators cannot produce more evidence against those suspected of crimes, then the solution is not to try to salvage something from such cases, but to work harder at building them.

Judges, too, ought to be committed to the values underlying the design of the legal system, especially as these relate to the fair and accurate resolution of criminal charges against individuals. If prosecutors can perhaps be forgiven for being overzealous about securing convictions of those suspected of crimes, given the adversary portion of their multifaceted role, judges should not be. Their principal function is to ensure a fair and orderly process, one that gives both sides the opportunity to make their case and dispute the opposing case.[38] This is not to deny, of course, that judges have other important responsibilities (e.g., to protect witnesses) or that they must balance competing demands. They surely have some responsibility to see to it that the guilty are punished, in addition to their responsibilities to ensure the innocent are not and that fair procedures are adhered to.[39] The ways in which these conflicting demands are managed in the context of trials is a fascinating subject. Fortunately, our focus is narrower, since it concerns the responsibilities judges have when they encounter criminal defendants who indicate a willingness to admit their guilt.

Arguably, judges in such cases act reasonably and properly if they provide a forum in which both the prosecution and defense can outline their respective cases and defendants can be questioned to ensure that they understand what rights they will waive if they enter guilty pleas. In most settlement hearings, we might assume that judges will hear admissions from defendants concerning the crimes with which they have been charged. In cases involving less serious crimes, I have urged employment by settlement-hearing judges of a "more likely guilty than not" evidence sufficiency

---

[38] See Sir P. Otton, "The Role of the Judge in Criminal Cases," in M. McConville and G. Wilson (eds.), *The Handbook of the Criminal Justice Process* (Oxford: Oxford University Press, 2002) 323. For extended discussion of the role of judges in criminal cases, with special attention to the question of whether it is accurate to characterize that role as "umpireal" in nature, see J. Jackson, "Judicial Responsibility in Criminal Proceedings," [1996] 49 *Current Legal Problems* 59. Jackson argues that it is not; that judges in common law jurisdictions have been given powers to direct and shape trials in myriad ways. Nonetheless, Jackson does not dispute the notion that judges must avoid taking sides in the criminal cases that come before them.

[39] See Jackson (n 38 above) 88.

standard. When the crimes alleged are more serious, it seems advisable for judges to utilize a more rigorous standard—one to the effect that the defendant is "very likely" guilty. Again, in many cases, whether they involve serious crimes or not, judges at settlement hearings are apt to find that the state's case meets the relevant evidence sufficiency standard and defendants will candidly admit their guilt. Of course, if the state's evidence does not satisfy the relevant sufficiency standard for one or more charges, judges are to dismiss them, even if this means they must dismiss all of them. Again, they are to be understood as doing so without prejudice to the prosecution. Prosecutors are permitted to subsequently reinstate some or all of the charges, assuming that they can amass more convincing evidence to support them. But judges at settlement hearings in many of the half-loaf cases might find that the evidence satisfies the sufficiency standard, though barely. What should judges do in such cases?

In Chapter 1, I suggested that judges who discover at settlement hearings that the evidence against defendants is considerably short of convincing beyond reasonable doubt would not act improperly in advising defendants of that fact. The role of judges, and especially of principled judges, is not to pressure defendants to enter guilty pleas, though doing so would reduce the strain on their crowded court dockets. It is instead to ensure that defendants are treated fairly—by receiving appropriate sentences in cases in which they admit their guilt, or by ensuring that defendants are guaranteed a full and fair hearing if they elect to go to trial. Principled judges would be troubled by the half-loaf cases, especially if defendants cannot tell a plausible story confirming their guilt, or, worse, seem to deny all or part of it. However, defendants advised by settlement-hearing judges that the prosecution's case against them appears less than decisive might nonetheless have their own reasons for acceding to guilty pleas, ones that the courts should respect. But no state officials, whether judges or prosecutors, should have the option of offering defendants in such cases anything more than modest and fixed sentence discounts in exchange for their guilty pleas.

Arguments in support of half-loaf plea bargaining

In the previous section, it was suggested that state officials should not be permitted to have recourse to the kinds of generous waiver rewards that are endemic to half-loaf plea bargaining. Such rewards are strikingly at odds with the underlying moral values upon which the criminal justice system is erected. If prosecutors cannot come up with evidence against the individuals they have charged with crimes that is conclusive or reasonably close to it, then prosecutors should proceed to trial with the evidence they have, or concede that the state has not done enough to warrant the infliction of criminal sanctions on those individuals. The judges who conduct settlement hearings in half-loaf cases might reasonably offer defendants their frank assessments of the strength of the evidence against them, even if this means subtly encouraging them to proceed with trial adjudication.

To some, the folly of hamstringing state officials in these ways will thus be revealed. In particular, if we prevent prosecutors from engaging in familiar forms of charge and sentence bargaining, they will be forced either to drop charges in many half-loaf cases or proceed to trials that they will sometimes, perhaps often, lose. On the assumption that many of the defendants in half-loaf cases are, in fact, guilty, either choice will produce unwelcome outcomes. Many individuals who deserve to be punished will escape punishment altogether. Beyond this, it also might be argued that denying prosecutors the option of offering more substantial waiver rewards will jeopardize their good relations with the police and criminal investigators on whom they crucially depend. If prosecutors, denied access to more substantial waiver rewards, drop charges in too many of the half-loaf cases, this will impact the morale of those who apprehend suspects and track down evidence against them. Who will want to help out prosecutors who are not given the tools to do their jobs, even if doing so means compromising a bit on the charges pursued or the sentences ultimately assigned? Again, some will steadfastly insist that some punishment of the guilty is better than no punishment at all.

The concern that prosecutors must be permitted to employ offers of substantial waiver rewards in order to maintain comity with the police or other officials who investigate crimes seems overblown. Granted, prosecutors must be careful not to alienate the other officials in the criminal justice system. But there will be an abundance of cases in which those other officials do their jobs competently and thus give prosecutors the evidence they need to effect guilty pleas or win trials. It seems doubtful that police and criminal investigators will suddenly become less conscientious in their tasks simply because other state officials have been denied the tools to forge deals in cases in which the evidence amassed against defendants is thin. In fact, we might reasonably worry that giving state officials the tools to press for pleas in such cases creates a climate in which lower levels of investigative effort are encouraged. If we permit state officials to extract guilty pleas from individuals against whom the evidence is weak, we are likely to find ourselves with more cases in which that is precisely what they must do. To put it bluntly, half-loaf plea bargaining might engender sloth on the part of criminal investigators.

Nevertheless, there are cases in which it appears that half-loaf plea bargaining is more defensible. We have seen these kinds of cases before. Sometimes there will be probative evidence against defendants which prosecutors will not be able to introduce or rely on should there be trials. The police may have uncovered highly incriminating evidence through questionable searches and seizures. Defendants' attorneys will move to have such evidence excluded, though there is little doubt that it implicates their clients. It might seem too easy in such cases to say that state officials should accept the unavailability of the evidence as the price the criminal justice system has to pay to balance the pursuit of justice against other societal values, such as the privacy of citizens. Though principled prosecutors will, for the most part, accept the rules and procedures of the criminal justice system and seek to abide by them, they might have their doubts about some of them. They would certainly not be alone in doubting the wisdom of excluding illegally obtained evidence regardless of its probative value, the extent to which its acquisition violated reasonable expectations of citizen privacy, or the seriousness of the crimes for which it would help prosecutors secure convictions.[40] Besides, even if principled prosecutors agree with the existing rules regarding such evidence—as they might well do—that would not completely resolve the dilemmas raised by these kinds of cases.

Consider also cases in which prosecutors discover that crucial witnesses against defendants are reluctant to take the stand or have been so traumatized by the crimes against them that they may prove ineffective if they do so. Victims of sexual assault or of gang violence may balk at testifying, either because they do not want to relive the trauma of the crimes committed against them on the witness stand or because they fear subsequent retaliation if they do so. Cases of these kinds will be more troublesome when it is not the identity of the perpetrators that is in question, but simply whether they committed the crimes of which they stand accused.[41] In some rape cases, for instance, the identity of the assailant will not be in doubt, though whether he can be shown to have acted as the state alleges might crucially depend on the willingness and ability of the victim to testify convincingly against him. Prosecutors might have good reasons for believing that defendants' crimes were real and serious, but realize that success in demonstrating these things in court depends on honest but balky or shaky witnesses.[42]

There are, in these kinds of cases, two distinguishable reasons why principled prosecutors might be tempted to compromise and accept half-loaves. On the one hand, they might believe that their doing so will give the perpetrators at least some of the punishment they deserve and thereby offer the victims some measure of satisfaction or vindication. Dropped charges or acquittals will do neither. On the other hand, prosecutors might believe that the defendants in question are dangerous individuals. Inducing them to plead guilty to lesser crimes or for reduced punishment will get them off the streets for some period of time, whereas forgoing prosecution or

---

[40] See L. Laudan, *Truth, Error, and Criminal Law: An Essay in Legal Epistemology* (Cambridge: Cambridge University Press, 2006) 185–93; M. R. Wilkey, "The Exclusionary Rule: Why Suppress Valid Evidence?" [1978] 62 *Judicature* 214; and D. H. Oaks, "Studying the Exclusionary Rule in Search and Seizure," [1970] 37 *U. Chi. L. Rev.* 665.

[41] I draw this distinction in "Criminal Record, Character Evidence, and the Criminal Trial," 14 *Legal Theory* [2008] 167, 169.

[42] F. C. Zacharias usefully discusses this kind of case in his "Justice in Plea Bargaining," [1998] 39 *Wm. & Mary L. Rev.* 1122, 1155–6. Zacharias assumes that the prosecutor who knows she has a crucial witness who is unlikely to appear at trial has to make the decision about how to proceed with plea bargaining all on her own. The settlement hearings I have proposed would make it more difficult for prosecutors to hide the fact that witnesses are unlikely to appear at defendants' trials, since the presiding judges would presumably inquire into their availability in determining the factual basis for any plea by defendants.

persisting in it and having trials acquit such individuals will leave them free to victimize others.

The first thing to say about these kinds of cases is that they are likely to constitute a subset, and perhaps a smallish one, of half-loaf cases. In the majority of half-loaf cases, prosecutors will not have access to incriminating evidence that will be unavailable to them should there be trials. Many perpetrators of crimes will be successful at destroying or concealing the evidence against them, or lucky in not leaving much evidence behind or having the police find it. In this larger portion of the half-loaf cases, all prosecutors will have is less than conclusive evidence against defendants. If the crimes in question are serious enough and the evidence is near-conclusive or moderately conclusive, prosecutors may have little choice but to proceed to trial and take their chances. Yet principled prosecutors should be reluctant to offer enticing charge or sentence bargains to salvage something from such cases. They will be aware of the disproportionate number of innocent defendants in this group of cases. They also will be committed to the societal preference for not punishing the innocent over punishing the guilty, as this preference is reflected in due process standards. They will therefore be wary of assuming that their own judgments about the likely guilt of defendants are sufficient grounds for attempting (through more generous sentence or charge bargains) to effect some punishment of them. They will believe their options are limited: Inform defendants that modest sentence discounts are available to them if they plead guilty, proceed to trial, or drop the charges, hoping, perhaps, to refile them should more evidence emerge.

Furthermore, not all of the cases for which prosecutors have incriminating evidence that will be unavailable at trial will prove to be fertile grounds for half-loaf plea bargaining. If the unavailable evidence is crucial to the state's case, such that without it the evidence falls considerably short of being conclusive or even near-conclusive, only the most extremely risk-averse defendants will consider guilty pleas. Most will proceed to trial and hope to gain outright acquittals. Only in cases in which the remaining evidence poses a significant threat to defendants will it make sense for prosecutors to seek some compromise. Of course, defendants against whom the state's case is significantly weakened might agree to plead guilty if prosecutors were permitted to strategically overcharge them or threaten them with trial penalties, or if the prohibitions defendants are alleged to have violated carry with them harshly disproportionate sanctions. But we are supposing that such features of plea bargaining or its context, though often ubiquitous in the real world of criminal justice, are absent here. This means that the cases ripe for half-loaf plea bargaining will be ones in which the available evidence menaces defendants, though it by no means guarantees their conviction with any certainty. That leaves us with a rather small group of cases, or so it would seem.

There is a further difficulty here as well. No matter how incriminating some evidence might appear to be, it is not until it has been introduced at trial, and subjected to contestation by the defense, that its probative value can fully and accurately be assessed. Damning witnesses might falter or fizzle on the stand. Physical evidence that seemed conclusive may turn out to be flawed or ambiguous. Knowing these things, it is not clear why we should be prepared to supply state officials with the tools to forge half-loaf plea bargains because, in advance of trials, they fervently believe that they have sufficient evidence of defendants' guilt to warrant their arranging some punishment or other of them.

We should also scrutinize closely the argument that enabling prosecutors to mete out some deserved punishment in half-loaf cases is better than having them obtain no punishment at all. Much depends on how substantial the waiver rewards used to effect that punishment turn out to be. Large ones will produce blatant falsehoods about what offenders have done or the seriousness of their crimes. Defendants will wind up pleading guilty to crimes that are very different or much less serious than the ones we are supposed to have good reasons for believing they committed. Proponents of half-loaf plea bargaining might respond to this by saying that the alternative of having prosecutors drop charges or proceed to trials, which they could lose, will likewise produce false accounts of what defendants have done or deserve. But this response is far from convincing. If charges are dropped, prosecutors (and the state on whose authority they act) do not take a stand on what defendants deserve; they simply forgo further prosecution for the time being. If defendants are acquitted, prosecutors need not concur with the verdict and cannot plausibly be construed as doing so. After all, they proceeded to trial and (presumably) made every effort to demonstrate the guilt of defendants on the more serious (and let us assume more accurate) charges. Of course, defendants against whom charges are dropped or who gain acquittals might declare that the system has exonerated them, but it is not obvious why that should trouble us. Even defendants who plead guilty sometimes stoutly and publicly maintain their innocence.

Furthermore, generous waiver rewards could result in offenders being assigned such a small portion of the punishment they deserve for their crimes that victims or their family members will be outraged, rather than satisfied, by the outcomes. A woman who has been brutally raped, for instance, might reasonably object that her attacker should not be allowed to plead guilty to simple assault or confinement, even if that is all prosecutors believe they can get, given the weaknesses in the state's case. If plea bargained outcomes diverge too far from deserved ones, they make a mockery of justice. What this suggests is that half-loaf plea bargains, if they occur at all, must be kept modest. Granted, prosecutors in some of these cases might be able to claim, with some cogency, that permitting defendants to walk will also not satisfy victims or their relatives. But it may be better to pursue trial conviction and fail than agree to something that fundamentally distorts the crimes committed or lets offenders off with a slap on the wrist. At the very least, it would seem that prosecutors in such cases ought to meet with victims or their relatives, explain the (mostly) unsatisfactory options available, and perhaps take seriously their views about what should be done.

It would also seem that in determining whether half a loaf is better than none at all, the probability of successful prosecution ought to be taken into account. Suppose that, for instance, a generous waiver reward would almost certainly yield a guilty plea to a sentence that is only 30 percent of what an offender deserves for his crime. Suppose also that a trial, while standing only a 70 percent chance of producing a conviction, would yield a sentence that was fully in accordance with what the offender deserves. Is the former option obviously superior to the latter one, viewed prospectively? I, for one, am not convinced that it is. Of course, as the percentage of deserved punishment produced by plea bargaining increases and the odds of trial success diminish, plea deals will be increasingly attractive. But the probabilities of trial success cannot go much lower or else why would any reasonably perceptive defendant agree to plead guilty at all? As we saw earlier, the state's case must be sufficient to menace the defendant or else the defendant will likely insist on going to trial. This, too, suggests that the superiority of negotiated settlements in these kinds of cases will only manifest itself if waiver rewards are kept from becoming too large.

The preceding point about probabilities also applies to half-loaf cases in which prosecutors might be moved to offer generous waiver rewards because they deem defendants to be dangerous individuals. Again, suppose that prosecutors will sometimes have good reasons for making such judgments about defendants. Defendants might have long and violent criminal histories. Further, let us suppose that the individuals accused of crimes have not been targeted by the police simply because of those histories; there is evidence implicating them for the crimes currently under investigation, though prosecutors know that some of it will be inaccessible should the case go to trial. There is, in such cases, something to be said for prosecutors arranging some punishment of these individuals, especially if it includes prison stints that remove them from the community for a substantial period of time. However, the weaker the evidence is against such individuals, the larger the sentence or charge discounts they will demand in exchange for pleas. Are certain but relatively short prison sentences all that valuable, on incapacitation grounds, compared with uncertain but considerably longer ones? Perhaps they are, but, in evaluating this, it would seem to matter how lengthy the compromise sentences turn out to be compared with the ones such individuals would receive if they were convicted at their trials. A 100 percent probability of a two-year prison sentence might be better than a 60 percent probability of a four-year one, if our concern is to incapacitate the dangerous. But the former might not be better than a 60 percent chance of a ten-year sentence, assuming that such a sentence is likely if the defendant is convicted at trial. Of course, if trial conviction probabilities are lower than 60 percent, prosecutors might be better off taking the bird in the hand, so to speak. But they cannot be much lower or, again, most defendants will risk trials and hope for outright acquittals. Indeed, there is some evidence that offenders who have significant histories of offending are just the sorts of individuals who demand trials because they have low risk aversion.[43]

---

[43] Bibas (n 10 above) 2509–10.

Furthermore, half-loaf plea bargaining will produce distortions in the criminal records of offenders, and this will complicate efforts to assign the recidivists among them longer sentences in the future. The substantial charge or sentence reductions afforded defendants against whom the evidence is shaky will inevitably make their crimes appear fewer or less serious than they really were, if and when it comes time to sentence them for subsequent offenses. This will make it harder for prosecutors to recommend longer sentences for dangerous individuals, or for judges to assign them. Of course, trials of such defendants also will sometimes produce distortions, and arguably worse ones, if they are wrongly acquitted. But trials will also produce convictions and, we might suppose, more accurate public records of what offenders have done. Moreover, if prosecutors in half-loaf cases resort to very generous waiver-reward offers in order to eke something from the initial charges they lodged, then plea bargaining will produce distortions in the criminal records of individuals that come close to those produced by outright acquittals. If, on the other hand, some of these kinds of defendants can be induced to plead guilty for modest waiver rewards, their criminal records will more accurately record the kinds and severity of the offenses they committed.

Finally, prosecutors who are tempted to compromise in half-loaf cases might not succeed in reducing crime in their communities because of the tenuous link between imprisonment and diminished offending. Some kinds of offenses are not reliably reduced in communities by imprisoning offenders, since those imprisoned will simply be replaced by other individuals who will step up to commit the crimes in question.[44] This suggests that prosecutors should be less inclined to accept half-loaf bargains, on grounds of incapacitation, in many cases of drug and property offenses. Gaining half a loaf in such cases does little to protect communities from dangerous individuals.

Elsewhere in the book, the possibility has been raised that prosecutors might be permitted to appeal to the courts for permission to offer more generous waiver rewards in a few, exceptional cases. It would be crucial to limit their abilities to do so and provide judges with clear criteria governing the bestowal of such rewards. Of the two kinds of cases in which it appears that larger-than-normal sentence reductions might be defensible, my sense is that cases in which vital evidence has been excluded by judges are the more interesting ones. Cases in which the state's evidence has been weakened because a witness is suddenly unavailable or unwilling to testify, though perhaps ripe for half-loaf plea bargaining, will be too varied in character to warrant the drawing of general conclusions. Perhaps key witnesses have been threatened or bribed by defendants, or have simply disappeared. But equally, perhaps key witnesses have been coached or pressured by the police or prosecutors to testify, and now that the trial is approaching, they realize that they are a lot less sure of the veracity of their

---

[44] F. E. Zimring and G. Hawkins, *Incapacitation: Penal Confinement and the Restraint of Crime* (New York: Oxford University Press, 1995) 43–56.

testimony than they initially led state officials to believe. We could not conclude, in other words, that if the witnesses in question were on hand to testify, the evidence against defendants would be conclusive. Also, as we have seen, it is hazardous, at best, to predict, in advance of their testimony, how any witness will fare under cross-examination. Recourse to substantial waiver rewards to salvage some sort of conviction from cases like these seems a questionable enterprise.

Suppose, however, that prosecutors were allowed to petition settlement-hearing judges for larger-than-normal waiver rewards to wrest convictions from cases in which evidence strongly suggestive, or even conclusive, of defendants' guilt had previously been excluded. Since the settlement-hearing judges might well have been the ones to rule the evidence inadmissible, they would have very good reasons to believe that the defendants in question were, in fact, guilty as charged. The judges would also recognize the ways and extent to which their earlier rulings critically weakened the prosecution's case. Of course, as we have seen, the remaining evidence must be such as to menace defendants, or else they will be unwilling to enter guilty pleas in exchange for more substantial sentencing lenity. But assume that there would be a few defendants willing to compromise on pleas because the evidence against them, while not as imposing as it used to be, is worrisome enough. Have we not, at long last, identified a class of cases in which we should consider giving state officials the authority to engage in half-loaf plea bargaining?

Maybe, but I am unconvinced that the difficulties and dangers such cases pose make it worth permitting prosecutors and judges to attempt to do so. First, it does not seem likely that there will be many such cases—not enough of them, perhaps, to make it worth our while to devise rules to govern them. Second, there are familiar difficulties in attempting to cabin the authority of judges to allow larger-than-normal waiver rewards. We might say that they should only be utilized in a small group of cases and adopt criteria that restrict them accordingly. But we might worry that state officials will attempt to evade the criteria or interpret them loosely in efforts to expand the use of such rewards. Third, there is something odd about a scheme in which judges are tasked with excluding evidence under certain circumstances, only to subsequently let it in the back door, so to speak, to justify the employment of larger-than-normal sentence reductions. In particular, we might worry that if the purpose of excluding such evidence is to discourage misconduct by state agents in searching for and seizing incriminating materials, then permitting other state agents to exploit knowledge of the existence of such evidence frustrates that purpose. In response, it might be argued that state officials will still pay some price for having initially overstepped their authority in acquiring the evidence, since they will have to offer more substantial waiver rewards to secure guilty pleas. Though that seems correct, again, we might wonder about whether this narrowly tailored exception to a general policy of fixed and modest waiver rewards is worth all of the fuss and bother, given the meager number of cases in which the exception will produce useful results.

The problem of innocent defendants

As we have seen, part of what is worrisome about the generous waiver rewards that prosecutors offer in the half-loaf cases is the possibility that they will induce defendants who are innocent of all or some of the charges against them to throw in the towel and plead guilty. In particular, for those defendants who already have criminal records, one more mark on their records is not that significant; avoiding imprisonment or lengthy confinement is entirely different. Substantial waiver rewards enable such defendants to minimize their losses. By contrast, the kinds of limited waiver rewards that I have maintained ought to be on offer would seem to put factually innocent defendants in a bind, since they will not be able to get as much for their guilty pleas. Yet if they go to trial and lose, which they might, they will wind up having to serve longer sentences, although not much longer ones. All in all, it might seem that the availability of more substantial waiver rewards is beneficial to innocent defendants who have no guarantee that trials will exonerate them.

Oren Gazal-Ayal has argued that limiting sentence reductions (and strongly discouraging charge bargaining) would actually help innocent defendants.[45] He begins with the sensible premise that the half-loaf cases are likely to contain a disproportionate number of innocent defendants. He then urges the adoption of caps on the magnitude of the sentence reductions on offer to defendants. The logic of his argument is this: If sentence reductions were capped at, say, 35 to 50 percent, most defendants in the weakest cases would not find it in their interest to enter guilty pleas. They would simply not see themselves as getting enough for doing so. Prosecutors would then face a stark choice: Go to trial and risk losing such cases—likely outcomes given the shaky character of the evidence—or drop the charges altogether and pursue other cases that are not fraught with evidentiary problems. Gazal-Ayal argues that in most cases, prosecutors would choose the latter alternative and that their doing so is preferable, given the disproportionately high number of innocent defendants in the group.

I have suggested that the sentence reductions on offer to defendants willing to admit their guilt should be more limited than Gazal-Ayal proposes. The modest sentence discounts I support would provide innocent defendants with even less incentive to enter guilty pleas, thus forcing the hand of prosecutors. I have also suggested that prosecutors would be unlikely to pursue half-loaf cases to trial when the offenses in question are low-level ones. There is not enough for them to gain by doing so, given the toll that would be exacted on their resources and the ready availability of lots of other low-level cases in which they could more easily amass convictions by attracting guilty pleas. Principled prosecutors, in particular, would be reluctant to persist in their efforts to inflict legal sanctions on defendants accused of low-level offenses against whom the evidence was spotty. They would recognize that the state had not met its burden of proof and that little of significance was at stake in continued efforts

---

[45] Gazal-Ayal (n 25 above) 2313–17.

to inflict punishment on individuals whose crimes were not all that serious to begin with. However, I am less confident than Gazal-Ayal that prosecutors, principled or otherwise, would drop charges when defendants demanded trials and the charges in question were more serious. With grave offenses, in particular, prosecutors might have little choice but to take their chances by proceeding to trial with the evidence they have. Either that or they would have to drop the charges for the time being, hoping to refile them later if more evidence became available. For their part, innocent defendants in such cases might fervently wish that more substantial waiver rewards were available than those I have defended, though they might have to be very large indeed to attract their guilty pleas. Yet though their predicament is regrettable, I am not convinced that permitting variable and substantial waiver rewards as a matter of common practice is the best solution, for the reasons already given.

However, the claim that prosecutors will not proceed with trials in half-loaf cases involving low-level offenses has been challenged by Josh Bowers.[46] His argument is that most innocents charged with crimes will be recidivists.[47] This is no mere coincidence, as we have already seen. When police are uncertain of the identities of the individuals who have committed crimes, they tend to focus their attention on known offenders. "Usual suspects policing," combined with questionable investigative tactics designed to build cases against such individuals, result in the charging of recidivists who may well be innocent of the crimes under investigation. Prosecutors will be disinclined to believe recidivists' protestations of innocence, so they will not tend to drop charges against them, even if they realize that the evidence the police have garnered is short of conclusive.[48] Further, prosecutors will recognize that many such defendants are in a bind, one produced by the poor quality of the legal representation available to them, the process costs they will have to absorb even if they gain acquittals at their trials, and the rules governing defendant testimony should they elect to go to trial. With regard to the lattermost point, all defendants have to choose between taking the stand in their own defense or remaining silent during their trials. If they take the stand, then, depending on the legal rules in existence concerning the introduction of character evidence, they risk the jury learning of their past misdeeds. Bowers writes in the context of United States evidence law, which is more permissive regarding the introduction of "character evidence" than is the law of other countries. Jurors who get wind of defendants' unsavory pasts will have more incentive to convict them on the current charges.[49] If such defendants chose not to testify at their trials, than that, too, might work to the state's advantage. Silent defendants who do not answer the charges and evidence against them might appear guilty to the jury.[50]

---

[46] See Bowers (n 4 above).   [47] Bowers (n 4 above) 1124–5.
[48] Bowers (n 4 above) 1128–30.   [49] Bowers (n 4 above) 1130–1.
[50] In the United States, prosecutors and judges are not permitted to remark upon the defendant's failure to testify as suggesting guilt, whereas in England and Wales, no such bar to comment by state officials exists. Still, it would not be odd for jurors to draw their own conclusions about the likely guilt of defendants who decline to testify, whether state officials draw their attention to it or not.

The savvy prosecutor who recognizes the dilemma recidivist defendants find them-selves in might therefore elect not to drop charges when defendants refuse to admit their guilt in exchange for modest sentence discounts. They will grasp the favorable odds of their prevailing at trials in spite of the weakness of the evidence. Of course, prosecutors in such cases will not really wish to go to trial. Yet if they persist in doing so in a few cases, word will spread that defendants should take the discounts available to them and plead guilty. Bowers' conclusion is that many actually innocent defend-ants will wind up worse off under any scheme that limits the size of waiver rewards, whether Gazal-Ayal's capped scheme or my own more restrictive one, than under schemes that permit prosecutors to offer large waiver rewards in half-loaf cases.

Bowers' analysis takes the legal status quo in the United States almost entirely as a given. Yet it is not clear why we should decline to defuse the dilemma faced by inno-cent recidivists charged with crimes in other ways than by permitting prosecutors to offer robust and variable waiver rewards. First, the United States would do well to follow the lead of other countries in making it much more difficult for prosecutors to attempt to impeach the testimony of defendants who take the stand during their trials through the introduction of their past criminal records. Indeed, there are persuasive reasons for doing so independently of its likely impact on plea bargaining.[51] Much of Bowers' case for large waiver rewards turns on the threat posed to innocent recidivists of prosecutors being able to introduce such impeachment evidence. Granted, pros-ecutors caught up in a narrow conviction-maximizing mentality might not hesitate to introduce defendants' past criminal records to impeach them should they take the stand in their own defense. But it is far from clear that principled prosecutors would follow their lead. Principled prosecutors, committed to the value of procedural jus-tice, would understand the potentially noxious influence of such impeachment tes-timony. This is not to say that principled prosecutors would never seek to introduce such evidence. They might if it served as an effective rebuttal to specific claims made by testifying defendants.[52] But principled prosecutors would be more cautious than Bowers assumes about poisoning defendants' chances of fair trials.

Second, as we have already noted, the indigent defense system in the United States is scandalously underfunded.[53] Not surprisingly, many innocent defendants, con-cerned that their defense attorney might not be up to the challenge of vigorously defending them, will be wary of going to trial. As Bowers himself notes, overworked, uncommitted, or incompetent defense attorneys might botch plea negotiations. But

---

[51] See, for instance, R. Friedman, "Character Impeachment Evidence: Psycho-Bayesian [!?] Analysis and a Proposed Overhaul," [1991] 38 *UCLA L. Rev.* 637.

[52] Federal Rule of Evidence 404(b) allows evidence of past crimes for "other purposes, such as proof of motive, opportunity, intent, preparation, plan, knowledge, identity, or absence of mistake or accident." Richard Uviller employs the acronym "KIPPOMIA" to refer to these exceptions. See his "Evidence of Character To Prove Conduct: Illusion, Illogic, and Injustice in the Courtroom," [1982] 130 *U. Pa. L. Rev.* 845, 877.

[53] See the references (n 10 above).

they are even more likely to make an absolute hash of defending their clients at trial.[54] Improving the indigent defense system would reduce the risks of going to trial and might embolden more innocent defendants to do so.

Third, surely more might be done to sensitize and educate the police about the hazards of "usual suspects" policing and the dangers of focusing too quickly and narrowly on individuals they regard as likely suspects.[55] Since it is policing that plays a key role in introducing innocent recidivists into the criminal justice pipeline to begin with, attempts to alter it might be the most effective way of avoiding miscarriages of justice. Not punishing the innocent at all is obviously preferable to punishing them less.

Fourth, although it might be difficult to eliminate process costs altogether, steps could be undertaken to reduce them by speeding up the onset of trials and perhaps by simplifying trials themselves, so that they are not such lengthy ordeals.[56] We could also consider less use of remand before trials, especially for individuals accused of nothing more than low-level offenses.

Finally, and perhaps most importantly, Bowers' argument does not provide much support for half-loaf plea bargaining. As he admits, his focus is primarily on low-level offenses regarding which, as we have seen, few officials in the criminal justice system wish to conduct trials. In these cases, which are the majority of cases processed by the criminal justice system, what really drives plea bargaining is not the weakness of the evidence against defendants, but the desire of prosecutors and judges to amass convictions while conserving their limited resources. Again, when the evidence supporting the guilt of defendants on such low-level charges is insufficient, principled prosecutors can simply drop the charges with few repercussions.

Concluding remarks

Despite the fact that half-loaf cases seem to invite prosecutors to depart from the kinds of veridical charging practices and modest waiver rewards I have urged throughout this book, closer examination of such cases reveals very limited support for their doing so. Many criminal cases involve low-level offenses and the primary motivating factor for negotiating settlements will be the conservation of state resources. Principled prosecutors will drop charges in such cases if the evidence supporting them is flimsy and defendants are not moved to plead guilty by the availability of minimal sentence reductions. Not only will prosecutors have less room to negotiate when the charges are more serious, principled ones will be reluctant to seek harsh criminal sanctions against individuals when the evidence that they have falls well short of the stringent

---

[54] Bowers (n 4 above) 1151–2.

[55] See Findley and Scott (n 12 above), for extended discussion of the ways in which police investigations can go wrong.

[56] See S. J. Schulhofer, "Is Plea Bargaining Inevitable?" [1984] 97 *Harv. L. Rev.* 1037, 1062–87.

standard set by the criminal law. Moreover, defendants in such cases will be more inclined to risk trials, especially if they are not overcharged or threatened with trial penalties.

Only in what turns out to be a small subset of half-loaf cases—ones in which prosecutors are in possession of incriminating evidence that will be unavailable to them at trial—does a plausible pretext exist for half-loaf plea bargaining. Yet if my arguments throughout this chapter are persuasive, the reasons prosecutors have to negotiate in such cases are exceptional and thus provide little support for robust forms of charge and sentence bargaining.

9

Plea Bargaining and Getting at the Truth

It would seem that a crucial feature of charge-adjudication schemes is their ability to help us discern the truth or falsity of the charges against individuals that have been levied by state officials. Punishment of the factually innocent is a grave injustice; in the vast majority of cases, whatever meager benefits it produces will be hugely outweighed by the burdens it imposes on the individuals wrongly punished and the public who must pay for it.[1] Non-punishment of the guilty is likewise highly undesirable. Justice is not done if they escape the punishment they deserve, and when their crimes are grave, intense distress is caused to victims, their families, and the public more generally. In cases in which the unpunished guilty have continuing criminal proclivities, the failure of the state to deter or incapacitate them means that they may well go on to victimize others.

Beyond accurately and reliably separating the innocent from the guilty, we want charge-adjudication schemes to help us assign appropriate sanctions to offenders. Ordinarily, they do this by refining the charges of which defendants are convicted and according to which they are sentenced. Whatever the goal of a sentencing scheme, the determination of sentences in specific cases should be made by a sensitive and informed weighing of the relevant factors surrounding crimes and offenders. Over- or under-punishment of offenders conveys falsehoods about the seriousness of their crimes or the danger they constitute to the community.

Broadly speaking, if the criminal justice system is to discern and convey truths—in the form of accurate verdicts and sentences keyed to offenders and their criminal acts—we must see to it that it performs three crucial tasks at a high level of proficiency. First, there must be trained officials who gather, sort, and preliminarily analyze evidence concerning apparent offenses. In most countries, police and criminal investigators perform this key function, though at times they do so in concert with prosecutors or judges. Second, there must be officials whose task it is to evaluate

---

[1] It might seem that punishment of the innocent produces no benefits whatsoever. But that is not quite correct. First, as long as the innocents punished can be made to appear guilty, then their punishment might make some marginal contribution to general deterrence. Second, in cases in which innocents punished have continuing criminal proclivities, their imprisonment may reduce crime via incapacitation.

the evidence that has been amassed and determine whether and which charges should be filed against individuals suspected of crimes. In most countries, prosecutors fulfill this role, though they may be aided by the police and judges. Third, there must be some authoritative means of resolving charges, of determining which, if any, are adequately supported by the evidence. Trials are often imagined to be this authoritative mechanism and in some countries they are. But, as we have seen, in other countries a more informal resolution of charges, usually in the form of plea bargaining, is the dominant mechanism.

Given the concerns of this book, the main focus in this chapter is on the authoritative means of resolving charges. Yet the evaluation of charge-adjudication schemes cannot be entirely disentangled from prior charging decisions made by state officials, or from the collection of evidence by police and other criminal investigators. More often than we would perhaps like to think, mistakes made by state officials in the early stages of criminal investigation defeat the ability of charge-adjudication schemes to produce accurate verdicts and appropriate sentences.[2] All of this is obvious and might go without saying, but I would not want my focus on charge adjudication to be taken as a sign of uncritical acceptance of the quality of the evidence with which it works and upon which it depends.

To some, it will seem absurd to suggest that either adversary trials or robust forms of plea bargaining aim at discovering and affirming truths about what individuals accused of crimes have actually done. Adversary trials are too much in the way of oppositional dramas to have truth be a reliable outcome. Both prosecutors and defense attorneys have powerful incentives to conceal or distort the truth, especially if doing so will enable them to prevail. If we want trials to get at the truth, we would do much better to move toward the inquisitorial versions of them that are the norm throughout much of Europe. In inquisitorial trials, prosecutors and defense attorneys play less prominent roles, and the judges who oversee the proceedings seem disinclined to permit tactics that distort the search for the truth.[3]

Especially in its more robust forms, plea bargaining's relation to the truth seems more tenuous still. The negotiated resolution of charges makes the truth or falsity of charges against individuals seem almost beside the point. What matters is what the interested parties—prosecutors, defendants (or their attorneys), and sometimes judges—are willing to agree on. Rather than having truth or falsity determined by flawed trial procedures, it is determined by mutual consent, which seems no kind of truth-seeking mechanism at all. The apex of absurdity is reached when it is possible

[2] See K. A. Findley and M. S. Scott, "The Multiple Dimensions of Tunnel Vision in Criminal Cases," [2006] 2006 *Wis. L. Rev.* 291.

[3] The contrasts between adversarial and inquisitorial systems, in relation to plea bargaining, are illuminated in Y. Ma, "Prosecutorial Discretion and Plea Bargaining in the United States, France, Germany, and Italy: A Comparative Perspective," [2002] 12 *International Criminal Justice Review* 22; T. Weigend, "Is the Criminal Process About Truth?: A German Perspective," [2003] 26 *Harv. J. L. & Pub. Pol'y* 157; and M. Langer, "From Legal Transplants to Legal Translations: The Globalization of Plea Bargaining and the Americanization Thesis in Criminal Procedure," [2004] 45 *Harv. Int'l L. J.* 1.

for prosecutors and defendants to engage in "fact bargaining," that is, negotiations about the facts that are to be appropriately captured by the charges.[4] Fact bargaining makes it seem as if no crime has been committed until the parties involved in the negotiations agree to stipulate what that crime is. It is hard to imagine a legal procedure more ill-suited to discovering the truth about the crimes individuals have or have not committed, and for assigning the guilty sentences that accurately convey the gravity of their crimes to the public.

Though these indictments of adversary trials and plea bargaining move too quickly, it is relatively easy to show that robust forms of plea bargaining are unreliable mechanisms for getting at the truth of what those charged with crimes have done. Demonstrating this in more detail is my aim in the first section of this chapter. The problems, as we shall see, do not stem entirely from the charge-adjudication procedures themselves. They also result from broader features of the criminal justice system, such as overcriminalization, overcharging, and, at times, the inadequacy of provisions for the criminal defense of the indigent. The next section addresses the question of whether adversary trials are likely to do any better. If they take the form that predominates in the United States, the answer is far from clear. Yet they need not take that form. Indeed, there is reason to believe that British criminal trials are better designed to get at the important truths about what those accused of crimes have or have not done. Nonetheless, trials of any kind are costly endeavors and they will often leave us guessing as to whether we have, in fact, gotten at or close to the truth.

One signal advantage to plea bargaining is that it holds out the prospect of inducing those accused of crimes to openly admit their guilt or implicate others. Whether it can be structured to do so without distorting the truth in other ways is the subject of the third section, in which we return to some familiar themes that have occupied us throughout the book. Specifically, the question of whether scaled-back versions of plea bargaining will enhance our ability to get at the truth, particularly compared with more freewheeling forms of the practice, is examined. It is contended that the potential of plea bargaining to reveal truths might be more fully exploited if various reforms were implemented.

Still, more restrained forms of plea bargaining will not eliminate all of the falsehoods generated by contemporary criminal justice systems concerning the crimes individuals have committed. Plea bargaining operates against the backdrop provided by the larger social system and the criminal law with its specific prohibitions and sentencing scheme. In some countries, social deprivation, overcriminalization, and

---

[4] See W. J. Stuntz, "Plea Bargaining and the Criminal Law's Disappearing Shadow," [2004] 117 *Harv. L. Rev.* 2548, 2559–60. See also S. J. Schulhofer and I. H. Nagel, "Plea Negotiations Under the Federal Sentencing Guidelines: Guideline Circumvention and its Dynamics in the Post-Mistretta Period," [1997] 91 *Nw. U. L. Rev.* 1284; and N. J. King, "Judicial Oversight of Negotiated Sentences in a World of Bargained Punishment," [2005] 58 *Stan. L. Rev.* 293. Andrew Ashworth and Mike Redmayne note the existence of fact bargaining in England and Wales, in *The Criminal Process*, 4th edition (Oxford: Oxford University Press, 2010) 300–1.

excessive sanctions distort the truthful outcomes achievable by plea bargaining, typically by suggesting that individuals have committed more or worse wrongs than they actually have. The fourth and concluding section identifies some of these distortions, ones that reforms in plea bargaining alone can do little to correct.

A preliminary point

The premise upon which this chapter depends might be queried by those who question how far truth is a value in the design of the criminal law and its allied institutions. Truth is obviously not the sole value of importance in the criminal justice system. It is widely understood that we are prepared to balance the search for the truth against other values, such as the protection of citizen privacy or the preservation of certain kinds of relationships.[5] The more interesting question is whether the search for the truth has anything more than derivative value in the criminal law. It might be claimed that we are interested in the truth of the charges against criminal defendants because we want to punish all and only those individuals who deserve it and do so in accordance with the seriousness of their crimes. Alternatively, it might be claimed that we seek to establish the truth of criminal charges against individuals because we want to employ our limited resources to reduce crimes in ways that are optimally effective and efficient. In short, truth is subordinate to the values of retribution or crime reduction, or perhaps some combination of the two.

There is much to be said for this position, but I think it goes too far. It is vitally important to us to know the truth about what crimes individuals have or have not committed because legal punishment, and the criminal law more generally, has an expressive function.[6] Individuals found guilty of crimes are censured by the state for their wrongdoing.[7] Their reputations are thereby tarnished, as they are publicly condemned for having violated norms thought necessary to society's functioning. Obviously, those punished have a considerable stake in the accuracy of this official rebuke of their actions, one that arguably extends beyond any hard treatment they will be made to endure because of their convictions. For better or worse, many of their fellow citizens will regard and treat them differently after they are convicted of crimes. This explains why individuals falsely convicted of crimes often speak first and foremost about "clearing their names and reputations." Sure, the sanctions they were made to wrongly endure were bad, but the stain on their reputations is, in a way, worse. We are intensely social creatures and what others think about us matters to us. The law-abiding public also has a significant stake in the accuracy of convictions and sentences. They serve as vital signals concerning whether, and to what extent,

---

[5] See L. Laudan, *Truth, Error, and Criminal Law: An Essay in Legal Epistemology* (Cambridge: Cambridge University Press, 2006) 4–5, and Weigend (n 3 above) 161–2.

[6] J. Feinberg, "The Expressive Function of Punishment," [1965] 49 *The Monist* 397.

[7] The element of "censure" in legal punishment is emphasized by Andrew von Hirsch. See, for instance, his *Censure and Sanctions* (Oxford: Clarendon Press, 1993).

we can trust and esteem our fellow citizens. In short, truth matters in the criminal law beyond ensuring that crime is reduced or offenders receive their just deserts because of what criminal convictions communicate about individuals to their fellow citizens.

The deficiencies of robust plea bargaining in getting at the truth

If our concern is to discern the truth or falsity of the criminal charges that have been lodged against individuals, then their cooperation is of undeniable value. On the plausible assumption that most criminal defendants are guilty of something, if not quite the precise crimes with which they have been charged, then ideally what we want them to do is admit their guilt and reveal to the authorities what they have done, why they have done it, and who else, if anyone, cooperated with them in doing it. Most other routes to the truth about what crimes occurred and how serious they were are longer, more arduous, and less certain. If those guilty of crimes can be brought to confess them openly and honestly, then not only will we save precious resources investigating crimes, we will also obtain a greater level of assurance that when we inflict punishment, we do so justifiably. Given the considerable moral hazards involved in punishing individuals, this higher level of assurance is not to be gainsaid. Granted, criminal trials require state officials to demonstrate beyond reasonable doubt that defendants are guilty of the crimes with which they have been charged. If that standard is truly and fully met, then the officials who impose punishment act defensibly in inflicting punishment on those convicted of crimes. Yet the standard of "beyond reasonable doubt" might be met more fully or even exceeded if defendants themselves candidly admit and fully disclose their crimes. In doing so they may reveal things that definitively affirm their guilt. We might therefore be able to say with some confidence that our punishing them is justified to a higher degree—"beyond all doubt," as it were.

The suggestion that the guilty might usefully incriminate themselves will be greeted with horror by some. My point is not that they should be forced to do so on pain of being held in contempt of court, and certainly not that they should be tortured or otherwise bullied into it. It is, instead, that there is a great deal to be said on behalf of such self-incrimination and therefore in finding ways to encourage, or at least not discourage, it. Indeed, in properly morally educated individuals, self-incrimination is not something that the authorities would have to squeeze out of them. It would occur, more or less spontaneously, perhaps even before persons were confronted by the authorities with plausible suspicions about what they had done.[8] After all, the

---

[8] The notion that individuals should answer to queries about their conduct when confronted by others who have reason to believe they have engaged in wrongdoing comes from R. K. Greenawalt, "Silence as a Moral and Constitutional Right," [1981] 23 *Wm. & Mary L. Rev.* 15.

proper response to one's wrongdoing, and especially one's serious wrongdoing, is remorse, acceptance of responsibility, apology, and attempts to repair whatever damage one has done.[9] It is not to flee, deny or conceal the truth, or offer self-serving and essentially false rationalizations of one's conduct. Beyond this, conscientious moral agents will acknowledge the justice of their being punished proportionally with the seriousness of their wrongs, even if they will not quite embrace the stigma and hard treatment that is an inevitable consequence. In a world much better than our own, sanctions for crimes might even be structured so that they enabled wrongdoers to focus on the defects in moral understanding or motivation that led to their misconduct, thereby undertaking meaningful self-reform.

We are, it seems clear, a long way from a world in which most criminal wrongdoers behave as we expect conscientious moral agents to. Those offenders who "admit" their crimes in the course of plea negotiations will often, we suspect, reveal as little about them as they have to in order to secure an acceptable resolution of their cases. Too often they will disclose only what their attorneys advise them to. And many will not embrace their punishment as their due, but simply as the inevitable consequence of their having been apprehended, charged, and persuaded to enter guilty pleas. What has gone wrong here, and what role might more robust forms of plea bargaining play in undermining our confidence that our procedures for determining guilt and innocence reliably get at the truth of what those charged with crimes have done?

The worrisome features of plea bargaining, especially as it exists in the United States, have been well-documented in previous chapters. Their implications for our ability to get at the truth can thus straightforwardly be teased out. Prosecutors have been provided with extraordinary tools to put pressure on those whom they believe are guilty of having committed crimes. Overlapping and redundant criminal statutes make strategic overcharging both easy and commonplace. Yet such overcharging, while effective at bending defendants to the will of prosecutors, guarantees that any link between the charges ultimately acceded to by most defendants and the truth of what they have done is tenuous, at best. Plea negotiations might ferret out all of the redundant or excessive charges, but equally they might not. Those few defendants who elect trial adjudication face long odds of prevailing. Even if they are guilty of only some of the charges that prosecutors have lodged against them, partial acquittals may not yield convictions on the precise set of charges of which they are guilty. Threatened trial penalties add to the pressure prosecutors bring to bear on those charged with crimes. It is conceivable that such penalties will yield negotiated outcomes that accurately reflect the crimes of those who agree to plead guilty, but it seems likely that quite often they will not.

Whatever else might be said against charge bargaining, at least it has some potential to produce convictions that correspond with the ways in which individuals have

---

[9] For an elegant account of the interconnections between blame, remorse, and repentance, see R. A. Duff, *Trials and Punishments* (Cambridge: Cambridge University Press, 1986) 57–70.

criminally behaved. Prosecutors who engage in charge-stacking might be convinced to pare charges back to those that actually reflect the criminal conduct of defendants. Fact bargaining, so-called, does not appear to have even this much to be said for it. Defendants who care little about how they have victimized others, or only care about minimizing their punishment, will be eager to cooperate with state officials in understating the number of their crimes or the seriousness of them. Prosecutors who care only about maximizing convictions efficiently might acquiesce in distortions of the reality of what offenders have done if offenders will admit their guilt to something and be done with it. Both sides might work assiduously to shield the truth from judges, and judges, for their part, might not be all that interested in finding out whether or how they have been misled.[10] Granted, we can conceive of negotiations about the facts that seem less insidious. Individuals who have been badly overcharged might respond (typically through their attorneys) by pointing out how the charges exaggerate or otherwise distort their crimes. They might also indicate a willingness to admit guilt to a charge or set of charges that captures more accurately their criminal conduct. Similarly, prosecutors might initially misapprehend the nature or severity of the accused person's criminal conduct. It would be entirely appropriate for the accused, through his or her attorney, to attempt to correct this mistaken apprehension, not so much to deny criminal culpability entirely, but to try and elicit charges that more closely reflect what actually occurred. I doubt that anyone would object to such discussions between the accused and state officials, since they do not amount to "fact bargaining" so much as "fact correction." Yet discussions of these kinds presume the existence of defendants who are willing to admit they have offended in some manner, if not quite the one initially captured in the charges against them. They also presuppose that prosecutors are willing to listen rather than simply pressure defendants to plead guilty. No doubt the stars occasionally align, and defendants and prosecutors of the right kinds meet up and "negotiate" about the facts in such a benign fashion. But these are not the kinds of negotiations that are of grave concern to critics of robust plea bargaining.

In short, it is apparent that prosecutors in the United States value the efficient resolution of cases more than the accuracy of the ultimate charges to which they acquiesce, at least when the crimes in question are not too serious.[11] When the evidence they have is short of conclusive, or when their caseloads are especially heavy, prosecutors routinely agree to drop what may be veridical charges to secure deals. Prosecutors also offer generous sentence reductions. There seems little concern to ensure that the sanctions thereby assigned to the vast majority of low-level offenders, and perhaps some mid-level ones, reflect in any very close way the precise crimes they have committed. Though he defends robust forms of plea bargaining on other grounds, Josh Bowers aptly sums up what many observers of the United States legal

---

[10] See King (n 4 above) 295–300.
[11] See J. Bowers, "Punishing the Innocent," [2008] 156 *U. Pa. L. Rev.* 1117, 1122.

system think about the strength of its commitment to getting at the truth: "That fact is that the criminal justice system no longer has much to do with transparent adversarial truth-seeking; it has far more to do with the opaque processing of (rightful or wrongful) recent arrests. Guilty pleas are thus no more than sterile administrative procedures, and plea bargaining is merely the mechanism that ensures that these procedures are carried out efficiently."[12] Efficient case-processing is what drives the plea bargaining system; truth is secondary, at best, and of little moment, at worst.

What is less often noticed about the considerable leverage accorded to prosecutors is its impact on the attitudes and behavior of the individuals caught up in the criminal justice system. It is one thing to have committed one or more offenses, to be apprehended and charged with them, and to face criminal sanctions that correspond with their seriousness. Few offenders will welcome this predicament, but if they are guilty and know it, they might have to admit that it is not an entirely unreasonable one for prosecutors to have put them in. But it is quite different to be guilty of one or more offenses and to find oneself in the grips of a rapacious prosecutor who threatens all manner of extremely harsh sanctions if one does not admit to at least some of them. Many defendants in such circumstances will feel themselves ill-used by prosecutors, and thus be less likely to cooperate or do so in anything but the most grudging fashion. Most of us, when accused of much worse wrongs than we have actually committed, or threatened with much worse penalties for them than our behavior warrants, react defensively, if not resentfully. We may deny having done anything wrong. Or we may simply refuse to cooperate with efforts to investigate our wrongdoing.

Those who defend the extraordinary powers given to prosecutors might argue that such powers enable them to muster dire threats against defendants, ones that are, in fact, quite effective at securing their cooperation. Faced with long sentences, many defendants "sing like canaries" in order to gain more acceptable outcomes for themselves. Perhaps, but overbearing prosecutorial tactics might lead other offenders to clam up, hunker down, and admit no more than they have to (or their attorneys advise them to). Further, there is some evidence that offenders who are treated brusquely by the authorities—especially those brought to heel with threats of long sentences by prosecutors who are uninterested in hearing, or contemptuous of, defendants' sides of the story—are less accepting of the legitimacy of their punishment and so poorer candidates for rehabilitation.[13]

Incidentally, other features of the US criminal justice system—ones independent of plea bargaining—also act as impediments to offenders candidly admitting their crimes during plea negotiations. Criminal prohibitions that overreach may do so, since offenders may believe that the state has no business criminalizing their conduct at all or punishing it to the extent that it does. Add to this the perception of inequitable enforcement of certain kinds of offenses, and many of those arrested and

---

[12]   Bowers (n 11 above) 1173.
[13]   See M. M. O'Hear, "Plea Bargaining and Procedural Justice," [2008] 42 *Ga. L. Rev.* 407, 420–2.

charged with crimes will be resentful of the authorities and, somewhat understanda-bly, uncooperative with them.[14] Finally, the prospect of unduly long sentences, many of them to be served under increasingly harsh penal conditions, gives individuals ample incentives to conceal their criminal acts and thereby minimize their punish-ment. Again, it is one thing to tell the truth if one faces reasonable punishment for one's crimes, and forms of it that, though unpleasant, do not seem calculated to crip-ple one's life-prospects. It is quite another to do so if it will plunge one into the abyss of contemporary imprisonment, with its spartan if not cruel conditions, and highly deleterious after-effects.[15]

Will adversary trials fare better?

The defects in plea bargaining's ability to get at the truth will be taken by some to confirm the advantages of adversary trials. Whatever else one says about them, trials are much more formal and public procedures for determining whether defendants are guilty, ones which might enable us better to discern the precise character of the actions in which individuals have engaged. Those charged with crimes begin with a presumption of innocence. State officials are then required to formally and publicly present their evidence supporting any and all charges and have it vigorously contested by the defense. Once the evidence has survived such testing, it must be powerful enough to convince a jury (or in bench trials, a judge), beyond reasonable doubt, of the guilt of defendants. The combination of the burden of proof on the state, the high standard of proof that its amassed evidence must meet, and the opportunity for defendants to challenge that evidence, is designed to make it difficult for the state to convict without a strong showing by its officials that defendants are very likely guilty of the crimes with which they have been charged. Still, proponents of trials must admit that defendants in a given case might be guilty as charged, in spite of the inabil-ity of the state to surmount the various obstacles to proving guilt that we put in its path. Indeed, those obstacles might have more to do with our desire to prevent unjust punishment of the innocent than with getting at the truth of what those charged with crimes have done.

There are, in fact, numerous reasons to doubt that adversary trials, as they are structured and conducted in the United States, are more reliable mechanisms for producing truthful verdicts and sentences than robust plea bargaining. As has been noted, both sides in adversary criminal trials have motives to frustrate the search for the truth and the means at their disposal to do so. Prosecutors do not like to lose,

---

[14] On inequitable enforcement, see W. J. Stuntz, "Race, Class, and Drugs," [1998] 98 *Colum. L. Rev.* 1795.

[15] On the effects of imprisonment on individuals' life-prospects, see B. Western, *Punishment and Inequality in America* (New York: Russell Sage, 2006). On the psychological harm wrought by imprison-ment, see C. Haney, *Reforming Punishment: Psychological Limits to the Pains of Imprisonment* (Washington, DC: American Psychological Association, 2009).

especially in high-profile cases. The list of ways in which they can, more or less deliberately, undermine the search for the truth is long and disheartening—use of inflam-
matory rhetoric, witness-coaching, striking of what they fear are sympathetic jurors,
downplaying (and in some cases outright concealment) of exculpatory evidence,
and introduction of defendants' past criminal records for purposes of impeachment,
among them.[16] Prosecutors in the United States also have significant resource advantages over defendants in most cases. They have the police and other investigators to
assist them in investigating crimes, and assistants to help them organize evidence and
research the law. Many criminal defendants are, by contrast, impoverished. As we
have seen in previous chapters, most observers of the indigent defense system in the
United States find it to be inadequate.[17] Adversary trials will succeed at discovering
the truth, if they can succeed in doing so at all, only if both sides have the resources
to put up a spirited fight. Yet many defendants enter such contests with overworked,
inexperienced, and sometimes reluctant or resentful defense attorneys. If adversary
trials are contests, then defendants appear to be routinely overmatched.

In addition, prosecutors have the powerful persuasive edge that goes with being
spokespersons for, and protectors of, the public interest.[18] This edge may be especially
potent in jury trials. As we have seen, there is evidence that jurors do not always grant
defendants the presumption of innocence.[19] Instead, they sometimes begin with the
assumption that those who have managed to get themselves charged in the first place
must be guilty of something—a not entirely unreasonable assumption in most cases,
as it turns out. This effectively translates into something like a presumption of guilt
that defendants must overcome.[20] It is hard to see how this will not work to the state's
advantage in getting prosecutors part way toward satisfying the standard of proof in
criminal cases. Yet that, in turn, means that the state will win cases on evidence that
is short of conclusive and some cases on what amounts to relatively weak evidence.[21]
To make matters worse, prosecutors can stack charges against defendants in ways that
will make it seem as if they must be guilty of something, thus effectively lowering the
barriers to conviction at trial.

---

[16] The ways in which US prosecutors can more or less deliberately defeat the search for the truth
are nicely cataloged by B. L. Gershman in "The Prosecutor's Duty to Truth," [2001] 14 *Geo. J. Legal
Ethics* 309.

[17] See S. J. Schulhofer, "Plea Bargaining as Disaster," [1992] 101 *Yale L. J.* 1979, 1988–90; F. H.
Easterbrook, "Plea Bargaining as Compromise," 101 *Yale L. J.* [1992] 1969, 1973–74; and T. W. Church,
Jr., "In Defense of 'Bargain Justice'," [1979] 13 *Law & Soc'y Rev.* 509, 522.

[18] See Gershman (n 16 above) 340–1.

[19] See M. J. Frank and D. Borschard, "The Silent Criminal Defendant and the Presumption of
Innocence: In the Hands of Real Jurors, is Either of Them Safe?" [2006] 10 *Lewis & Clark L. Rev.* 237,
249–51, and Findley and Scott (n 2 above) 340–1

[20] Defendants are unlikely to fare better with bench trials, since long experience will inform judges
that most defendants are guilty.

[21] Statistics seem to bear this out, with prosecutors winning the vast majority (over 80 percent) of the
felony cases that go to trial. See W. J. Stuntz, "The Pathological Politics of Criminal Law," [2001] 100
Mich. L. Rev. 505, 570. See also Findley and Scott (n 2 above) 341.

Defense attorneys' livelihoods depend on their winning cases, or at least on their appearing to put up a good fight on their clients' behalf. They, too, will seek to prevent consideration of probative evidence against their clients or downplay its significance. Defense attorneys can also elect to simply chip away at the state's evidence without putting forward an affirmative defense that better illuminates what happened in a given case. And their clients do not have to say a thing one way or the other during the course of their trials, even though they will often be in a better position than anyone to reveal to the court what actually occurred. Moreover, their silence at trial cannot be cited by the prosecution as evidence of their guilt. Even defendants who are wholly or partly innocent (partly, in the sense that they are guilty of some criminal misconduct though they have been overcharged by prosecutors) may be advised that it is in their best interests not to take the stand on their own behalf and explain to the jury (or judge in the case of a bench trial) their version of the events under investigation. Again, this will be especially true for innocent defendants who have past records which might be revealed once they testify.[22] But it may also be true for defendants who, for one reason or another, may not make good witnesses on their own behalf.[23] Defendants who have been overcharged, but who are guilty of some of the charges against them, may also find that it is in their best interests to remain silent and have their attorneys challenge the admissibility of damning evidence, seek to discredit truthful witnesses, and divert the jury's attention from probative evidence. These tactics are, at best, contingently related to truth-finding and, at worst, counter to it, especially if they produce full acquittals of partly guilty defendants.

It might be claimed that zealous advocacy by the prosecution and defense is the best means available for getting at the truth of what individuals charged with crimes have actually done.[24] Having each side's version of events challenged fully and vigorously, though far from perfect, is nonetheless the most reliable method we have for discovering the truth when facts are contested. An analogy might be drawn between trials and the scientific method. Scientists advance hypotheses about the causes or effects of natural phenomena and other scientists subject those hypotheses to rigorous examination. Out of this process, scientific truth gradually emerges. So it is with trials, with one or both sides advancing hypotheses about contested events and then having to endure vigorous challenges to their claims.

The problem with this analogy, as David Luban points out, is that the scientific method disallows the parties debating a hypothesis to conceal or distort evidence, even if doing so would help them to prevail.[25] Science proceeds by the disinterested

---

[22] Bowers (n 11 above) 1130. See also R. O. Lempert, S. R. Gross, and J. S. Liebman, *A Modern Approach to Evidence Law*, 3rd edition (St Paul, Minn.: West, 2000) 327–9.

[23] S. J. Schulhofer, "Some Kind Words for the Privilege Against Self-Incrimination," [1991–92] 26 *Val. U. L. Rev.* 311.

[24] David Luban develops and critiques this argument in *Lawyers and Justice: An Ethical Study* (Princeton, NJ: Princeton University Press, 1988) 68–74. See also Weigend (n 3 above) 159.

[25] Luban (n 24 above) 69–70.

pursuit of the truth, or it is supposed to. Prosecutors and defense attorneys seem, and are expected to be, more self-interested or client-interested than disinterested (where the prosecutor's "client" might be understood as the general public). Admittedly, prosecutors have a duty to pursue justice, but, as Abbe Smith points out, they will typically believe that they are doing so by securing the convictions of defendants, all of whom they tend to believe are guilty.[26] If the idea is that the truth-concealing practices that the two sides utilize will cancel out and leave the truth exposed, then Luban's quip that "there is no earthly reason to think that this will happen" seems apropos.[27] Juror confusion or compromise is an equally likely result, one that may not yield anything approaching a verdict that squares with the facts.[28]

The decision by defendants to pursue trial adjudication of the charges against them appears to have one clear advantage if our aim is to discern the truth about what they have or have not done. If defendants are convicted at trial, they can subsequently appeal their convictions. In cases of wrongful convictions, the appeal process offers at least the prospect of correction and ultimate vindication of the truth. Once plea bargain agreements are entered into by defendants and affirmed by the courts, there are typically no further appeals and so no possibility of subsequent "corrections" in cases in which individuals have wrongly admitted their guilt or falsely done so out of fear of even worse legal consequences should they proceed to trial and lose. Though this is an important point on behalf of trial adjudication, the truth-revealing advantages of conviction appeals may be more apparent than real. Relatively few conviction appeals are successful outside of capital cases, and this presumably includes many individuals whose convictions were wholly or partially mistaken.[29] Moreover, appeal courts can reverse convictions that were veridical. The jury got it right but the appellate court reverses the conviction and orders a new trial because of some procedural error before or during the trial. Such outcomes might accord with important norms of procedural justice but obviously do not show that the larger trial process is adept at getting at the truth.

The conclusions toward which this and the preceding section point are dispiriting: Neither trials nor plea bargaining, as they exist in the United States, appear to be reliable methods for discerning the important truths with which it seems that the criminal justice system ought to be concerned. Perhaps we should infer from this that

---

[26] See A. Smith, "Can You Be a Good Person and a Good Prosecutor?" [2001] 14 Geo. J. Legal Ethics 355, 378.

[27] Luban (n 24 above) 70.

[28] See M. Damaska, "Truth in Adjudication," [1998] 49 Hastings L. J. 289, 294–5. Damaska suggests that properly structured discussions in which all viewpoints are allowed a hearing might yield better outcomes when people deliberate about values and rules rather than about facts. When the facts are in dispute, participants with contrary viewpoints must be convinced that they are mistaken. When that does not occur, compromises aimed at breaking deadlocks are likely outcomes.

[29] See A. W. Alschuler, "The Supreme Court and the Jury: Voir Dire, Peremptory Challenges, and the Review of Jury Verdicts," [1989] 56 U. Chi. L. Rev. 153, 213–18; and Findley and Scott (n 2 above) 348–53.

charge-adjudication procedures there do not have truth as their goal; they really are designed to serve some other purpose, such as the resolution of social conflicts.[30]

Fortunately, we can imagine improvements in adversary trials that would enhance their abilities to discern the truth of what those accused of crimes have or have not done. Among the modifications that would help in this regard are the following: preparation by the prosecution of a full evidence dossier that would be made available to defendants and their attorneys prior to trial; better explanations of key legal concepts to jurors; a requirement that defendants testify at their trials (or have the refusal to do so noted as evidence against them); tighter controls on the introduction into evidence of a defendant's past criminal record; less exclusion of probative evidence on the grounds that it was improperly obtained; and a requirement that juries explain and justify their verdicts.[31]

Adversary trials in England and Wales already incorporate some of these features and have others besides that seem promising if our concern is to uncover the truth about what those facing charges have done. British judges play more active roles by sometimes taking it upon themselves to question witnesses. In the Crown Courts, where more serious cases are tried, judges summarize the evidence before the verdict goes to the jury. This seems an enormously useful practice in that it helps jurors sort through what might have been a complicated presentation of claims and counterclaims.[32] Also, British adversary trials seem more dignified than their United States counterparts, with much less scope given to prosecutors or defense attorneys to badger witnesses, grandstand in front of the jury, or engage in rhetorical flourishes that distract the jurors from the task at hand.[33] The lawyers on both sides in British trials are supposed to conduct themselves in ways that appear impartial. In the words of one commentator: "It is the cogency of the argument that holds sway rather than the personality of the advocate."[34] Further, the far superior legal help and advice given to the accused, at all stages of the investigation and adjudicative process, is apt to make for more vigorous contestation of the evidence against the accused and thus a fairer contest, of sorts, between the state and those individuals who elect trial adjudication.[35]

---

[30] Weigend (n 3 above) embraces this view, though not without some ambivalence (pp. 172–3). There are other possibilities, of course, including more radically skeptical approaches which appear to deny the possibility of truth at all. For useful discussion of such approaches, see Damaska (n 28 above) 290–4.

[31] For an extended discussion of changes in the structure and conduct of adversary trials which might make them better at discerning the truth, see Laudan (n 5 above).

[32] However, the concern has been expressed that judges might exhibit subtle or not so subtle forms of bias in questioning witnesses or summarizing the evidence. See M. E. Collett and M. B. Kovera, "The Effects of British and American Trial Procedures on the Quality of Juror Decision-Making," [2003] 27 L. & Hum. Behavior 403.

[33] See J. Jackson, "The Adversary Trial and Trial by Judge Alone," in M. McConville and G. Wilson (eds.), The Handbook of the Criminal Justice Process (Oxford: Oxford University Press, 2002) 335, 339.

[34] S. Solley, "The Role of the Advocate," in McConville and Wilson (n 33 above) 311, 317.

[35] See N. Lefstein, "In Search of Gideon's Promise: Lessons from England and the Need for Federal Help," [2004] 55 Hastings L. J. 835.

However, it is not obvious that the truth will emerge from such contests, or that we will be in a better position to know when, and to what extent, it has done so. Even if we judge British trials to be superior to American ones in discerning and making public truths about what those accused of crimes have actually done, and believe that trials in both countries are susceptible to further refinement in producing accurate verdicts, we might have to accept the fact that trials will never offer as much assurance that we have gotten at the truth in the absence of the kinds of confessions from defendants that often precede or accompany guilty pleas. If defendants can be induced to talk about their (and perhaps others') crimes, in ways that they might be disinclined to do during trials, then we will gain vital confirming evidence about what occurred and, just as importantly, what did not. This is not to say that defendants who admit their guilt will never conceal aspects of their criminal conduct nor distort their roles in the events under investigation. They undoubtedly will. But even half or partial truths might help state officials and the public fill in some of the gaps in their understanding of those events, gaps that they would otherwise have to fill by guesswork based on whatever other evidence they have been able to adduce. We are thus led to consider whether, and to what extent, the reforms in plea bargaining proposed throughout this book will be truth-discerning.

Could plea bargaining be made to better get at the truth?

In his illuminating comparative examination of truth-seeking in the criminal law, Thomas Weigend posits that plea bargaining is ill-matched with the inquisitorial legal systems of Europe because they treat getting at the substantive truth of what defendants have done as their *raison d'être*.[36] Plea bargaining, he claims, fits better within legal systems that construe charge adjudication as a means to resolving disputes between state officials and those whom they suspect of crimes. As long as the dispute can be resolved to everyone's satisfaction, whether the resolution reflects in any very close way the crimes of the accused is not of much significance.

Assuming that plea bargaining must take the form it does currently in the United States, the logic of Weigend's position seems unassailable. If we allow prosecutors to strategically overcharge defendants, threaten them with trial penalties, and offer them substantial and variable waiver rewards in the form of both charge and sentence reductions, then plea bargaining will not in any dependable way hit upon the truth of what defendants have done or punish them pursuant to (all and only) their crimes. It is worth noting, however, that limited forms of plea bargaining have increasingly made inroads in countries with inquisitorial legal systems.[37] What are we to make of this? If Weigend's contentions are correct, then plea bargaining's emergence constitutes a corruption of such legal systems. Plea bargaining simply cannot be squared with legal

---

[36] Weigend (n 3 above) 171.
[37] See Langer (n 3 above) 39–53 for discussion of plea bargaining in Germany and Italy.

procedures aimed at discerning truths about what individuals charged with crimes have done.

There is another possibility, however. Perhaps the forms of plea bargaining that have emerged in some European countries are sufficiently restrained so that they do not subvert in fundamental ways the search for the truth. My aim in this section is not to substantiate this conjecture with detailed reference to specific legal systems and the ways in which they have permitted non-trial adjudication a limited role in charge adjudication. Instead, my aim is the more limited one of showing how restrained forms of plea bargaining are, at least in principle, capable of getting at the truth in ways superior to more robust forms of it.

How is it possible to make a plea-negotiation scheme more conducive to discerning truths about what those charged with crimes have actually done? One thing we would have to do is strongly discourage, if not eliminate entirely, strategic overcharging by prosecutors. As we have seen, the point of this practice is not to arrive at charges that accurately reflect the crimes individuals have committed, but to put pressure on them to plea guilty rather than go to trial. Suppose, then, that the prosecutors who confronted suspected offenders charged them in ways that sought to do no more than capture fairly and accurately the criminal conduct in which it appeared they had engaged.[38] In accordance with the procedure outlined in Chapter 1, defendants who wished to plead guilty would have the option of asking for a settlement hearing before a judge at which all sides spoke to the charges and the evidence for them. Assuming that the judge was not prepared to dismiss all of the charges after the hearing, the judge would set a presumptive sentence for each of the charges remaining in place. That sentence would be the one defendants could expect to receive if, after the hearing, they decided not to plead guilty and instead elected trial adjudication at which they were found guilty. Any post-trial adjustment to the presumptive sentence would have to be justified by the judge and would be subject to appeal. This procedure was designed to preclude either prosecutors or judges from imposing additional penalties on defendants for electing trial adjudication. The elimination of trial penalties is truth-preserving because such penalties are extra increments of punishment unrelated to the criminal charges of which individuals stand accused. As such, they distort the severity of offenders' sentences in cases in which they are convicted after trials.

During settlement hearings before a judge, defendants would have the opportunity to contest the charges and present their side of the story. Again, since defendants who request such hearings would usually do so because they were prepared to

---

[38] The problem, as we saw in Chapter 1, is that in countries with overlapping and duplicative criminal statutes, it will be easy for prosecutors to claim that they are doing no more than charging individuals with crimes for which there is convincing evidence when, in fact, they are doing so to put pressure on them to accede to guilty pleas. The solution, short of the wholesale revision of criminal codes, might be to make concurrent sentences the norm in most multiple-charge cases, thereby reducing the incentives state officials have to overcharge.

admit their guilt, they would be expected to participate actively in the hearings and answer questions posed to them by the presiding judge. They would have various incentives for doing so. A few might hope to convince the judge of their innocence on the charges. Others might maintain that, while guilty of some criminal conduct, they have been charged inappropriately. Yet others would hope to persuade the judge that though they are guilty as charged, they are not as culpable for what they have done as it appears and are thus deserving of sentences lower in the relevant sentencing range. Finally, some defendants would wish simply to acknowledge their guilt and apologize to the victims of their crimes as well as to the larger community. Of course, some defendants would lie or otherwise shade the truth to make themselves look less culpable. But presiding judges would have access to the written record of the case, along with affidavits filed by victims stating their version of the events at issue. Also, the prosecutor would be on hand to counter false or misleading statements by defendants.

We are thus brought to the central question that will occupy us in this section: Which scheme of available waiver rewards would better comport with our desire to get at the truth of the charges against criminal defendants? One which permitted prosecutors to offer substantial and variable rewards to defendants in exchange for their guilty pleas once presumptive sentences for them had been set, or one which strictly limited their abilities to do so? Let us suppose that the former, more robust scheme involved both the possibility of negotiated charge and sentence reductions, whereas the latter, more modest scheme, strongly discouraged charge and fact bargaining and either capped or fixed sentence reductions at modest levels.

If our concern is to have a charge-adjudication scheme that enables us to get at the truth of what criminal defendants have done, then the problems with substantial and variable waiver rewards are readily apparent. Once it is assumed that prosecutors charge veridically, then charge bargaining would tend to yield inaccurate outcomes. If prosecutors have persuasive evidence that individuals are guilty of numerous crimes, but agree to drop a subset of them in exchange for guilty pleas, then they conspire with defendants in perpetrating falsehoods. In a few cases, it might turn out that defendants were actually innocent of the dropped charges. But it is fanciful to believe that the paring away of charges will typically yield such felicitous outcomes. In what is likely to be the majority of cases, the ultimate disposition of charge-bargained cases will be misleading. Individuals guilty of doing several bad things, perhaps several very bad things, would be neither convicted of them nor punished for them.

It might be objected that the elimination of charge bargaining would also produce some falsehoods. If prosecutors were discouraged from dropping charges in cases in which the evidence was suggestive but short of conclusive, then cautious defendants might plead guilty to charges of which they were innocent. Also, bolder defendants might proceed to trial and, in some cases, incorrectly be found guilty of charges of which they were innocent. We might hope that trial adjudication will filter out most of the mistaken charges, but we know that it will not always do so. If prosecutors were permitted to charge bargain in such cases, they could agree to drop charges for which the evidence was weak in exchange for guilty pleas to charges for which the evidence was much stronger.

But the falsehoods produced when prosecutors make honest mistakes are different from those produced when they know or suspect that they have the evidence to convict defendants and drop charges anyway in order to secure guilty pleas to other charges. In the latter kinds of cases, prosecutors know, or at least have good reasons to believe, that they are perpetrating falsehoods. This will especially be true when they drop charges in order to conserve their resources, rather than because the evidence for them is fragile. In such cases, prosecutors and defendants will knowingly participate in the creation of a false public record of the crimes that the latter have committed. However, if prosecutors refuse to drop false charges which they believe are supported by the evidence, and defendants cave in and plead guilty to them or are found guilty of them after trials, then that is altogether different. Prosecutors in such cases will be inadvertently, rather than deliberately, responsible for the perpetration of falsehoods. Only if charge bargaining is limited to charges for which the evidence is considerably short of conclusive can prosecutors claim that they are not knowingly perpetrating falsehoods. And even then they will have to strongly suspect that they are sometimes doing so, since not all of the charges they might be tempted to drop will, in fact, turn out to be false. If prosecutors believe in the charges they have levied against defendants, then the thing to do if guilty pleas on such charges are not forthcoming is to let trial adjudication take its course. If prosecutors do not believe that the evidence supports the charges they have filed, then they should drop them because they recognize that no jury should find the evidence convincing beyond reasonable doubt.

In response, it might be contended that false outcomes are false outcomes. What does it matter if prosecutors (and sometimes defendants or their attorneys) knowingly produce some while at other times inadvertently produce others? To this I would say that it makes all the difference in the world to say to prosecutors "Do your jobs as best you can while seeking to minimize mistaken convictions" as opposed to "Be prepared to participate in the creation of falsehoods, when doing so enables you to conserve your scarce resources or eke out some kind of conviction from a set of charges only some of which you believe are veridical."

The falsehoods perpetrated by sentence bargaining, especially when it involves the offer of large and variable waiver rewards, are also readily apparent. The whole point of having a hearing before a judge once charges are announced is to arrive at an accurate presumptive sentence, one reflecting the facts of a case as they are known at the time, as well as the pertinent characteristics of defendants. Slight downward departures from such sentences, in the form of modest, fixed waiver rewards, are one thing. They will not tend to suggest that defendants have committed significantly less serious crimes than they, in fact, have. But the larger these downward departures are allowed to become, the more they will suggest that defendants have offended in some way other than they did. Sentence discounts of 50 to 75 percent badly distort the truth about what offenders have done. Yet such discounts are neither unheard of nor uncommon in the United States.[39]

Keep in mind that we are presuming both veridical charging and conscientious efforts by judges to set appropriate presumptive sentences at pre-trial hearings. Allowing the negotiation of large and variable waiver rewards, in such a context, is contrary to the truth-discerning and truth-perpetrating functions of these other important features of the criminal justice system. In the absence of full defendant confessions, state officials will not be certain that they are imposing appropriate criminal sanctions on the guilty. But they will know that they have done all that they can to investigate crimes, charge individuals fairly, and impose fitting sanctions on those who agree to plead guilty. The availability of large and variable waiver rewards confounds the workings of this otherwise orderly process.

It will be objected that substantial and variable waiver rewards have a clear advantage in what we hope are the relatively rare cases in which innocent defendants plead guilty to the charges against them.[40] In such cases, the significantly reduced sentences that these unfortunate individuals receive will, at the very least, make their "crimes" appear less serious and thus minimize the falsehoods perpetrated by their pleas. Modest and fixed sentence discounts, by contrast, will saddle such defendants with longer sentences and thus contribute to the appearance of their having committed worse crimes. Falsehoods might be falsehoods, but some are greater than others. Robust waiver rewards at least have the virtue of minimizing them in false-plea cases.

The problem with this argument, though, is that it ignores the fact that large and variable waiver rewards might induce more guilty pleas by the innocent than would more modest ones. Faced with more substantial discrepancies between trial and negotiated outcomes, more innocent defendants will likely opt for the latter. By contrast, more innocent defendants might elect trial adjudication if they cannot gain as much by acceding to guilty pleas. Prosecutors would then have to decide whether the evidence against such defendants was strong enough to proceed to trial. In a number of cases, they would decide to proceed, but not in all. If the charges were dropped, the outcomes would correspond with the truth, on the assumption that the defendants in question are, in fact, innocent. Moreover, prosecutors would not win all of the cases that went to trial. Even if we assume, for the sake of argument, that they would win

---

[39] See Bowers (n 11 above) 1142–5 for a discussion of leniency in sentencing in plea bargaining cases, especially when the crimes in question are lower-level offenses. As Bowers makes clear, plea bargained cases also produce non-custodial sentences where trials might produce custodial ones, or sentences to time already served while awaiting trial. See also Schulhofer (n 17 above) 1993, where he claims that those who plead guilty receive sentences from "twenty-five to seventy-five percent lower than those imposed on comparable defendants convicted at trial." As I have noted elsewhere, however, Schulhofer's figures do not distinguish foregone waiver rewards and trial penalties and thus the contribution each makes to the higher sentences assigned to those convicted after trials.

[40] Again, as Bowers (n 11 above) notes, the most common defendants wrongly charged with crimes will be those with prior records, at 1124–32.

a majority of such cases, the fact that they would lose some reduces further the edge that robust waiver rewards have in such cases. Moreover, the vast majority of criminal defendants will not be innocent. Robust waiver rewards will work against the combination of veridical charging and carefully set presumptive sentences in producing outcomes that align with the evidence that state officials have been able to amass against guilty defendants.

Nevertheless, waiver rewards of any size, even modest ones, distort the truth about the severity of offenders' crimes to some extent, at least on the assumption that presumptive sentences set by judges in pre-trial hearings discern those truths for the most part. On the rare occasions when presumptive sentences are revised post-trial, the revisions will also, we should assume, better reflect the gravity of offenders' crimes. Yet it seems clear that the modestly discounted sentences resulting from guilty pleas could only be claimed to come "close enough" to relaying to the public the "truth" about the seriousness of offenders' crimes. But why settle for "close enough" when, with a little more effort, we could nail down the truth with greater precision? Of course, we might not want to literally force every criminal defendant to go to trial. Those willing to confess or plead guilty could be allowed to do so, but they should not be granted sentence discounts. Instead they should receive their presumptive sentences.

One problem with this line of argument is that it assumes that adversary trials can be made to yield convictions as often as plea bargaining will yield guilty pleas. But that seems unlikely, especially if we are imagining improved adversary trials in which defendants are provided with effective legal counsel, among other things.[41] If criminal defendants had only the two options of pleading guilty for no sentence discounts or going to trial, then some who would be willing to plead guilty for modest sentence discounts would elect trial adjudication and wrongly be acquitted. Perhaps this would not apply to many. Most defendants would be guilty and prosecutors would retain many of the usual advantages that help them win trials. Still, trials would occasionally produce mistaken acquittals where plea bargaining would have produced guilty pleas. We thus face a choice: Is it better to have a charge-adjudication system that yields more convictions but somewhat less accurate sentences, or one that yields fewer convictions but more accurate sentences? Which of these systems gives us more of the truth? The answer appears to depend on the number of occasions on which trials will yield mistaken acquittals. The more they did so, the better modest forms of plea bargaining will look.

Also, plea bargaining is likely to produce some increase in the number of cases processed by the criminal justice system, relative to the number that will be produced

---

[41] Ashworth and Redmayne (n 4 above) report acquittal rates of 45 percent in the Crown Courts of England and Wales (p. 294). This rate might be, in part, attributable to the better defense representation provided to British criminal defendants, representation which does a more effective job of putting the state's case to the test during trials. It could be argued, of course, that most of the defendants acquitted are, in fact, innocent. But that seems unlikely.

by trials. Again, trials are expensive and time-consuming enterprises and thus deplete the resources state officials have at their disposal to process cases. Assume that when trials produce accurate guilty verdicts, they likewise produce sentences that better reflect all of the relevant elements of the crimes committed by individuals. Nonetheless, a system that limited defendants' options to pleading guilty and receiving their presumptive sentences or going to trial would likely see some increase in the demand for trials. That increased demand would, in turn, yield some decrease in the overall number of convictions obtained. Again, we confront a trade-off: Is it better to have a system that produces more accurate sentences for the offenders it manages to convict, or one that produces somewhat less accurate sentences, though by no means wholly inaccurate ones, for a larger group of offenders? The answer to this question might depend on the magnitude of the increased number of cases that plea bargaining would enable state officials to process relative to those they could process via trial adjudication. If the magnitude was significant, then that would seem to count in plea bargaining's favor.

Beyond these points, it seems fair to say that adversary trials, due to their oppositional nature, will leave state officials, and therefore the citizens on whose behalf they act, less certain that when they impose legal punishment on individuals, they do so justifiably. Under the modest waiver-reward scheme I defend, defendants who are willing to enter guilty pleas appear before a judge and submit to questioning. Their answers to the questions posed will often, though not invariably, confirm their guilt and provide crucial evidence about their level of culpability for their crimes. State officials will therefore receive the vital assurance that any fitting punishment they impose is justified. We can imagine, I suppose, that those same defendants, in the course of adversary trial proceedings, would take the stand and reveal things confirming their guilt or level of culpability. But it seems more likely that their attorneys would counsel them not to do so, or that defendants, of their own volition, would be disinclined to do so. Adversary trials, whatever their form, are set up to be contests of sorts between the state and criminal defendants (or the attorneys who represent them). Both sides have motivations to play up their version of events and discredit competing ones. Even if we suppose that some of the more troubling truth-distorting tactics common to adversary trials in the United States were utilized less often by the contestants, trials would nonetheless present juries or judges with conflicting accounts of the events at issue. The relevant fact-finders will have to sort through these accounts, comparing them with the evidence at hand. Though more often than not they will arrive at accurate verdicts and sentences, sometimes they will not. In some cases—and we probably do not know how many—juries will announce mistaken or confused verdicts. And less often we will know that trials have produced accurate verdicts and sentences because less often we will have unvarnished admissions of guilt from defendants' own mouths.

Full-on inquisitorial trials, with their more relentless searches for the truth of what happened in criminal cases, might produce verdicts and sentences that are only marginally more truthful than those obtained from limited forms of plea bargaining. That might explain why some European countries have moved toward permitting prosecutors or judges more discretion in offering defendants modest waiver rewards in exchange for confessions or guilty pleas, at least when the charges in question are not terribly serious.[42] It simply may not make sense to employ expensive and burdensome charge-adjudication mechanisms when the crimes in question are minor and modest waiver rewards can do well enough, and perhaps better, at ferreting out the truth of what occurred and assigning appropriate sentences to those willing to admit their guilt.

Admittedly, when the charges in question carry with them the possibility of lengthy imprisonment, with its myriad costs and harmful effects on individuals, then more concerted efforts to arrive at the truth might seem more desirable.[43] Yet even in such cases, something short of full trials might be worth considering for defendants who candidly admit their guilt. As we have seen, one option would be to require prosecutors in the more serious cases to submit complete evidence dossiers to the judges overseeing them, as well as to the defense.[44] Judges at settlement hearings could then be required to ensure that the evidence meets a high standard of proof—such as that the evidence "very likely" would yield a conviction at trial—before setting presumptive sentences and accepting any confessions or guilty pleas. If judges believed the evidence insufficient to warrant accepting admissions of guilt, they would be required to inform both sides of their findings. Prosecutors, in particular, would then face difficult decisions about how or whether to proceed to trial. Presumably, in most such cases, they would be disinclined to do so, especially if they faced the very real prospect of summary rulings against them once they had presented their evidence in court. These more elaborate safeguards in serious cases should assure us that settlement hearings would suffice to protect the presumably rare innocent defendants who, for some reason, were inclined to plead guilty to one or more of the serious charges against them.

Finally, it is worth noting that other changes in the criminal justice system might further enhance the ability of a limited plea-negotiation scheme to get at the truth of what offenders have done. The elimination or significant curtailment of morals offenses, along with their tendency to generate inequities in policing and prosecution, might lessen some of the alienation or resentment many offenders feel toward the criminal law. If the criminal law focused more narrowly on the prohibition of acts genuinely harmful to others, and saw to the equitable enforcement of these more

---

[42] Notably, the sentence reductions received by defendants who admit their guilt tend to be significantly lower in Germany than in the United States. See J. I. Turner, "Judicial Participation in Plea Negotiations: A Comparative View," [2006] 54 Am. J. Comp. L. 199, 235.

[43] Langer (n 3 above) reports that sentence bargaining in Italy is limited to minor offenses where a defendant's sentence does not exceed five years' imprisonment after a waiver reward is granted (p. 50). Similarly, in Argentina, Langer notes that negotiated sentences cannot exceed six years' imprisonment (p. 54).

[44] Both are common practices in Germany. See Turner (n 42 above) 230.

defensible prohibitions, then fewer criminal defendants could plausibly regard the crimes for which they were arrested as something other than real wrongs. They also could not point to better-situated members of society who routinely escaped prosecution for similar kinds of offenses. Offenders would then have less cause to withhold their cooperation with the authorities and might more readily admit their crimes. Admissions of guilt and acceptance of responsibility for crimes might also be more forthcoming if current forms of lengthy and harsh legal punishment were abandoned in favor of shorter sentences served under more constructive conditions. Though punishment will never be pleasant, its destructive tendencies could be ameliorated in ways that would make it easier for offenders to embrace it as justified and a plausible pathway toward reform.

Truth and the limits of charge-adjudication schemes

My defense of settlement hearings and limited sentence concessions for defendants willing to plead guilty as mechanisms for getting at the truth has so far occurred against an idealized background. For one thing, I have not given much weight to the very real possibility that existing sentencing schemes might be either indefensibly lenient or, more likely, unduly harsh. Yet it is apparent that defective sentencing schemes will tend to produce distortions of the truth by making offenders' crimes appear either less or more serious than they really are. Saying this is consistent with acknowledging that there may not be a single, most defensible way to set sentences for the various kinds of criminal offenses. In particular, what is known as the "anchoring problem" in sentencing theory suggests that it is unlikely that there is a sentencing scheme that is uniquely proportionate with the full range of criminal offenses.[45] It does not follow, of course, that there are no indefensible sentencing schemes. If a given society assigns draconian penalties to relatively minor offenses, then it communicates something misleading, if not utterly false, about the wrongs committed by the individuals convicted of such offenses. The same is true if it punishes serious offenses with a proverbial slap on the wrist.

Charge-adjudication procedures might initially seem helpless to correct, in any systematic way, the falsehoods borne of poorly conceived sentencing schemes. However, it could be argued that substantial and variable waiver rewards would at least have the virtue of limiting the falsehoods perpetrated by unduly harsh sentencing schemes. Such rewards would mitigate the sentences handed down and so make offenders' crimes seem like the less serious ones that we are supposing they are. Modest waiver rewards would not have that laudable effect. Though that seems correct as far as it goes, it should also be apparent by now that robust waiver-reward

---

[45] For discussion of the anchoring problem, see von Hirsch (n 7 above) 36–46.

schemes will reduce sentencing falsehoods haphazardly. They will also more often suggest that like offenders have committed crimes that are vastly different from one another. The best way to make plea bargaining consistently truth-perpetrating is to wed it to a defensible sentencing scheme and then make sure that it does not upset such a scheme by making sentences subject to wide-ranging negotiation.

Charge-adjudication procedures are likewise at the mercy of other truth-distorting features of criminal justice systems and the larger social systems in which they operate. As we have seen, severe social deprivation can be understood as diminishing, without reducing entirely, the culpability of offenders for their crimes.[46] Yet some legal systems do not recognize social deprivation as a partial excuse for criminal conduct or as a mitigating factor in sentencing.[47] Criminal convictions of the desperately poor will therefore make them appear worse persons than they really are. Also, though most legal systems incorporate an insanity defense, they may not treat mental illness that does not rise to the level of insanity as an excusing factor in crime or a mitigating one in sentencing. On the plausible assumption that those who suffer from significant forms of mental illness are less culpable for their criminal actions than those who do not, convictions of the mentally ill might convey partial falsehoods about them and the seriousness of their crimes. More controversially, it has been argued that otherwise sophisticated legal systems prohibit and punish the harmful acts of the poor, while not prohibiting or not enforcing laws against the equally, if not more, harmful actions of the rich and powerful.[48] The actions of the socially marginalized are thus made to appear the only or most salient threats to the safety and security of their fellow citizens. But this appearance is misleading, though it is one that charge-adjudication schemes will be largely helpless to do anything about.

Finally, it seems clear that some of the truths accurately discerned by charge-adjudication schemes will turn out to be of dubious value. Again, the criminal law in any existing society might prohibit and punish perfectly reasonable and harmless kinds of conduct. This possibility is not limited to tyrannical political regimes, though it is perhaps more common to them. The criminal law in many liberal democratic societies arguably exceeds its moral remit, prohibiting conduct that is not in any very significant or direct way harmful (or threatening) to the legitimate interests of other individuals.[49] We might be able to uncover lots of truths about

---

[46] See my *Rethinking Imprisonment* (Oxford: Oxford University Press, 2007) 84–98.

[47] Social deprivation, even when severe, is not treated by United States law as constituting duress, that is, a situation of genuinely hard choice. For useful discussion of duress and social deprivation, see S. J. Morse, "Deprivation and Desert," in W. C. Heffernan and J. Kleinig (eds.), *From Social Justice to Criminal Justice: Poverty and the Administration of Criminal Law* (New York: Oxford University Press, 2000) 114.

[48] See J. Reiman, *The Rich Get Richer and the Poor Get Prison,* 8th edition (Boston: Allyn and Bacon, 2006) 70–100, and B. Hudson, "Punishing the Poor: Dilemmas of Justice and Difference," in Heffernan and Kleinig (n 47 above) 189.

[49] See D. Husak, *Overcriminalization: The Limits of the Criminal Law* (Oxford: Oxford University Press, 2008).

what individuals charged with such morally suspect crimes have done, but only an unsophisticated legal positivism would hold these truths to be worth the resources used in pursuing them and the human suffering wrought by doing so. The value of the truths discerned and made public by charge-adjudication schemes is thus, to some extent, dependent upon the quality of the laws they help to enforce.

Charge-adjudication schemes, no matter how accurate or reliable, are, by their very natures, limited truth-discerning mechanisms. They might be capable of finding and affirming nominal truths about what those charged with crimes have or have not done. But they cannot tell us whether such nominal truths are ultimately worth pursuing or have the potential to mislead us. To get at those deeper and more subtle kinds of truths, we must have recourse to normative theories of the criminal law and the larger political and social order in which it functions.

Epilogue

In drawing discussion in the book to a close, two practical issues warrant some attention. One of them arises from my insistence that waiver rewards in the form of sentence discounts generally should be kept fixed and modest—no more than, say, 10 percent of the presumptive sentences announced during settlement hearings. Such a proposal makes sense for criminal sanctions that are meted out in quantitative terms, whether they involve time spent in custody, on probation, or dollar amounts of fines. But for many of the individuals charged with crimes, the overriding concern is to avoid, and not just minimize, custodial sanctions.[1] They will admit guilt—and might only do so—if they believe that state officials will assign them non-custodial penalties. Yet it is not apparent how such fairly common cases can be accommodated within the kind of waiver-reward scheme which I have maintained is most defensible. It would seem that if the judge at a settlement hearing determines, for instance, that a defendant presumptively should receive a 30-day jail term if found guilty of the crime with which she is charged, then the most my scheme would offer such a defendant is a reduction in her term of custody. This might make the scheme appear too inflexible and thus unresponsive to the real world of offender motivations that state officials confront.

In responding to this, it is important to set to one side the possibility that existing sentencing schemes too often or readily make offenders eligible for custodial sentences. It may well be that some legal systems resort to imprisonment too often and this fact inclines observers to think that the negotiated settlements that enable some offenders to avoid confinement are good and noble things. But suppose that more defensible sentencing schemes are in place such that the individuals who are assigned sentences involving short terms of custody are likely to deserve them given their crimes. Judges at settlement hearings would presumably discern this and set presumptive sentences accordingly. Under these assumptions, it might be questioned whether plea negotiations should be permitted to convert one kind of sentence into another kind.[2] In particular, if an individual's crime merits custody as a sanction, then it might seem that the most we should grant her in exchange for a guilty plea is some small discount in the term of her custody.

Still, in the spirit of compromise, another possibility might be envisioned. Suppose that once it is determined that an offender presumptively should be assigned a minimal sentence in custody of, say, no more than 30 days, a "conversion rule" is

---

[1] See, for instance, M. Heumann, *Plea Bargaining: The Experiences of Prosecutors, Judges, and Defense Attorneys* (Chicago: University of Chicago Press, 1977) 70.

[2] A point raised, though not insisted upon, by A. W. Alschuler, in "The Trial Judge's Role in Plea Bargaining," [1976] 76 *Colum. L. Rev.* 1059, 1124.

activated. The rule permits a short custody sentence to be converted to some mutu-ally agreed-upon—or better, some fairly standardized—non-custodial sentence that is commensurately burdensome. After all, once it is determined that an offender's crime warrants a de minimis term in custody, it does not seem troublesome to assign the offender some non-custodial sentence that is comparable in severity. Of course, it would be crucial not to permit negotiations about whether the offender's crime merits the de minimis presumptive custody sentence in the first place. That is some-thing to be determined by the judge based on the evidence concerning the offender's crime and her level of culpability in committing it. Once it is so determined, then, and only then, might the conversion rule become applicable.

This brings us to a second practical issue. As noted at the outset, proposals to mod-ify the framework within which the negotiated settlement of criminal charges occurs are sometimes met with the objection that participants in plea bargaining schemes who have had more leeway in negotiating guilty pleas have vested interests in keep-ing things the way they are. They will therefore work to frustrate the implemen-tation of any reforms, especially ones aimed at reining in the discretion that they have come to expect and rely upon. Also, reforms that look good in theory some-times have unexpected outcomes in practice. For instance, in an effort to reduce the discretion judges had to determine sentences, the Federal Sentencing Guidelines were developed and adopted in many jurisdictions throughout the United States. Yet the Guidelines had the unanticipated effect of enlarging the powers of prosecutors because they made charging decisions the paramount factor in the determination of defendants' sentences.[3] The Guidelines debacle is seen by many as a cautionary tale for those who would tinker with the negotiated plea system.

Of these two concerns about reforming plea bargaining, the former seems more worrisome. It goes without saying that we should think about how changes in plea bargaining practices could backfire or have unexpected consequences. But once we have done so, the only thing to do if we are convinced they are needed is to try them out and see what happens. If need be, we can adopt further changes. Moreover, in planning reforms, we can learn and take heart from the more restrained forms of negotiated settlements that exist in many countries. Some of these have existed for some time, which attests to their practical viability.

However, if state officials, criminal defendants, and their attorneys all have a stake in frustrating efforts at reform, then that is an altogether different matter. These are the actors who must be convinced to accede to any alterations in the system. If they are unanimous in their opposition to changes, it seems unlikely that reforms will be enacted or successful. It is worth pausing to see how the interests of these diverse parties coalesced around erecting the robust plea bargaining scheme that exists in

---

[3] See J. Standen, "Plea Bargaining in the Shadow of the Guidelines," [1993] 81 *Cal. L. Rev.* 1471.

the United States. Doing so will put us in a better position to discern the prospects of proposed modifications to it.

The story of this remarkable convergence of interests is perhaps best told by Milton Heumann.[4] On Heumann's account, United States judges, prosecutors, defendants, and their attorneys all find that plea bargaining in its current form coincides with their interests. It is easy to see why prosecutors would adhere to this view, especially given the extraordinary power robust forms of plea bargaining give them to induce guilty pleas from those they have charged with crimes. In a world where prosecutors can overcharge, add charges subsequent to failed plea negotiations, threaten trial penalties, and offer generous charge and sentence waiver rewards, plea bargaining enables them to process cases efficiently and thereby maximize the number of convictions they can wrest from their limited resources. And they can do all of this with limited oversight from other criminal justice officials, though in theory, of course, judges can decline to go along with the sentence concessions prosecutors offer to defendants. Yet judges, as it turns out, are not all that inclined to rock the boat once defendants and prosecutors have agreed upon a set of charges and a sentencing recommendation. Trials are burdensome to judges as well as to prosecutors. Moreover, trials force judges to make rulings on evidence or procedure that might subsequently be overturned on appeal. Judges, who generally dislike being overruled by higher courts, therefore have an additional incentive to go along with negotiated criminal settlements, since once plea agreements are finalized, there are scant grounds for appealing them.

Most criminal defendants, for reasons we have already seen, have little interest in seeking trial adjudication of the charges against them. In part this is because the vast majority of them are guilty, though perhaps not quite as they have been charged. Trials offer many defendants little hope for acquittal and the prospect of significantly longer sentences if they are convicted. And since most of them are accused of relatively low-level offenses and many already have criminal records, the real prizes to be won are the avoidance of jail or prison time altogether, or short stints in confinement if imprisonment cannot be avoided. Plea bargaining enables defendants to garner these prizes. Prosecutors, for the most part, want convictions; they are less concerned with the length of sentences assigned to defendants, especially when their crimes are not serious.[5]

Defense attorneys might emerge from law school eager to challenge every aspect of the state's case against their clients and thereby furnish them with stalwart legal representation. But they soon discover that neither the facts nor the law is on their side. Few of the cases they take on or are assigned pose significant factual or legal issues. Many are "dead bang," meaning that defendants are simply and rather obviously

[4] Heumann (n 1 above). See also L. Mather, *Plea Bargaining or Trial?* (Lexington, Mass.: Lexington Books, 1979).

[5] A point made by Josh Bowers as well, in "Punishing the Innocent," [2008] 156 *U. Pa. L. Rev.* 1117, 1141.

guilty as charged. Further, defense attorneys who dare to file motions challenging the state's evidence or who stubbornly hold out for better deals before advising their clients to accept them may face the ire of prosecutors or judges in subsequent cases. Defense attorneys learn that an amicable relationship with prosecutors and judges is the ticket to gaining more concessions for their clients. Finally, the high number of indigent defendants in the criminal justice system means that many of them will be represented by overworked public defenders or underpaid appointed ones. Neither type of defender will be inclined to encourage their clients to opt for burdensome trials, especially if the prospects of acquittal are dim.

Given the ways in which robust forms of plea bargaining serve the interests of all of the principal actors in the United States criminal justice system, it is no wonder that it has become an entrenched way of resolving criminal charges. The reforms urged in previous chapters would impact prosecutors most directly. They would be deprived of trial penalties in all of their forms, charge bargaining would be strongly discouraged, and the waiver rewards on offer would be modest and rarely subject to manipulation by them. There is no point in denying that prosecutors would have the most to lose from such reforms and thus the most powerful motivations for resisting them. It would not be much in the way of principled resistance, at least if my arguments in preceding chapters have been convincing. There are simply not very persuasive reasons for handing prosecutors the tools to threaten criminal defendants with dire consequences for refusing to admit their guilt. Also, most cases would still be resolved without trials, since few defendants would perceive it to be in their interests to insist on them. The burdens on prosecutors posed by trials would increase somewhat, although to what extent is probably unknown. However, some of the defendants who would elect trial adjudication would be those against whom the state's evidence was considerably short of conclusive. As we saw in Chapter 8, principled prosecutors could, and probably should, limit the trial burdens posed by such cases by dropping charges in many of them, unless or until more evidence becomes available.

Fortunately, the other main actors in the criminal justice system would not be as adversely affected by the reforms I have proposed and might actually benefit from them. Judges would bear the additional burdens of having to conduct settlement hearings. Yet these burdens would partially be compensated for by not having to conduct mostly meaningless plea colloquies. Also, settlement hearings would require judges to assume more active roles in the resolution of criminal charges. Whether this would be perceived by most of them as an unwanted chore or an attractive opportunity is not clear. There would be a greater scope for them to review the factual basis for charges, something which they are supposed to do in any case but which most observers doubt that they do very often. Furthermore, since most cases would still be resolved without trials, the proposed reforms are consistent with the interests judges have in avoiding trial adjudication.

Next, consider how criminal defendants would be affected by the suggested reforms. They would not have to go to trial if they did not see it as in their interests to do so. Most presumably would not. Granted, substantial and variable waiver rewards would no longer be on offer from prosecutors. This might mean that defendants would face somewhat longer sentences for any guilty pleas they entered. But defendants would no longer be menaced by trial penalties and subject, as often, to strategic overcharging. They would also presumably benefit from having judges scrutinize the evidence for the charges against them at settlement hearings. Duplicative, overlapping, or groundless charges might thereby be eliminated. Moreover, defendants would have a chance at settlement hearings to explain their side of things, something which they are not really encouraged to do at plea colloquies. All of this suggests that defendants' interests would be at least as well served by limiting the non-trial resolution of criminal charges as by maintaining it in its current forms.

Finally, since the proposed reforms would be unlikely to result in significant increases in trial demand by defendants, defense attorneys—even overworked ones—would not have reasons for resisting them. They might even welcome the reforms, since settlement hearings would provide them with more meaningful opportunities to question the state's charges and the evidence for them. Moreover, prosecutors would lack the means for penalizing defense attorneys who challenged their charging decisions and sentencing recommendations, since they would no longer have the degree of control over charges and sentences that they currently possess. All of this, it seems, bodes well for gaining defense attorney acquiescence in the proposed changes.

Prosecutors are probably the most politically influential actors in the United States criminal justice system. Criminal defendants have few influential spokespersons willing to speak on their behalf, and state and federal legislators seem disinclined to listen even if they did. Defense attorneys are represented by bar associations, but so, to some extent, are prosecutors. Also, the politicization of criminal justice has made the legislators who control so much of criminal justice policy more responsive to prosecutors than to the lawyers who represent criminal offenders.[6] Judges have generally been reticent to step into the political fray. This, too, leaves the field open for prosecutors to promote their perceived interests and they have not been reticent about doing so.

Reading the tea leaves, then, the short-term prospects for the reform of plea bargaining in the United States appear somewhat dreary. The same is true, it must be acknowledged, for the prospects of other needed reforms in the larger criminal justice system. But that does not mean that we should refrain from making the case for them as best we can. In relation to plea bargaining in particular, I hope to have shown the implausibility of claims to the effect that it must continue in its current form because alternatives to it are unwise or infeasible.

The good news is that comparable plea bargaining practices are not well entrenched elsewhere in the world. In many countries, they are relatively new, or if not exactly

---

[6] See W. J. Stuntz, "The Pathological Politics of Criminal Law," [2001] 100 *Mich. L. Rev.* 505, 528–38.

recent in origin, their open acknowledgment and formalization is.[7] Moreover, in many of these countries, prosecutors are not granted such formidable powers to intimidate defendants and their attorneys. We thus might reasonably hope that the more restrained forms of plea bargaining that appear most defensible will ultimately prevail.

---

[7] See the remarkable story of the denial by official authorities of plea bargaining's existence in England and Wales in the 1970s in J. Baldwin and M. McConville, "Plea Bargaining and Plea Negotiations in England," [1979] 13 *L. & Soc'y Rev.* 287, 302. See also their *Negotiated Justice: Pressures to Plead Guilty* (London: Martin Robertson, 1977).

Bibliography

Acorn, A. E. (1991) "Similar Fact Evidence and the Principle of Inductive Reasoning: Makin Sense," 11 *O. J. L. S.* 63.

Adelstein, R. and Micelli, T. J. (2001) "Toward a Comparative Economics of Plea Bargaining," 11 *European Journal of Law and Economics* 47.

Alschuler, A. (1968) "The Prosecutor's Role in Plea Bargaining," 36 *U. Chi. L. Rev.* 50.

—— (1976) "The Trial Judge's Role in Plea Bargaining, Part I," 76 *Colum. L. Rev.* 1059.

—— (1979) "Plea Bargaining and its History," 79 *Colum. L. Rev.* 1.

—— (1981) "The Changing Plea Bargaining Debate," 69 *Cal. L. Rev.* 652.

—— (1983) "Implementing the Criminal Defendant's Right to Trial: Alternatives to the Plea Bargaining System," 50 *U. Chi. L. Rev.* 931.

—— (1989) "The Supreme Court and the Jury: Voir Dire, Peremptory Challenges, and the Review of Jury Verdicts," 56 *U. Chi. L. Rev.* 153.

—— (1997) "A Peculiar Privilege in Historical Perspective," in R. H. Helmholz, et al. (eds.), *The Privilege Against Self-Incrimination: Its Origins and Development* (Chicago: University of Chicago Press) 181.

—— and Deiss, A. B. (1994) "A Brief History of the Criminal Jury in the United States," 61 *U. Chi. L. Rev.* 867.

Amar, A. R. (1997) *The Constitution and Criminal Procedure* (New Haven, Conn.: Yale University Press).

Andenaes, J. (1966) "The General Preventive Effects of Punishment," 114 *U. Pa. L. Rev.* 949.

Anderson, D. A. (1999) "The Aggregate Burden of Crime," 42 *J. L. & Econ.* 611.

Anderson, J. L. (1999) "Annulment Retributivism: A Hegelian Theory of Punishment," 5 *Legal Theory* 363.

Anonymous (1972) "Note: Restructuring the Plea Bargain," 82 *Yale L. J.* 286.

Ashworth, A. and Redmayne M. (2010) *The Criminal Process*, 4th edition (Oxford: Oxford University Press).

Bagaric, M. and Ameraskara, K. (2001) "Feeling Sorry?—Tell Someone Who Cares: The Irrelevance of Remorse in Sentencing," 40 *The Howard Journal* 364.

Baker, D. (2008) "Constitutionalizing the Harm Principle," 27 *Criminal Justice Ethics* 3.

Baldwin, J. and McConville, M. (1977) *Negotiated Justice: Pressures to Plead Guilty* (London: Martin Robertson).

—— (1979) "Plea Bargaining and Plea Negotiation in England," 13 *L. & Soc'y Rev.* 287.

Becker, G. (1968) "Crime and Punishment: An Economic Approach," 76 *Journal of Political Economics* 169.

Beeman, Y. A. (1987) "Note: Accomplice Testimony Under Contingent Plea Agreements," 72 *Cornell L. Rev.* 799.

Bentham, J. (1935) *An Introduction to the Principles of Morals and Legislation*, P. Wheelright (ed.) (Garden City NY: Doubleday, Doran, and Company) (Original 1789).

Beres, L. S. (1994) "Civil Contempt and the Rational Contemnor," 69 *Ind. L. J.* 722.

Bibas, S. (2004) "Plea Bargaining Outside the Shadow of Trial," 117 *Harv. L. Rev.* 2463.

—— and Bierschbach, R. A. (2004) "Integrating Remorse and Apology into Criminal Procedure," 114 *Yale L. J.* 85.

Bowers, J. (2007) "Punishing the Innocent," 156 *U. Pa. L. Rev.* 1117.

Braithwaite, J. (1999) "Restorative Justice: Assessing Optimistic and Pessimistic Accounts," 25 *Crime and Justice: A Review of Research* 1.

Bronaugh, R. (1998) "Is There a Duty to Confess?" 98 *American Philosophical Association Newsletter on Philosophy and Law* 86.

Brunk, C. (1979) "The Problem of Voluntariness and Coercion in the Negotiated Plea," 13 *L. & Soc'y Rev.* 527.

Cahill, M. T. (2007) "Retributive Justice in the Real World," 85 *Wash. U. L. Rev.* 815.

Cavadino, M. and Dignan, J. (2006) *Penal Systems: A Comparative Approach* (London: Sage Publications).

Church, Jr., T. W. (1979) "In Defense of 'Bargain Justice'," 13 *L. & Soc'y Rev.* 509.

Cole, D. (1999) *No Equal Justice: Race and Class in the American Criminal Justice System* (New York: New Press).

Collett, M. E. and Kovera, M. B. (2003) "The Effects of British and American Trial Procedures on the Quality of Juror Decision-Making," 27 *L. & Hum. Behavior* 403.

Currie, E. (1998) *Crime and Punishment in America* (New York: Henry Holt).

Damaska, M. (1998) "Truth in Adjudication," 49 *Hastings L. J.* 289.

Delgado, R. (1985) "Rotten Social Background: Should the Criminal Law Recognize a Defense of Severe Environmental Deprivation?" 3 *L. & Ineq.* 9.

Dolinko, D. (1986) "Is There a Rationale for the Privilege Against Self-Incrimination?" 33 *UCLA L. Rev.* 1063.

Duff, R. A. (1977) "Psychopathy and Moral Understanding," 14 *American Philosophical Quarterly* 189.

—— (1986) *Trials and Punishments* (Cambridge: Cambridge University Press).

—— (1998) "Dangerousness and Citizenship," in A. Ashworth and M. Wasik (eds.) *Fundamentals of Sentencing Theory* (Oxford: Clarendon Press) 141.

—— (2001) *Punishment, Communication and Community* (Oxford: Oxford University Press).

——, Farmer, L., Marshall, S., and Tadros, V. (2007) *The Trial on Trial, Vol. 3: Towards a Normative Theory of the Criminal Trial* (Oxford: Hart Publishing).

Darbyshire, P. (2000) "The Mischief of Plea Bargaining and Sentencing Rewards," 2000 *Crim. L. Rev.* 895.

Doob, A. and Webster, C. M. (2003) "Sentence Severity and Crime: Accepting the Null Hypothesis," 30 *Crime and Justice: A Review of Research* 143.

Easterbrook, F. H. (1983) "Criminal Procedure as a Market System," 12 *J. Legal Stud.* 289.

—— (1992) "Plea Bargaining as Compromise," 101 *Yale L. J.* 1969.

Ewin, R. E. (1992) "Loyalty and Virtues," 42 *Philosophical Quarterly* 403.

—— (1993) "Loyalties, and Why Loyalty Should be Ignored," 12 *Criminal Justice Ethics* 6.

Feeley, M. M. (1979) *The Process Is the Punishment: Handling Cases in a Lower Criminal Court* (New York: Russell Sage Foundation).

Feinberg, J. (1965) "The Expressive Function of Punishment," 49 *The Monist* 397.

—— (1984) *Harm to Others* (New York: Oxford University Press).

—— (1986) *Harm to Self* (New York: Oxford University Press).

—— (1990) *Harmless Wrongdoing* (New York: Oxford University Press).

Findlay, K. A., and Scott, M. S. (2006) "The Multiple Dimensions of Tunnel Vision in Criminal Cases," 2006 *Wis. L. Rev.* 291.

Fine, C. and Kennett, J. (2004) "Mental Impairment, Moral Understanding, and Criminal Responsibility: Psychopathy and the Purposes of Punishment," 27 *International Journal of Law and Psychiatry* 425.

Fisher, G. (2003) *Plea Bargaining's Triumph: A History of Plea Bargaining in America* (Stanford, Calif.: Stanford University Press).

Fisher, S. Z. (1987–8) "In Search of the Virtuous Prosecutor: A Conceptual Framework," 15 *Am. J. Crim. L.* 197.

—— (1993–94) "Just the Facts Ma'am: Lying and the Omission of Exculpatory Evidence in Police Reports," 28 *New Eng. L. Rev.* 1.

Frank, M. J., and Borschard, D. (2006) "The Silent Criminal Defendant and the Presumption of Innocence: In the Hands of Real Jurors, is Either of them Safe?" 10 *Lewis & Clark L. Rev.* 237.

Freeman, R. (1996) "Why Do So Many Young American Men Commit Crimes and What Might We Do About It?" 10 *Journal of Economic Perspectives* 25.

Freidman, R. (1991) "Character Impeachment Evidence: Psycho Bayesian [!?] Analysis and a Proposed Overhaul," 38 *UCLA L. Rev.* 637.

Garland, D. (2001) *The Culture of Control: Crime and Social Order in Contemporary Society* (Chicago: University of Chicago Press).

Garvey, S. P. (1999) "Punishment as Atonement," 46 *UCLA L. Rev.* 1801.

Gazal-Ayal, O. (2006) "Partial Ban on Plea Bargains," 27 *Cardozo L. Rev.* 2295.

Gershman, B. L. (1992) "The New Prosecutors," 53 *Pitt. L. Rev.* 393.

—— (2001a) "Prosecutorial Ethics and Victims' Rights: The Prosecutor's Duty of Neutrality," 14 *Geo. J. Legal Ethics* 559.

—— (2001b) "The Prosecutor's Duty to Truth," 14 *Geo. J. Legal Ethics* 309.

Gerstein, R. S. (1970) "Privacy and Self-Incrimination," 80 *Ethics* 87.

Gifford, D. B. (1983) "Meaningful Reform of Plea Bargaining: The Control of Prosecutorial Discretion," 1983 *U. Ill. L. Rev.* 37.

Goldman, A. (1979) "The Paradox of Punishment," 9 *Philosophy and Public Affairs* 42.

Green, B. A. (1999) "Why Should Prosecutors Seek Justice?" 26 *Fordham Urb. L. J.* 607.

Greenawalt, R. K. (1981) "Silence as a Moral and Constitutional Right," 23 *Wm. & Mary L. Rev.* 15.

Gross, H. (1979) *A Theory of Criminal Justice* (New York: Oxford University Press).

Guidorizzi, D. D. (1998) "Should We Really 'Ban' Plea Bargaining? The Core Concerns of Plea Bargaining Critics," 47 *Emory L. J.* 753.

Hagan, J. and Dinovitzer, R. (1999) "Collateral Consequences of Punishment for Children, Communities, and Prisoners," 26 *Crime and Justice: A Review of Research* 121.

Hampton, J. (1991) "A New Theory of Retribution," in R. G. Frey and C. W. Morris (eds.), *Liability and Responsibility: Essays in Law and Morals* (Cambridge: Cambridge University Press) 377.

Haney, C. (2009) *Reforming Imprisonment: Psychological Limits to the Pains of Imprisonment* (Washington, DC: American Psychological Association).

Harris, G. C. (2000) "Testimony for Sale: The Law and Ethics of Snitches and Experts," 28 *Pepp. L. Rev.* 1.

Hart, H. L. A. (1961) *The Concept of Law* (Oxford: Clarendon Press).

Hawkins, G. (1972) "Punishment as a Moral Educator," in R. J. Gerber and P. D. McAnany (eds.), *Contemporary Punishment: Views, Explanations, and Justifications* (Notre Dame, Ind.: University of Notre Dame Press) 120.

Heffernan, W. C. and Kleinig, J. (2000) *From Social Justice to Criminal Justice: Poverty and the Administration of the Criminal Law* (New York: Oxford University Press).

Heumann, M. (1977) *Plea Bargaining: The Experiences of Prosecutors, Judges, and Defense Attorneys* (Chicago: University of Chicago Press).

Hochschild, J. (1991) "The Politics of the Estranged Poor," 101 *Ethics* 560.

Hudson, B. (2000) "Punishing the Poor: Dilemmas of Justice and Difference," in Heffernan and Kleinig, *From Social Justice to Criminal Justice: Poverty and the Administration of Criminal Law* 189.

Husak, D. (2004) "Guns and Drugs: Case Studies in the Principled Limits of the Criminal Sanction," 23 *Law and Philosophy* 437.

—— (2008) *Overcriminalization: The Limits of the Criminal Law* (Oxford: Oxford University Press).

—— and de Marneffe, P. (2005) *The Legalization of Drugs* (Cambridge: Cambridge University Press).

Jackson, J. (1996) "Judicial Responsibility in Criminal Proceedings," 49 *Current Legal Problems* 59.

—— (2002) "The Adversary Trial and Trial by Judge Alone," in McConville and Wilson, *The Handbook of the Criminal Justice Process* 335.

Jareborg, N. (1998) "Why Bulk Discounts in Multiple Offence Sentencing?" in A. Ashworth and M. Wasik (eds.), *Fundamentals of Sentencing Theory* (Oxford: Clarendon Press), 129.

Jonakait, R. (2003) *The American Jury System* (New Haven, Conn.: Yale University Press, 2003).

King, N. J. (1995) "Constitutional Limits on Successive and Excessive Penalties," 144 *U. Pa. L. Rev.* 101.

—— (2005) "Judicial Oversight of Negotiated Sentences in a World of Bargained Punishment," 58 *Stan. L. Rev.* 293.

Kipnis, K. (1976) "Criminal Justice and the Negotiated Plea," 86 *Ethics* 93.

Kleinig, J. (2008) Ethics and Criminal Justice: An Introduction (Cambridge: Cambridge University Press).

Langbein, J. (1980) "Torture and Plea Bargaining," 58 *Public Interest* 43.

Langer, M. (2004) "From Legal Transplants to Legal Translations: The Globalization of Plea Bargaining and the Americanization Thesis in Criminal Procedure", 45 *Harv. Int'l L. J.* 1.

Laudan, L. (2006) *Truth, Error, and Criminal Law* (Cambridge: Cambridge University Press).

—— and Allen, R. J. (2011) "The Devastating Impact of Prior Crimes Evidence and Other Myths of the Criminal Justice Process", 101 *J. Crim. L. & Criminology* 493.

Lazarus, L. (2004) *Contrasting Prisoners' Rights: A Comparative Examination of Germany and England* (Oxford: Oxford University Press).

Lee, C. K. Y. (1994) "Prosecutorial Discretion, Substantial Assistance, and the Federal Sentencing Guidelines," 42 *UCLA L. Rev.* 105.

—— (1997) "From Gatekeepers to Concierge: Reigning in the Federal Prosecutor's Expanding Power Over Substantial Assistance Departures," 50 *Rutgers L. Rev.* 199.

Lefstein, N. (2004) "In Search of Gideon's Promise: Lessons from England and the Need for Federal Help," 55 *Hastings L. J.* 835.

Leipold, A. D. (1996) "Rethinking Jury Nullification," 82 Va. L. Rev. 253.

Lempert, R. O., Gross, S. R., and Liebman, J. S. (2000) *A Modern Approach to Evidence Law*, 3rd edition (St Paul, Minn.: West).

Lippke, R. L. (2006) "Mixed Theories of Punishment and Mixed Offenders: Some Unresolved Tensions," 32 *Southern Journal of Philosophy* 273.

—— (2007) *Rethinking Imprisonment* (Oxford: Oxford University Press).

—— (2008a) "To Waive or Not to Waive: The Right to Trial and Plea Bargaining," 2 *Criminal Law and Philosophy* 181.

—— (2008b) "No Easy Way Out: Dangerous Offenders and Preventive Detention," 27 *Law and Philosophy* 383.

—— (2008c) "Criminal Record, Character Evidence, and the Criminal Trial," 14 *Legal Theory* 167.

—— (2010) "Punishing the Guilty, Not Punishing the Innocent," 7 *Journal of Moral Philosophy* 462.

—— (2011) "Retributive Sentencing, Multiple Offenders, and Bulk Discounts," in M. D. White (ed.), *Retributivism: Essays in Theory and Policy* (Oxford: Oxford University Press) 212.

Luban, D. (1988) *Lawyers and Justice: An Ethical Study* (Princeton, NJ: Princeton University Press).

Ma, Y. (2002) "Prosecutorial Discretion and Plea Bargaining in the United States, France, Germany, and Italy: A Comparative Perspective," 12 *International Criminal Justice Review* 22.

Markel, D. (2001) "Are Shaming Punishments Beautifully Retributive? Retributivism and the Implications for the Alternative Sanctions Debate," 54 *Vand. L. Rev.* 2157.

Mather, L. M. (1979) *Plea Bargaining or Trial? The Process of Criminal Case Disposition* (Lexington, Mass.: Lexington Books).

Mathiesen, T. (2000) *Prison On Trial*, 2nd edition (Winchester, UK: Waterside Press).

Maxfield, L. D. and Kramer, J. H. (1998) "Substantial Assistance: An Empirical Yardstick Gauging Equity in Current Federal Policy and Practice," 11 *Federal Sentencing Reporter* 6.

McConville, M. and Mirsky, C. L. (2005) *Jury Trials and Plea Bargaining: A True History* (Oxford: Hart Publishing).

—— and Wilson, G. (2002) *The Handbook of the Criminal Justice Process* (Oxford: Oxford University Press).

McCoy, C. (1993) *Politics and Plea Bargaining: Victims' Rights in California.* (Philadelphia: University of Pennsylvania Press).

—— (2005) "Plea Bargaining as Coercion: The Trial Penalty and Plea Bargaining Reform," 50 *Criminal Law Quarterly.*

Meares, T. L. (1995) "Rewards for Good Behavior: Influencing Prosecutorial Discretion and Conduct with Financial Incentives," 64 *Fordham L. Rev.* 851.

Micelli, T. J. (1996) "Plea Bargaining and Deterrence: An Institutional Approach," 3 *European Journal of Law and Economics* 249.

Moore, M. (1998) *Placing Blame: A General Theory of the Criminal Law* (New York: Oxford University Press).

Morris, H. (1968) "Persons and Punishment," 52 *The Monist* 475.

Morris, N. (1982) *Madness and the Criminal Law* (Chicago: University of Chicago Press).

Morse, S. J. (2000) "Deprivation and Desert," in Heffernan and Kleinig, *From Social Justice to Criminal Justice: Poverty and the Administration of Criminal Law* 114.

Mueller, C. and Kirkpatrick, L. C. (2003) *Evidence*, 3rd edition (New York: Aspen Publishers).

Murphy, J. (1972) "Moral Death: A Kantian Essay on Psychopathy," 82 *Ethics* 284.

—— (1973) "Marxism and Retribution," 2 *Philosophy and Public Affairs* 217.

—— (1997) "Repentance, Punishment, and Mercy," in A. Etzioni and D. E. Carney (eds.), *Repentance: A Comparative Perspective* (Lanham, Md.: Rowman and Littlefield, 1997) 143.

Nagin, D. (1998a) "Criminal Deterrence Research at the Outset of the Twenty-First Century," 23 *Crime and Justice: A Review of Research* 1.

—— (1998b) "Deterrence and Incapacitation," in M. Tonry (ed.), *The Handbook of Crime and Punishment* (New York: Oxford University Press) 345.

Nozick, R. (1974) *Anarchy, State, and Utopia* (New York: Basic Books).

Oaks, D. H. (1970) "Studying the Exclusionary Rule in Search and Seizure," 37 *U. Chi. L. Rev.* 665.

O'Hear, M. (2008) "Plea Bargaining and Procedural Justice," 42 *Ga. L. Rev.* 407.

Otton, P. (2002) "The Role of the Judge in Criminal Cases," in McConville and Wilson, *The Handbook of the Criminal Justice Process* 323.

Park, R. (1998) "Character at the Crossroads," 49 *Hastings L. J.* 738.

Partington, M. (2003) *An Introduction to the English Legal System*, 2nd edition (Oxford: Oxford University Press).

Philips, M. (1981–82) "The Question of Voluntariness in the Plea Bargaining Controversy: A Philosophical Clarification," 16 *L. & Soc'y Rev.* 207.

Punch, M. (2000) "Police Corruption and Its Prevention," 8 *European Journal of Criminal Policy and Research* 301.

Rawls, J. (1999) "A Kantian Conception of Equality," in S. Freeman (ed.), *John Rawls: Collected Papers* (Cambridge, Mass.: Harvard University Press) 257.

Redmayne, M. (2009) "Theorizing the Criminal Trial," 12 *New Crim. L. Rev.* 287.

Reiman, J. (2006) *The Rich Get Richer and the Poor Get Prison: Ideology, Class, and Criminal Justice* (Boston: Allyn and Bacon).

Richman, D. C. (1996) "Cooperating Defendants: The Costs and Benefits of Purchasing Information from Scoundrels," 8 *Federal Sentencing Reporter* 292.

Ryberg, J. (2005) "Retributivism and Multiple Offending," 11 *Res Publica* 213.

Sadurski, W. (1985) *Giving Desert Its Due* (Dordrecht, Netherlands: D. Reidel).

Sanchirico, C. W. (2001) "Character Evidence and the Object of Trial," 101 *Colum. L. Rev.* 1227.

Schulhofer, S. (1984) "Is Plea Bargaining Inevitable?" 97 *Harv. L. Rev.* 1037.

—— (1991) "Some Kind Words for the Privilege Against Self-Incrimination," 26 *Val. U. L. Rev.* 311.

—— (1992) "Plea Bargaining as Disaster," 101 *Yale L. J.* 1979.

—— and Nagel, I. H. (1997) "Plea Negotiations Under the Federal Sentencing Guidelines: Guideline Circumvention and its Dynamics in the Post-Mistretta Period," 91 *Nw. U. L. Rev.* 1284.

Scott, R. E. and Stuntz, W. J. (1992) "Plea Bargaining as Contract," 101 *Yale L. J.* 1909.

Sher, G. (1987) *Desert* (Princeton, NJ: Princeton University Press).

Smith, A. (2001) "Can You Be a Good Person and a Good Prosecutor?" 14 *Geo. J. Legal Ethics* 355.

Smith, N. (2008) *I Was Wrong: The Meanings of Apologies* (Cambridge: Cambridge University Press).

Solley, S. (2002) "The Role of the Advocate," in McConville and Wilson, *The Handbook of the Criminal Justice Process* 311.

Standen, J. (1993) "Plea Bargaining in the Shadow of the Guidelines," 81 *Cal. L. Rev.* 1471.

Stuntz, W. J. (1998) "Race, Class, and Drugs," 98 *Colum. L. Rev.* 1795.

—— (2001) "The Pathological Politics of Criminal Law," 100 *Mich. L. Rev.* 505.

—— (2004) "Plea Bargaining and the Criminal Law's Disappearing Shadow," 117 *Harv. L. Rev.* 2548.

Thalberg, I. (1963) "Remorse," 72 *Mind* 545.

Tillers, P. (1998) "What is Wrong with Character Evidence?" 49 *Hastings L. J.* 781.

Tonry, M. (1992) "Proportionality, Parsimony, and Interchangeability of Punishments," in R. A. Duff, S. Marshall, and R. P. Dobash (eds.), *Penal Theory and Penal Practice* (Manchester, UK: Manchester University Press) 59.

—— (2004) *Thinking about Crime: Sense and Sensibility in American Penal Culture* (Oxford: Oxford University Press).

—— (2008) "Learning from the Limitations of Deterrence Research," 37 *Crime and Justice: A Review of Research* 279.

Tudor, S. K. (2008a) "Why Should Remorse be a Mitigating Factor in Sentencing," 2 *Criminal Law and Philosophy* 241.

—— (2008b) "Remorse, Reform, and the Real World: Reply to Lippke," 2 *Criminal Law and Philosophy* 269.

Turner, J. I. (2006) "Judicial Participation in Plea Negotiations: A Comparative Perspective," 54 *Am. J. Comp. L.* 199.

Turner, M. G., Sundt, J. L., Applegate, B. K., and Cullen, F. T. (1995) "'Three Strikes and You're Out' Legislation: A National Assessment," 59 *Federal Probation* 16.

Uviller, H. R. (1973) "The Virtuous Prosecutor in Quest of an Ethical Standard: Guidance from the ABA," 71 *Mich. L. Rev.* 1145.

—— (1982) "Evidence of Character to Prove Conduct: Illusion, Illogic, and Injustice in the Courtroom," 130 *U. Pa. L. Rev.* 845.

Vamos, N. (2009) "Please Don't Call it 'Plea Bargaining'," 2009 *Crim. L. Rev.* 617.

Vogel, M. (2007) *Coercion to Compromise: Plea Bargaining, the Courts, and the Making of Political Authority* (Oxford: Oxford University Press).

von Hirsch, A. (1992) "Proportionality in the Philosophy of Punishment," 16 *Crime and Justice: A Review of Research* 55.

—— (1993) *Censure and Sanctions* (Oxford: Clarendon Press).

—— and Maher, L. (1998) "Should Penal Rehabilitationism be Revived?" in A. von Hirsch and A. Ashworth (eds.), *Principled Sentencing: Readings on Theory and Policy*, 2nd edition (Oxford: Hart Publishing).

——, Bottoms, A. E., Burney, E., and Wikstrom P. O. (1999) *Criminal Deterrence and Sentence Severity: An Analysis of Recent Research* (Oxford: Hart Publishing).

—— and Ashworth, A. (2005) *Proportionate Sentencing: Exploring the Principles* (Oxford: Oxford University Press).

Waldron, J. (1981) "A Right to Do Wrong," 92 *Ethics* 21.

Ward, R. and Davies, O. M. (2004) *The Criminal Justice Act 2003: A Practitioner's Guide* (Bristol, UK: Jordan Publishing).

Weigend, T. (2003) "Is the Criminal Process About Truth? A German Perspective," 26 *Harv. J. L. & Public Pol'y* 157.

Weinstein, I. (1999) "Regulating the Market for Snitches," 47 *Buff. L. Rev.* 563.

Wertheimer, A. (1979a) "Freedom, Morality, Plea Bargaining, and the Supreme Court," 8 *Philosophy and Public Affairs* 203.

—— (1979b) "The Prosecutor and the Gunman," 89 *Ethics* 269.

Western, B. (2006) *Punishment and Inequality in America* (New York: Russell Sage).

Whitman, J. Q. (2003) *Harsh Justice: Criminal Punishment and the Widening Divide Between America and Europe* (Oxford: Oxford University Press).

Wilkey, M. R. (1978) "The Exclusionary Rule: Why Suppress Valid Evidence?" 62 *Judicature* 214.

Young, R. and Sanders, A. (2004) "The Ethics of Prosecution Lawyers," 7 *Legal Ethics* 190.

Zacharias, F. C. (1998) "Justice in Plea Bargaining," 39 *Wm. & Mary L. Rev.* 1122.

Zimring, F. E. (1998) "Toward a Jurisprudence of Youth Violence," 23 *Crime and Justice: A Review of Research* 477.

—— and Hawkins, G. (1995) *Incapacitation: Penal Confinement and the Restraint of Crime* (New York: Oxford University Press).

—— and —— (1997) *Crime Is Not the Problem: Lethal Violence in America* (Oxford: Oxford University Press).

Index